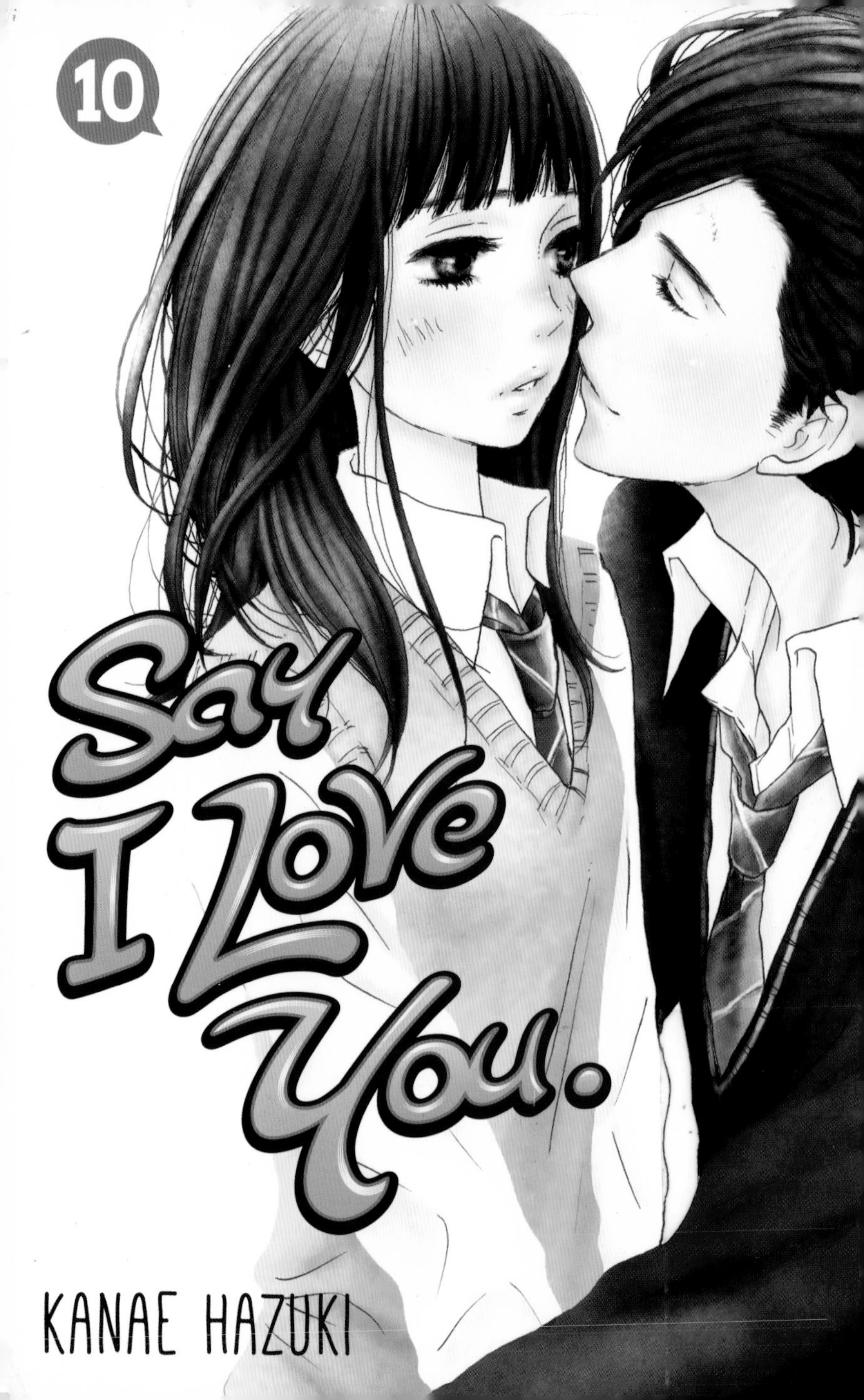
10
Say I Love You.
KANAE HAZUKI

Say I Love You.

10

by
Kanae
Hazuki

Kanae Hazuki
presents

Chapter 37

Chapter 38

Chapter 39

Chapter 40

CHARACTERS

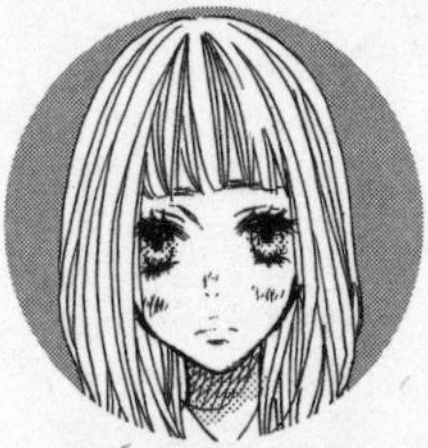

Mei Tachibana

A girl who hasn't had a single friend, let alone a boyfriend, in sixteen years, and has lived her life trusting no one. She finds herself attracted to Yamato, who, for some reason, just won't leave her alone, and they start dating.

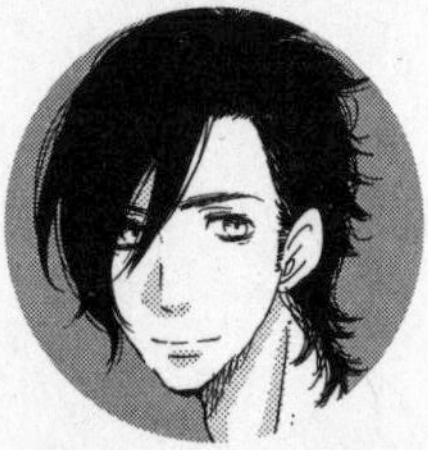

Yamato Kurosawa

The most popular boy at Mei's school. He has the love of many girls, yet for some reason, he is obsessed with Mei, the brooding weirdo girl from another class.

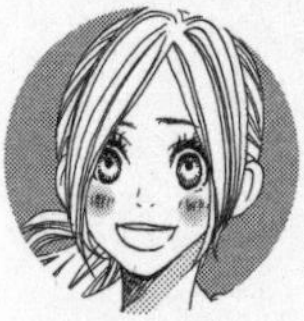

Mei's first friend. Unlike the other kids, she treats Mei like a normal person. She had a thing for Yamato, but now she is head over heels for his friend Nakanishi.

Asami

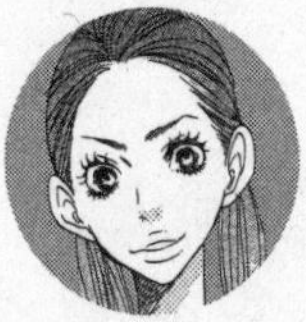

Mei's first rival. She had a crush on Yamato and was jealous of Mei, but now they are close friends. She is currently dating Masashi, who always loved her.

Aiko

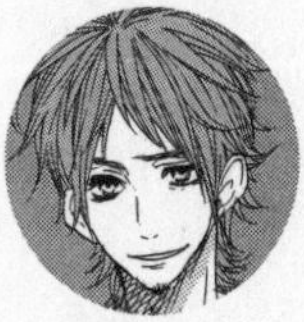

Yamato's brother and a hairstylist. He helped Mei out for the fireworks show and the beauty contest. He recently overcame his emotional scars and is starting out on a new romantic venture.

Daichi

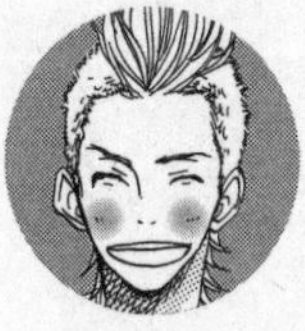

Yamato's classmate from middle school who had been the victim of bullying. For his own reasons, he started high school a year late. He likes Mei and told her so, but...?

Kai

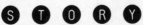

STORY

Mei Tachibana spent sixteen years without a single friend or boyfriend, but then, for some reason, Yamato Kurosawa, the most popular boy in school, took a liking to her. Mei was drawn in by Yamato's kindness and sincerity, and now they have entered the second year of their relationship. Mei panicked when Yamato won the grand prize at the school festival contest and went on a date with Megumi, but because of it all, she learned the depth of Yamato's love. After that, she learned more about Yamato's brother Daichi, who had given her a lot of help—she finds out about his past love and the scars in his heart. Knowing that, and seeing him as he finally faces a new romance, helps Mei mature a little more.

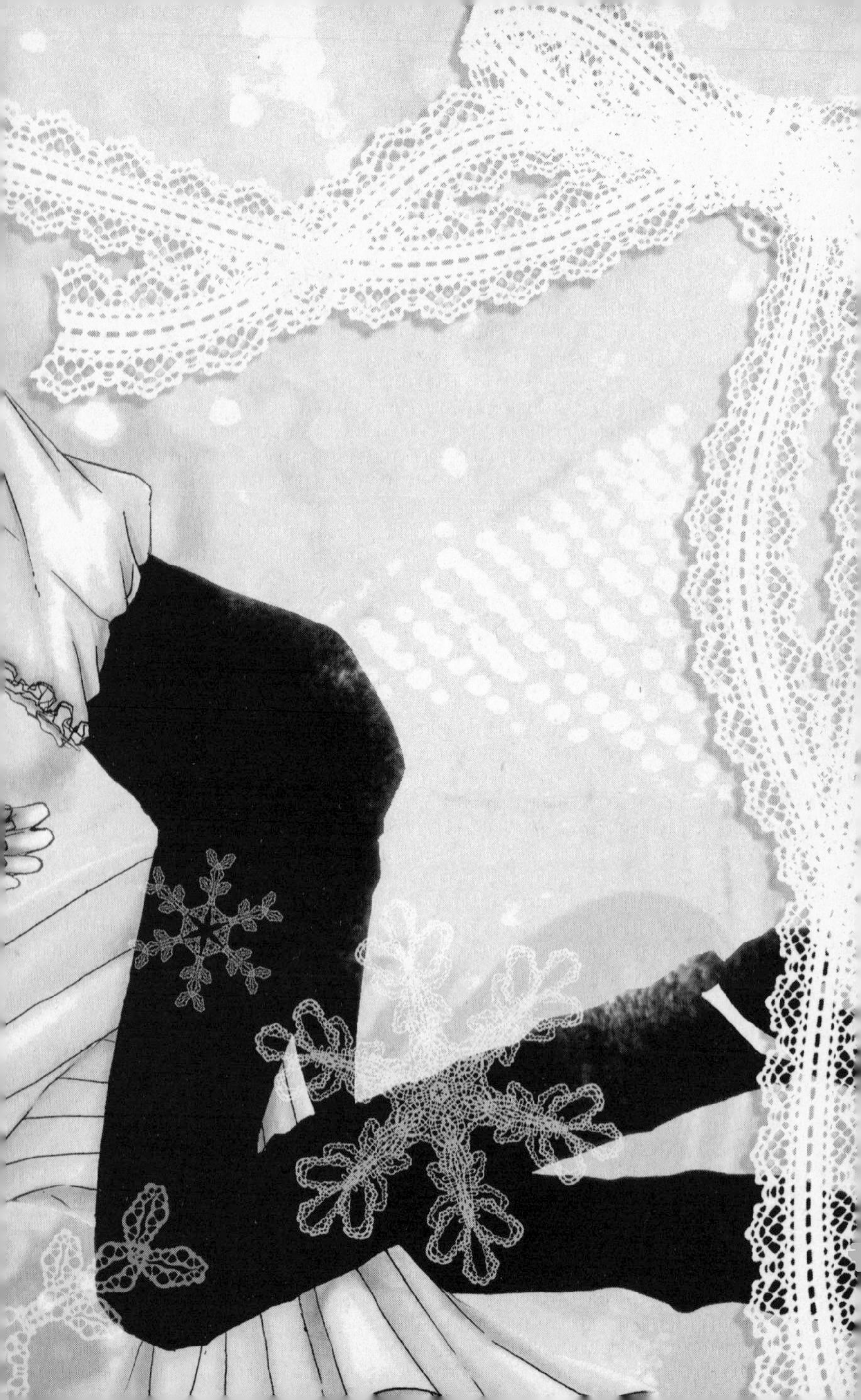

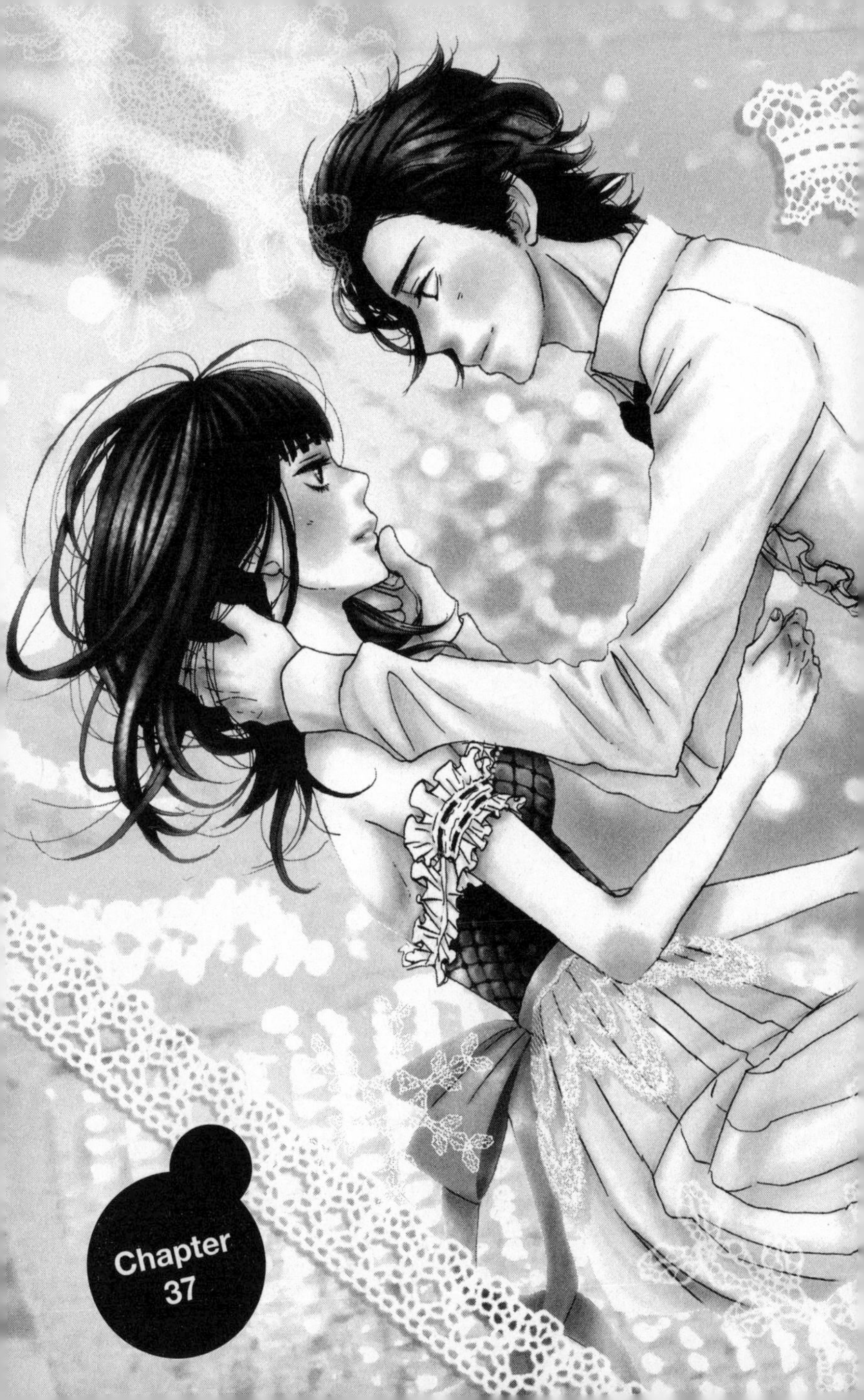
Chapter
37

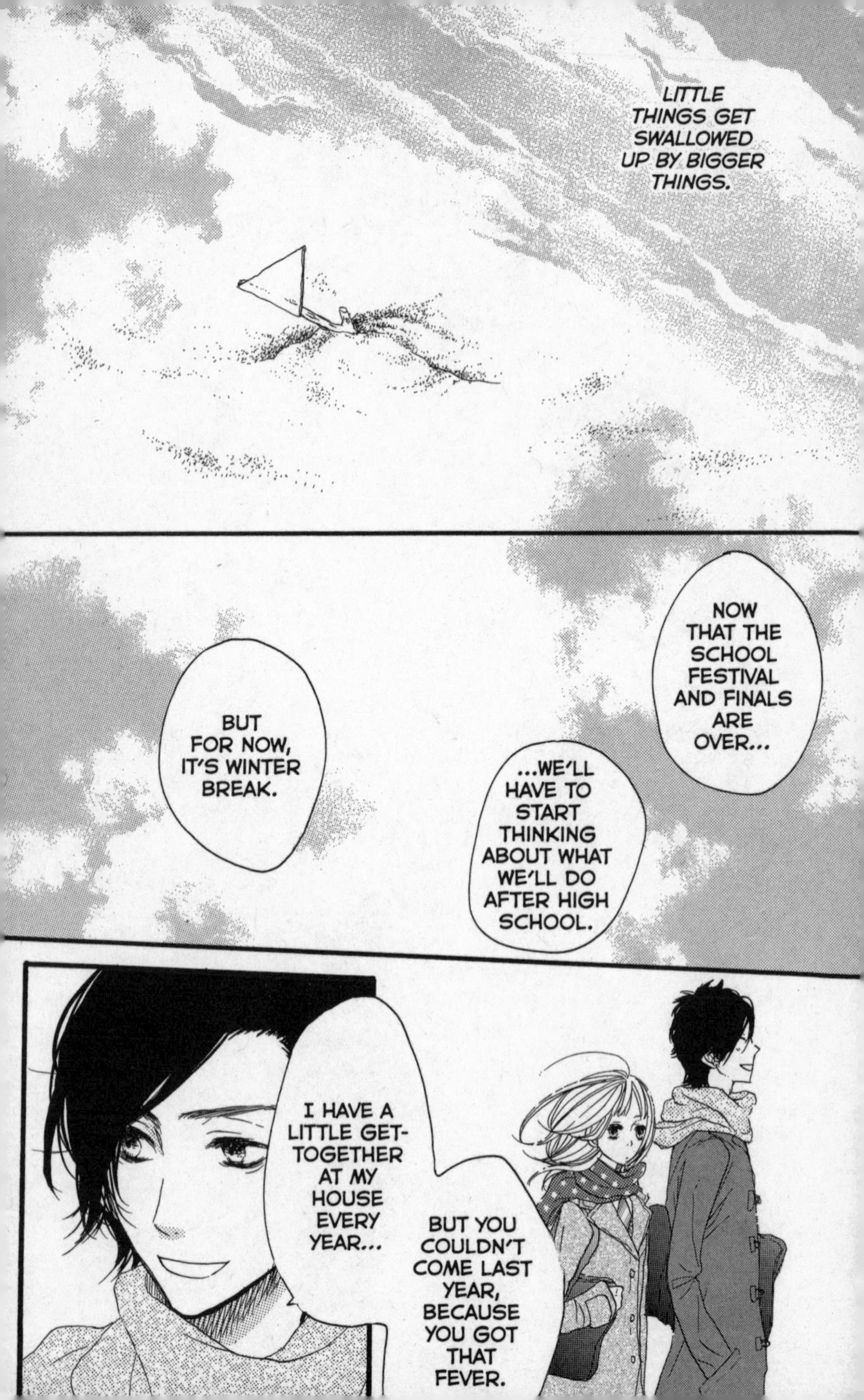
LITTLE THINGS GET SWALLOWED UP BY BIGGER THINGS.
NOW THAT THE SCHOOL FESTIVAL AND FINALS ARE OVER...
...WE'LL HAVE TO START THINKING ABOUT WHAT WE'LL DO AFTER HIGH SCHOOL.
BUT FOR NOW, IT'S WINTER BREAK.
I HAVE A LITTLE GET-TOGETHER AT MY HOUSE EVERY YEAR...
BUT YOU COULDN'T COME LAST YEAR, BECAUSE YOU GOT THAT FEVER.

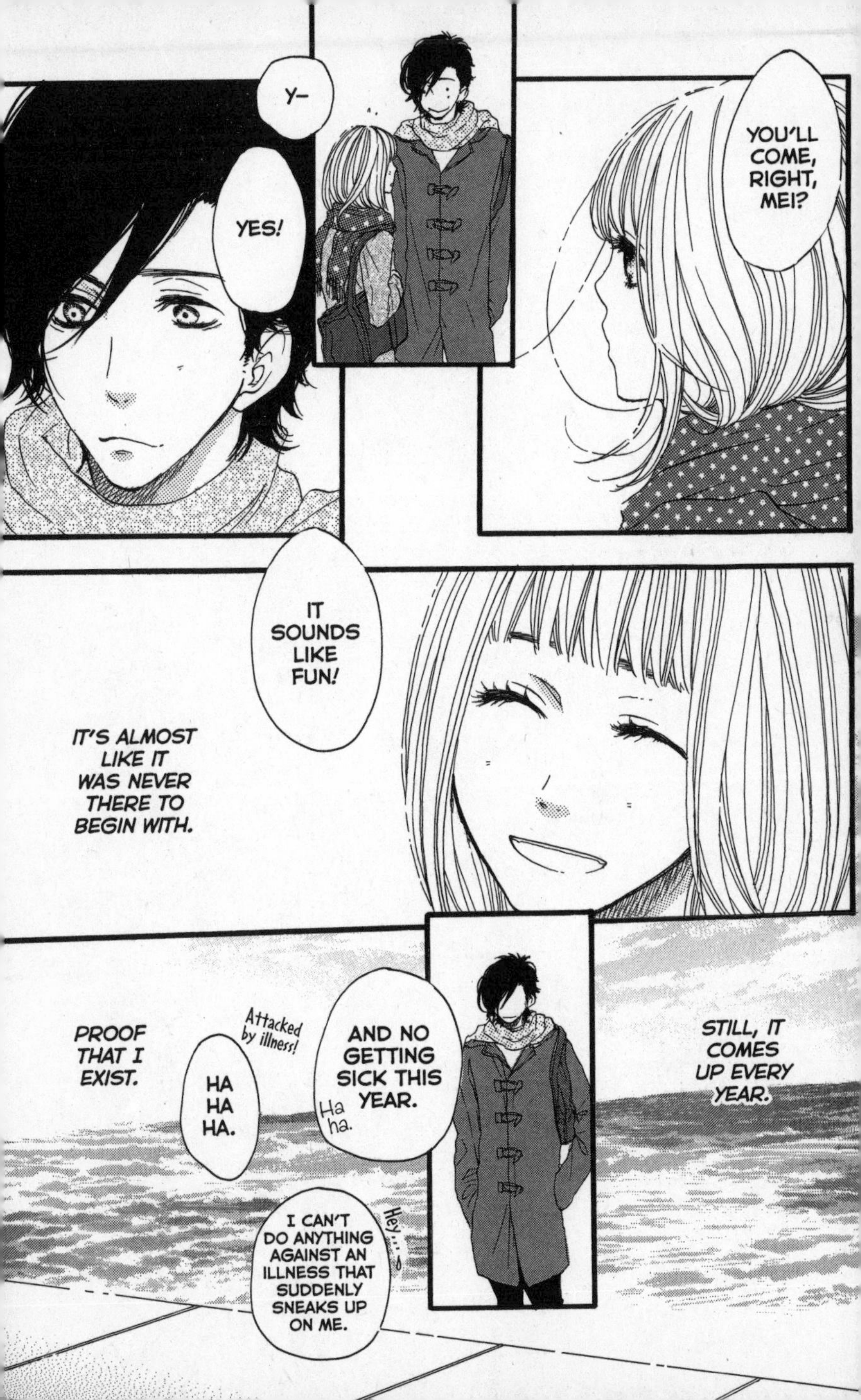
YOU'LL COME, RIGHT, MEI?
Y–
YES!
IT SOUNDS LIKE FUN!
IT'S ALMOST LIKE IT WAS NEVER THERE TO BEGIN WITH.
STILL, IT COMES UP EVERY YEAR.
AND NO GETTING SICK THIS YEAR.
Ha ha.
Attacked by illness!
HA HA HA.
Hey...
I CAN'T DO ANYTHING AGAINST AN ILLNESS THAT SUDDENLY SNEAKS UP ON ME.
PROOF THAT I EXIST.

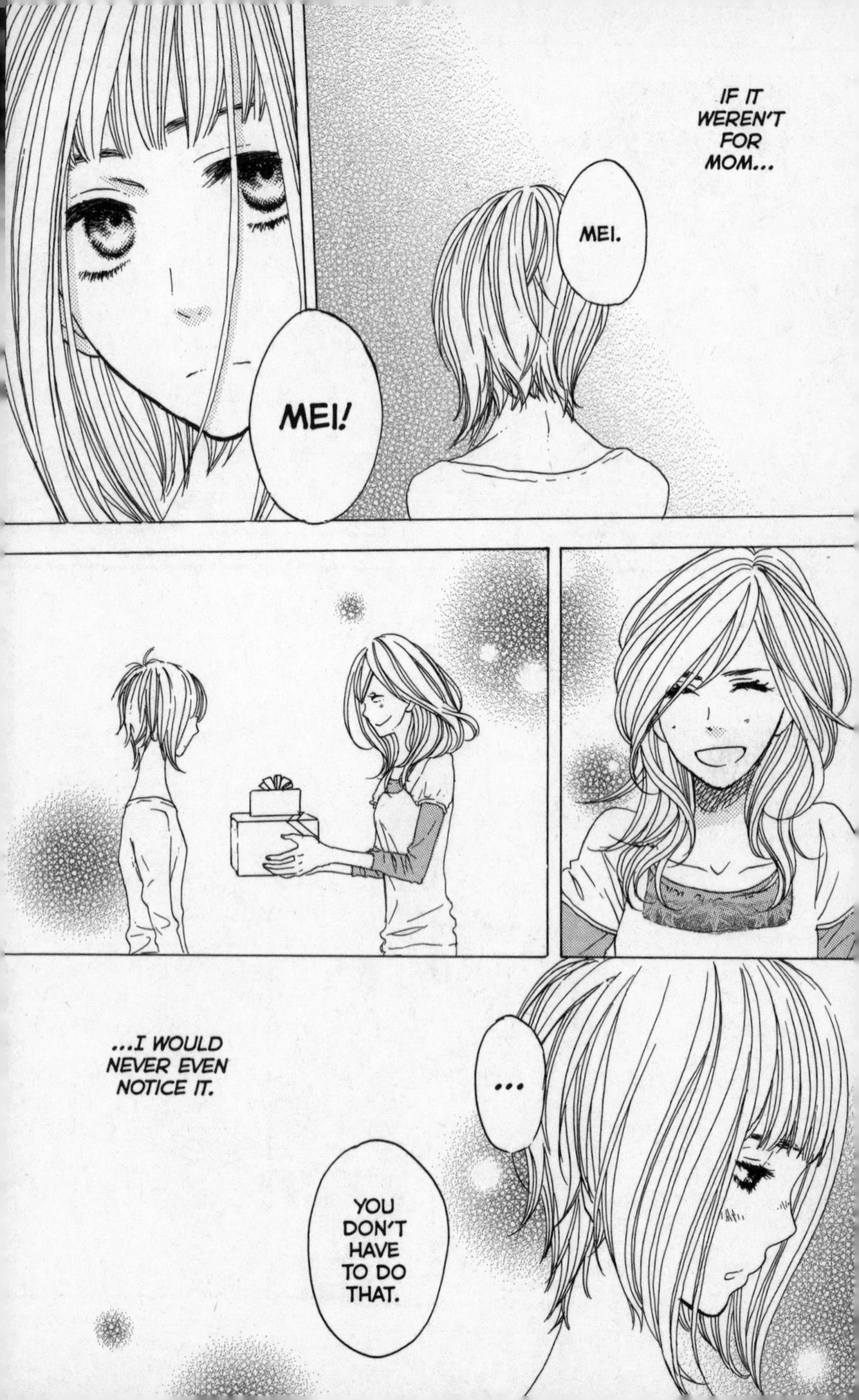
IF IT WEREN'T FOR MOM...
MEI.
MEI!
...
...I WOULD NEVER EVEN NOTICE IT.
YOU DON'T HAVE TO DO THAT.

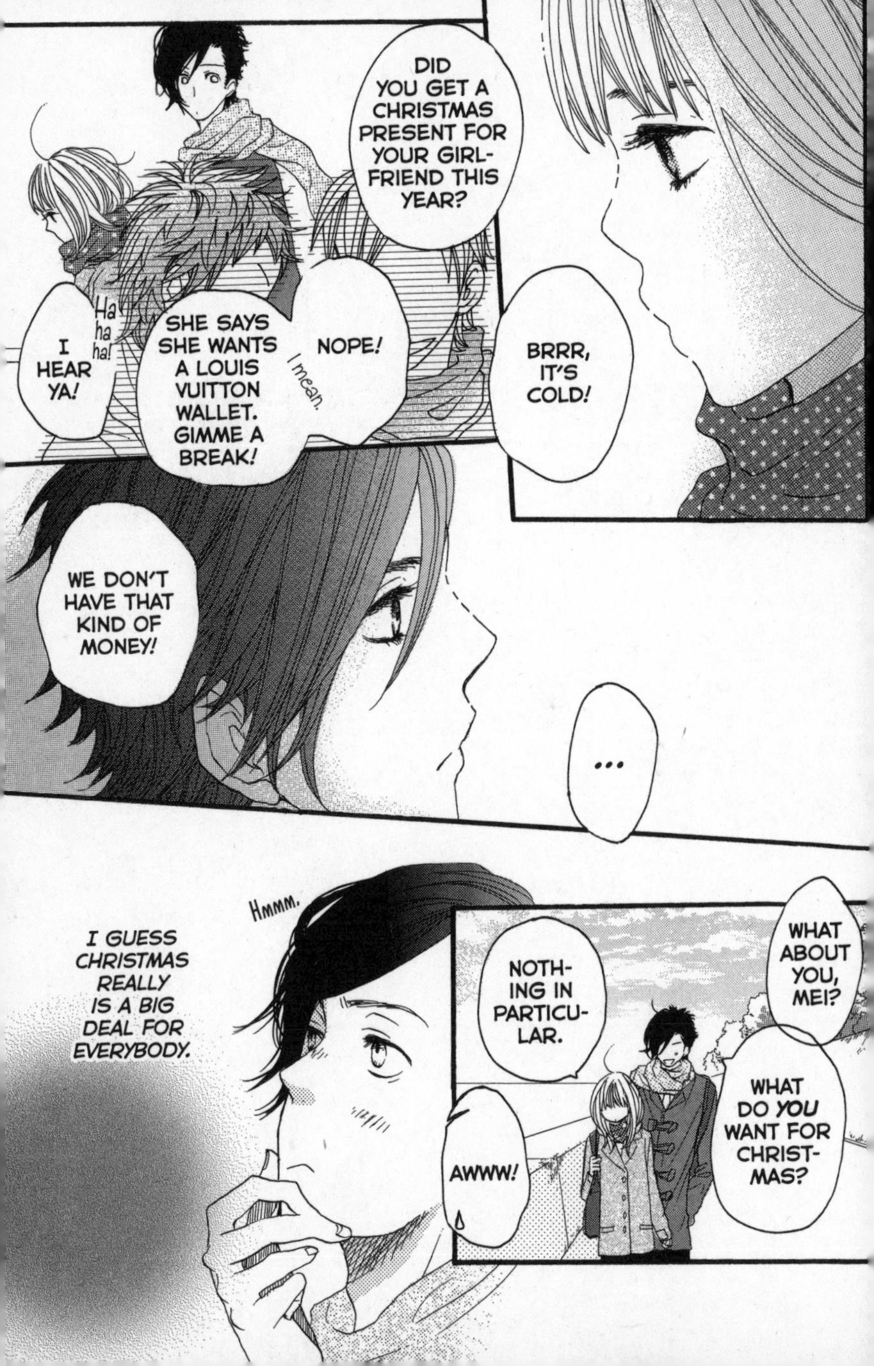
BRRR, IT'S COLD!
DID YOU GET A CHRISTMAS PRESENT FOR YOUR GIRL-FRIEND THIS YEAR?
NOPE!
I mean.
SHE SAYS SHE WANTS A LOUIS VUITTON WALLET. GIMME A BREAK!
Ha ha ha!
I HEAR YA!
WE DON'T HAVE THAT KIND OF MONEY!
...
WHAT ABOUT YOU, MEI?
WHAT DO *YOU* WANT FOR CHRIST-MAS?
NOTH-ING IN PARTICU-LAR.
AWWW!
Hmmm.
I GUESS CHRISTMAS REALLY IS A BIG DEAL FOR EVERYBODY.

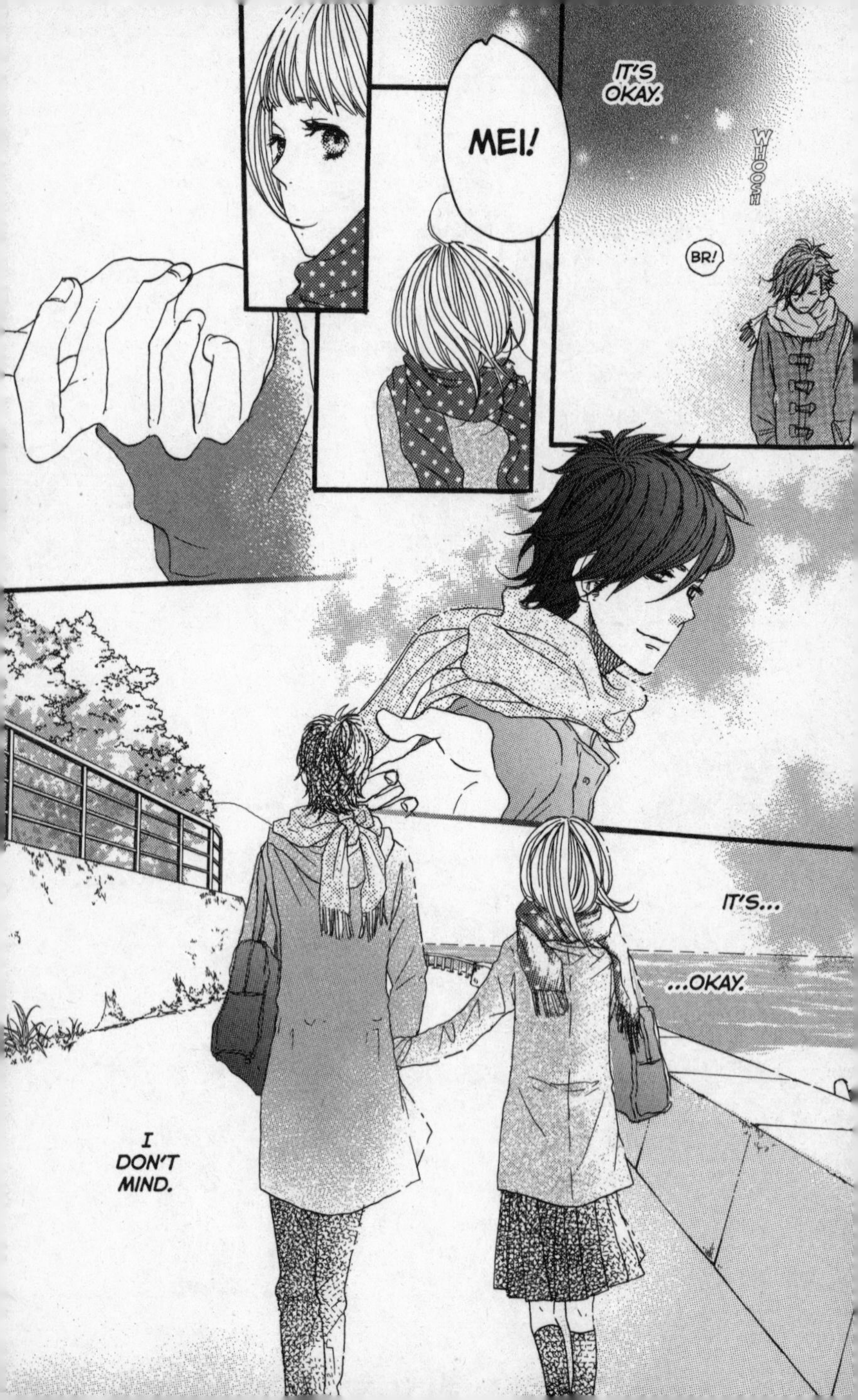
IT'S OKAY.
WHOOSH
BR!
MEI!
IT'S...
...OKAY.
I DON'T MIND.

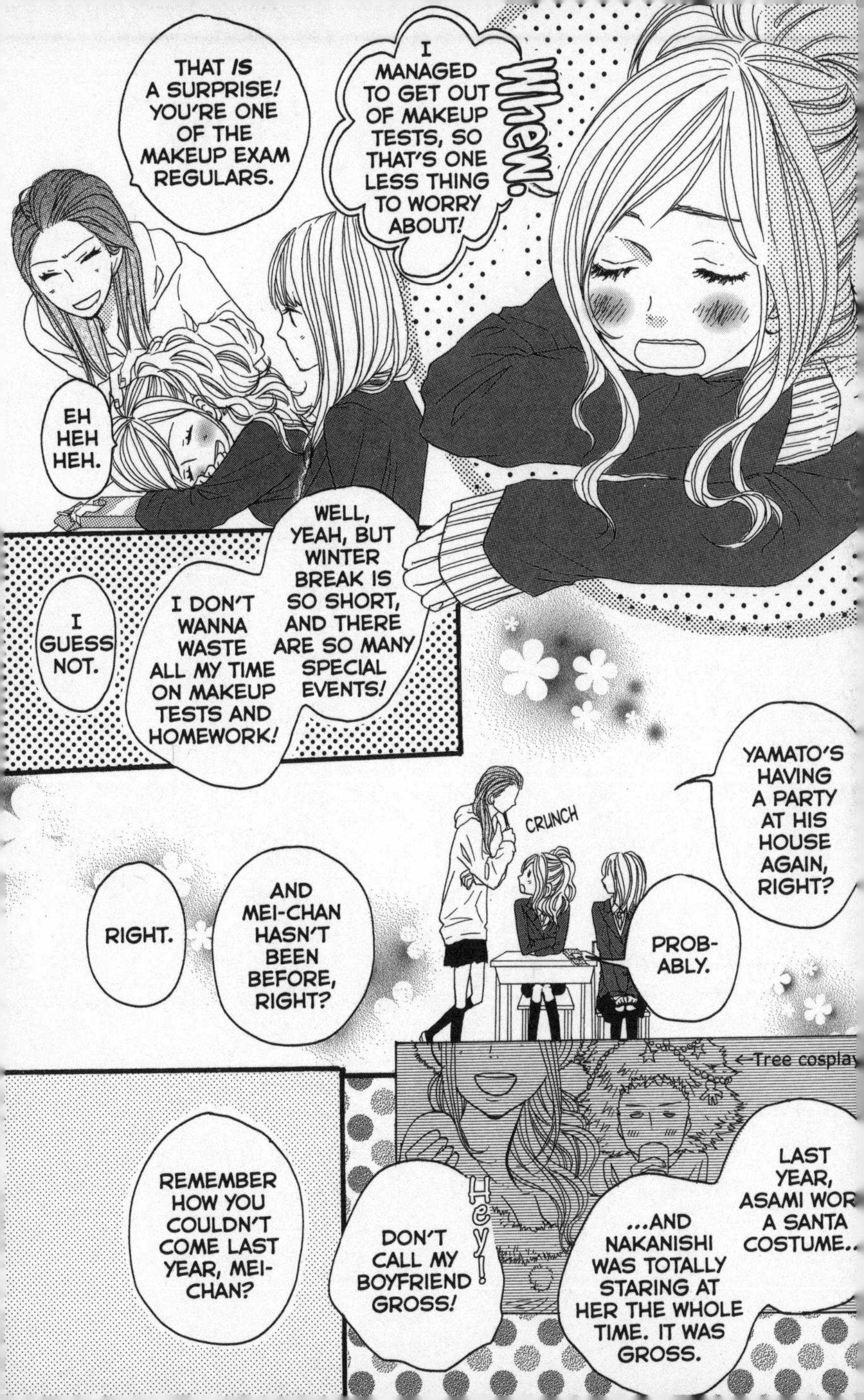
Whew!
I MANAGED TO GET OUT OF MAKEUP TESTS, SO THAT'S ONE LESS THING TO WORRY ABOUT!
THAT *IS* A SURPRISE! YOU'RE ONE OF THE MAKEUP EXAM REGULARS.
EH HEH HEH.
WELL, YEAH, BUT WINTER BREAK IS SO SHORT, AND THERE ARE SO MANY SPECIAL EVENTS!
I DON'T WANNA WASTE ALL MY TIME ON MAKEUP TESTS AND HOMEWORK!
I GUESS NOT.
YAMATO'S HAVING A PARTY AT HIS HOUSE AGAIN, RIGHT?
PROB-ABLY.
CRUNCH
AND MEI-CHAN HASN'T BEEN BEFORE, RIGHT?
RIGHT.
LAST YEAR, ASAMI WOR A SANTA COSTUME..
...AND NAKANISHI WAS TOTALLY STARING AT HER THE WHOLE TIME. IT WAS GROSS.
←Tree cosplay
Hey!
DON'T CALL MY BOYFRIEND GROSS!
REMEMBER HOW YOU COULDN'T COME LAST YEAR, MEI-CHAN?

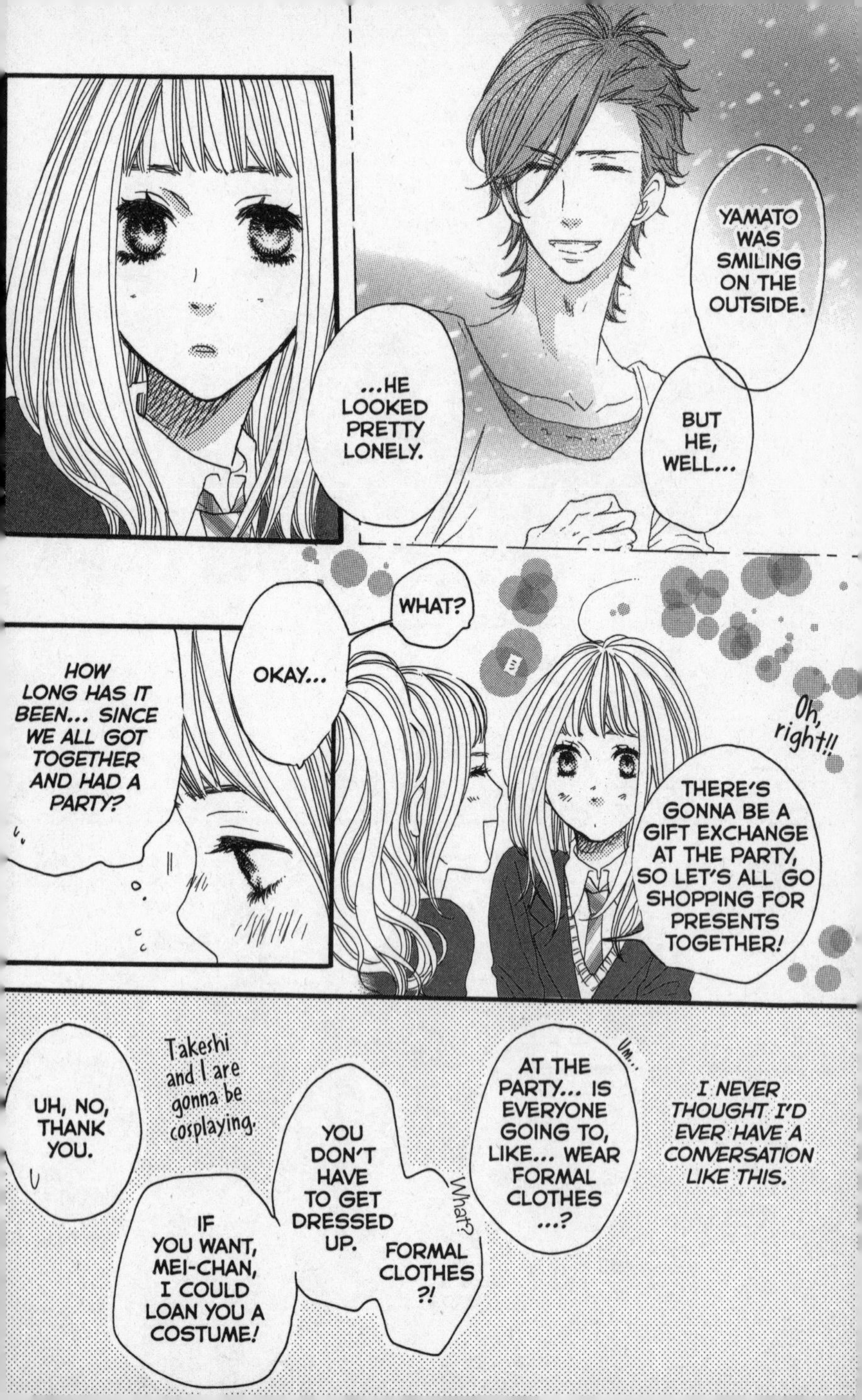
YAMATO WAS SMILING ON THE OUTSIDE.
BUT HE, WELL...
...HE LOOKED PRETTY LONELY.
Oh, right!!
THERE'S GONNA BE A GIFT EXCHANGE AT THE PARTY, SO LET'S ALL GO SHOPPING FOR PRESENTS TOGETHER!
WHAT?
OKAY...
HOW LONG HAS IT BEEN... SINCE WE ALL GOT TOGETHER AND HAD A PARTY?
I NEVER THOUGHT I'D EVER HAVE A CONVERSATION LIKE THIS.
Um...
AT THE PARTY... IS EVERYONE GOING TO, LIKE... WEAR FORMAL CLOTHES ...?
What?
FORMAL CLOTHES ?!
YOU DON'T HAVE TO GET DRESSED UP.
Takeshi and I are gonna be cosplaying.
IF YOU WANT, MEI-CHAN, I COULD LOAN YOU A COSTUME!
UH, NO, THANK YOU.

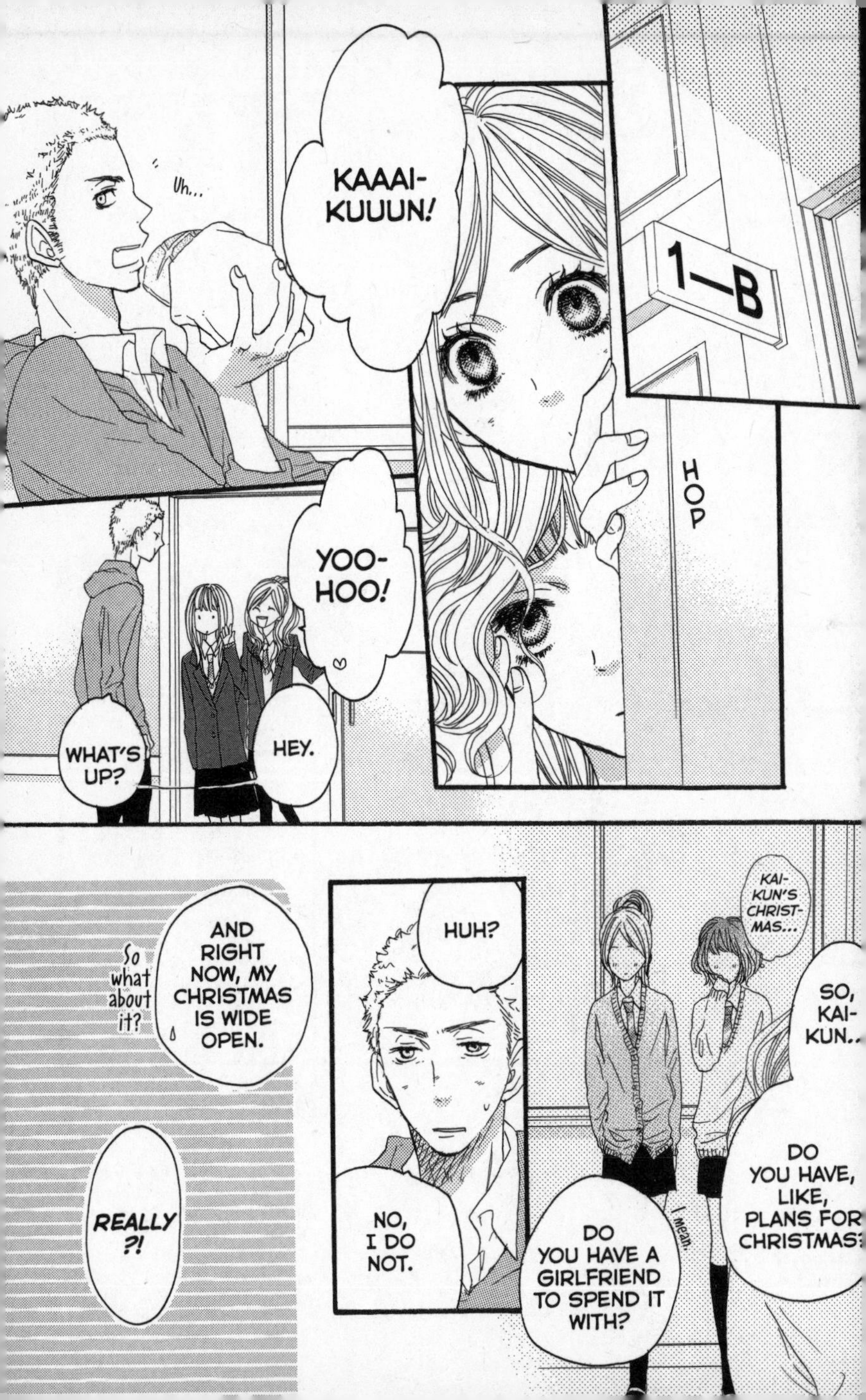
1—B
KAAAI-KUUUN!
HOP
Uh...
YOO-HOO!
HEY.
WHAT'S UP?
KAI-KUN'S CHRISTMAS...
SO, KAI-KUN..
DO YOU HAVE, LIKE, PLANS FOR CHRISTMAS?
I mean,
DO YOU HAVE A GIRLFRIEND TO SPEND IT WITH?
HUH?
NO, I DO NOT.
AND RIGHT NOW, MY CHRISTMAS IS WIDE OPEN.
So what about it?
REALLY?!

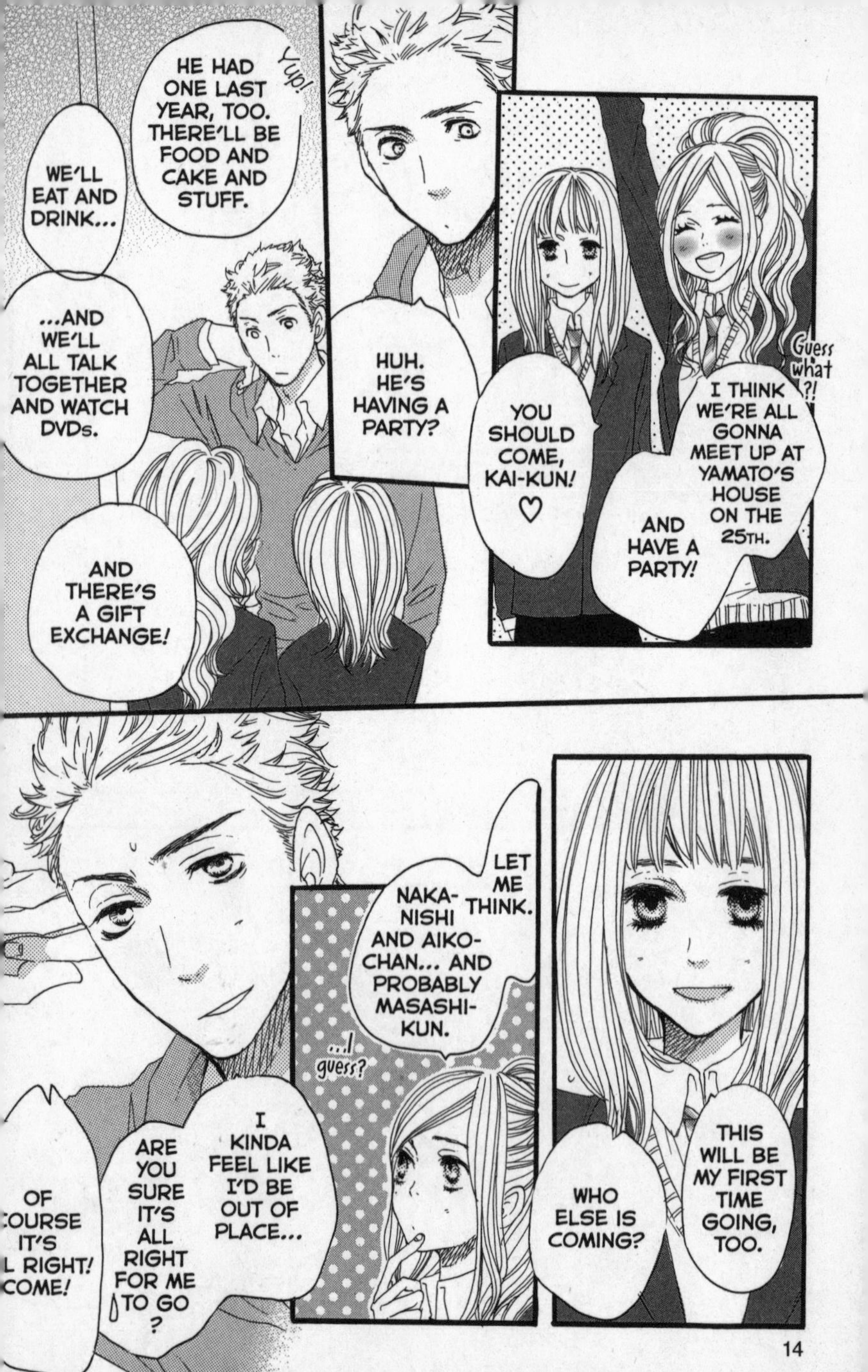
Guess what?!
I THINK WE'RE ALL GONNA MEET UP AT YAMATO'S HOUSE ON THE 25TH.
AND HAVE A PARTY!
YOU SHOULD COME, KAI-KUN! ♡
HUH. HE'S HAVING A PARTY?
Yup!
HE HAD ONE LAST YEAR, TOO. THERE'LL BE FOOD AND CAKE AND STUFF.
WE'LL EAT AND DRINK...
...AND WE'LL ALL TALK TOGETHER AND WATCH DVDs.
AND THERE'S A GIFT EXCHANGE!
THIS WILL BE MY FIRST TIME GOING, TOO.
WHO ELSE IS COMING?
LET ME THINK.
NAKA-NISHI AND AIKO-CHAN... AND PROBABLY MASASHI-KUN.
...I guess?
I KINDA FEEL LIKE I'D BE OUT OF PLACE...
ARE YOU SURE IT'S ALL RIGHT FOR ME TO GO?
OF COURSE IT'S L RIGHT! COME!

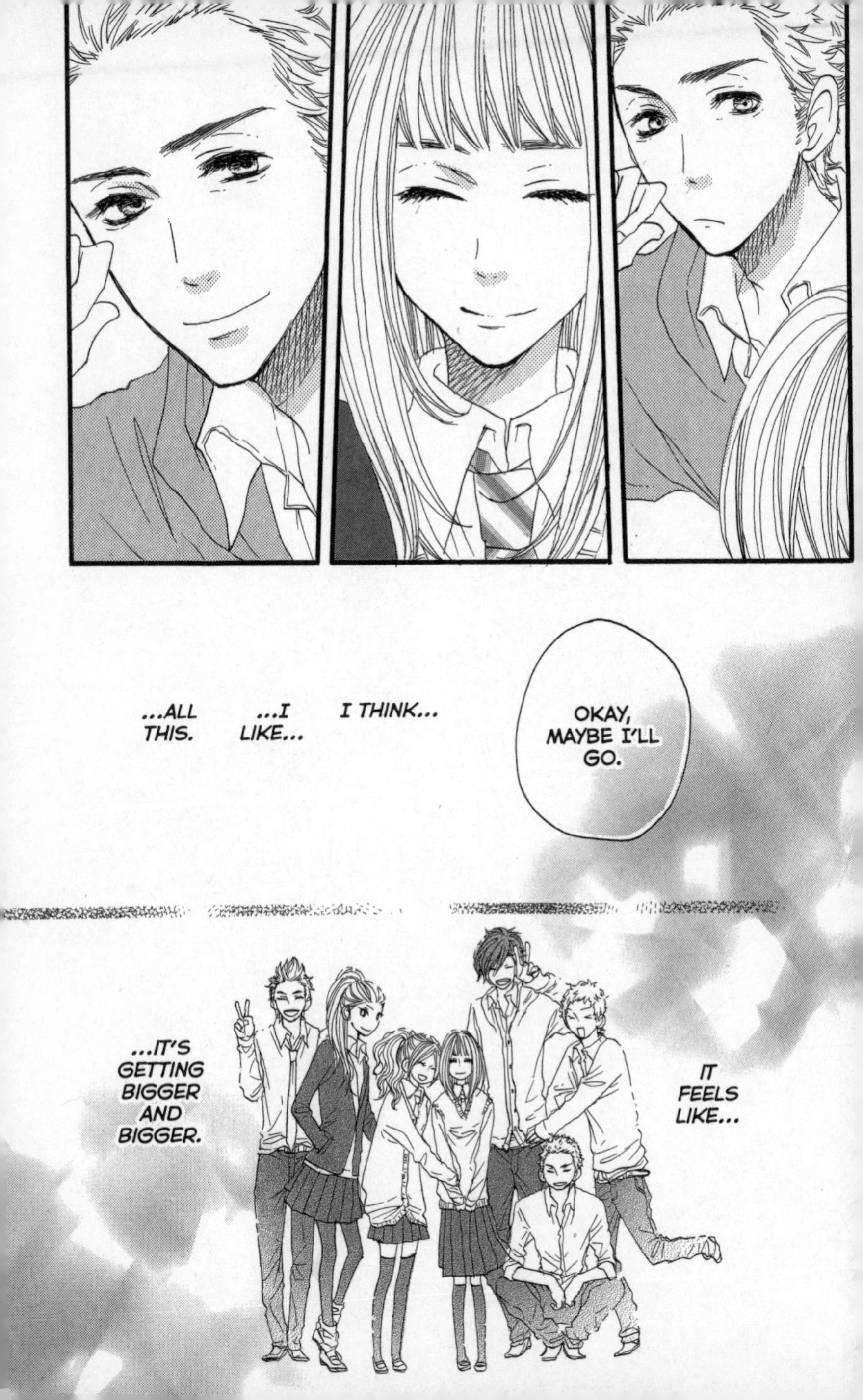
OKAY, MAYBE I'LL GO.
I THINK...
...I LIKE...
...ALL THIS.
IT FEELS LIKE...
...IT'S GETTING BIGGER AND BIGGER.

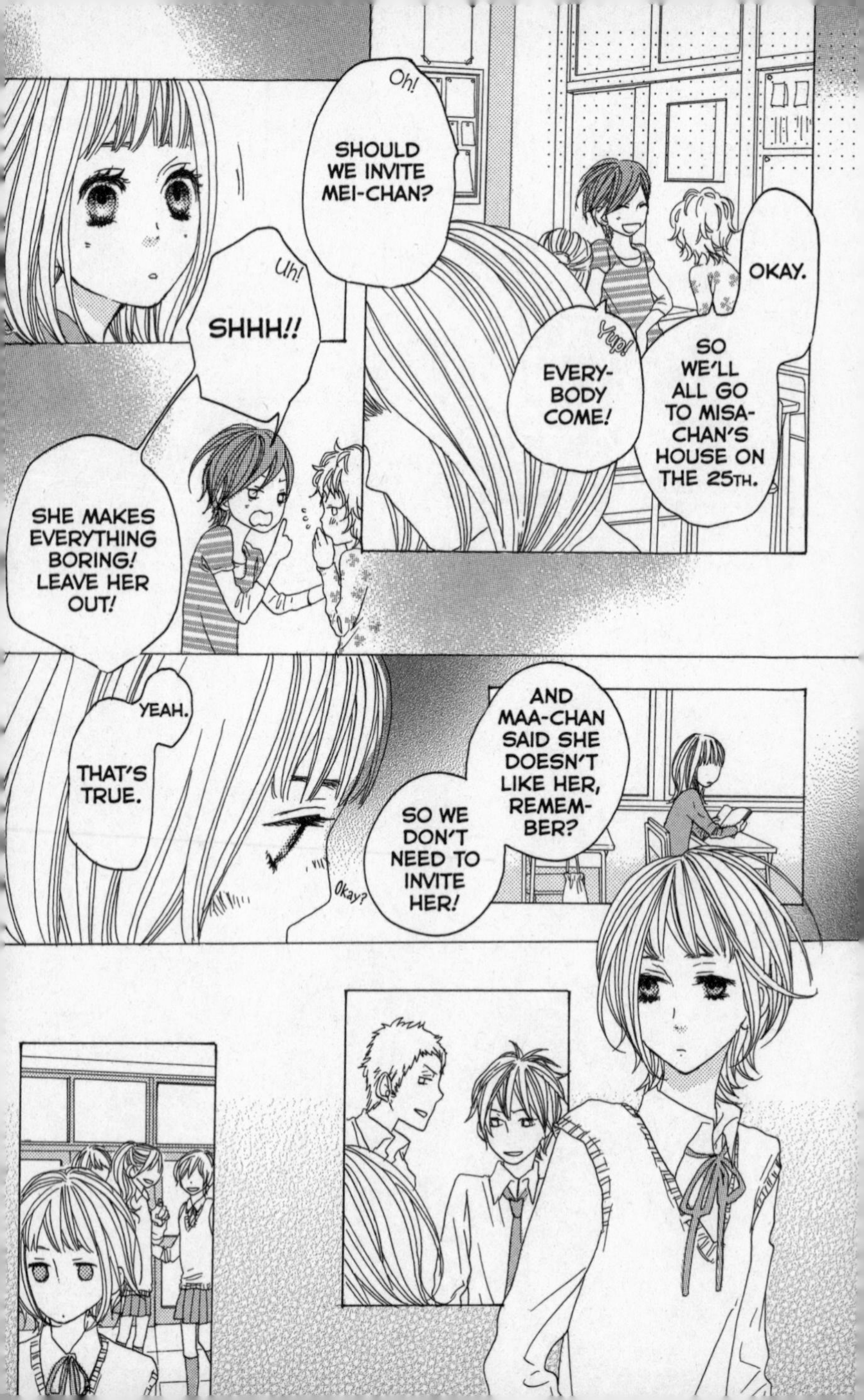
OKAY.
SO WE'LL ALL GO TO MISA-CHAN'S HOUSE ON THE 25TH.
Yup!
EVERY-BODY COME!
Oh!
SHOULD WE INVITE MEI-CHAN?
Uh!
SHHH!!
SHE MAKES EVERYTHING BORING! LEAVE HER OUT!
AND MAA-CHAN SAID SHE DOESN'T LIKE HER, REMEMBER?
SO WE DON'T NEED TO INVITE HER!
Okay?
YEAH.
THAT'S TRUE.

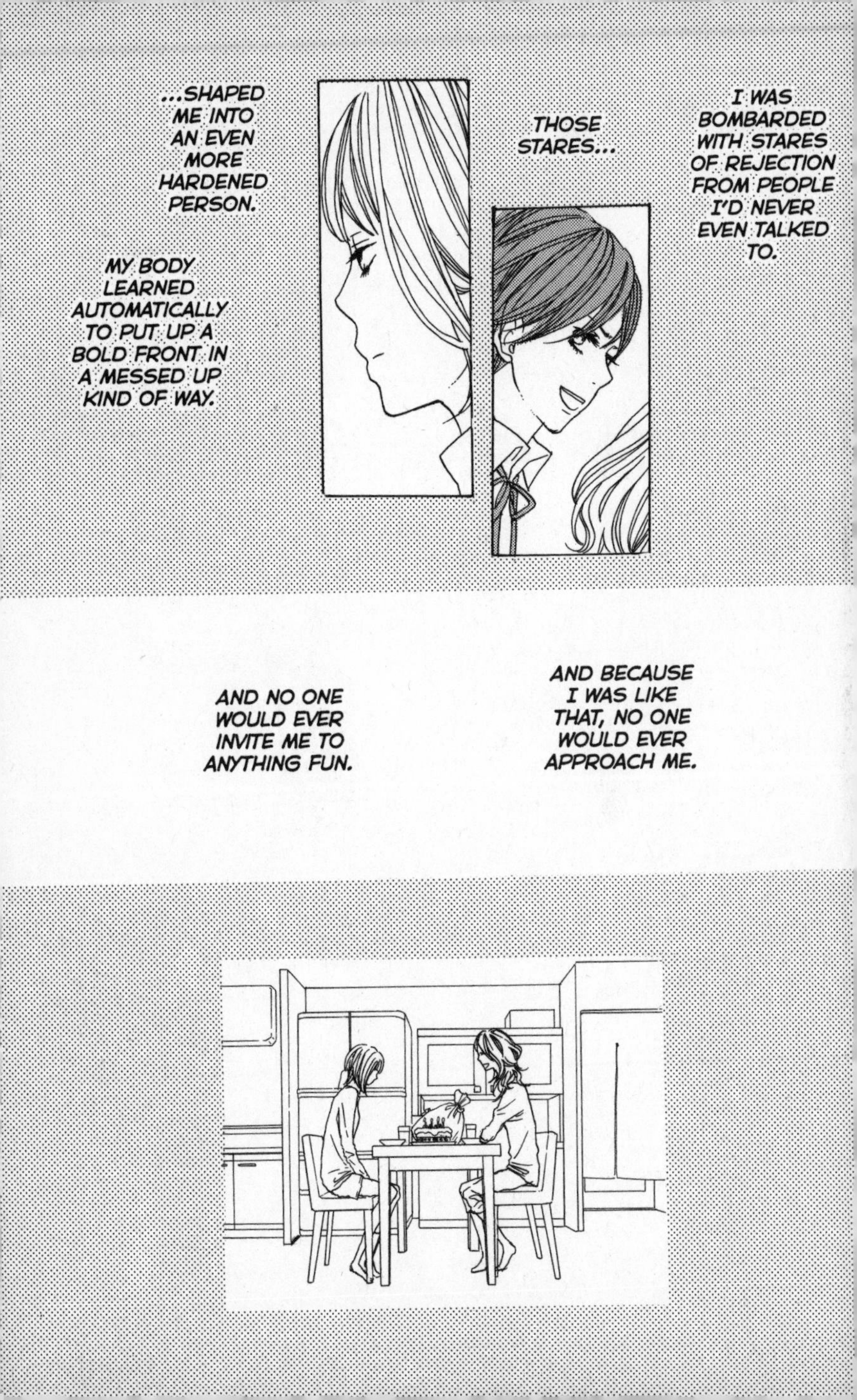
I WAS BOMBARDED WITH STARES OF REJECTION FROM PEOPLE I'D NEVER EVEN TALKED TO.
THOSE STARES...
...SHAPED ME INTO AN EVEN MORE HARDENED PERSON.
MY BODY LEARNED AUTOMATICALLY TO PUT UP A BOLD FRONT IN A MESSED UP KIND OF WAY.
AND BECAUSE I WAS LIKE THAT, NO ONE WOULD EVER APPROACH ME.
AND NO ONE WOULD EVER INVITE ME TO ANYTHING FUN.

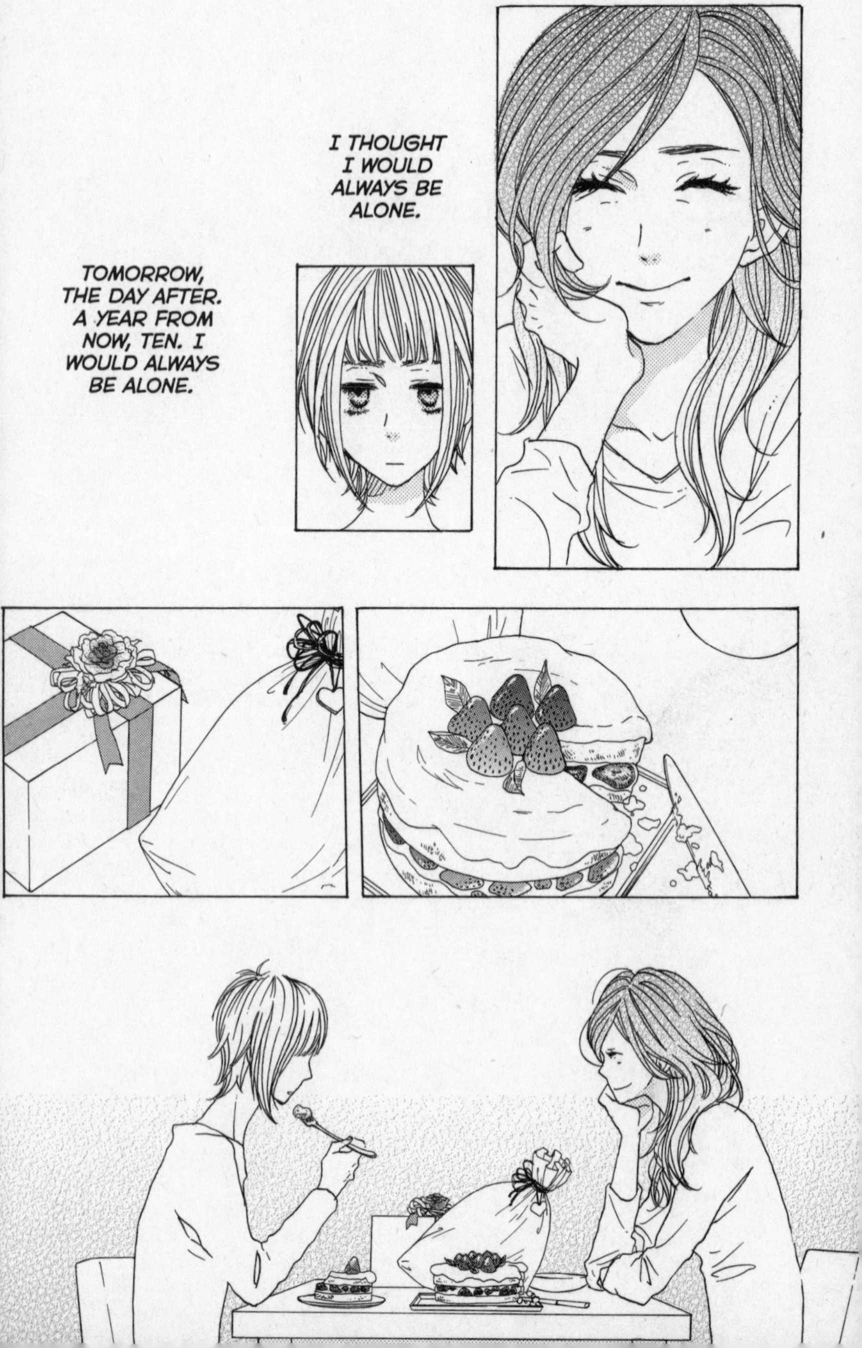
I THOUGHT I WOULD ALWAYS BE ALONE.
TOMORROW, THE DAY AFTER. A YEAR FROM NOW, TEN. I WOULD ALWAYS BE ALONE.

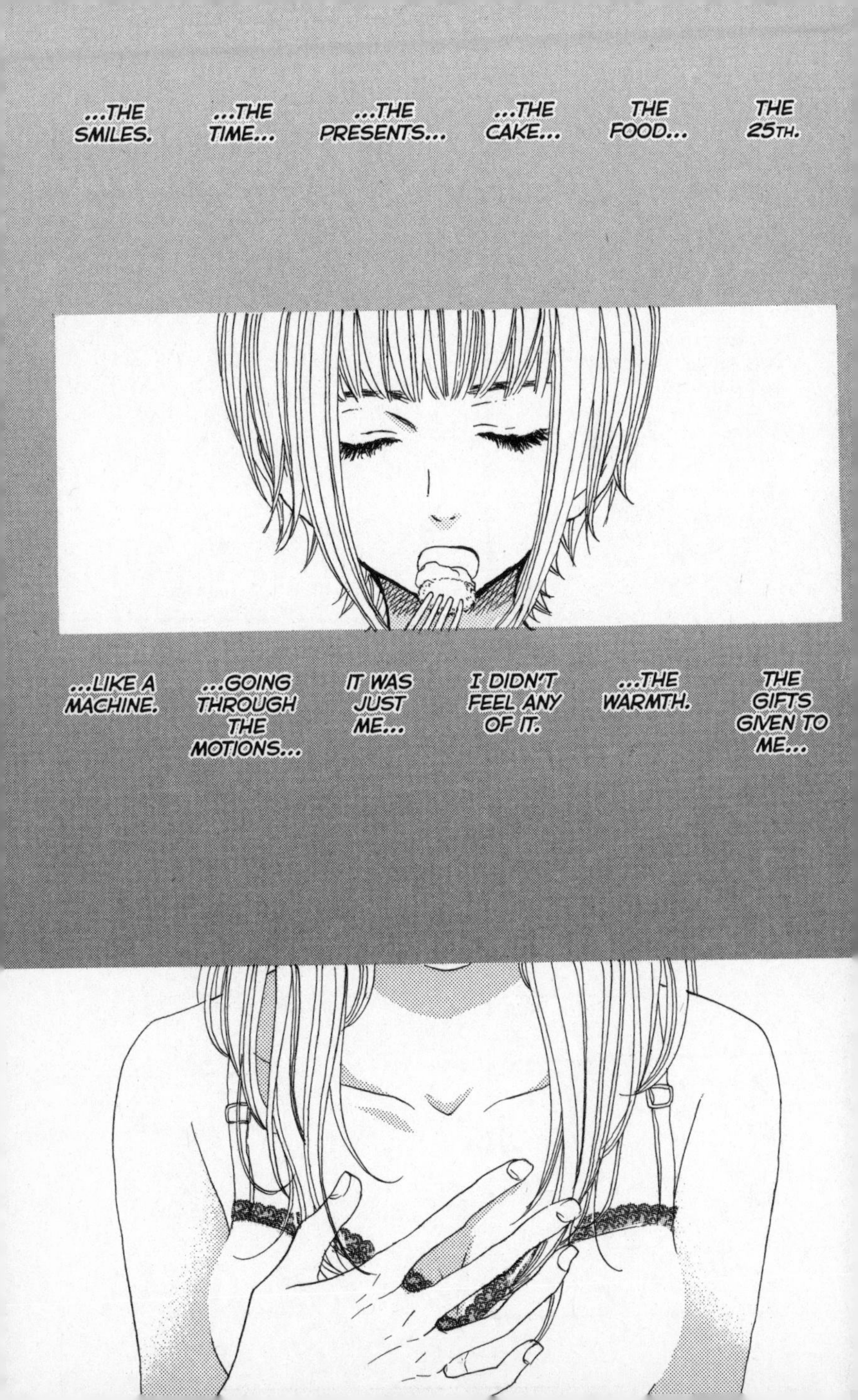
THE 25TH.
THE FOOD...
...THE CAKE...
...THE PRESENTS...
...THE TIME...
...THE SMILES.
THE GIFTS GIVEN TO ME...
...THE WARMTH.
I DIDN'T FEEL ANY OF IT.
IT WAS JUST ME...
...GOING THROUGH THE MOTIONS...
...LIKE A MACHINE.

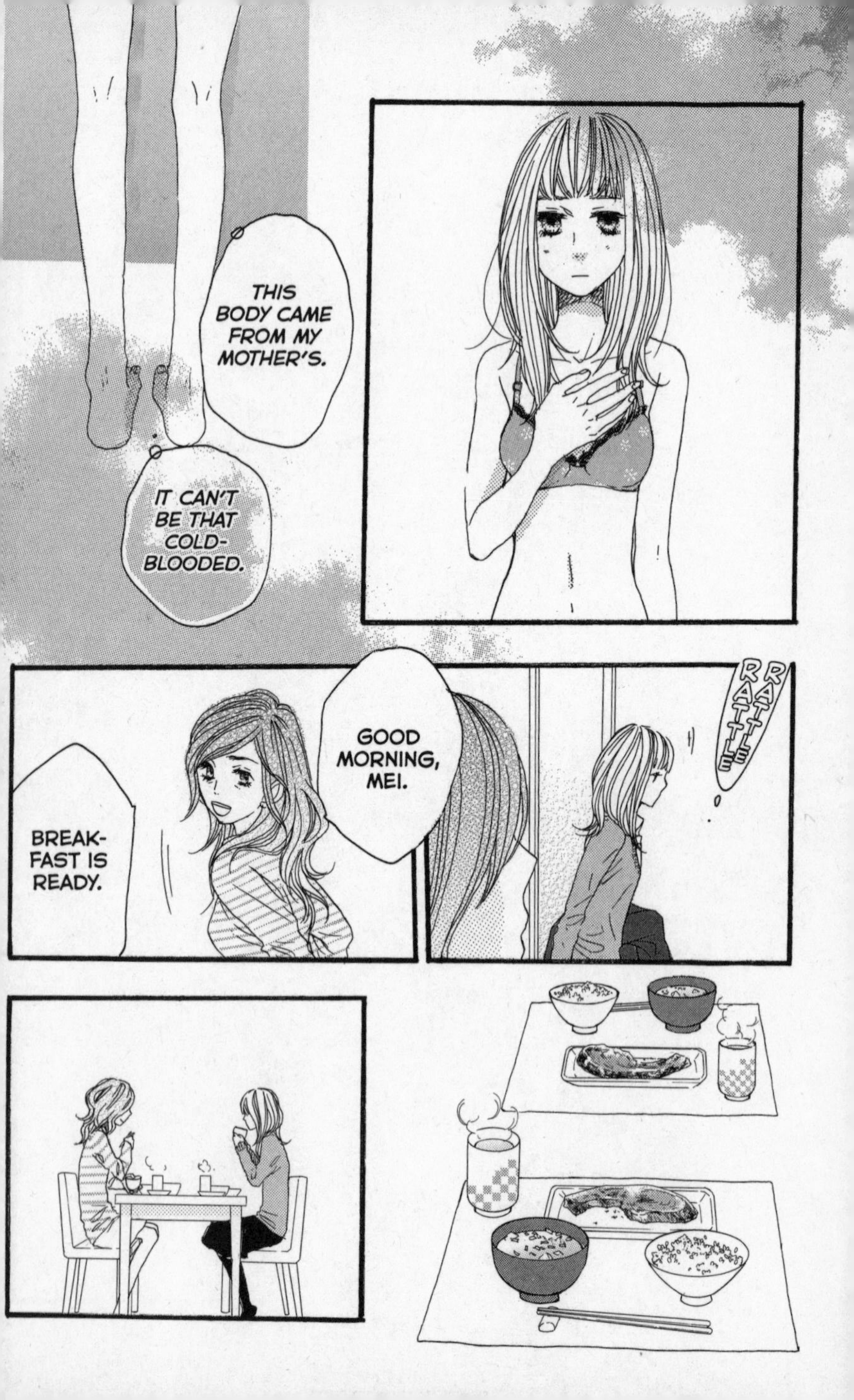
THIS BODY CAME FROM MY MOTHER'S.
IT CAN'T BE THAT COLD-BLOODED.
RATTLE RATTLE
GOOD MORNING, MEI.
BREAK-FAST IS READY.

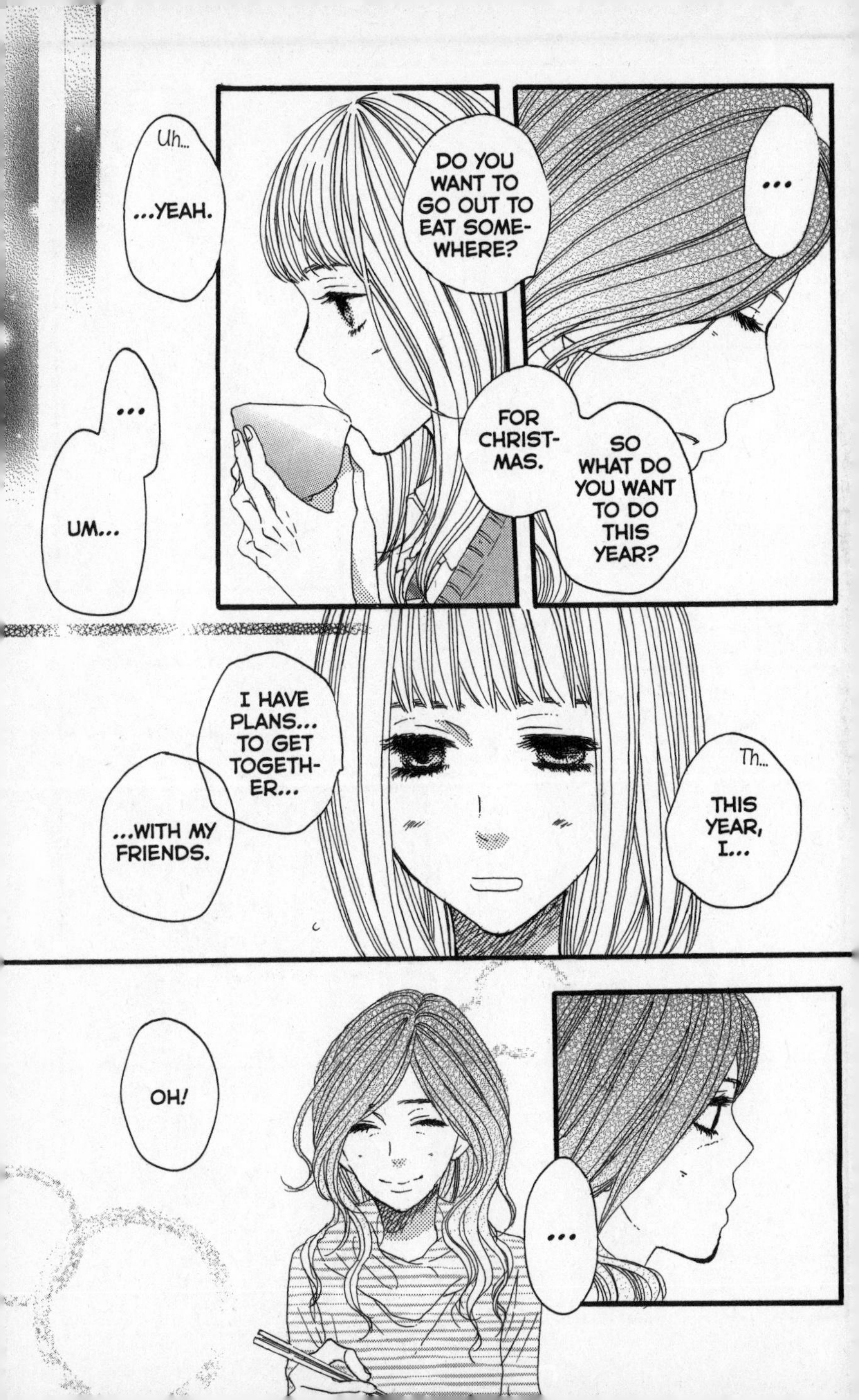
...
SO WHAT DO YOU WANT TO DO THIS YEAR?
FOR CHRIST-MAS.
DO YOU WANT TO GO OUT TO EAT SOME-WHERE?
Uh... ...YEAH.
...
UM...
Th... THIS YEAR, I...
I HAVE PLANS... TO GET TOGETH-ER...
...WITH MY FRIENDS.
...
OH!

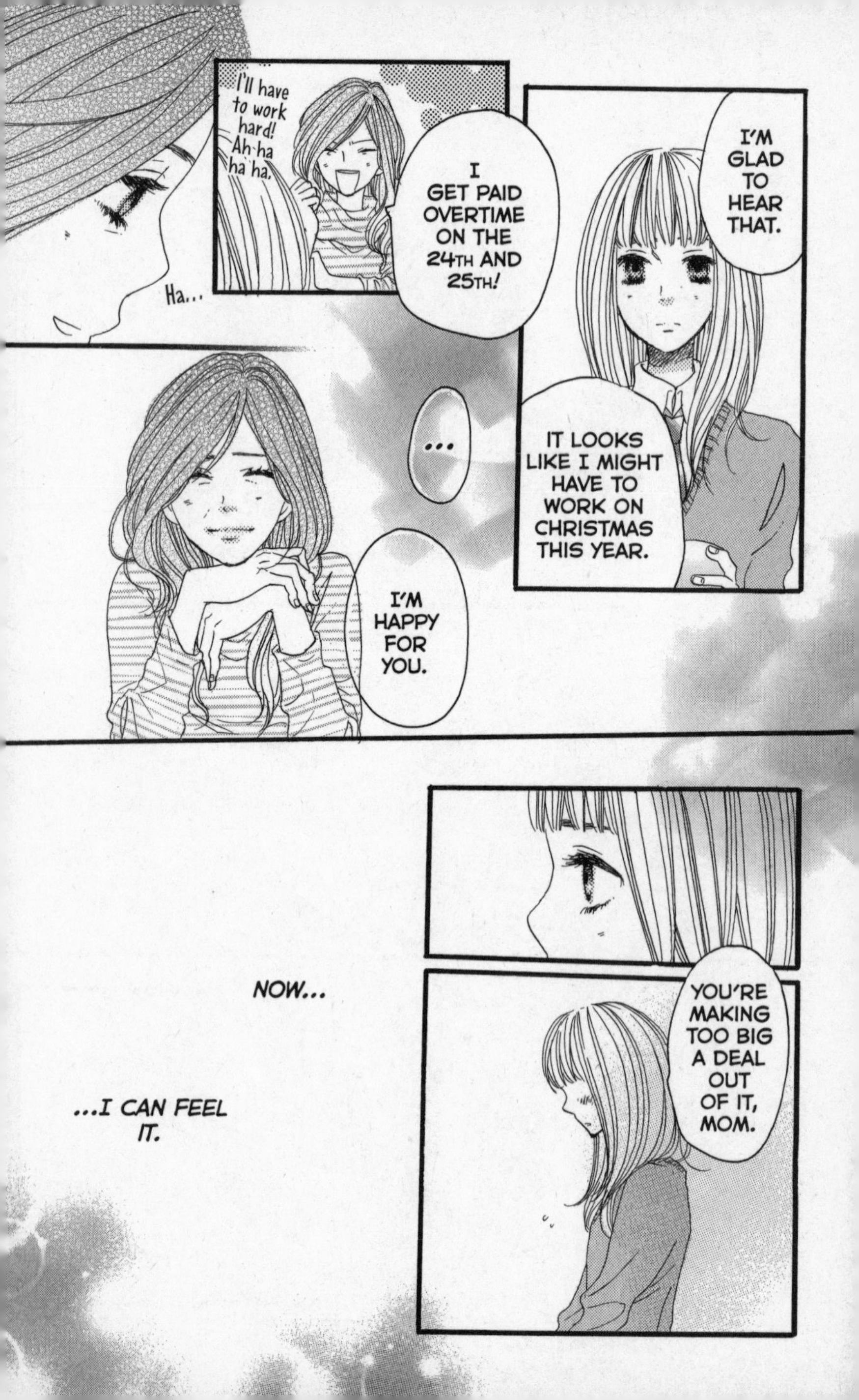
I'M GLAD TO HEAR THAT.
IT LOOKS LIKE I MIGHT HAVE TO WORK ON CHRISTMAS THIS YEAR.
I GET PAID OVERTIME ON THE 24TH AND 25TH!
I'll have to work hard! Ah-ha ha ha.
Ha...
...
I'M HAPPY FOR YOU.
YOU'RE MAKING TOO BIG A DEAL OUT OF IT, MOM.
NOW...
...I CAN FEEL IT.

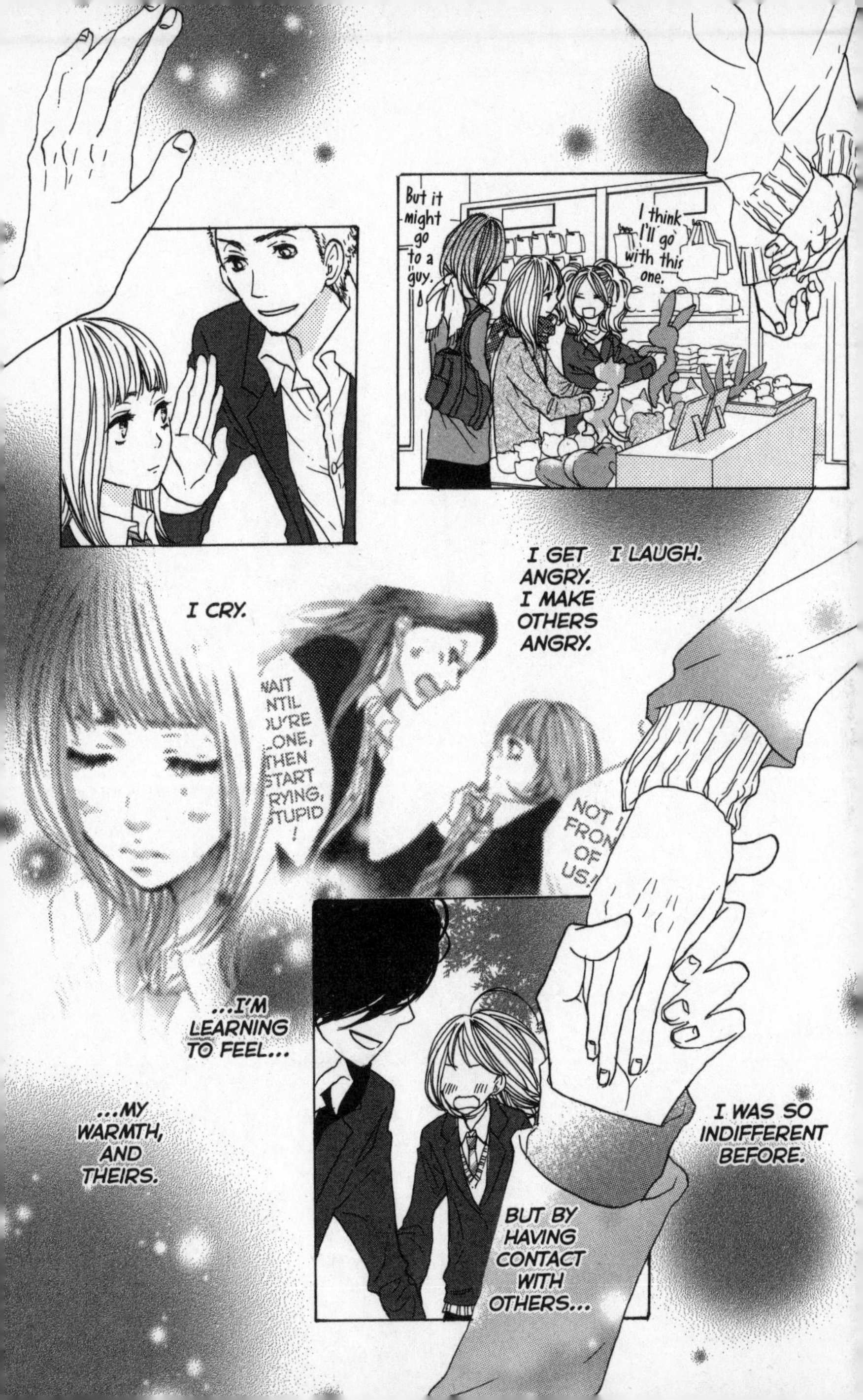
I think I'll go with this one.
But it might go to a guy.
I LAUGH.
I GET ANGRY. I MAKE OTHERS ANGRY.
NOT FRON OF US!
NAIT NTIL OU'RE ONE, THEN START RYING, STUPID!
I CRY.
I WAS SO INDIFFERENT BEFORE.
BUT BY HAVING CONTACT WITH OTHERS...
...I'M LEARNING TO FEEL...
...MY WARMTH, AND THEIRS.

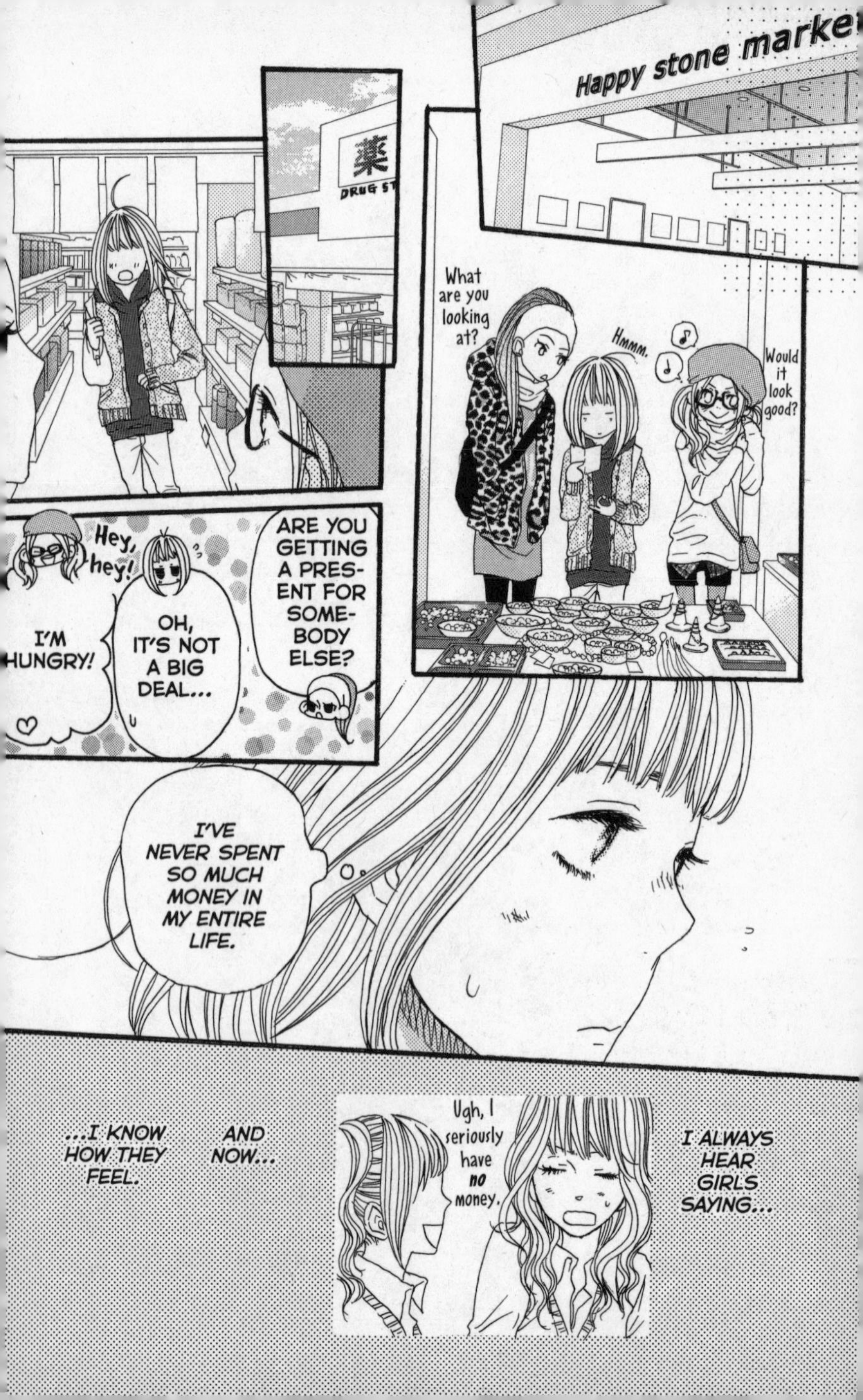
Happy stone market
DRUG ST
Would it look good?
Hmmm.
What are you looking at?
ARE YOU GETTING A PRESENT FOR SOMEBODY ELSE?
OH, IT'S NOT A BIG DEAL...
Hey, hey!
I'M HUNGRY!
I'VE NEVER SPENT SO MUCH MONEY IN MY ENTIRE LIFE.
I ALWAYS HEAR GIRLS SAYING...
Ugh, I seriously have no money.
AND NOW...
...I KNOW HOW THEY FEEL.

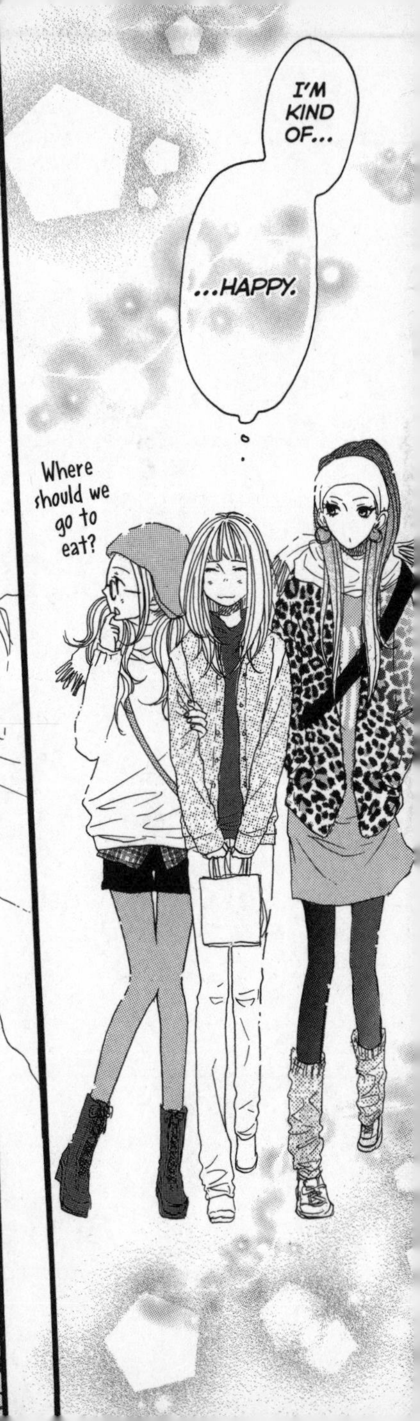
I'M KIND OF...
...HAPPY.
Where should we go to eat?

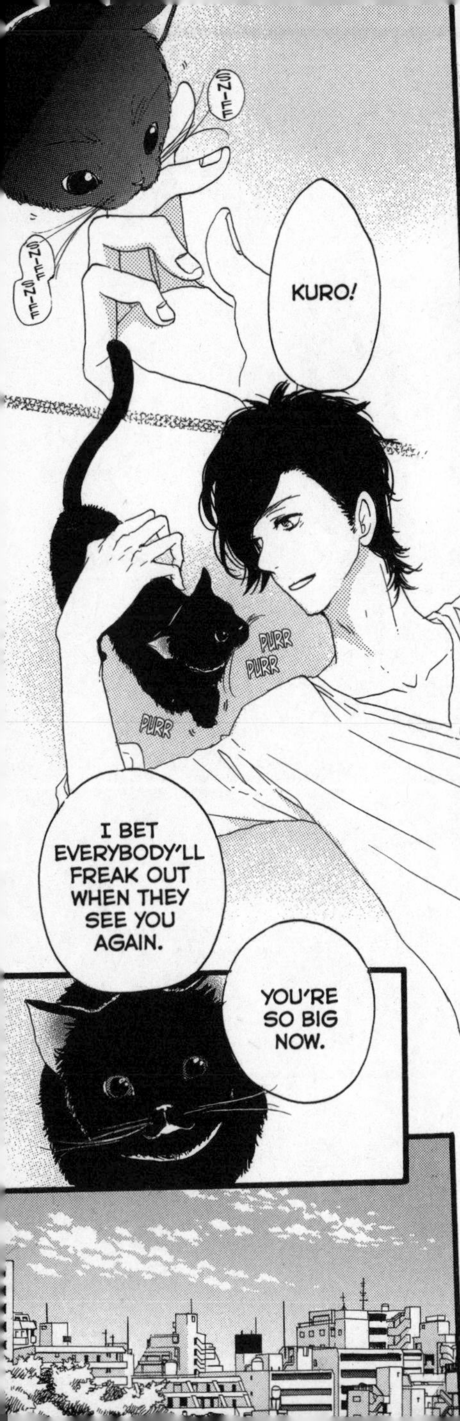
SNIFF
KURO!
SNIFF SNIFF
PURR PURR
PURR
I BET EVERYBODY'LL FREAK OUT WHEN THEY SEE YOU AGAIN.
YOU'RE SO BIG NOW.

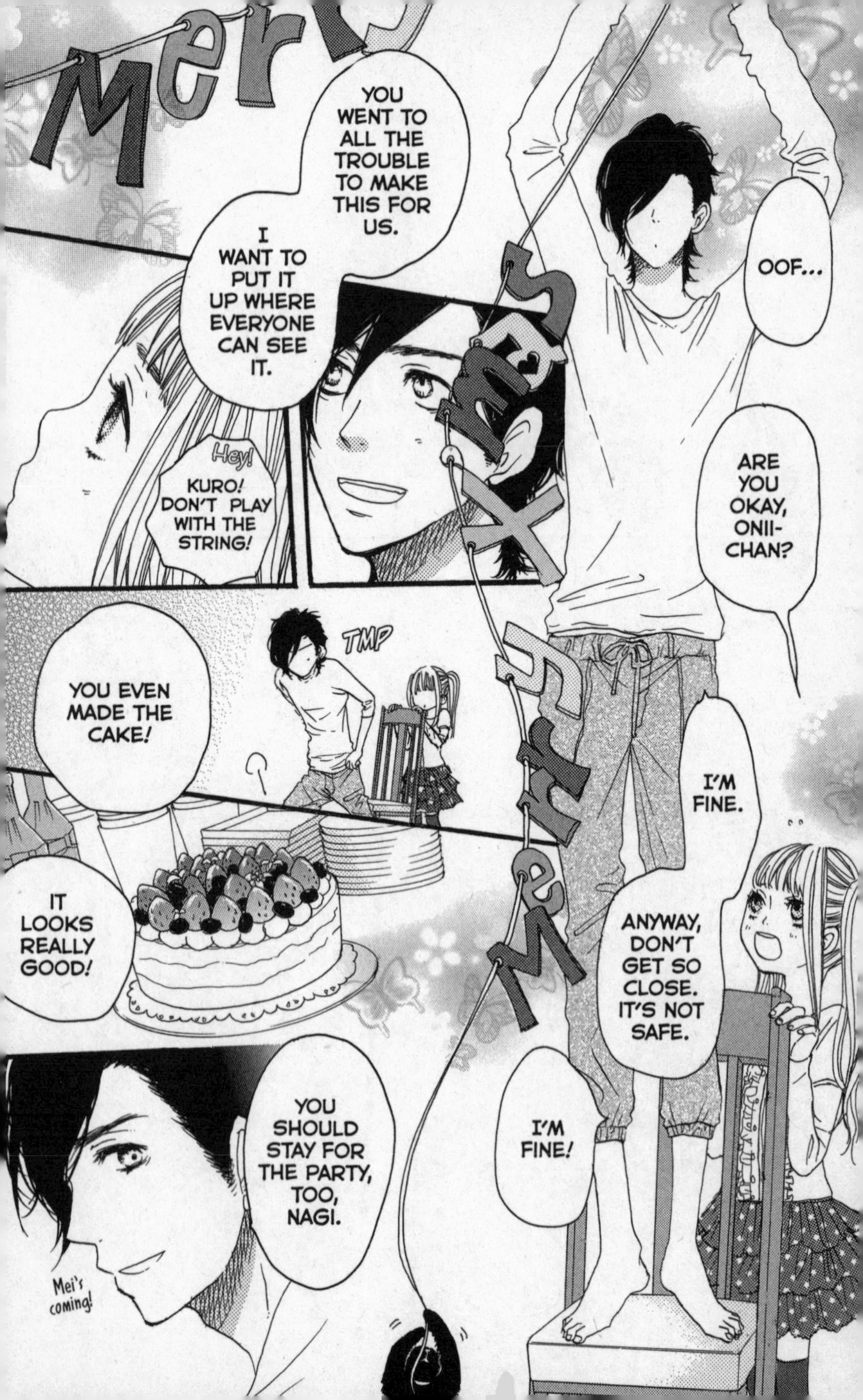
OOF...
ARE YOU OKAY, ONII-CHAN?
I'M FINE.
ANYWAY, DON'T GET SO CLOSE. IT'S NOT SAFE.
I'M FINE!
Merry
YOU WENT TO ALL THE TROUBLE TO MAKE THIS FOR US.
I WANT TO PUT IT UP WHERE EVERYONE CAN SEE IT.
Hey!
KURO! DON'T PLAY WITH THE STRING!
Xmas
Merry
TMP
YOU EVEN MADE THE CAKE!
IT LOOKS REALLY GOOD!
YOU SHOULD STAY FOR THE PARTY, TOO, NAGI.
Mei's coming!

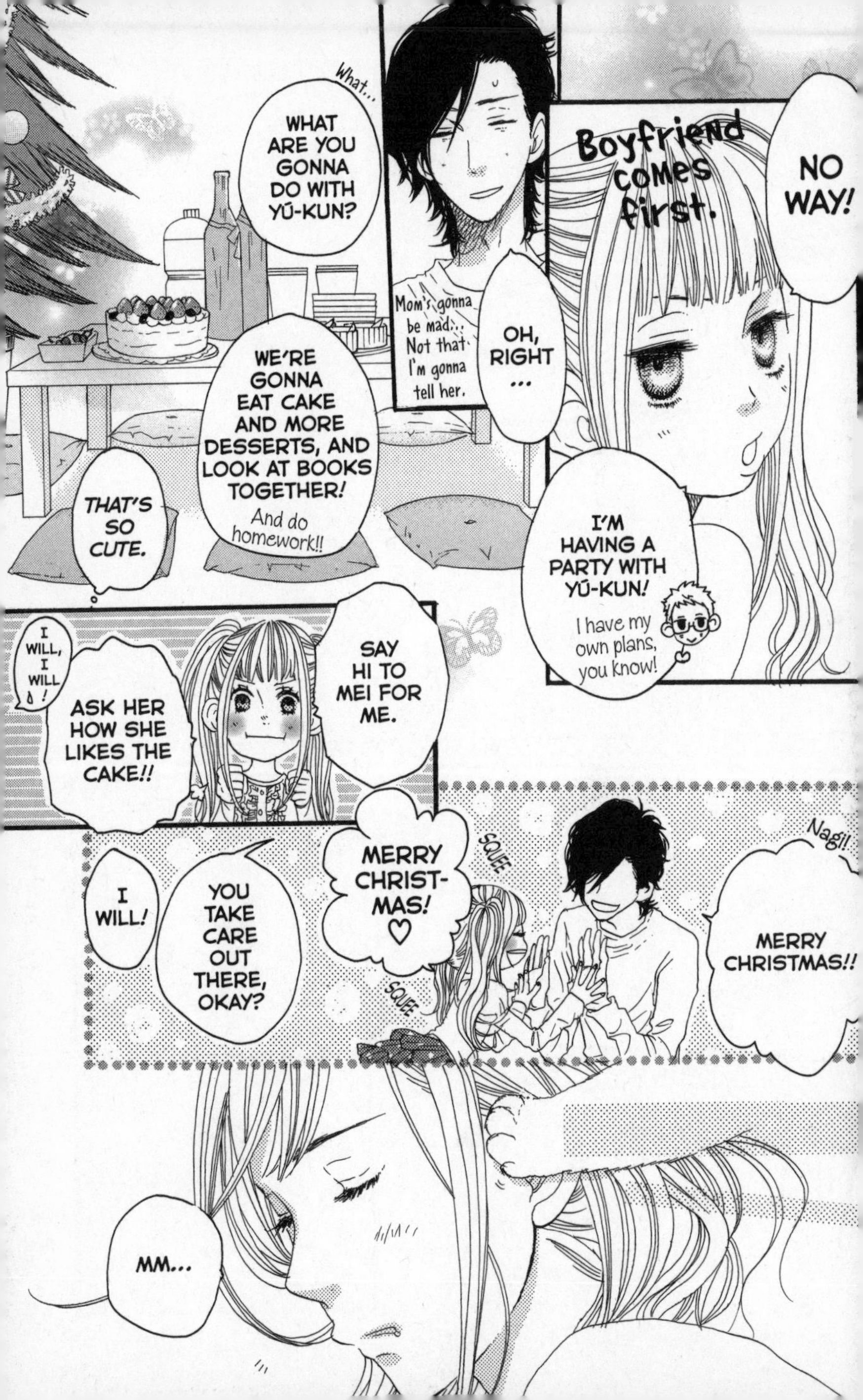
NO WAY!
Boyfriend comes first.
I'M HAVING A PARTY WITH YŪ-KUN!
I have my own plans, you know!
OH, RIGHT...
Mom's gonna be mad... Not that I'm gonna tell her.
What...
WHAT ARE YOU GONNA DO WITH YŪ-KUN?
WE'RE GONNA EAT CAKE AND MORE DESSERTS, AND LOOK AT BOOKS TOGETHER!
And do homework!!
THAT'S SO CUTE.
SAY HI TO MEI FOR ME.
ASK HER HOW SHE LIKES THE CAKE!!
I WILL, I WILL!
Nagi!!
MERRY CHRISTMAS!!
SQUEE
SQUEE
MERRY CHRIST-MAS! ♡
YOU TAKE CARE OUT THERE, OKAY?
I WILL!
MM...

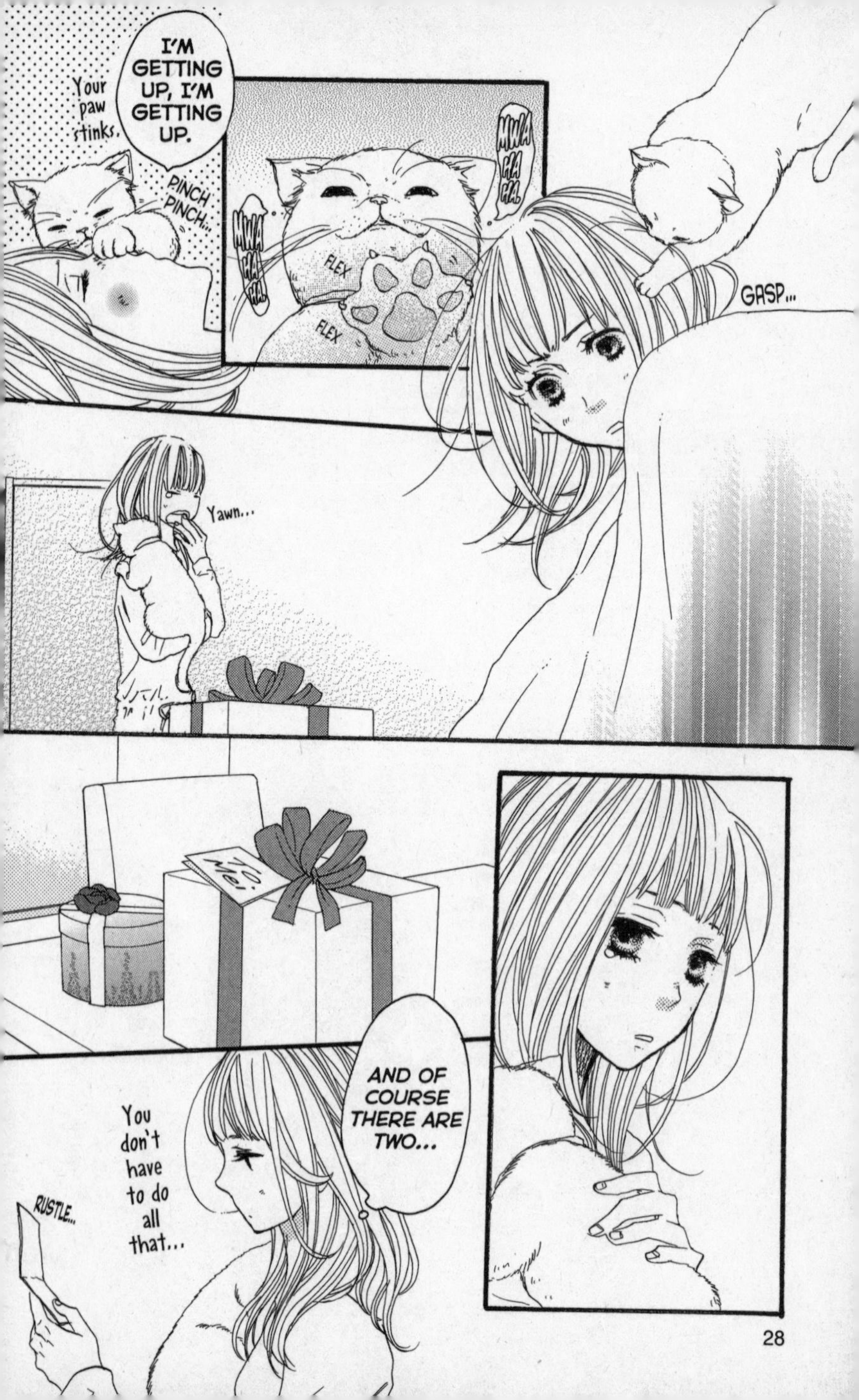
GASP...
MWA HA HA.
MWA HA HA.
FLEX
FLEX
PINCH PINCH...
I'M GETTING UP, I'M GETTING UP.
Your paw stinks.
Yawn...
To: Me!
AND OF COURSE THERE ARE TWO...
You don't have to do all that...
RUSTLE...

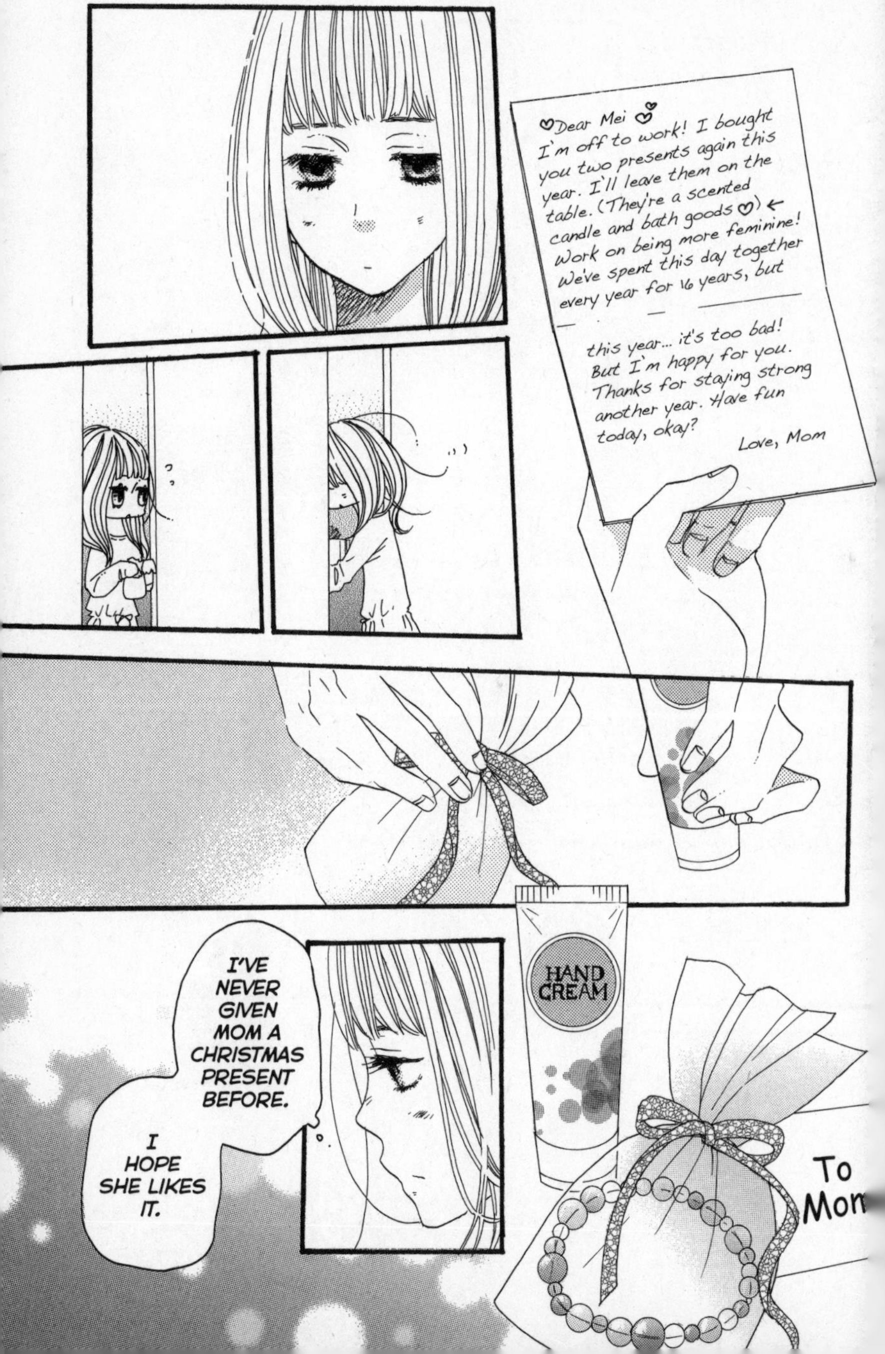
Dear Mei
I'm off to work! I bought you two presents again this year. I'll leave them on the table. (They're a scented candle and bath goods) ←
Work on being more feminine!
We've spent this day together every year for 16 years, but
this year... it's too bad! But I'm happy for you. Thanks for staying strong another year. Have fun today, okay?
Love, Mom
HAND CREAM
To Mom
I'VE NEVER GIVEN MOM A CHRISTMAS PRESENT BEFORE.
I HOPE SHE LIKES IT.

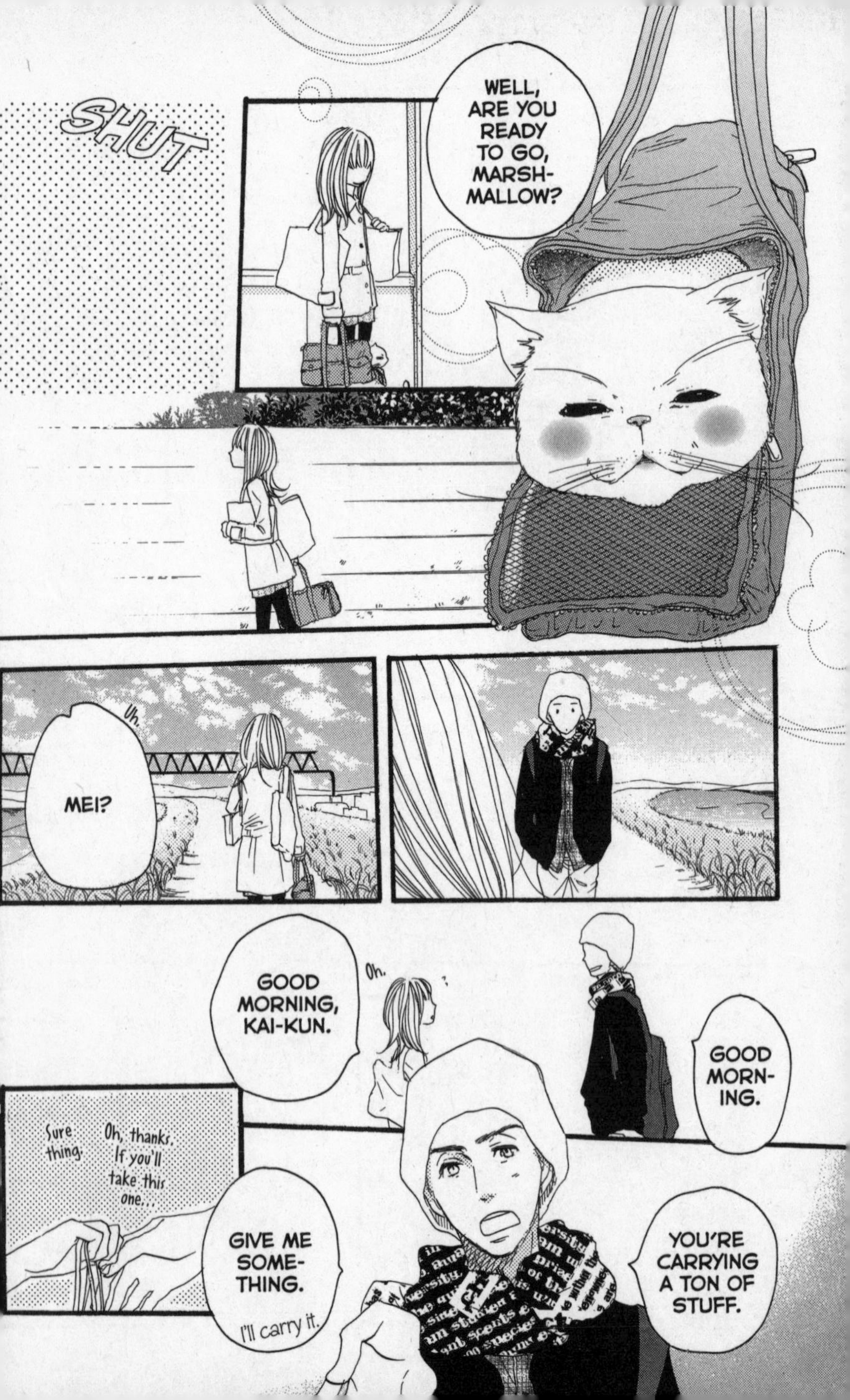
WELL, ARE YOU READY TO GO, MARSH-MALLOW?
SHUT
Uh.
MEI?
GOOD MORN-ING.
Oh.
GOOD MORNING, KAI-KUN.
YOU'RE CARRYING A TON OF STUFF.
GIVE ME SOME-THING.
I'll carry it.
Oh, thanks. If you'll take this one...
Sure thing.

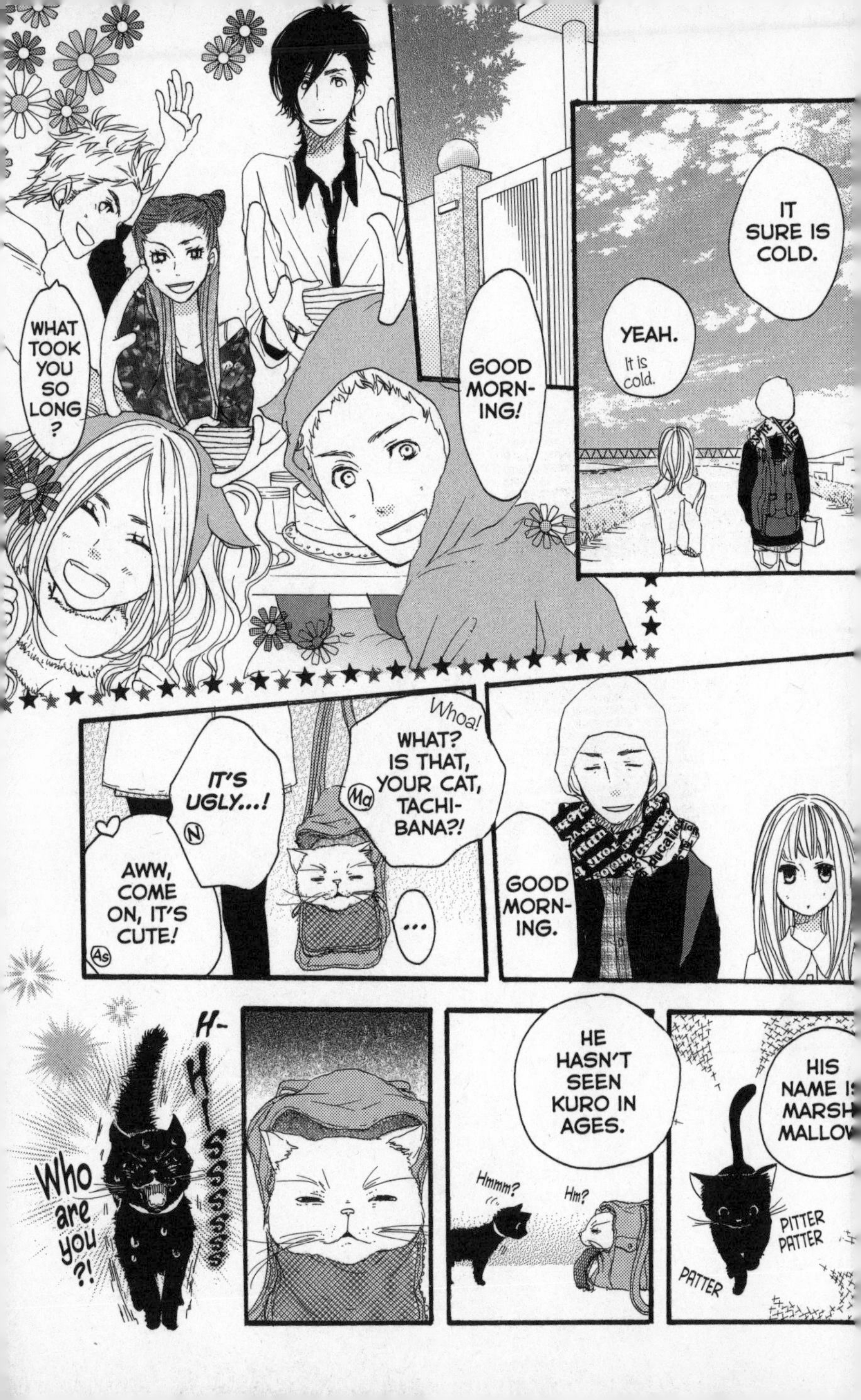
IT SURE IS COLD.
YEAH.
It is cold.
GOOD MORNING!
WHAT TOOK YOU SO LONG?
GOOD MORNING.
Whoa!
WHAT? IS THAT, YOUR CAT, TACHIBANA?!
IT'S UGLY...!
AWW, COME ON, IT'S CUTE!
...
HIS NAME IS MARSH MALLOW
PITTER PATTER
PATTER
HE HASN'T SEEN KURO IN AGES.
Hmmm?
Hm?
H-HISSSSSS
Who are you?!

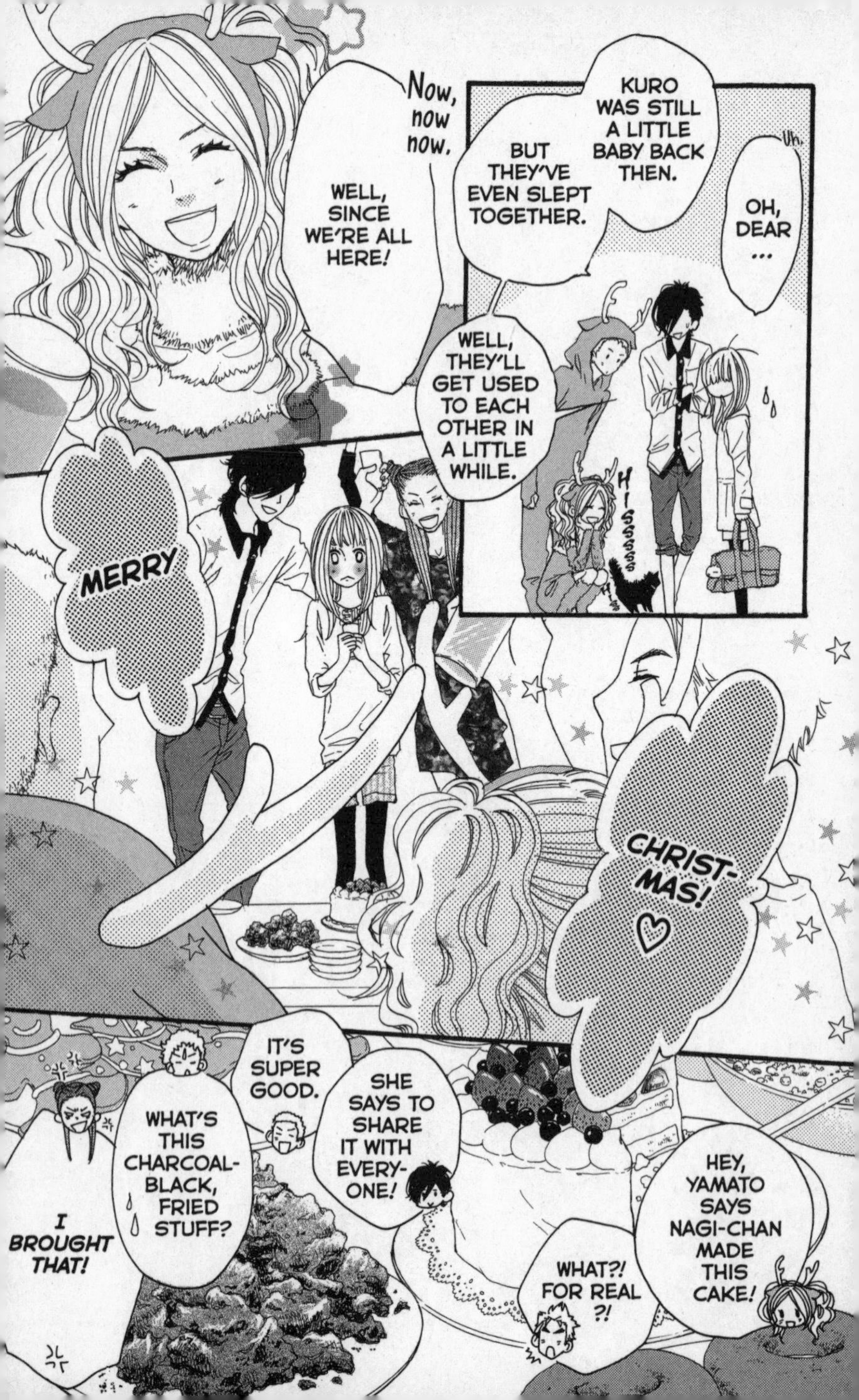
KURO WAS STILL A LITTLE BABY BACK THEN.
Uh.
OH, DEAR...
BUT THEY'VE EVEN SLEPT TOGETHER.
WELL, THEY'LL GET USED TO EACH OTHER IN A LITTLE WHILE.
HISSSSS
HISS
Now, now now.
WELL, SINCE WE'RE ALL HERE!
MERRY
CHRIST-MAS! ♡
HEY, YAMATO SAYS NAGI-CHAN MADE THIS CAKE!
WHAT?! FOR REAL?!
SHE SAYS TO SHARE IT WITH EVERY-ONE!
IT'S SUPER GOOD.
WHAT'S THIS CHARCOAL-BLACK, FRIED STUFF?
I BROUGHT THAT!

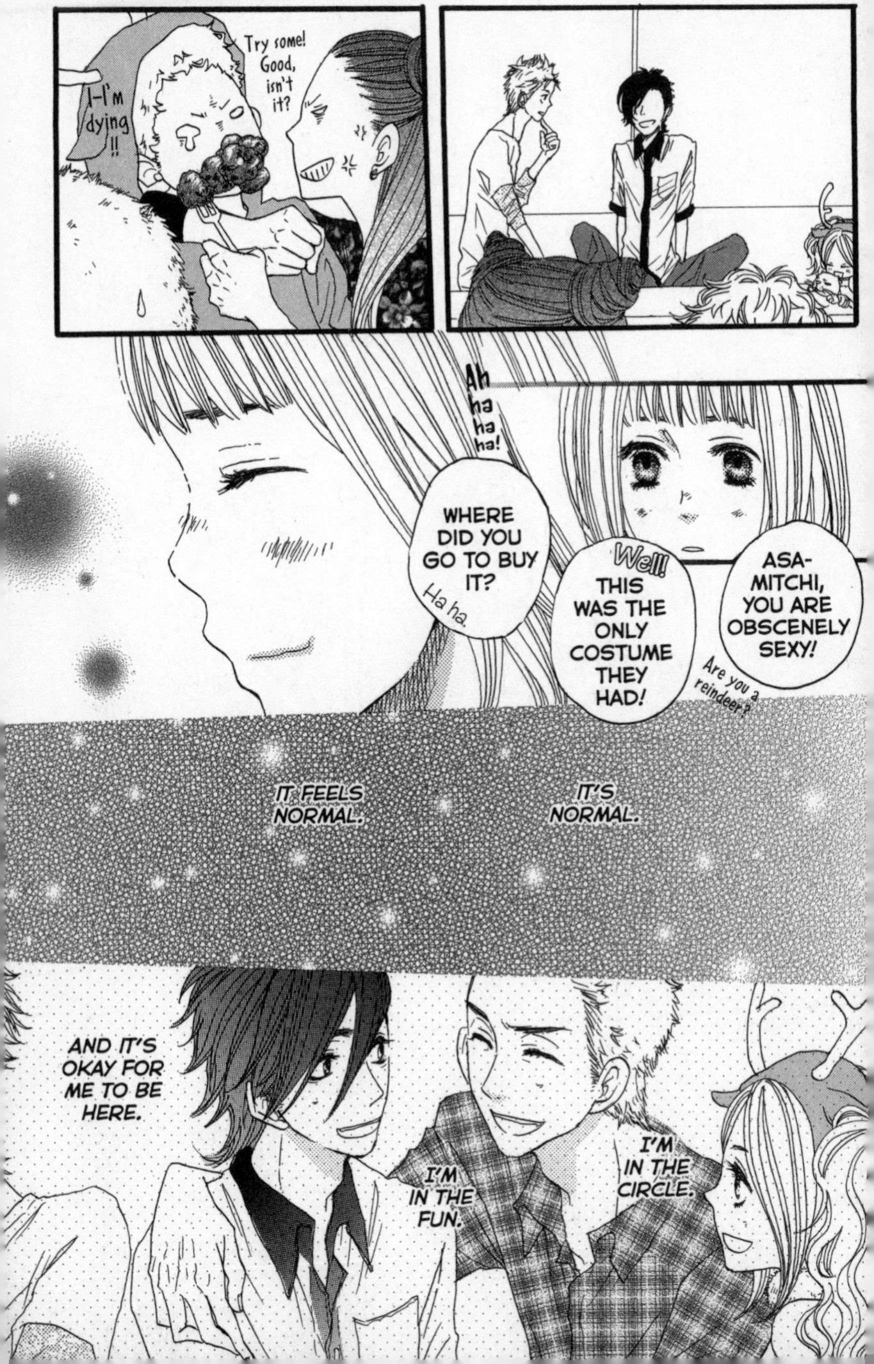
Try some! Good, isn't it?
I-I'm dying!!
ASA-MITCHI, YOU ARE OBSCENELY SEXY!
Are you a reindeer?
Well! THIS WAS THE ONLY COSTUME THEY HAD!
Ah ha ha ha!
WHERE DID YOU GO TO BUY IT?
Ha ha.
IT'S NORMAL.
IT FEELS NORMAL.
I'M IN THE CIRCLE.
I'M IN THE FUN.
AND IT'S OKAY FOR ME TO BE HERE.

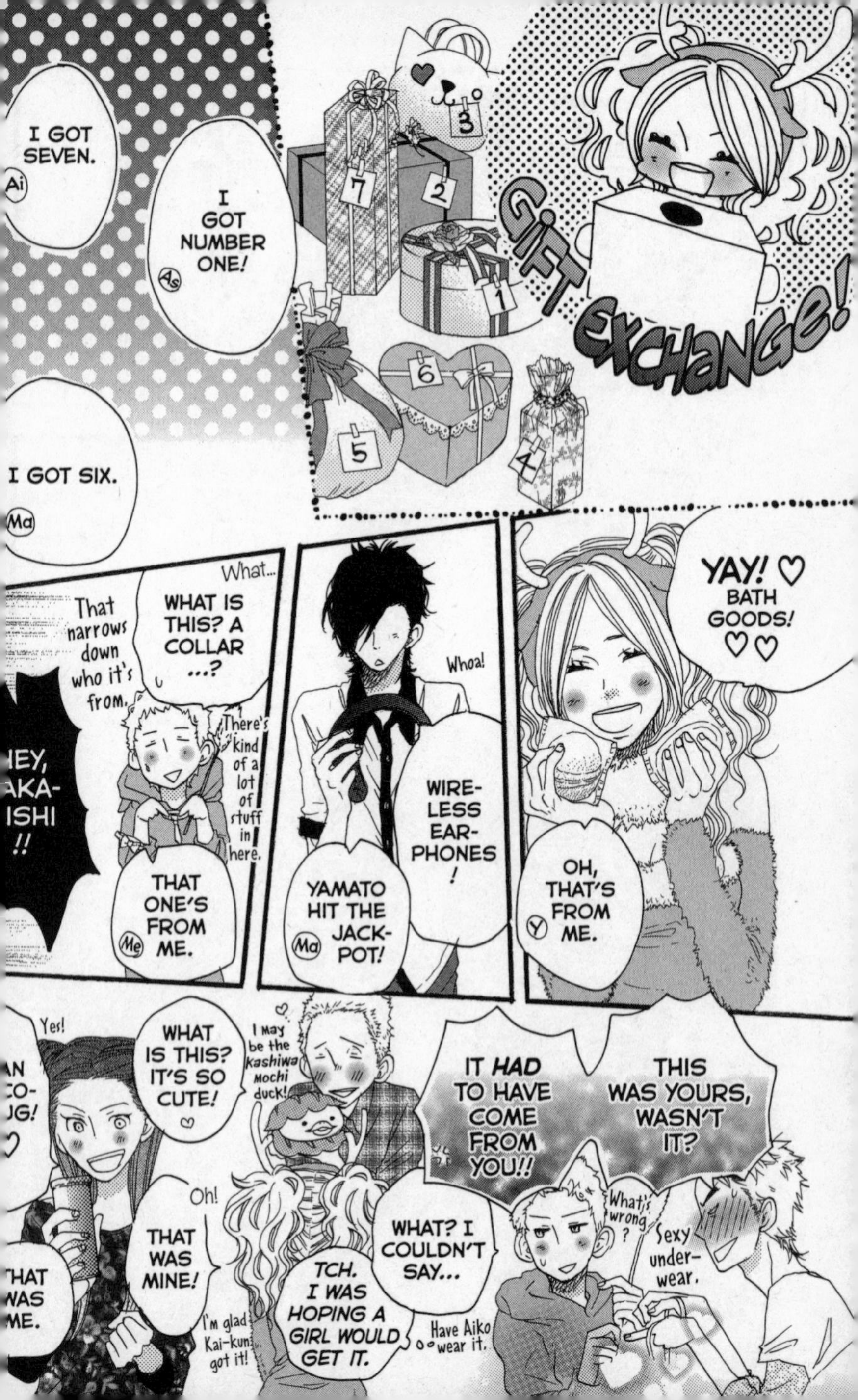
GIFT EXCHANGE!
I GOT NUMBER ONE!
I GOT SEVEN.
I GOT SIX.
YAY! ♡ BATH GOODS! ♡ ♡
OH, THAT'S FROM ME.
Whoa!
WIRELESS EARPHONES!
YAMATO HIT THE JACKPOT!
What...
WHAT IS THIS? A COLLAR ...?
That narrows down who it's from.
There's kind of a lot of stuff in here.
THAT ONE'S FROM ME.
HEY, AKA-ISHI!!
THIS WAS YOURS, WASN'T IT?
IT HAD TO HAVE COME FROM YOU!!
Sexy underwear.
What's wrong?
WHAT? I COULDN'T SAY...
Have Aiko wear it.
TCH. I WAS HOPING A GIRL WOULD GET IT.
I may be the kashiwa mochi duck!
WHAT IS THIS? IT'S SO CUTE!
Oh!
THAT WAS MINE!
I'm glad Kai-kun got it!
Yes!
HAT WAS ME.

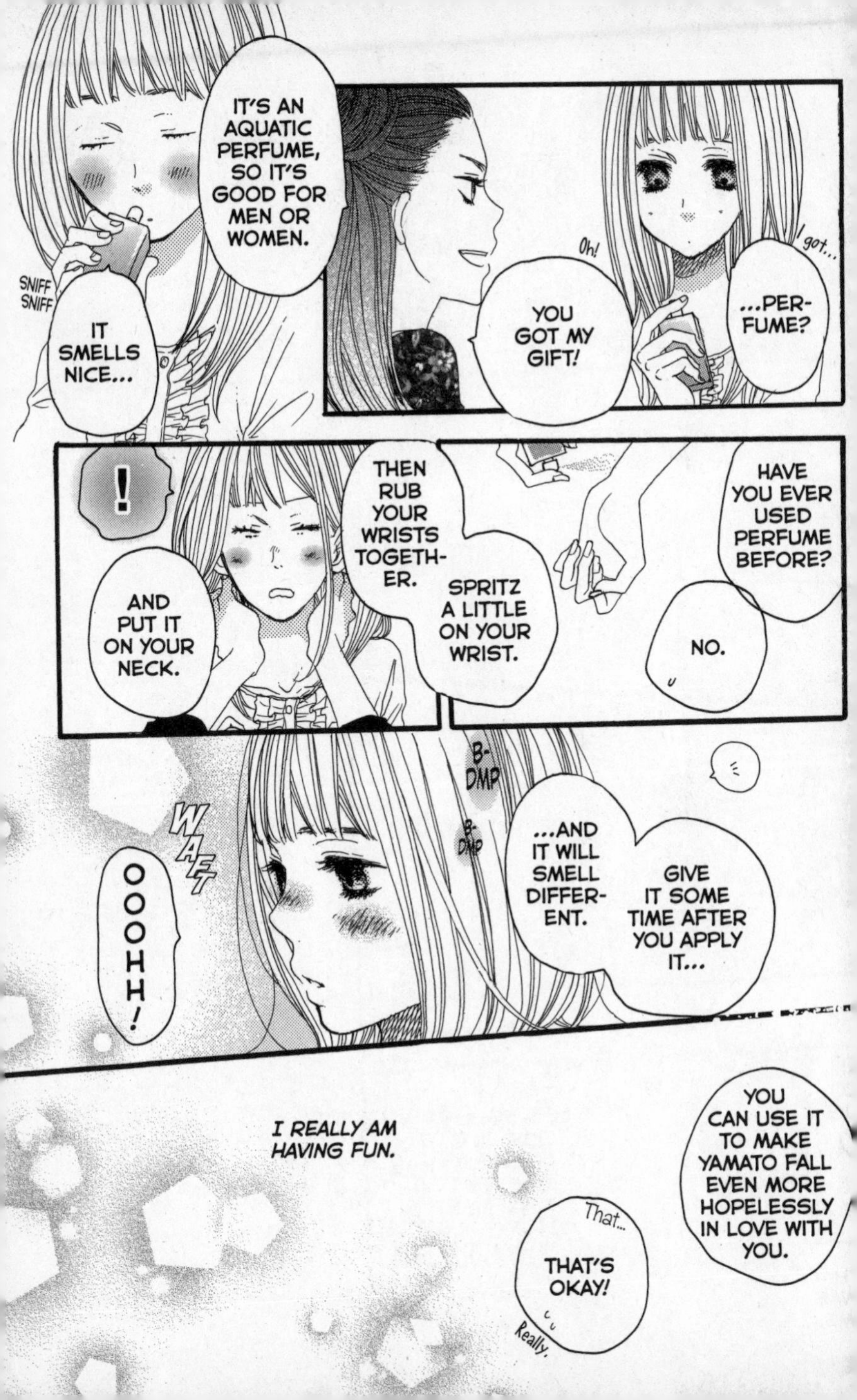
I got...
...PER-FUME?
Oh!
YOU GOT MY GIFT!
IT'S AN AQUATIC PERFUME, SO IT'S GOOD FOR MEN OR WOMEN.
SNIFF SNIFF
IT SMELLS NICE...
HAVE YOU EVER USED PERFUME BEFORE?
NO.
SPRITZ A LITTLE ON YOUR WRIST.
THEN RUB YOUR WRISTS TOGETH-ER.
!
AND PUT IT ON YOUR NECK.
GIVE IT SOME TIME AFTER YOU APPLY IT...
...AND IT WILL SMELL DIFFER-ENT.
B-DMP
B-DMP
WAFT
OOOOHH!
YOU CAN USE IT TO MAKE YAMATO FALL EVEN MORE HOPELESSLY IN LOVE WITH YOU.
That...
THAT'S OKAY!
Really.
I REALLY AM HAVING FUN.

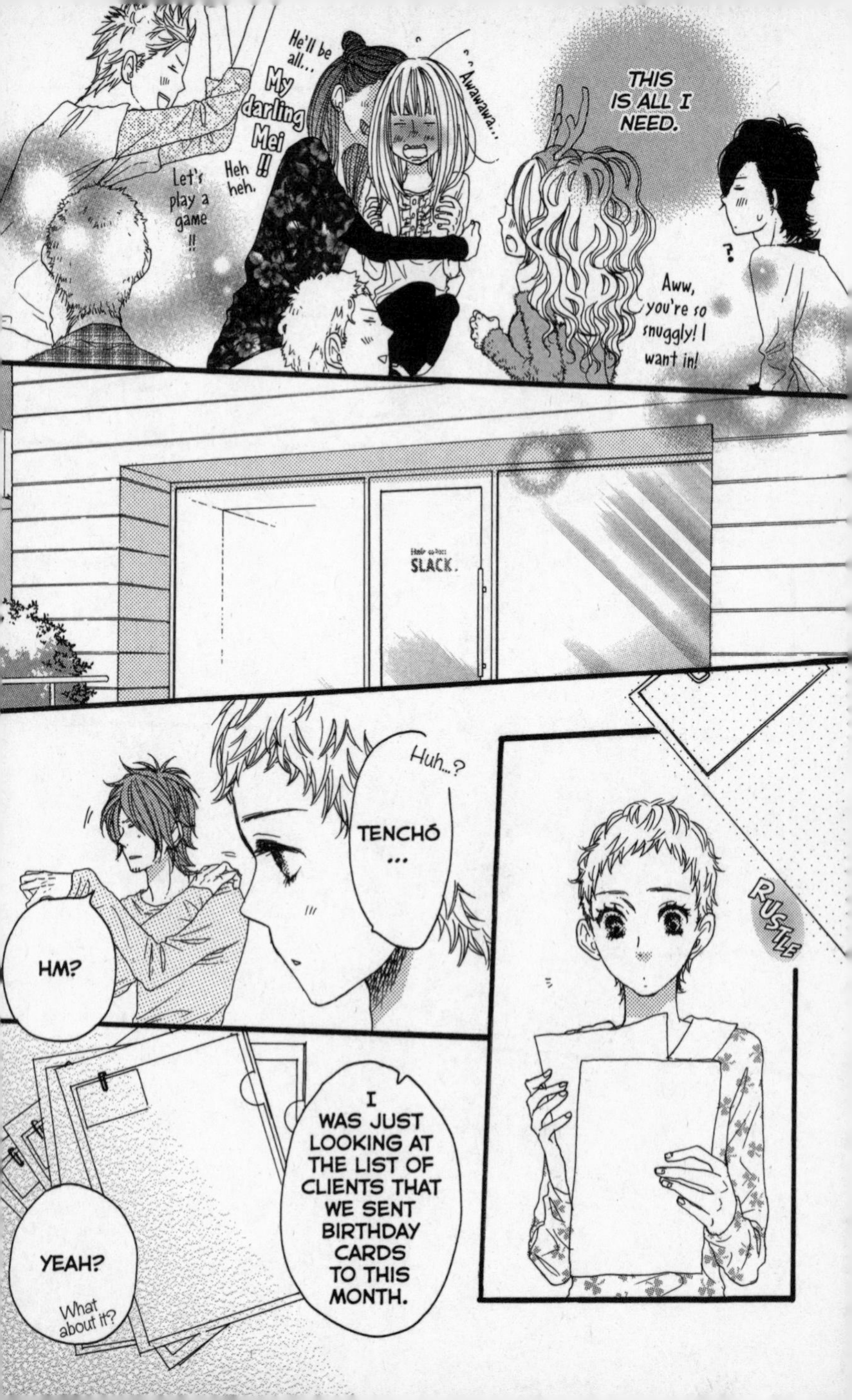
THIS IS ALL I NEED.
?
Aww, you're so snuggly! I want in!
Awawawa...
He'll be all... My darling Mei!!
Heh heh.
Let's play a game!!
SLACK.
RUSTLE
Huh...?
TENCHŌ...
HM?
I WAS JUST LOOKING AT THE LIST OF CLIENTS THAT WE SENT BIRTHDAY CARDS TO THIS MONTH.
YEAH?
What about it?

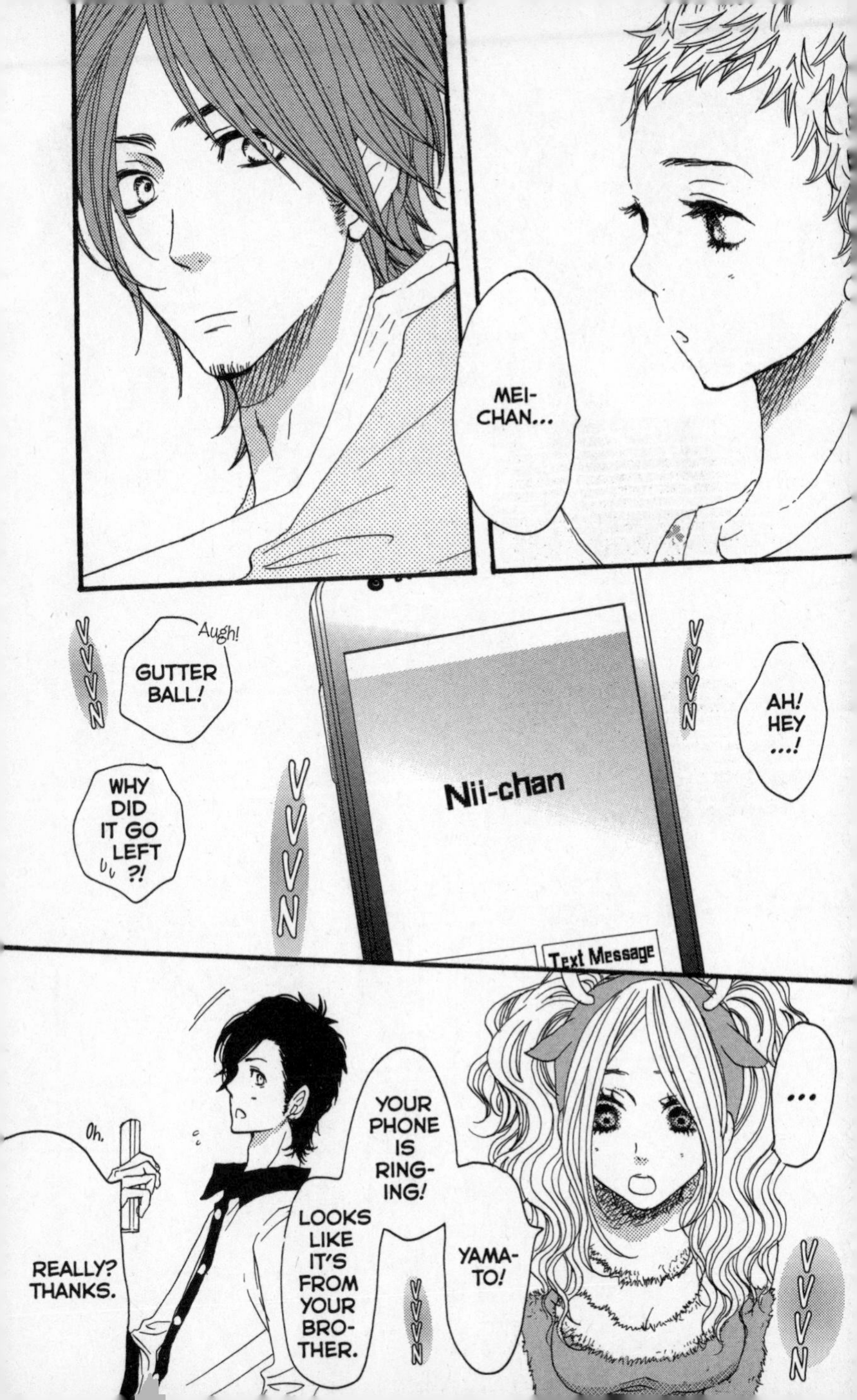
MEI-CHAN...
VVVN
AH! HEY ...!
Nii-chan
Text Message
VVVN
Augh!
GUTTER BALL!
VVVN
WHY DID IT GO LEFT ?!
...
VVVN
YOUR PHONE IS RINGING!
YAMATO!
LOOKS LIKE IT'S FROM YOUR BROTHER.
VVVN
Oh.
REALLY? THANKS.

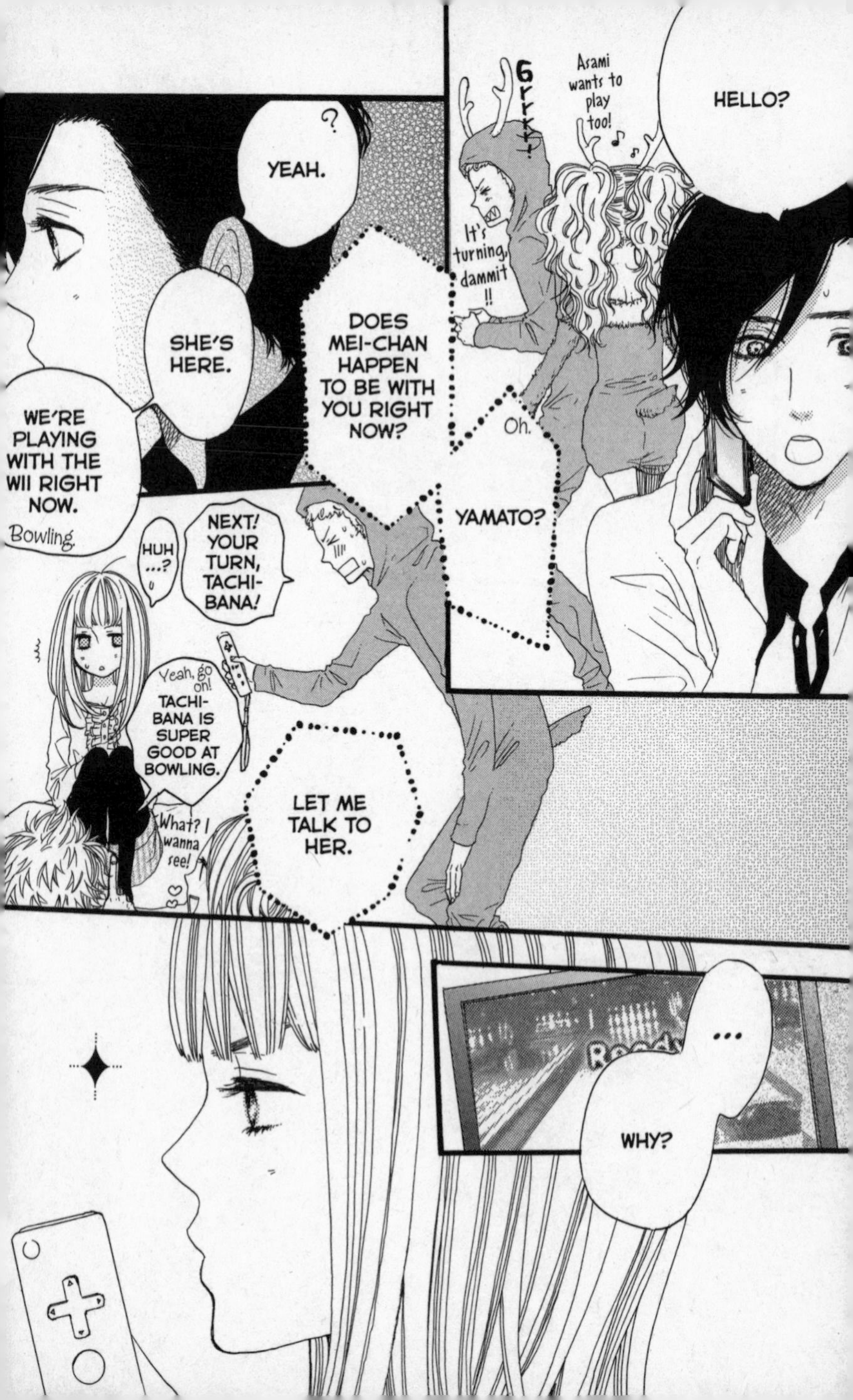
HELLO?
Asami wants to play too!
Grrrr
It's turning, dammit!!
Oh.
YAMATO?
DOES MEI-CHAN HAPPEN TO BE WITH YOU RIGHT NOW?
?
YEAH.
SHE'S HERE.
WE'RE PLAYING WITH THE WII RIGHT NOW.
Bowling.
LET ME TALK TO HER.
NEXT! YOUR TURN, TACHIBANA!
HUH ...?
Yeah, go on! TACHIBANA IS SUPER GOOD AT BOWLING.
What? I wanna see!
...
WHY?

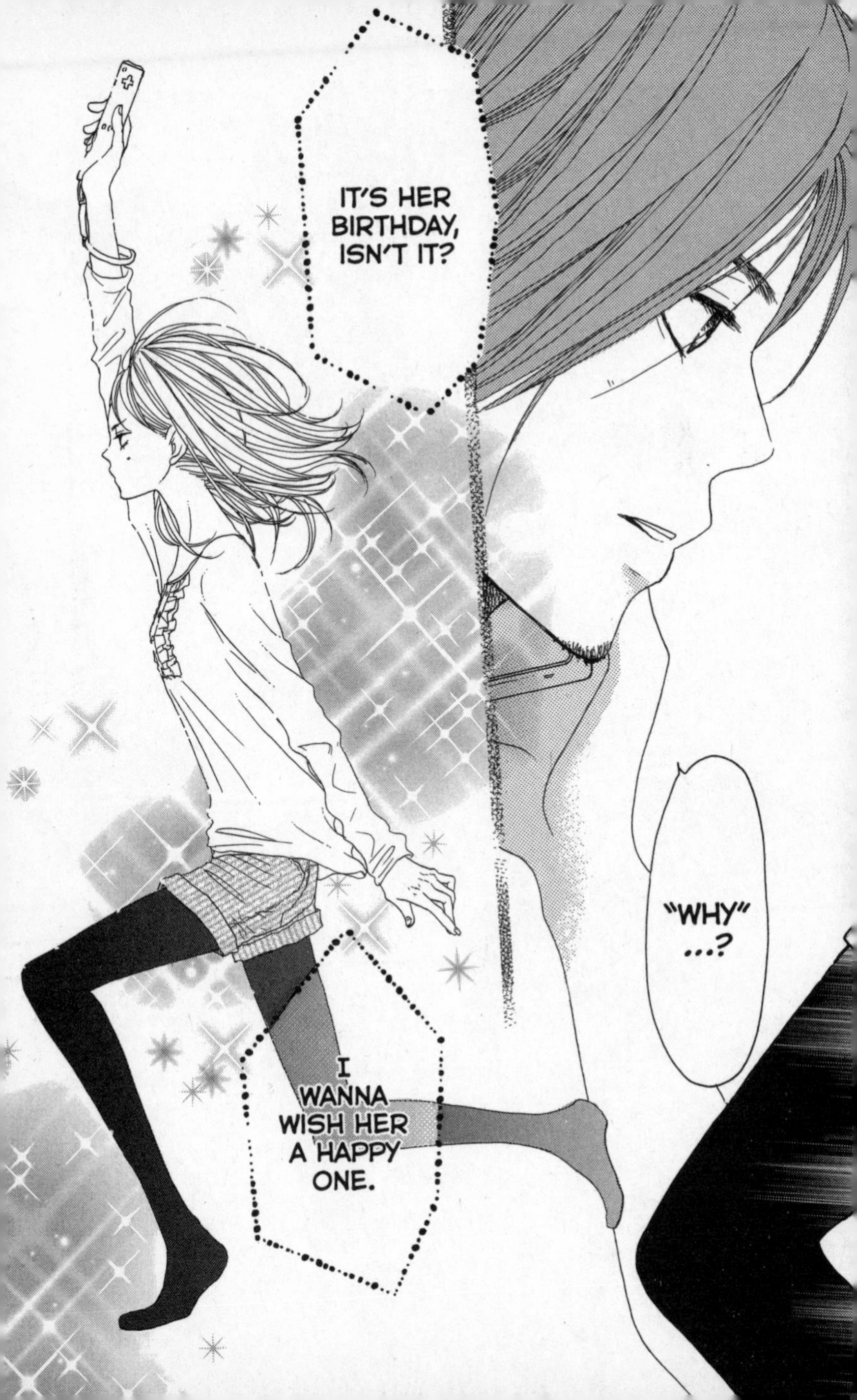
IT'S HER BIRTHDAY, ISN'T IT?
"WHY" ...?
I WANNA WISH HER A HAPPY ONE.

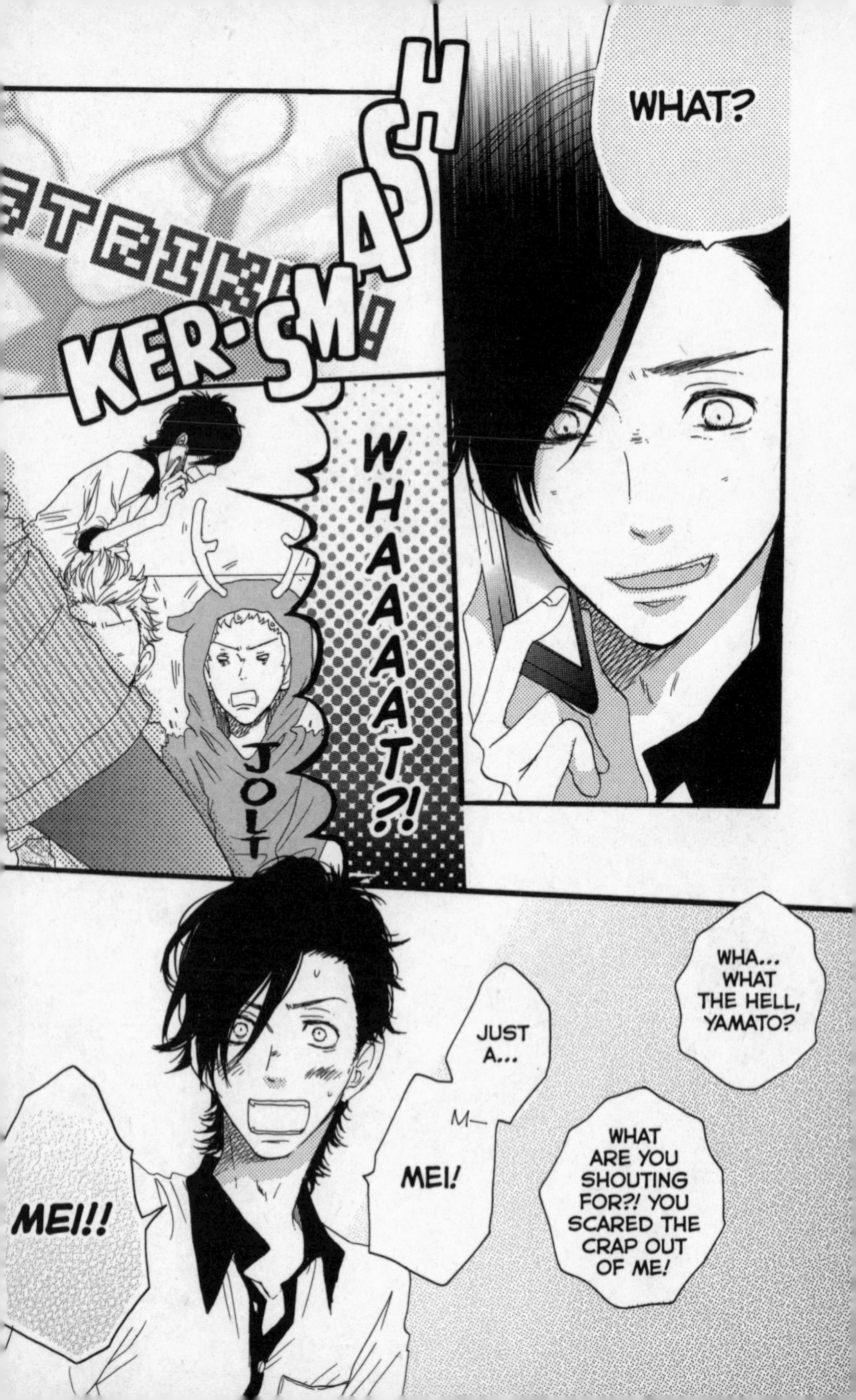
WHAT?
KER-SMASH!
WHAAAAAT?!
JOLT
WHA... WHAT THE HELL, YAMATO?
WHAT ARE YOU SHOUTING FOR?! YOU SCARED THE CRAP OUT OF ME!
JUST A...
M—
MEI!
MEI!!

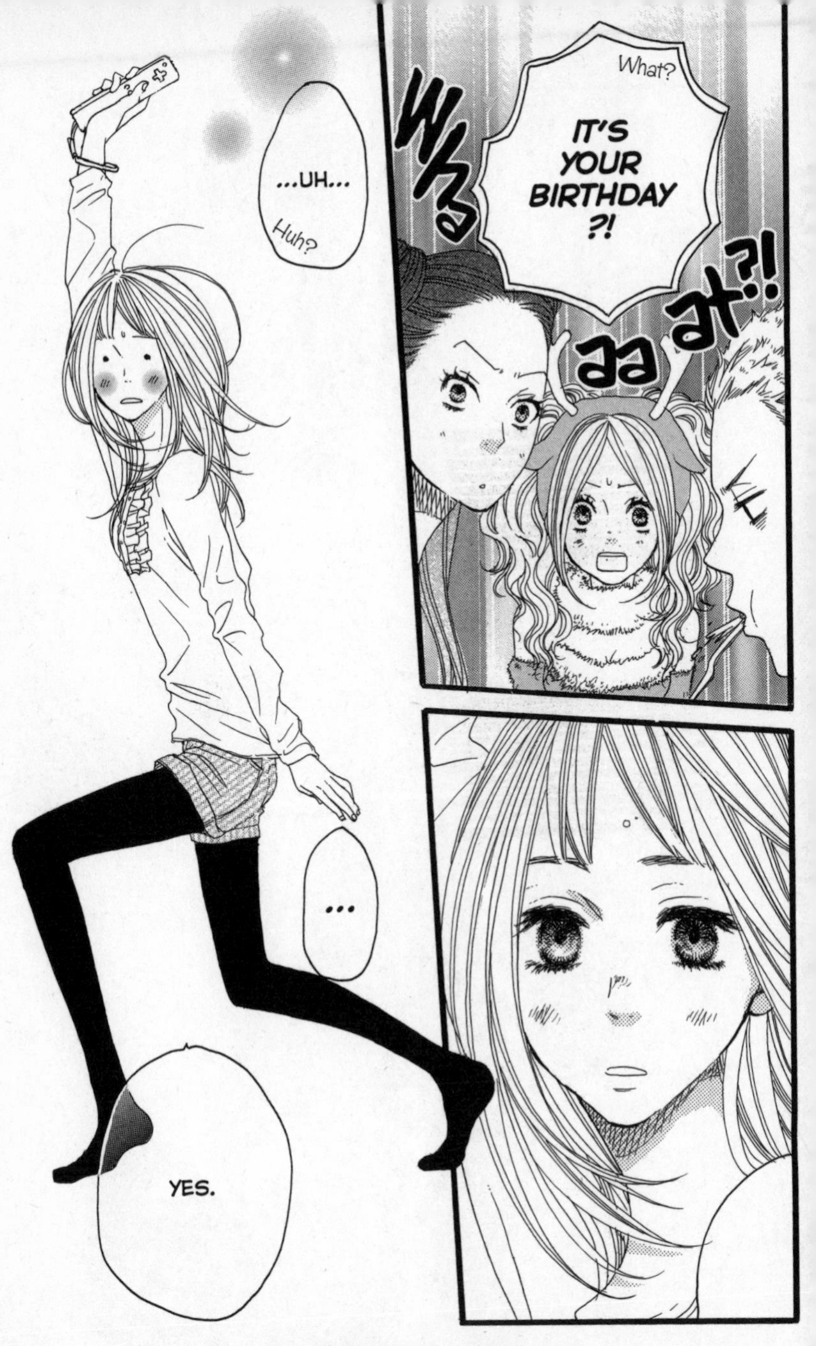
What?
IT'S YOUR BIRTHDAY?!
Wha
aa?!
...UH...
Huh?
...
YES.

Chapter 37 — End

Chapter
38

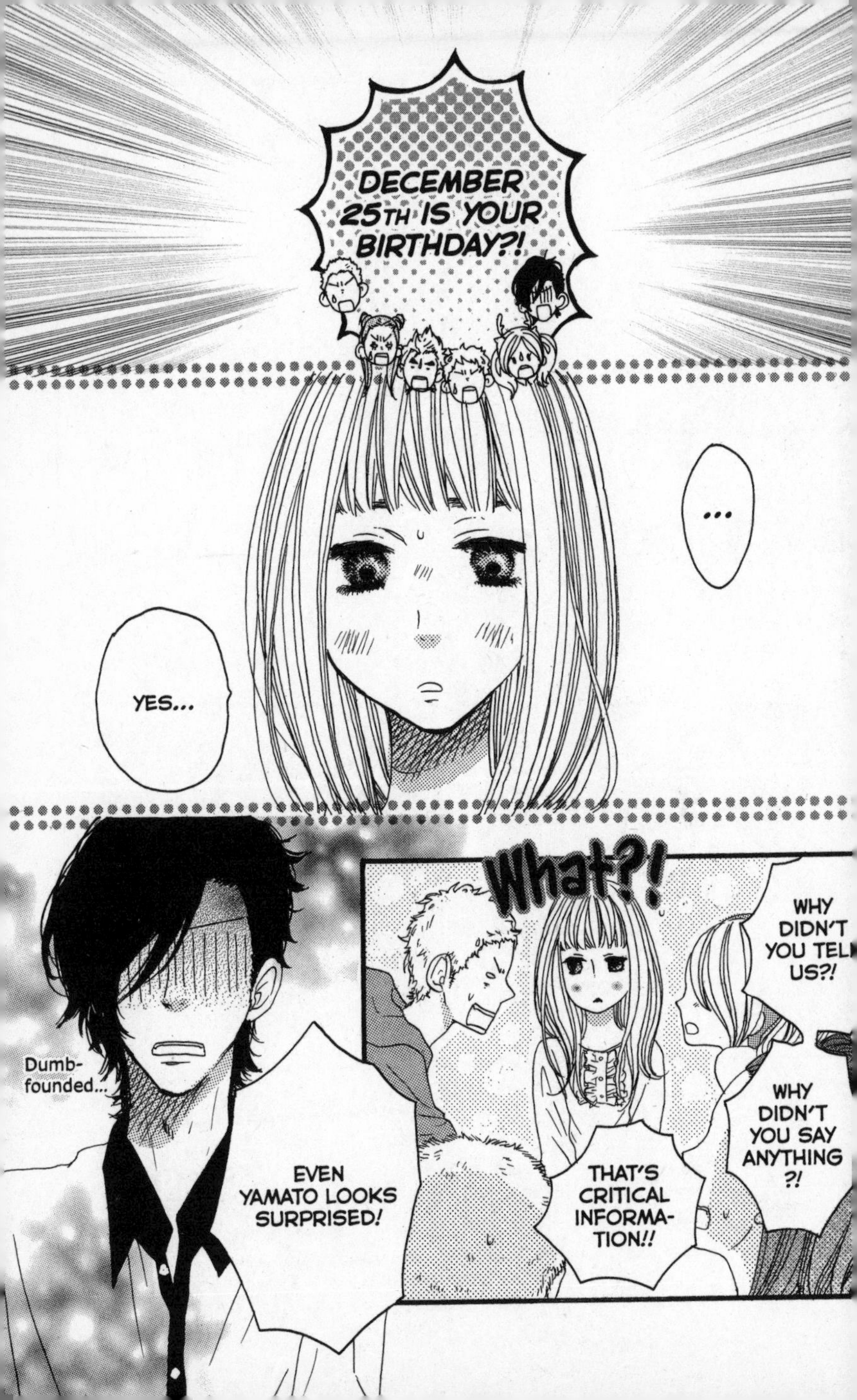
DECEMBER 25TH IS YOUR BIRTHDAY?!
...
YES...
What?!
WHY DIDN'T YOU TELL US?!
WHY DIDN'T YOU SAY ANYTHING?!
THAT'S CRITICAL INFORMATION!!
Dumbfounded...
EVEN YAMATO LOOKS SURPRISED!

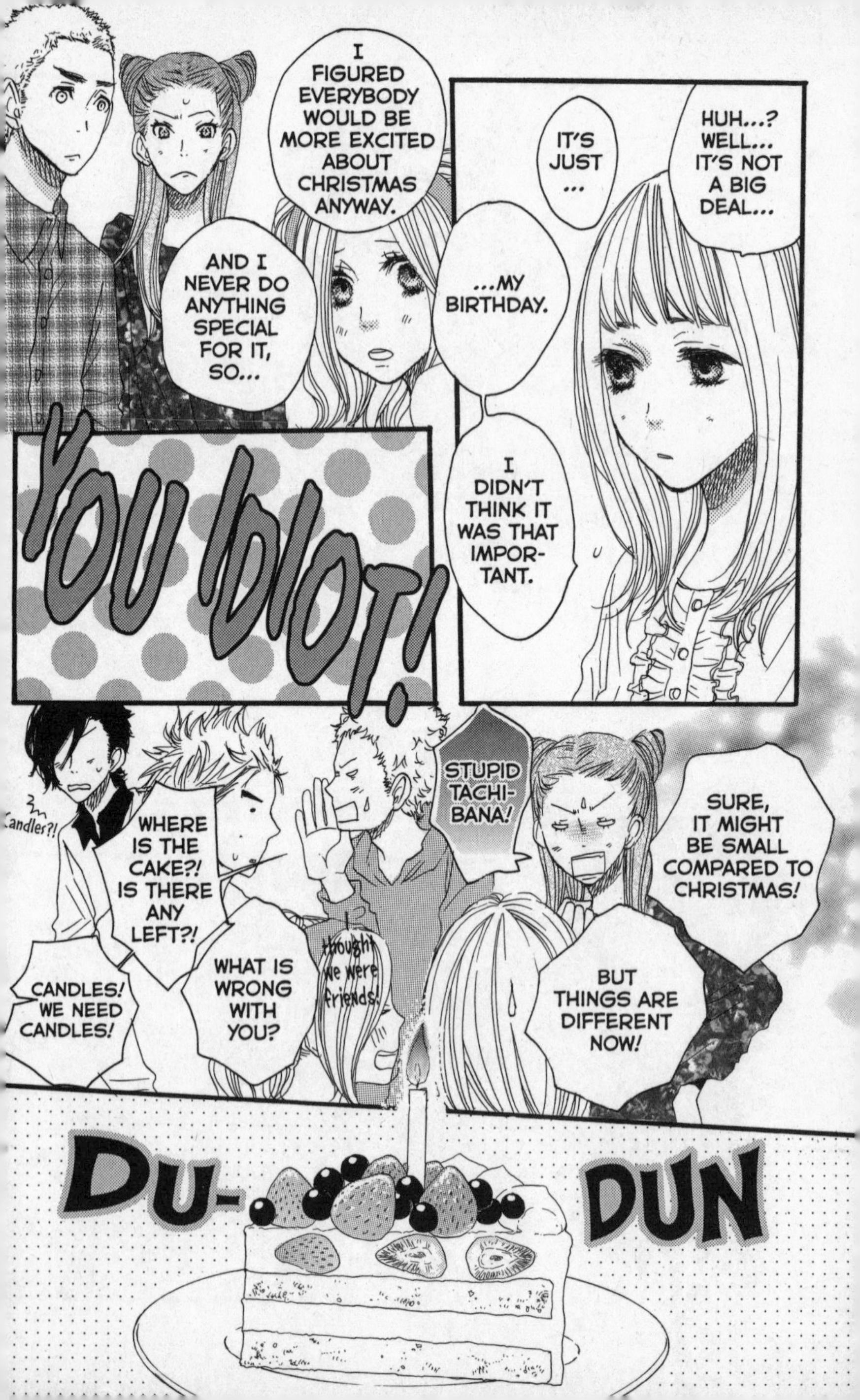
HUH...? WELL... IT'S NOT A BIG DEAL...
IT'S JUST ...
...MY BIRTHDAY.
I DIDN'T THINK IT WAS THAT IMPOR- TANT.
I FIGURED EVERYBODY WOULD BE MORE EXCITED ABOUT CHRISTMAS ANYWAY.
AND I NEVER DO ANYTHING SPECIAL FOR IT, SO...
YOU IDIOT!
SURE, IT MIGHT BE SMALL COMPARED TO CHRISTMAS!
BUT THINGS ARE DIFFERENT NOW!
STUPID TACHI- BANA!
thought we were friends!
WHERE IS THE CAKE?! IS THERE ANY LEFT?!
WHAT IS WRONG WITH YOU?
Candles?!
CANDLES! WE NEED CANDLES!
DU- DUN

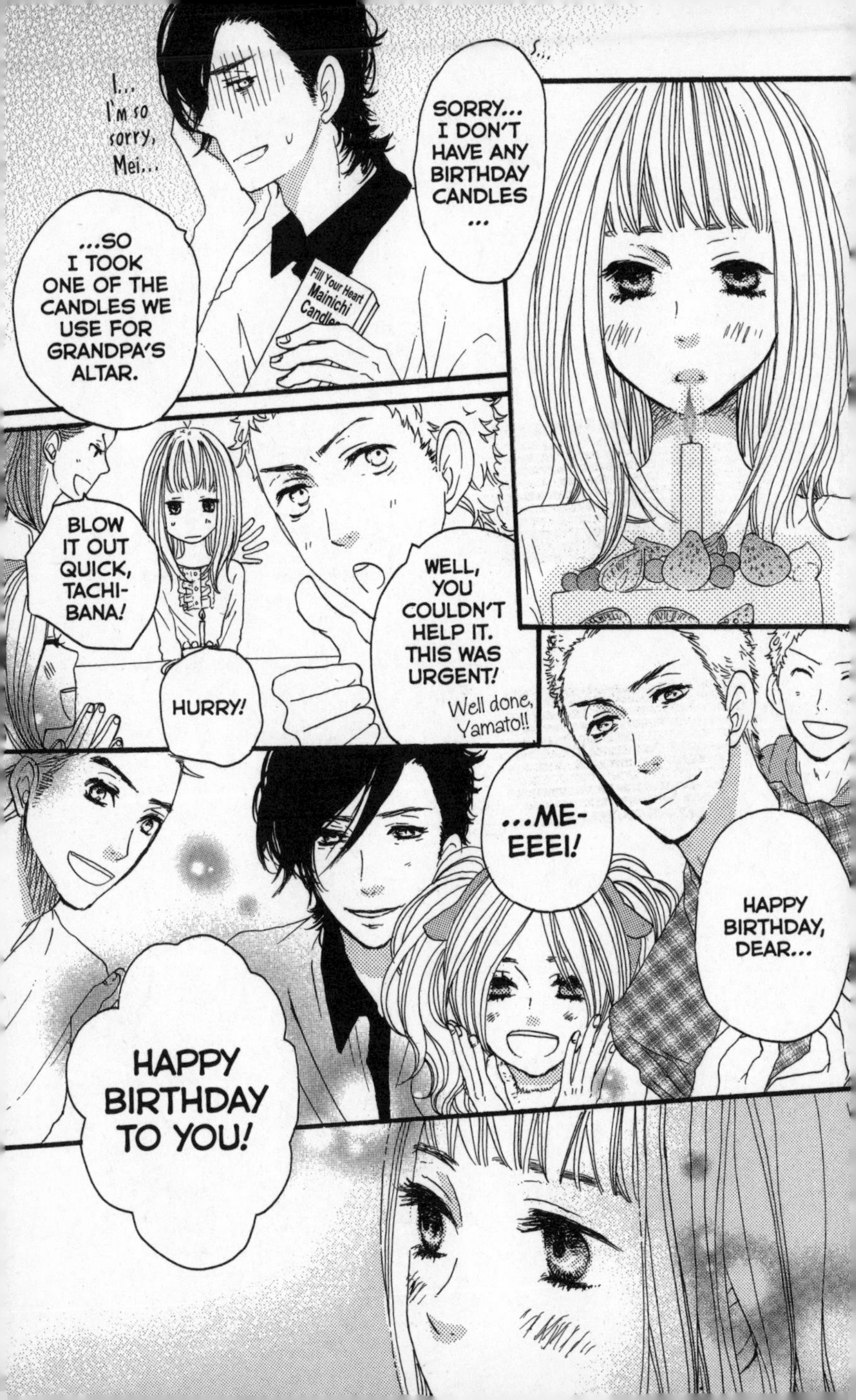
S...
SORRY... I DON'T HAVE ANY BIRTHDAY CANDLES...
I... I'm so sorry, Mei...
...SO I TOOK ONE OF THE CANDLES WE USE FOR GRANDPA'S ALTAR.
Fill Your Heart Mainichi Candles
WELL, YOU COULDN'T HELP IT. THIS WAS URGENT!
Well done, Yamato!!
BLOW IT OUT QUICK, TACHIBANA!
HURRY!
HAPPY BIRTHDAY, DEAR...
...ME-EEEI!
HAPPY BIRTHDAY TO YOU!

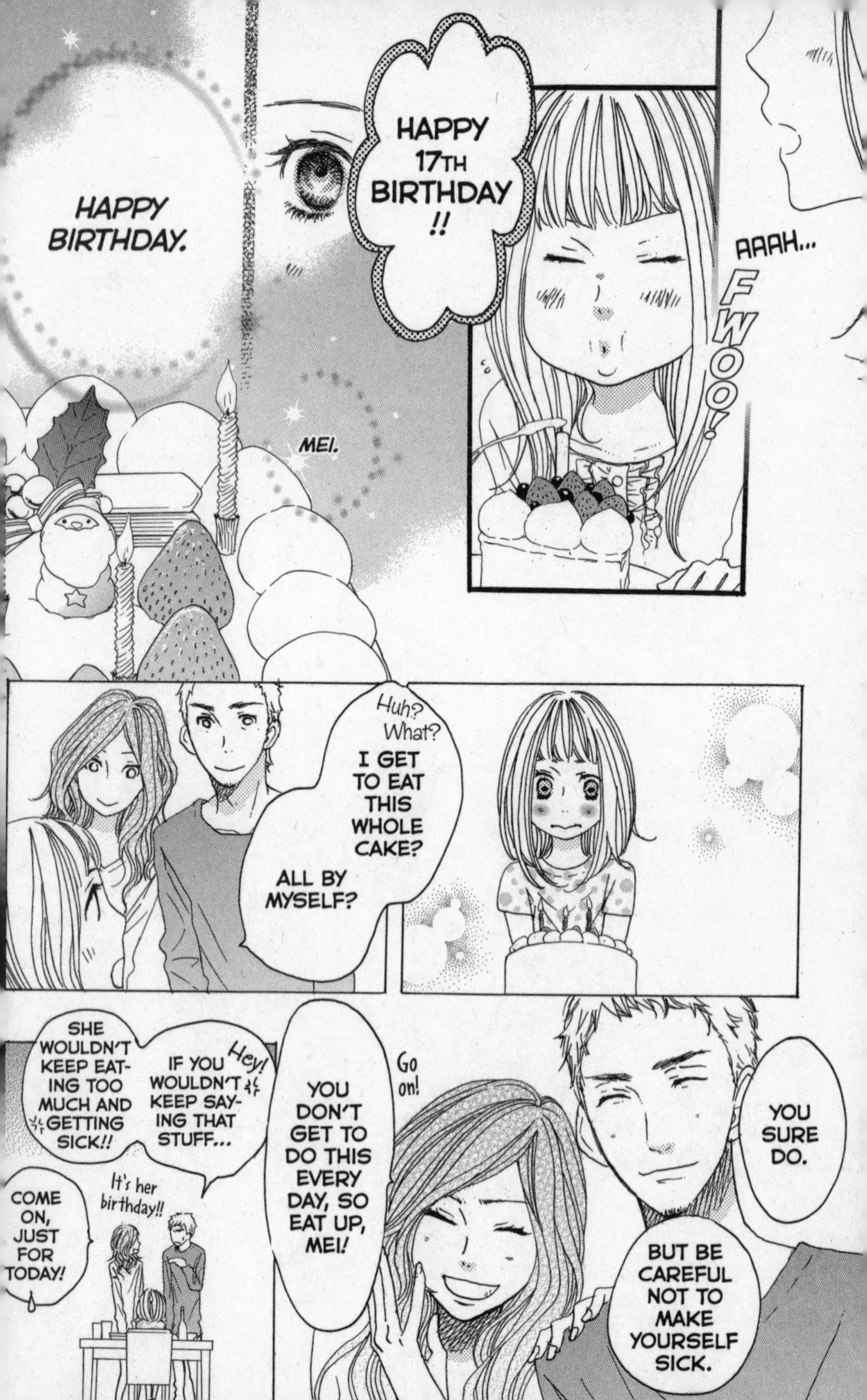
AAAH...
FWOOO!
HAPPY 17TH BIRTHDAY!!
HAPPY BIRTHDAY.
MEI.
Huh? What?
I GET TO EAT THIS WHOLE CAKE?
ALL BY MYSELF?
YOU SURE DO.
BUT BE CAREFUL NOT TO MAKE YOURSELF SICK.
Go on!
YOU DON'T GET TO DO THIS EVERY DAY, SO EAT UP, MEI!
Hey!
IF YOU WOULDN'T KEEP SAYING THAT STUFF...
SHE WOULDN'T KEEP EATING TOO MUCH AND GETTING SICK!!
It's her birthday!!
COME ON, JUST FOR TODAY!

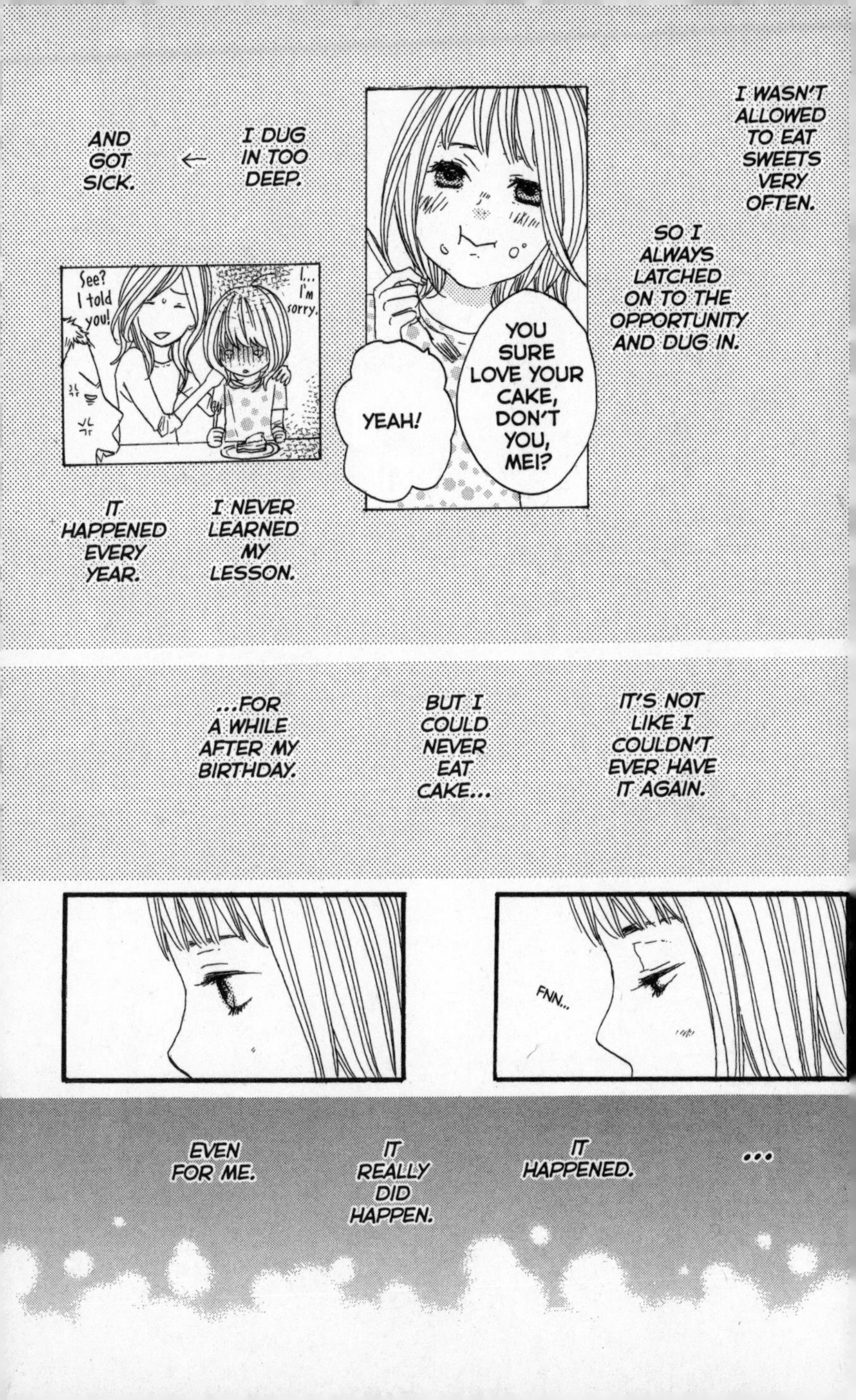
I WASN'T ALLOWED TO EAT SWEETS VERY OFTEN.
SO I ALWAYS LATCHED ON TO THE OPPORTUNITY AND DUG IN.
YOU SURE LOVE YOUR CAKE, DON'T YOU, MEI?
YEAH!
I DUG IN TOO DEEP.
AND GOT SICK.
I... I'm sorry.
See? I told you!
I NEVER LEARNED MY LESSON.
IT HAPPENED EVERY YEAR.
IT'S NOT LIKE I COULDN'T EVER HAVE IT AGAIN.
BUT I COULD NEVER EAT CAKE...
...FOR A WHILE AFTER MY BIRTHDAY.
FNN...
...
IT HAPPENED.
IT REALLY DID HAPPEN.
EVEN FOR ME.

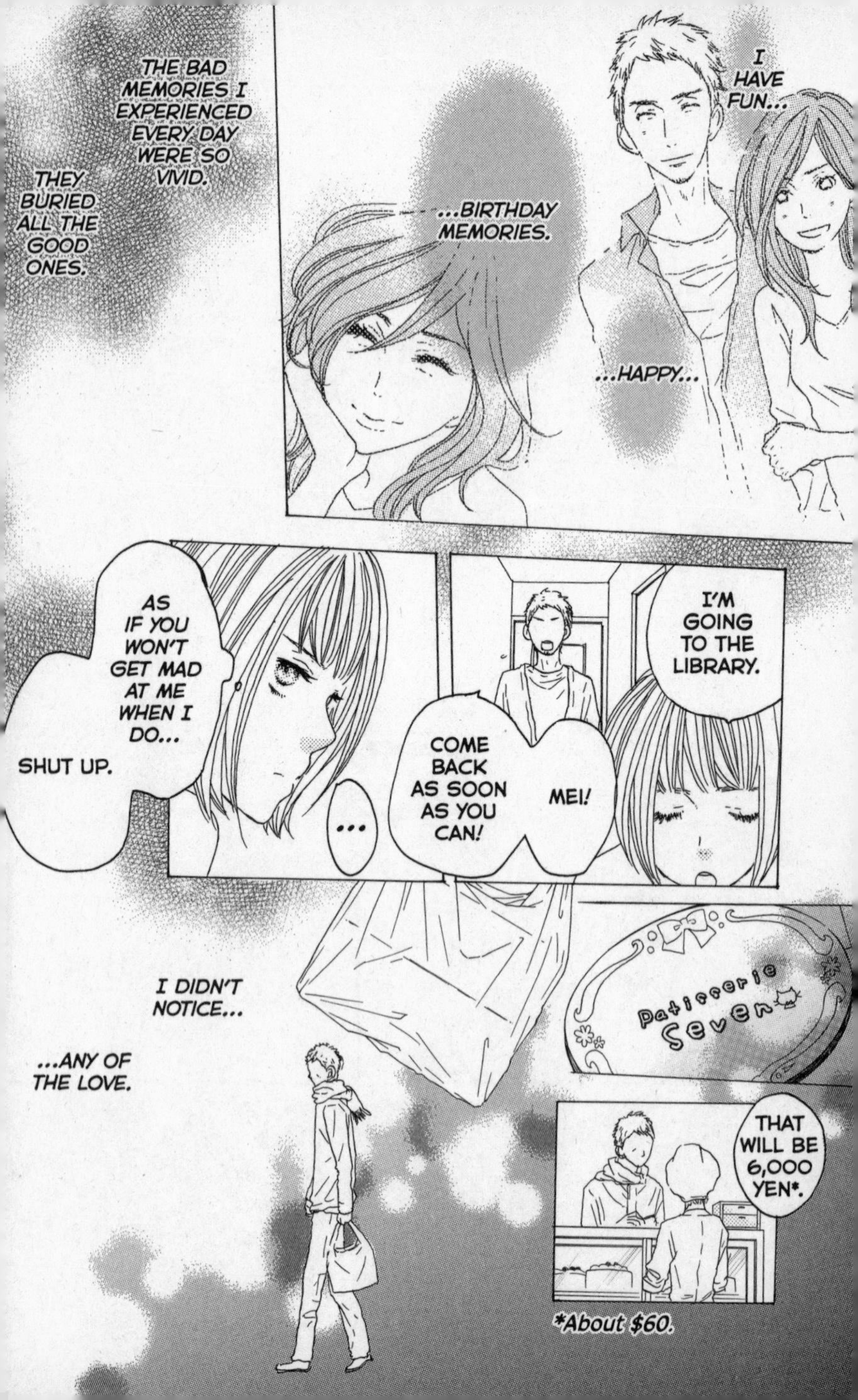
I HAVE FUN...
...HAPPY...
...BIRTHDAY MEMORIES.
THE BAD MEMORIES I EXPERIENCED EVERY DAY WERE SO VIVID.
THEY BURIED ALL THE GOOD ONES.
I'M GOING TO THE LIBRARY.
MEI!
COME BACK AS SOON AS YOU CAN!
...
AS IF YOU WON'T GET MAD AT ME WHEN I DO...
SHUT UP.
Patisserie Seven
THAT WILL BE 6,000 YEN*.
I DIDN'T NOTICE...
...ANY OF THE LOVE.
*About $60.

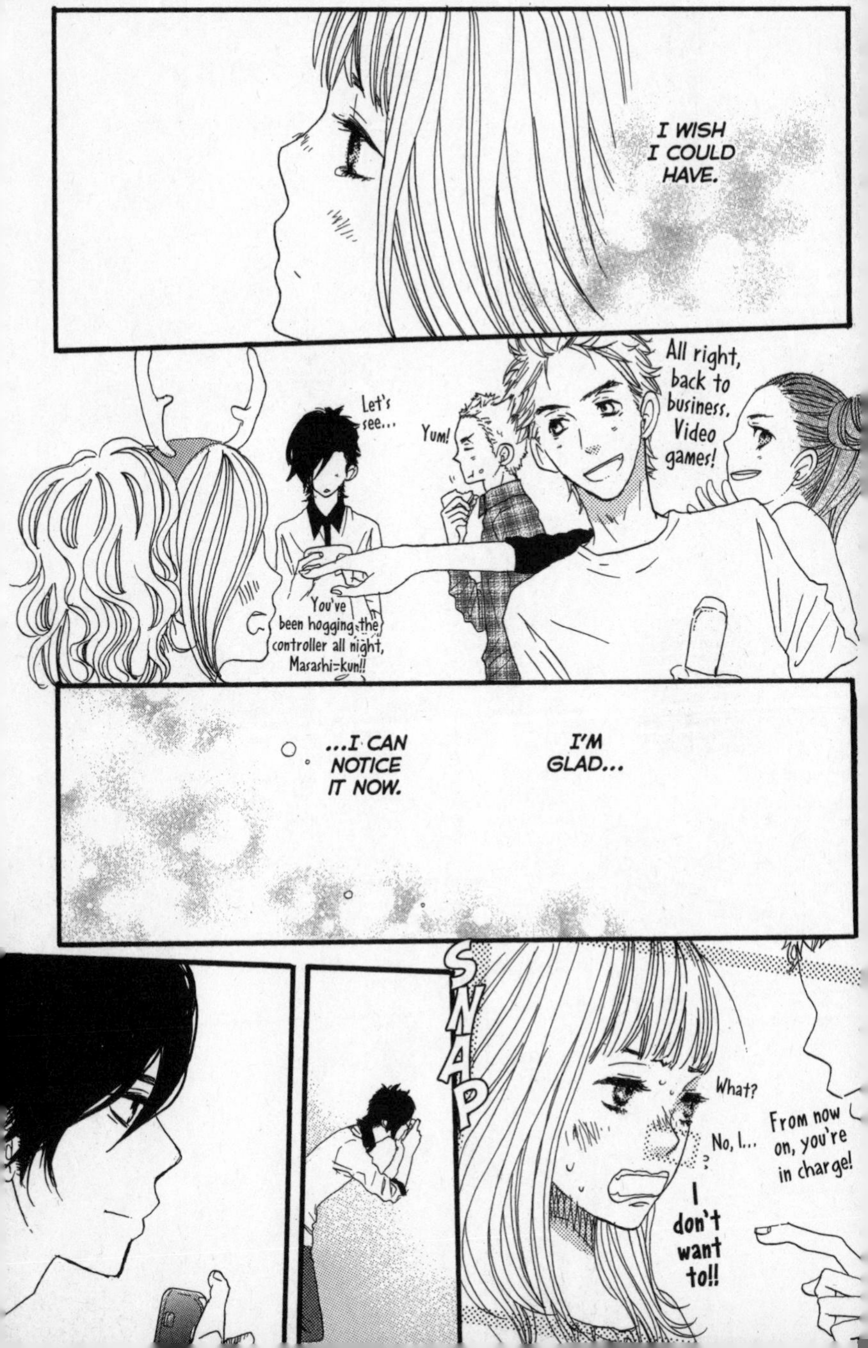
I WISH I COULD HAVE.
All right, back to business. Video games!
Yum!
Let's see...
You've been hogging the controller all night, Masashi-kun!!
I'M GLAD...
...I CAN NOTICE IT NOW.
From now on, you're in charge!
What?
No, I...
I don't want to!!
SNAP

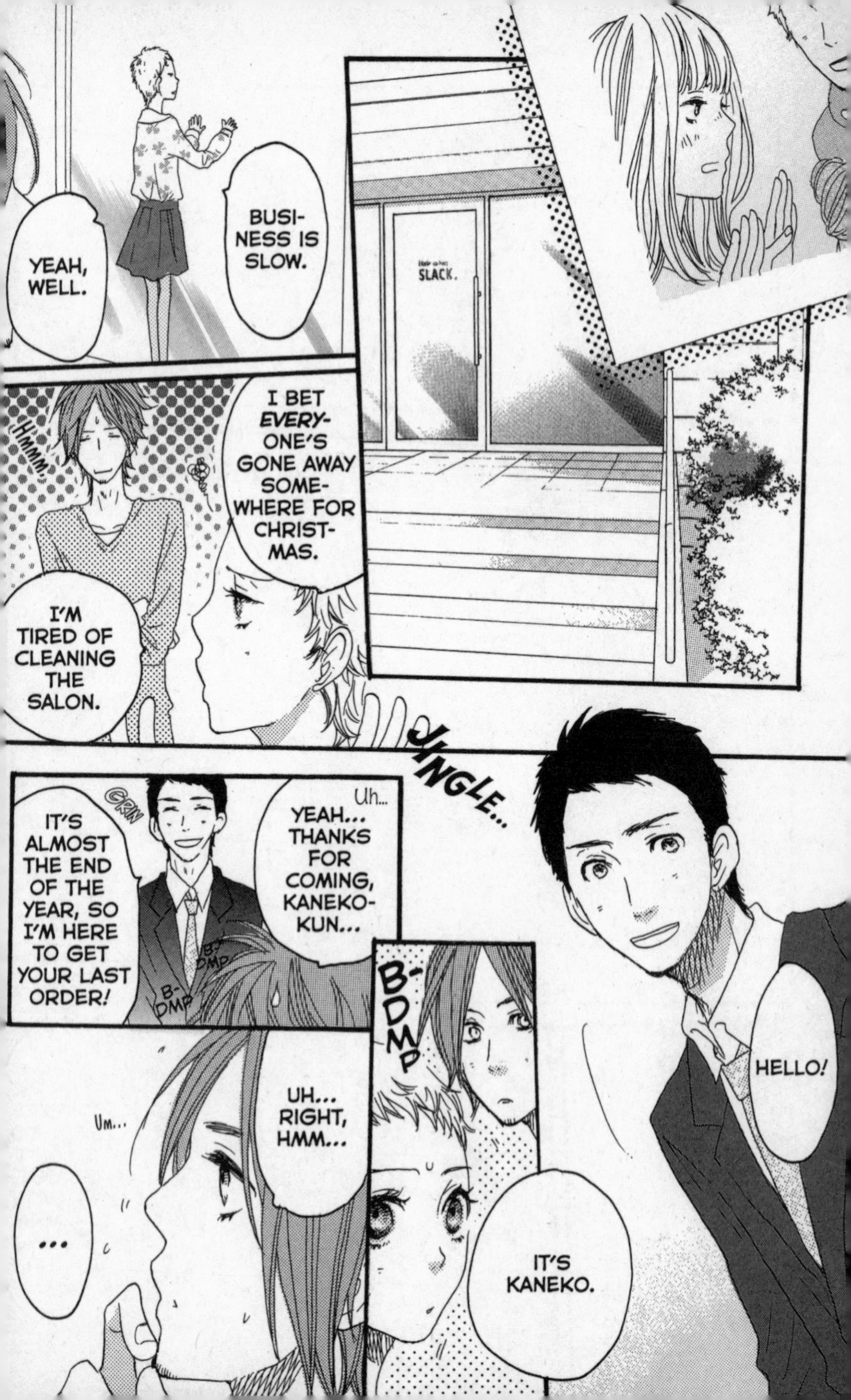
SLACK.
BUSI-NESS IS SLOW.
YEAH, WELL.
I BET EVERY-ONE'S GONE AWAY SOME-WHERE FOR CHRIST-MAS.
HMMM.
I'M TIRED OF CLEANING THE SALON.
JINGLE...
HELLO!
IT'S KANEKO.
Uh...
YEAH... THANKS FOR COMING, KANEKO-KUN...
GRIN
IT'S ALMOST THE END OF THE YEAR, SO I'M HERE TO GET YOUR LAST ORDER!
B-DMP
B-DMP
B-BDMP
UH... RIGHT, HMM...
UM...
...

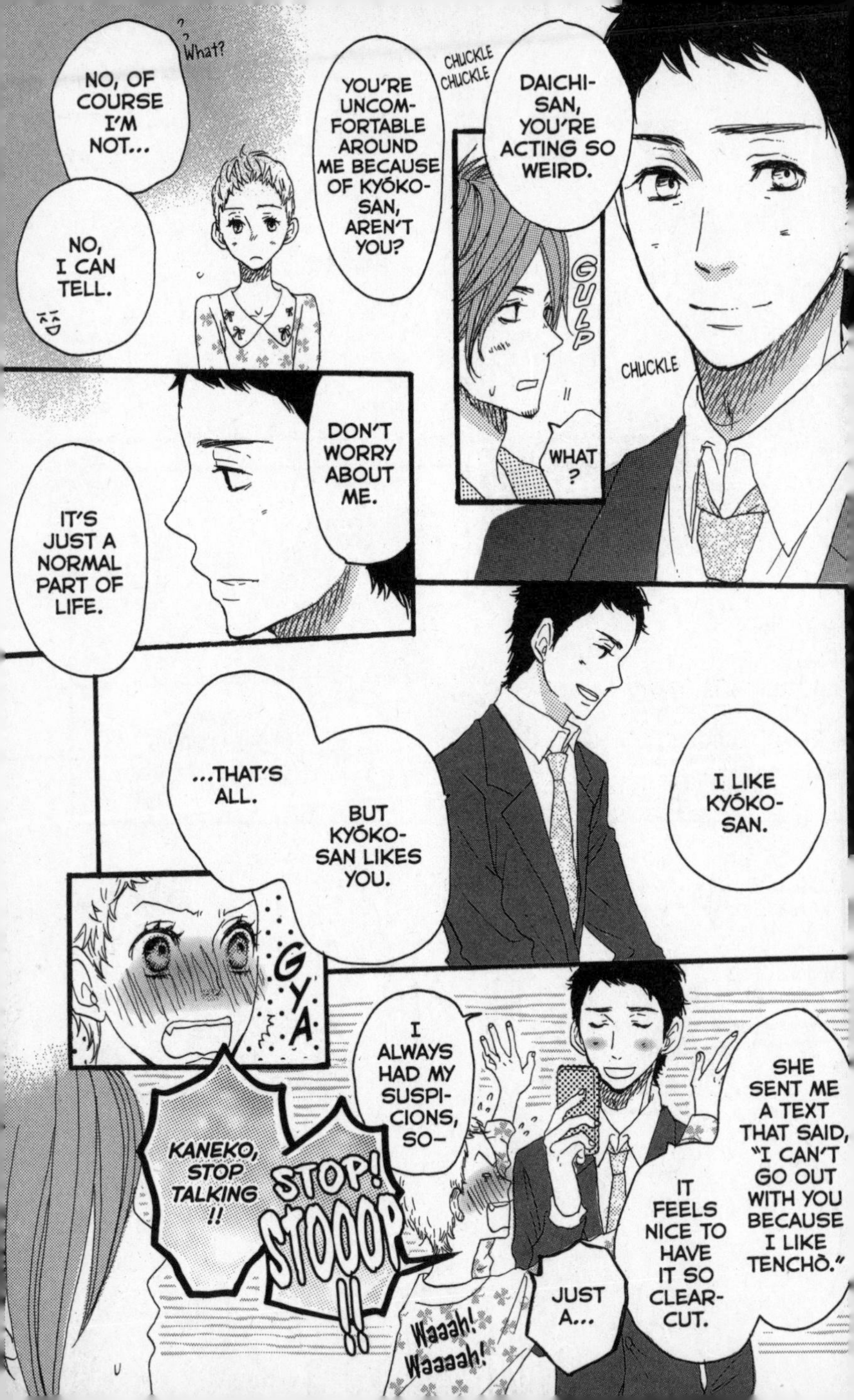
DAICHI-SAN, YOU'RE ACTING SO WEIRD.
CHUCKLE CHUCKLE
CHUCKLE
GULP
WHAT?
YOU'RE UNCOM-FORTABLE AROUND ME BECAUSE OF KYŌKO-SAN, AREN'T YOU?
What?
NO, OF COURSE I'M NOT...
NO, I CAN TELL.
DON'T WORRY ABOUT ME.
IT'S JUST A NORMAL PART OF LIFE.
I LIKE KYŌKO-SAN.
BUT KYŌKO-SAN LIKES YOU.
...THAT'S ALL.
GYA
SHE SENT ME A TEXT THAT SAID, "I CAN'T GO OUT WITH YOU BECAUSE I LIKE TENCHŌ."
I ALWAYS HAD MY SUSPI-CIONS, SO–
IT FEELS NICE TO HAVE IT SO CLEAR-CUT.
JUST A...
STOP! STOOOP!!
Waaah! Waaaah!
KANEKO, STOP TALKING!!

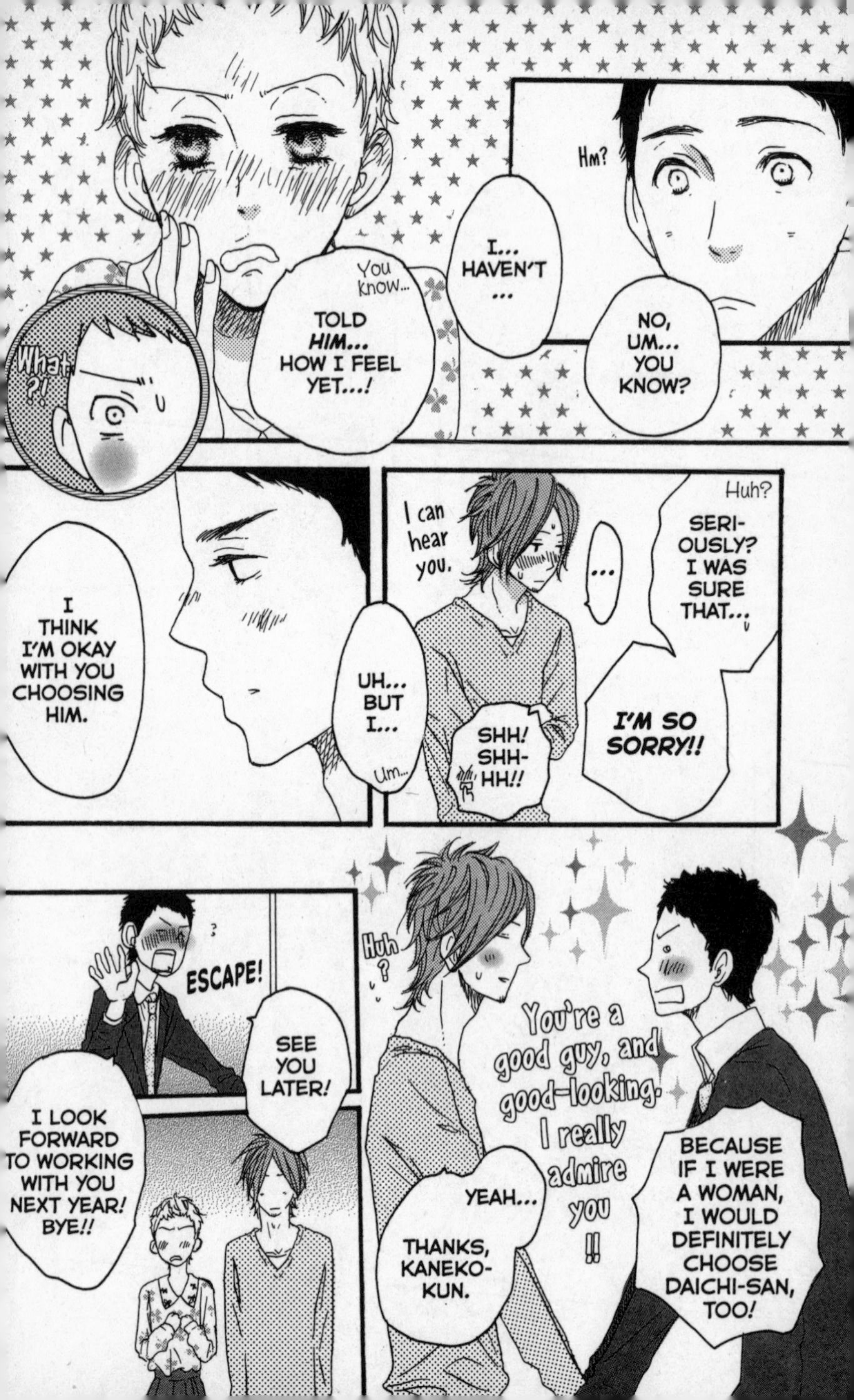
Hm?
NO, UM... YOU KNOW?
I... HAVEN'T ...
You know...
TOLD HIM... HOW I FEEL YET...!
What?!
Huh?
SERIOUSLY? I WAS SURE THAT...
...
I can hear you.
I'M SO SORRY!!
SHH! SHH-HH!!
UH... BUT I...
Um...
I THINK I'M OKAY WITH YOU CHOOSING HIM.
You're a good guy, and good-looking. I really admire you!!
BECAUSE IF I WERE A WOMAN, I WOULD DEFINITELY CHOOSE DAICHI-SAN, TOO!
Huh?
YEAH...
THANKS, KANEKO-KUN.
ESCAPE!
SEE YOU LATER!
I LOOK FORWARD TO WORKING WITH YOU NEXT YEAR! BYE!!

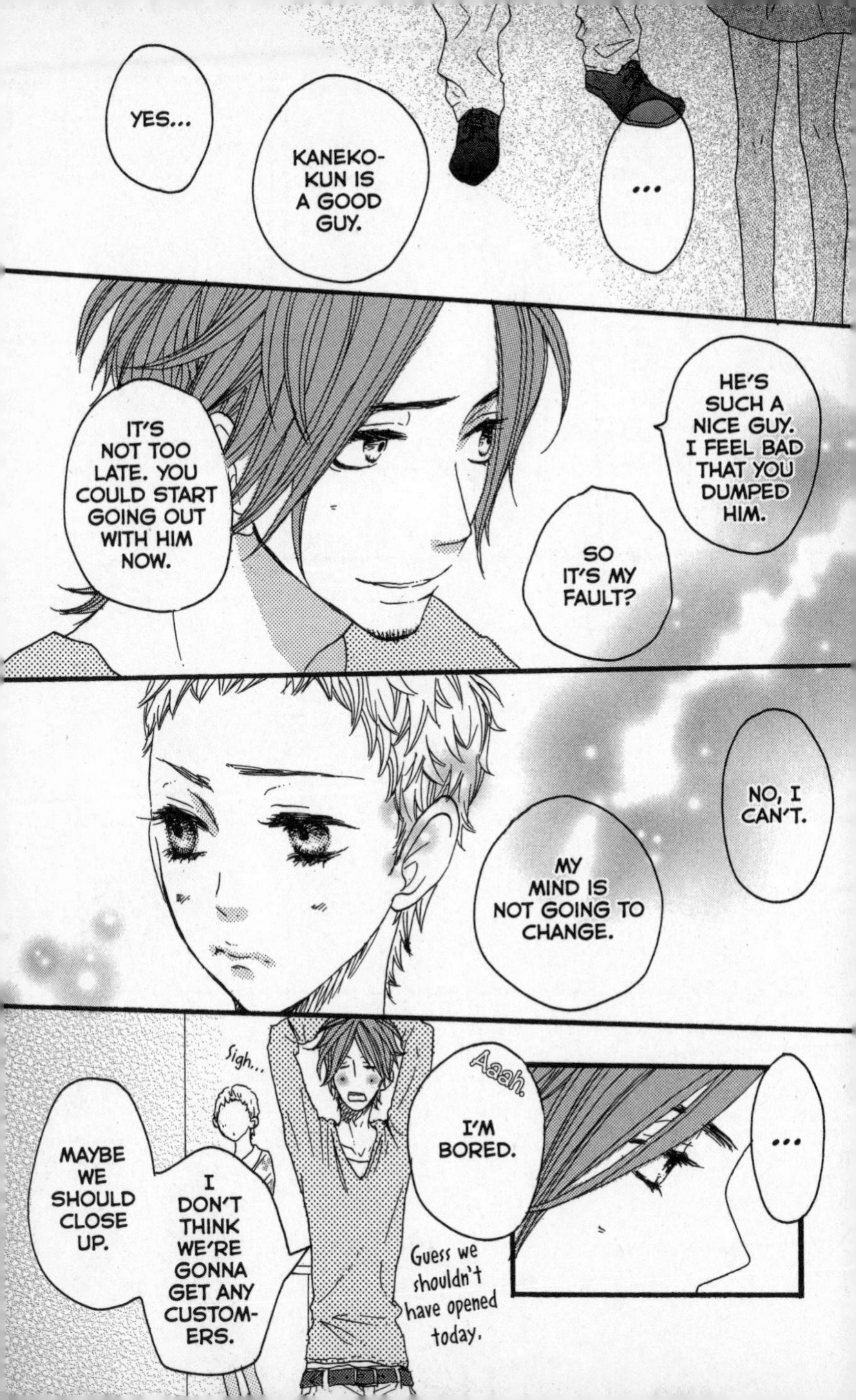
...
KANEKO-KUN IS A GOOD GUY.
YES...
HE'S SUCH A NICE GUY. I FEEL BAD THAT YOU DUMPED HIM.
SO IT'S MY FAULT?
IT'S NOT TOO LATE. YOU COULD START GOING OUT WITH HIM NOW.
NO, I CAN'T.
MY MIND IS NOT GOING TO CHANGE.
...
Aaah.
I'M BORED.
Sigh...
Guess we shouldn't have opened today.
I DON'T THINK WE'RE GONNA GET ANY CUSTOM-ERS.
MAYBE WE SHOULD CLOSE UP.

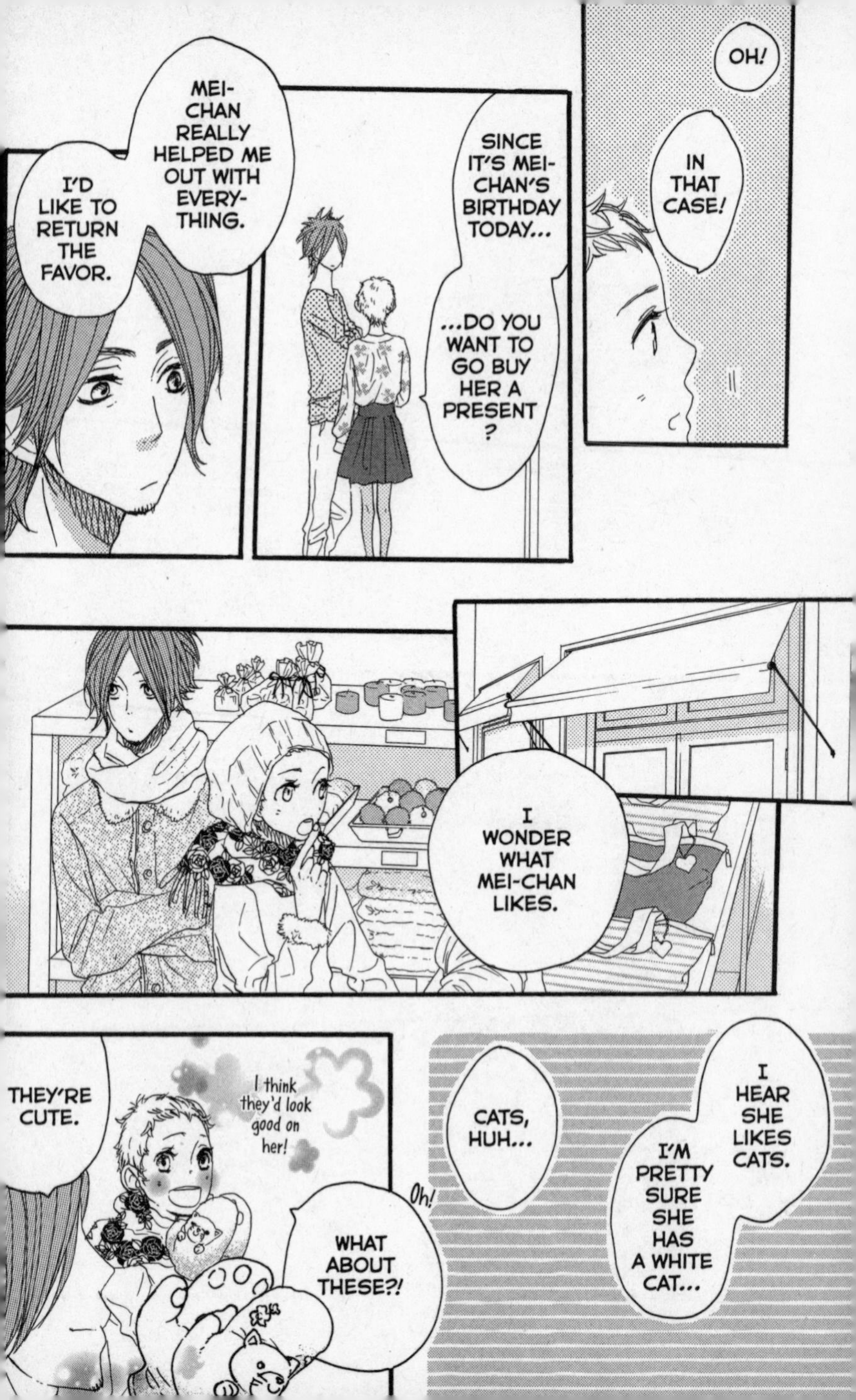
OH!
IN THAT CASE!
SINCE IT'S MEI-CHAN'S BIRTHDAY TODAY...
...DO YOU WANT TO GO BUY HER A PRESENT?
MEI-CHAN REALLY HELPED ME OUT WITH EVERYTHING.
I'D LIKE TO RETURN THE FAVOR.
I WONDER WHAT MEI-CHAN LIKES.
I HEAR SHE LIKES CATS.
I'M PRETTY SURE SHE HAS A WHITE CAT...
CATS, HUH...
Oh!
WHAT ABOUT THESE?!
I think they'd look good on her!
THEY'RE CUTE.

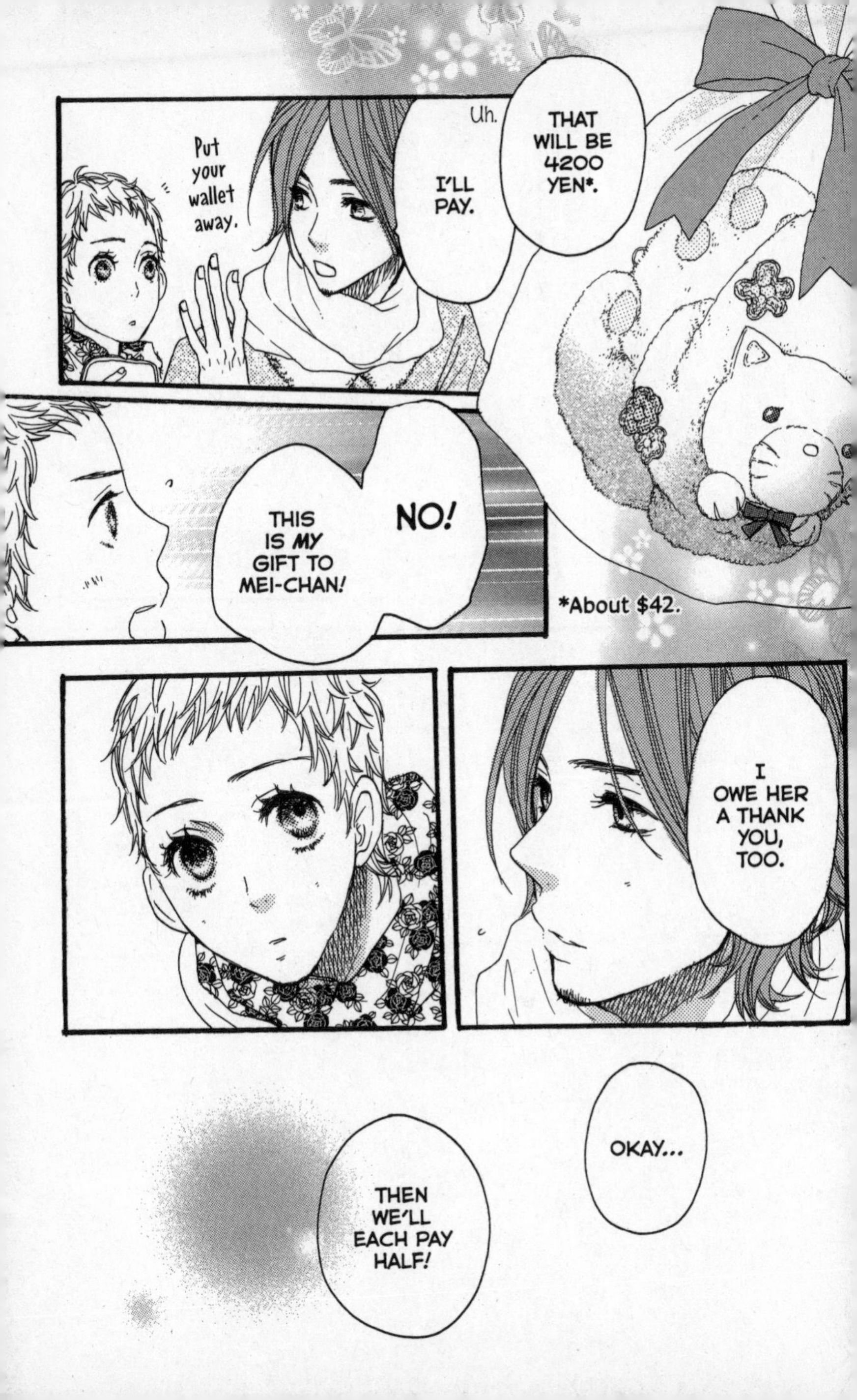
THAT WILL BE 4200 YEN*.
Uh.
I'LL PAY.
Put your wallet away.
NO!
THIS IS MY GIFT TO MEI-CHAN!
*About $42.
I OWE HER A THANK YOU, TOO.
OKAY...
THEN WE'LL EACH PAY HALF!

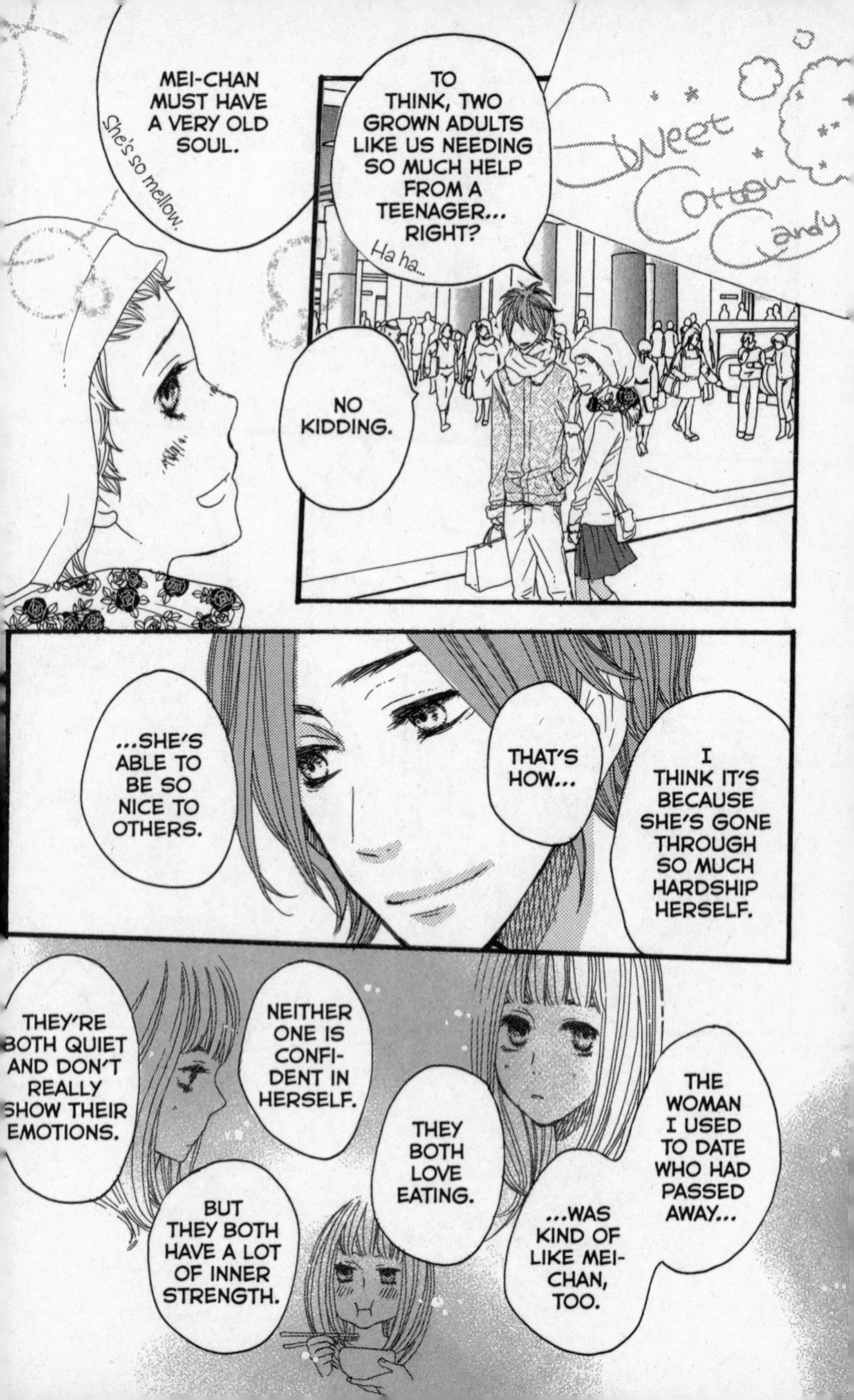
Sweet Cotton Candy
TO THINK, TWO GROWN ADULTS LIKE US NEEDING SO MUCH HELP FROM A TEENAGER... RIGHT?
Ha ha...
NO KIDDING.
MEI-CHAN MUST HAVE A VERY OLD SOUL.
She's so mellow.
I THINK IT'S BECAUSE SHE'S GONE THROUGH SO MUCH HARDSHIP HERSELF.
THAT'S HOW...
...SHE'S ABLE TO BE SO NICE TO OTHERS.
THE WOMAN I USED TO DATE WHO HAD PASSED AWAY...
...WAS KIND OF LIKE MEI-CHAN, TOO.
NEITHER ONE IS CONFI-DENT IN HERSELF.
THEY'RE BOTH QUIET AND DON'T REALLY SHOW THEIR EMOTIONS.
THEY BOTH LOVE EATING.
BUT THEY BOTH HAVE A LOT OF INNER STRENGTH.

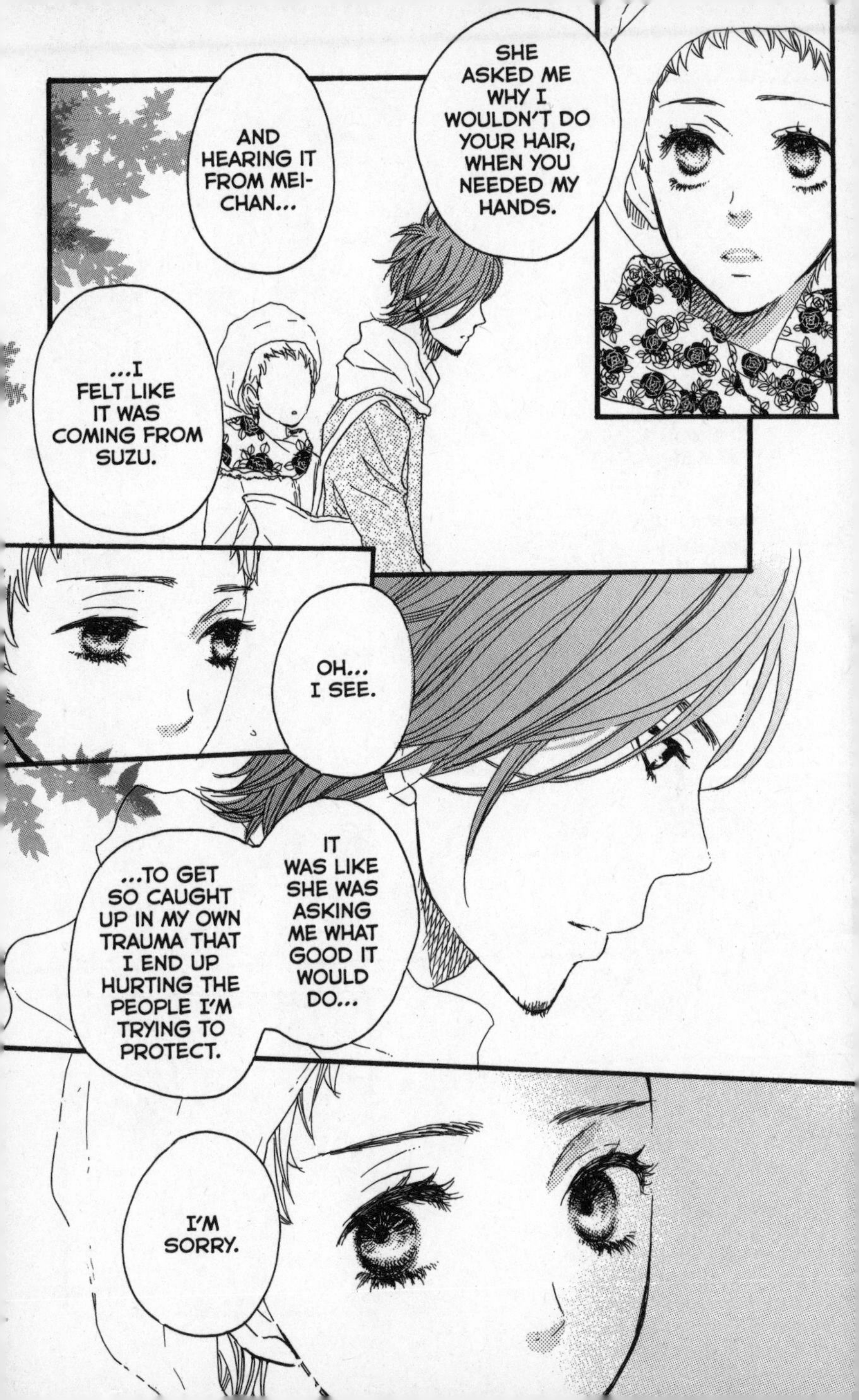
SHE ASKED ME WHY I WOULDN'T DO YOUR HAIR, WHEN YOU NEEDED MY HANDS.
AND HEARING IT FROM MEI-CHAN...
...I FELT LIKE IT WAS COMING FROM SUZU.
OH... I SEE.
IT WAS LIKE SHE WAS ASKING ME WHAT GOOD IT WOULD DO...
...TO GET SO CAUGHT UP IN MY OWN TRAUMA THAT I END UP HURTING THE PEOPLE I'M TRYING TO PROTECT.
I'M SORRY.

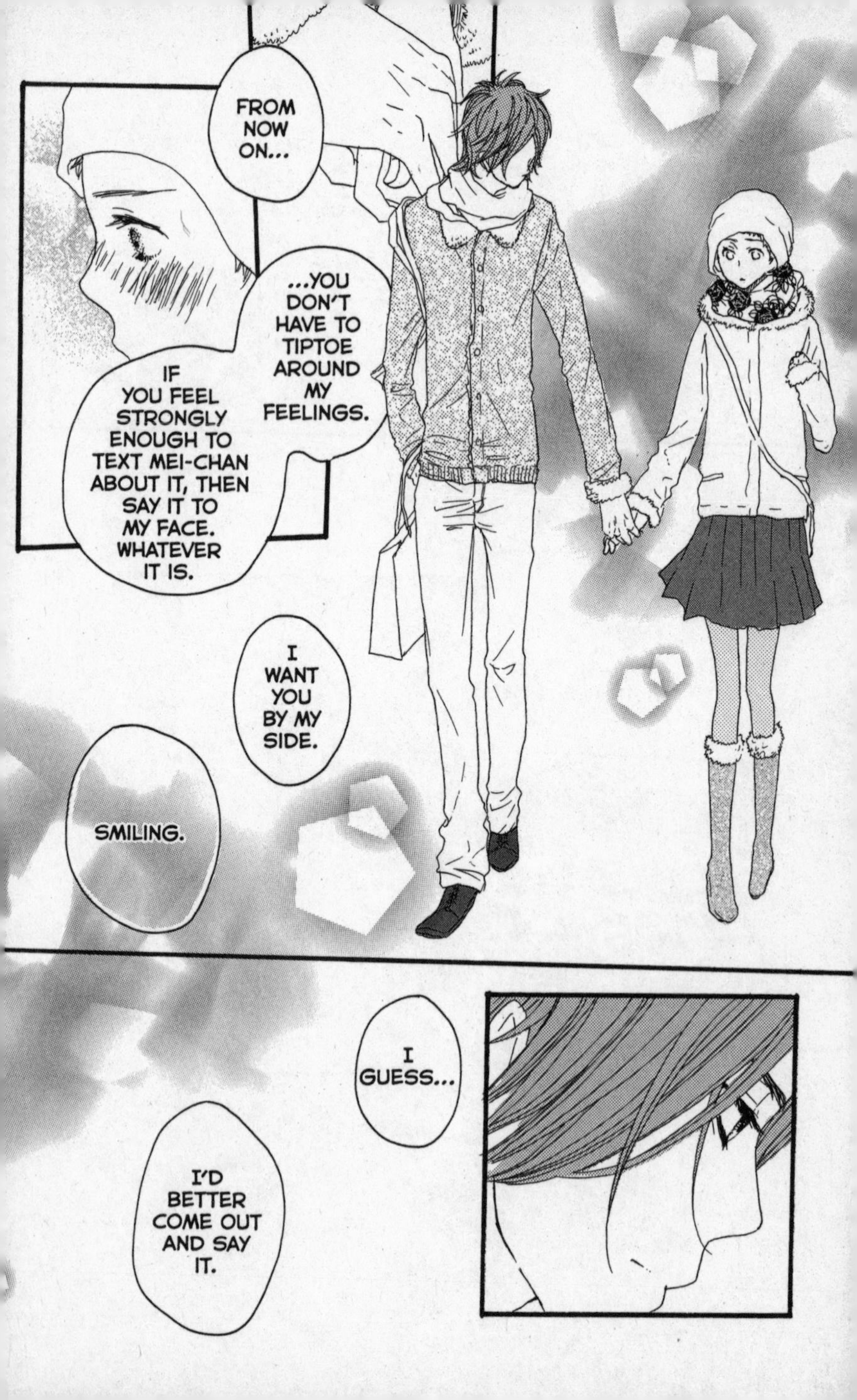
FROM NOW ON...
...YOU DON'T HAVE TO TIPTOE AROUND MY FEELINGS.
IF YOU FEEL STRONGLY ENOUGH TO TEXT MEI-CHAN ABOUT IT, THEN SAY IT TO MY FACE. WHATEVER IT IS.
I WANT YOU BY MY SIDE.
SMILING.
I GUESS...
I'D BETTER COME OUT AND SAY IT.

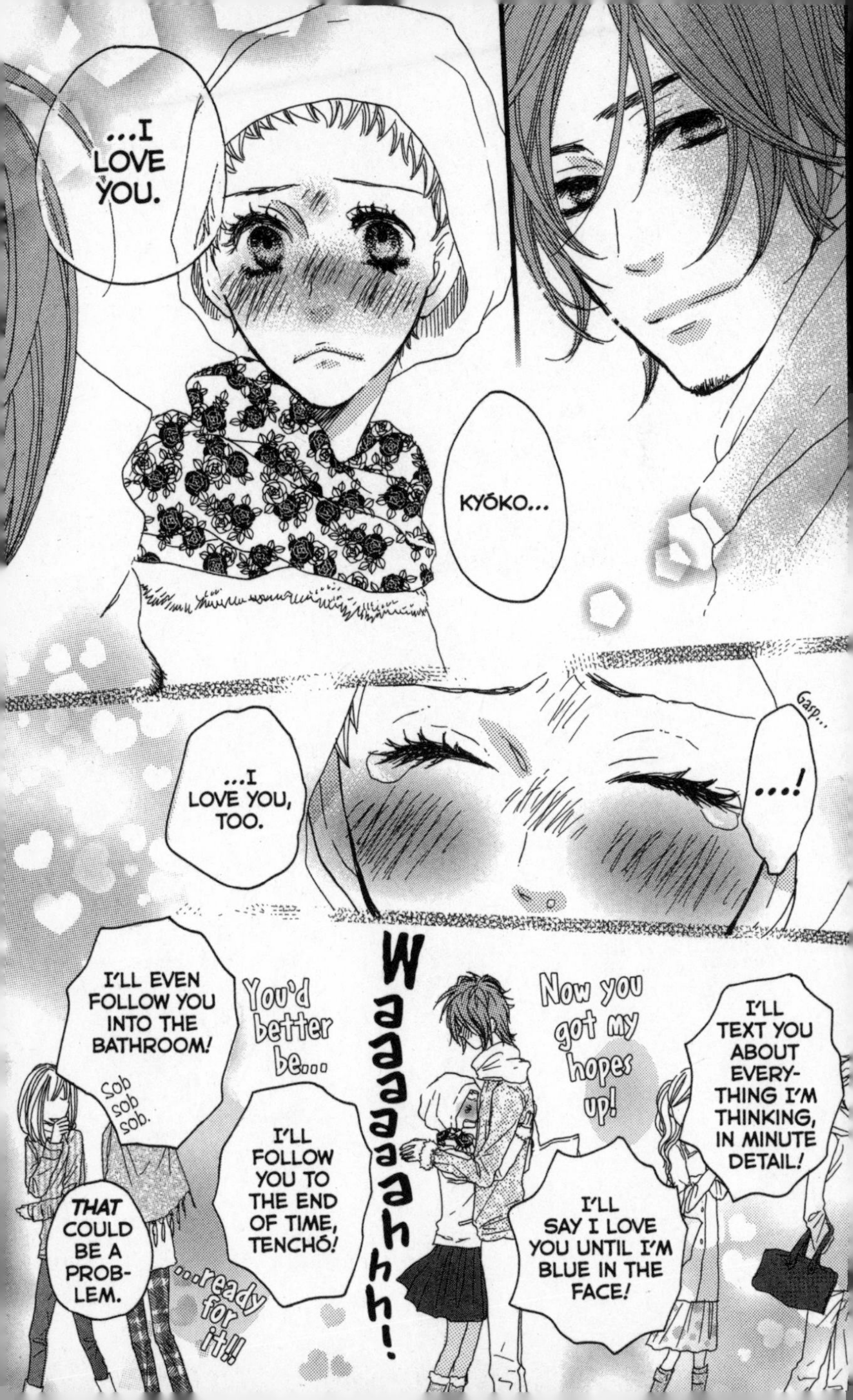

KYŌKO...
...I LOVE YOU.
Gasp...
...!
...I LOVE YOU, TOO.
I'LL TEXT YOU ABOUT EVERY-THING I'M THINKING, IN MINUTE DETAIL!
Now you got my hopes up!
I'LL SAY I LOVE YOU UNTIL I'M BLUE IN THE FACE!
Waaaaaaahhh!
I'LL FOLLOW YOU TO THE END OF TIME, TENCHŌ!
You'd better be... ...ready for it!!
I'LL EVEN FOLLOW YOU INTO THE BATHROOM!
Sob sob sob.
THAT COULD BE A PROB-LEM.

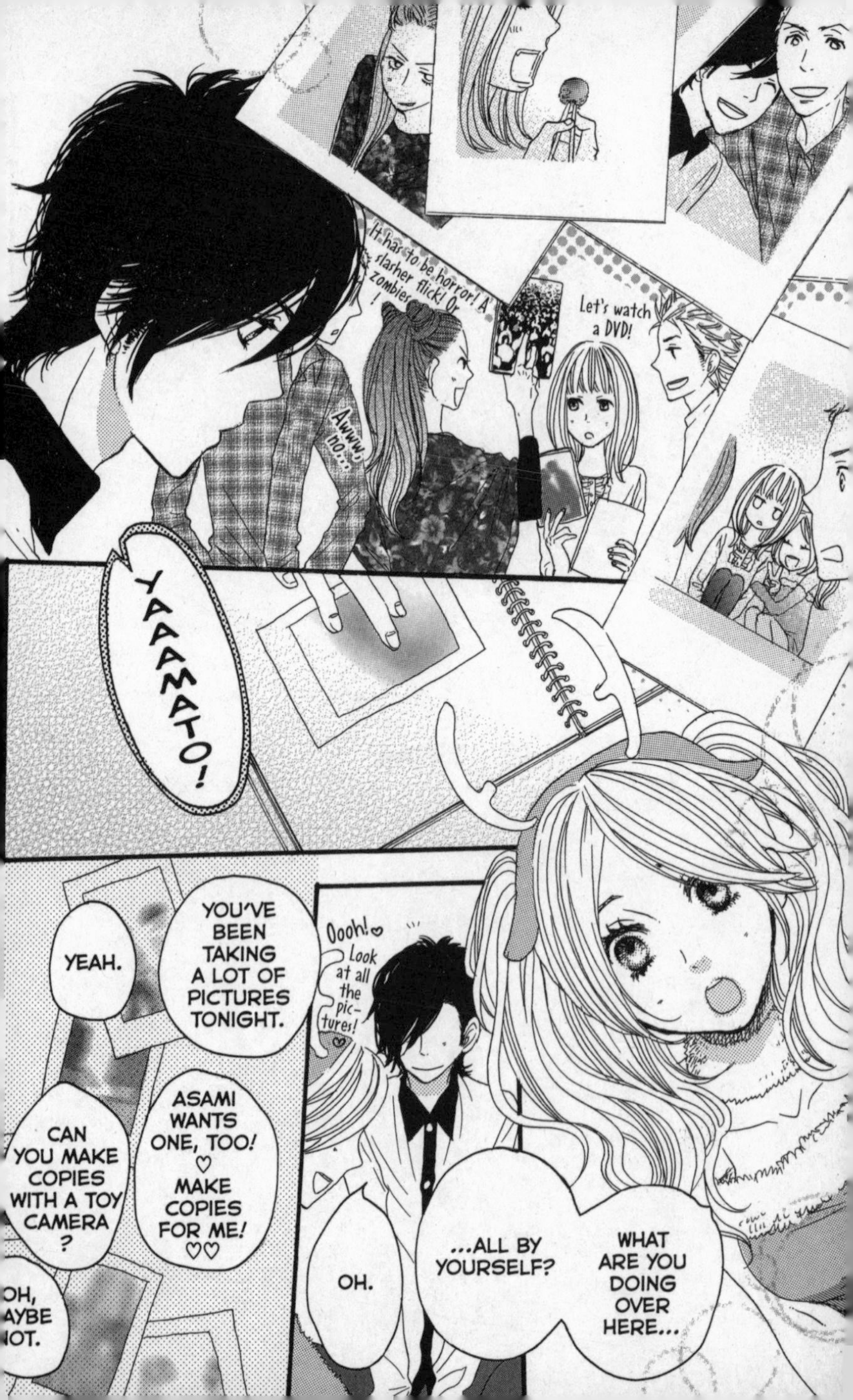
Let's watch a DVD!
It has to be horror! A slasher flick! Or zombies!
Awww, no...
YAAAMATO!
WHAT ARE YOU DOING OVER HERE...
...ALL BY YOURSELF?
OH.
Oooh! ♡ Look at all the pictures! ♡
YOU'VE BEEN TAKING A LOT OF PICTURES TONIGHT.
YEAH.
ASAMI WANTS ONE, TOO! ♡ MAKE COPIES FOR ME! ♡♡
CAN YOU MAKE COPIES WITH A TOY CAMERA?
OH, AYBE NOT.

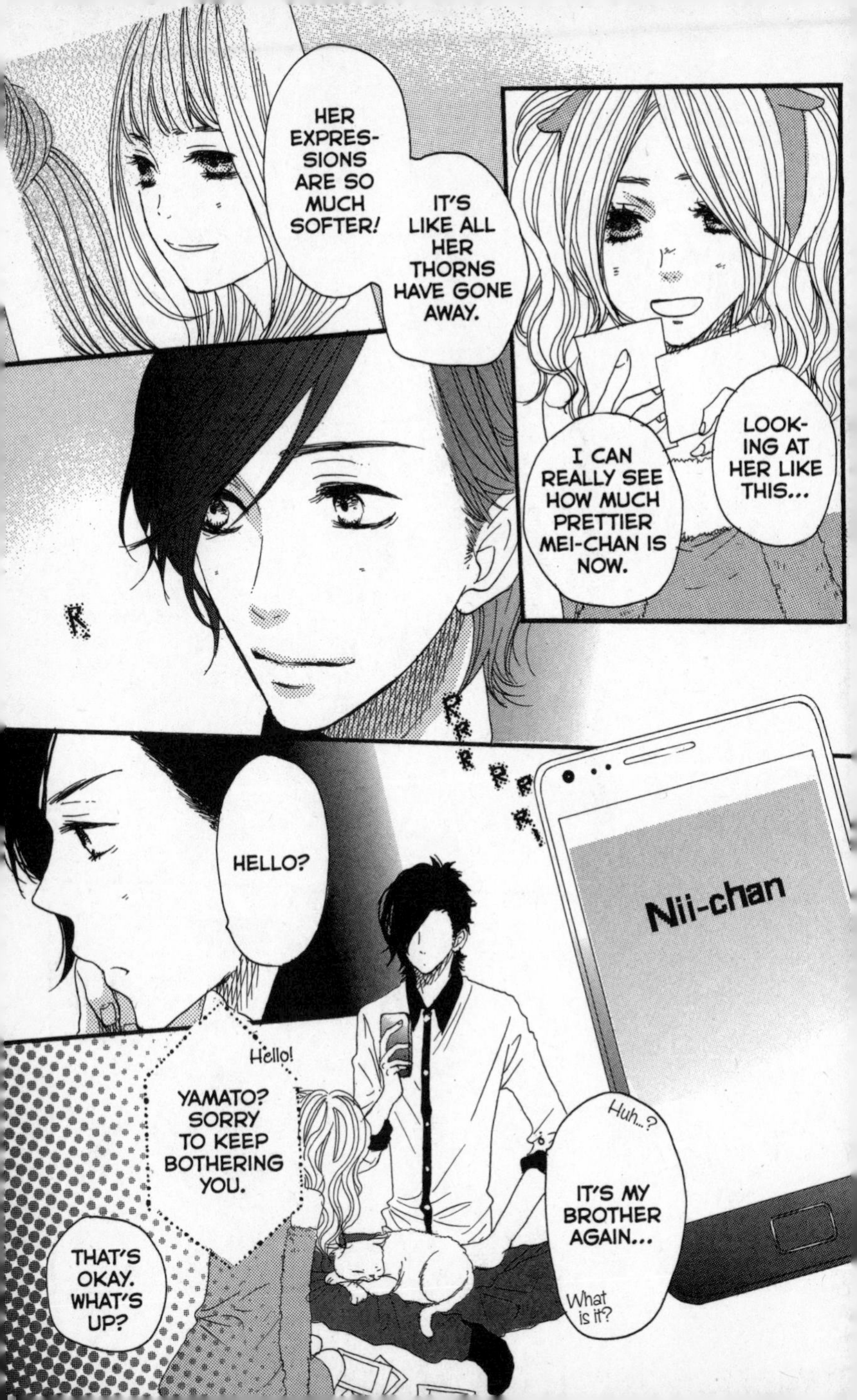
LOOKING AT HER LIKE THIS...
I CAN REALLY SEE HOW MUCH PRETTIER MEI-CHAN IS NOW.
HER EXPRESSIONS ARE SO MUCH SOFTER!
IT'S LIKE ALL HER THORNS HAVE GONE AWAY.
R
RRRR
Nii-chan
HELLO?
Huh...?
IT'S MY BROTHER AGAIN...
What is it?
Hello!
YAMATO? SORRY TO KEEP BOTHERING YOU.
THAT'S OKAY. WHAT'S UP?

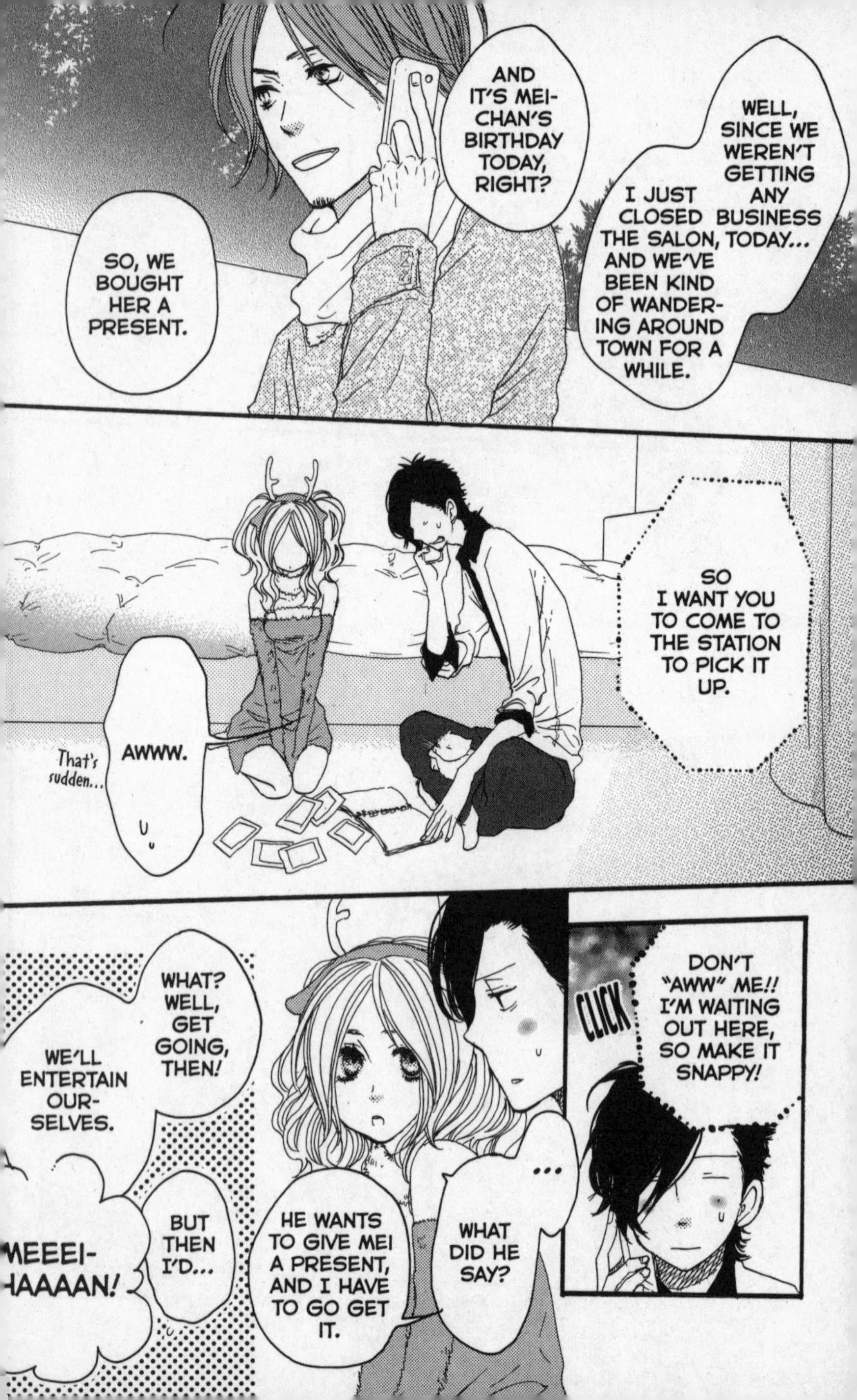
WELL, SINCE WE WEREN'T GETTING ANY BUSINESS TODAY...
I JUST CLOSED THE SALON, AND WE'VE BEEN KIND OF WANDERING AROUND TOWN FOR A WHILE.
AND IT'S MEI-CHAN'S BIRTHDAY TODAY, RIGHT?
SO, WE BOUGHT HER A PRESENT.
SO I WANT YOU TO COME TO THE STATION TO PICK IT UP.
AWWW.
That's sudden...
CLICK
DON'T "AWW" ME!! I'M WAITING OUT HERE, SO MAKE IT SNAPPY!
...
WHAT DID HE SAY?
HE WANTS TO GIVE MEI A PRESENT, AND I HAVE TO GO GET IT.
WHAT? WELL, GET GOING, THEN!
WE'LL ENTERTAIN OURSELVES.
BUT THEN I'D...
MEEEI-HAAAAN!

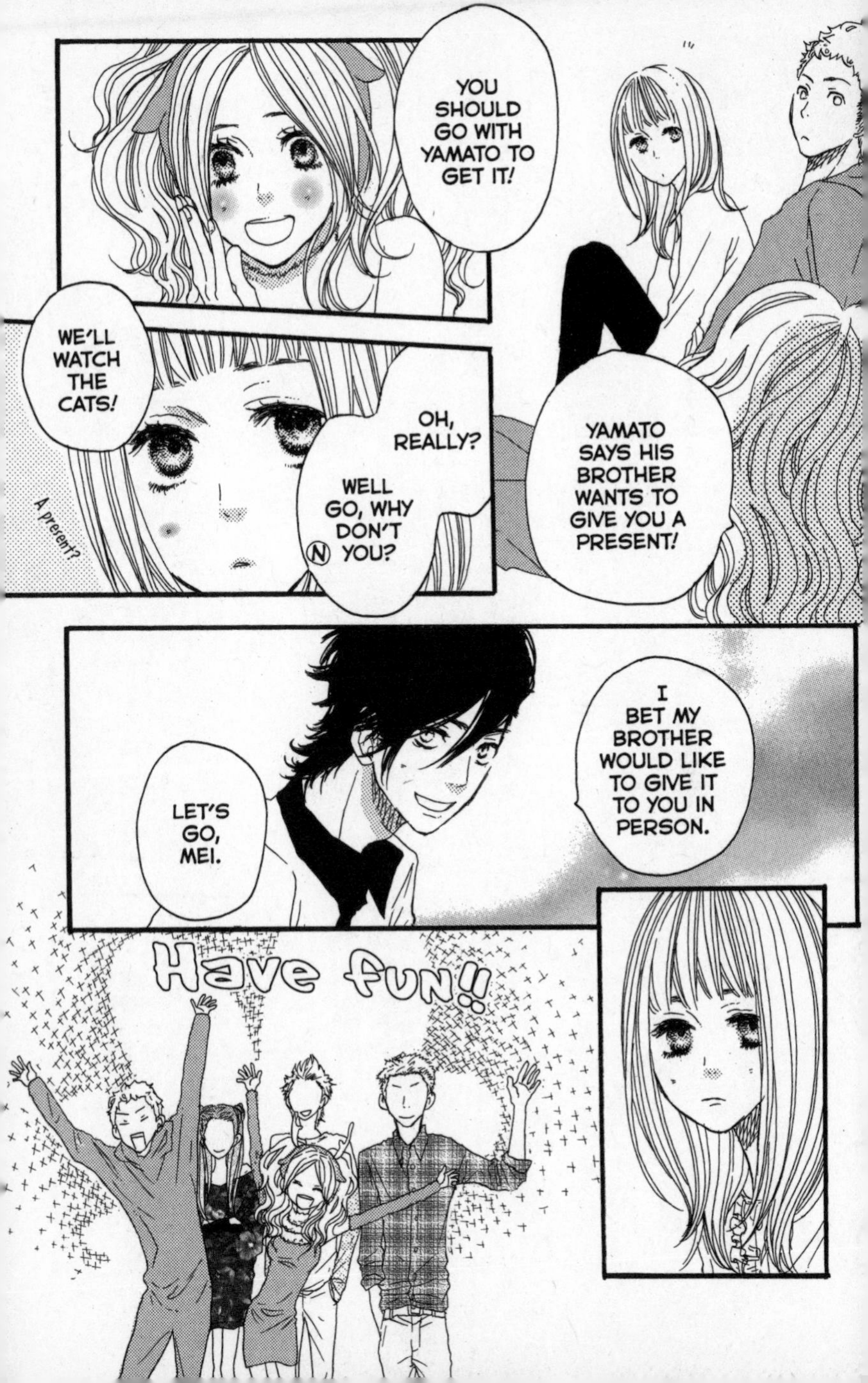
YAMATO SAYS HIS BROTHER WANTS TO GIVE YOU A PRESENT!
YOU SHOULD GO WITH YAMATO TO GET IT!
OH, REALLY?
WELL GO, WHY DON'T YOU?
WE'LL WATCH THE CATS!
A present?
I BET MY BROTHER WOULD LIKE TO GIVE IT TO YOU IN PERSON.
LET'S GO, MEI.
Have fun!!

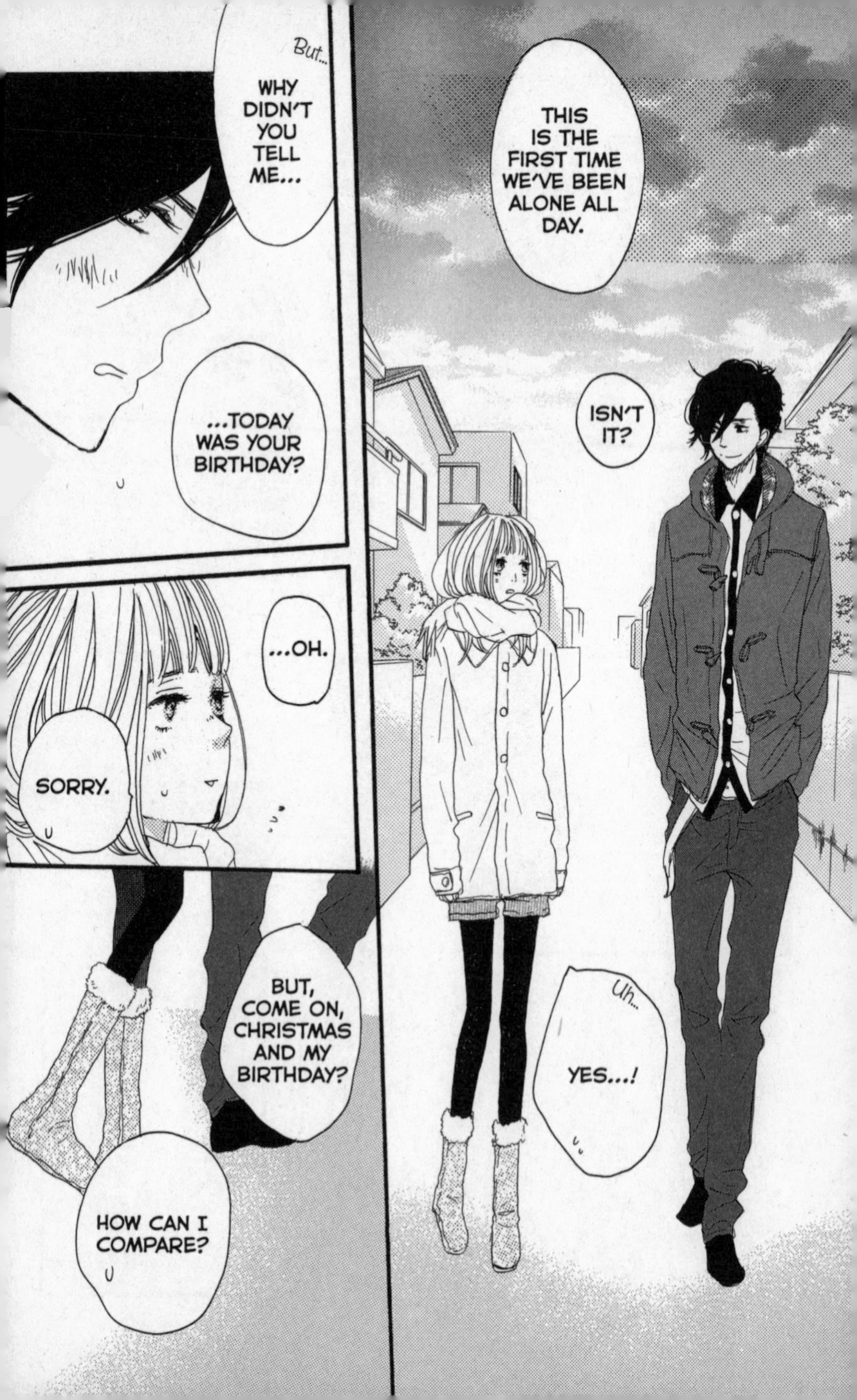
THIS IS THE FIRST TIME WE'VE BEEN ALONE ALL DAY.
ISN'T IT?
Uh...
YES...!
But...
WHY DIDN'T YOU TELL ME...
...TODAY WAS YOUR BIRTHDAY?
...OH.
SORRY.
BUT, COME ON, CHRISTMAS AND MY BIRTHDAY?
HOW CAN I COMPARE?

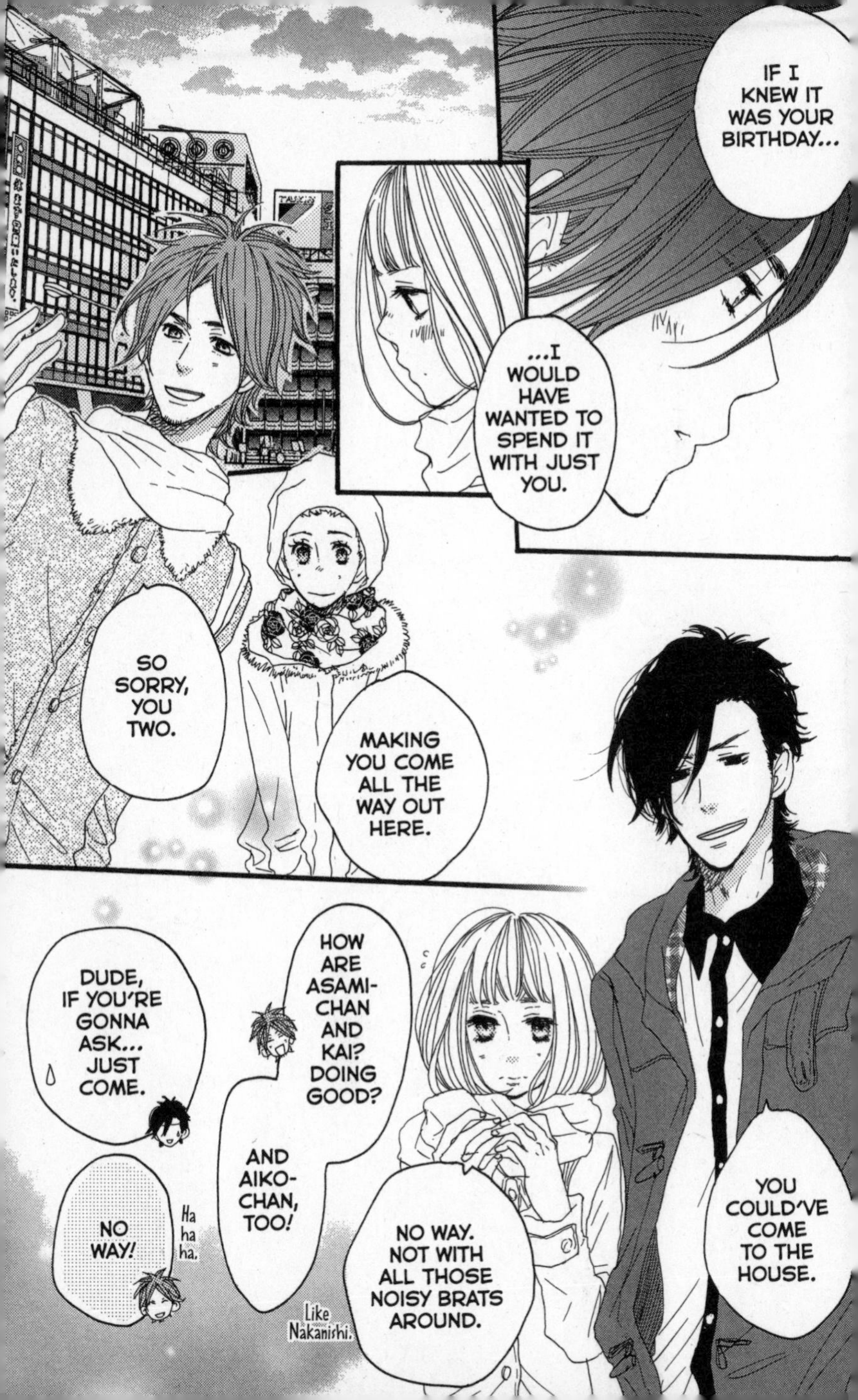
IF I KNEW IT WAS YOUR BIRTHDAY...
...I WOULD HAVE WANTED TO SPEND IT WITH JUST YOU.
SO SORRY, YOU TWO.
MAKING YOU COME ALL THE WAY OUT HERE.
YOU COULD'VE COME TO THE HOUSE.
NO WAY. NOT WITH ALL THOSE NOISY BRATS AROUND.
Like Nakanishi.
HOW ARE ASAMI-CHAN AND KAI? DOING GOOD?
AND AIKO-CHAN, TOO!
DUDE, IF YOU'RE GONNA ASK... JUST COME.
NO WAY!
Ha ha ha.

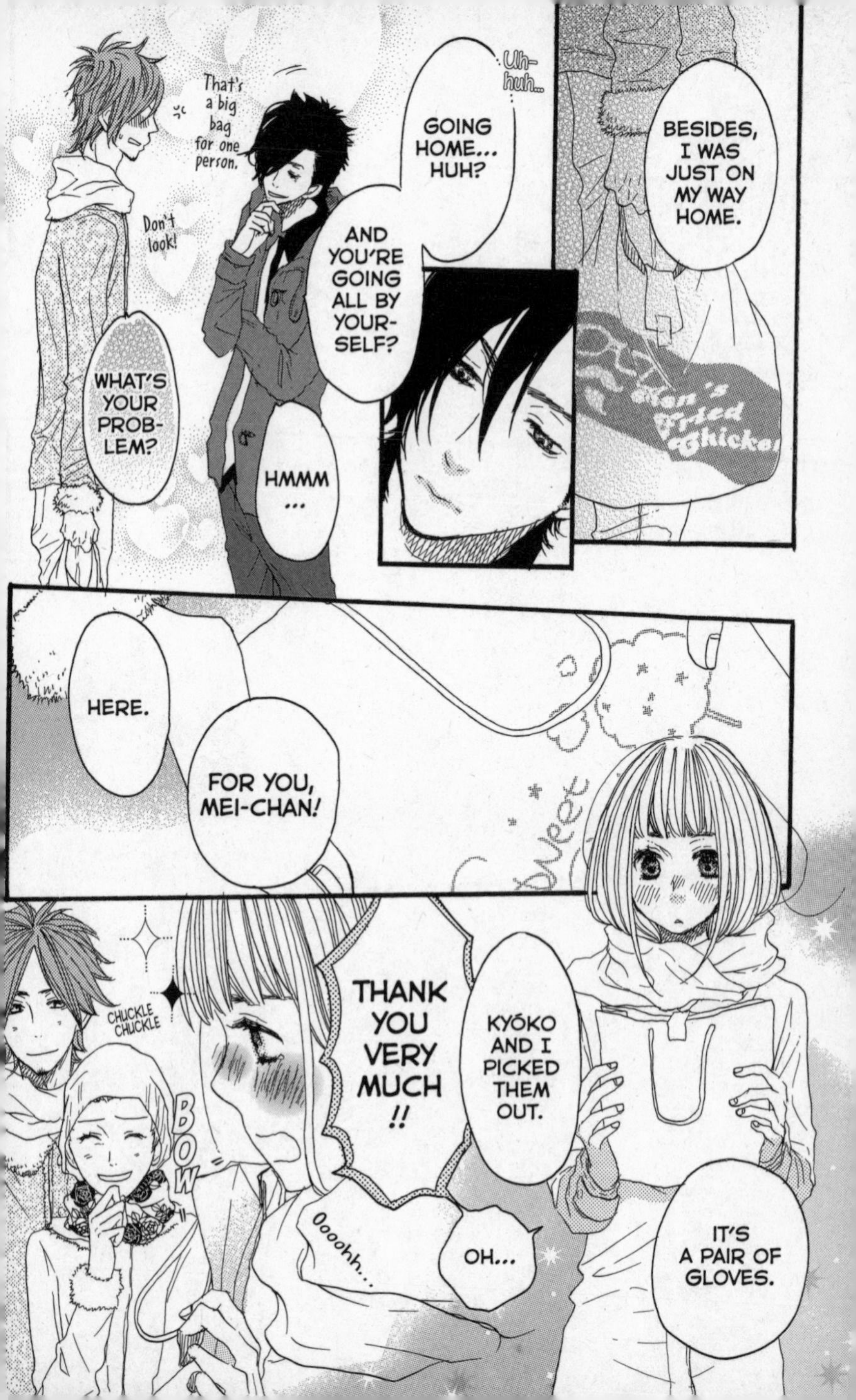

BESIDES, I WAS JUST ON MY WAY HOME.
Uh-huh...
GOING HOME... HUH?
AND YOU'RE GOING ALL BY YOURSELF?
That's a big bag for one person.
HMMM...
Don't look!
WHAT'S YOUR PROBLEM?
HERE.
FOR YOU, MEI-CHAN!
Sweet
IT'S A PAIR OF GLOVES.
KYŌKO AND I PICKED THEM OUT.
OH...
THANK YOU VERY MUCH!!
Ooooh...
BOW
CHUCKLE CHUCKLE

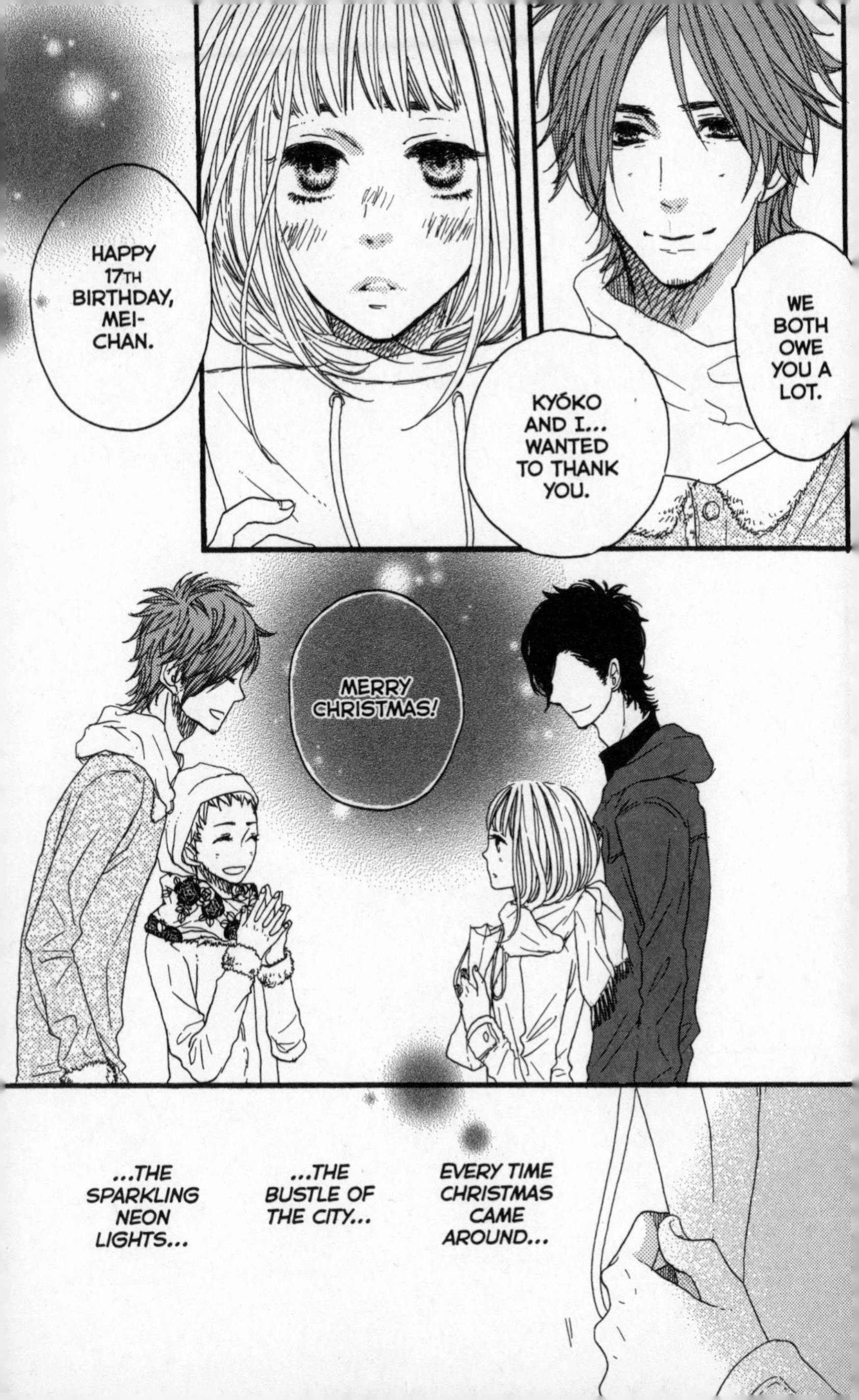
WE BOTH OWE YOU A LOT.
KYŌKO AND I... WANTED TO THANK YOU.
HAPPY 17TH BIRTHDAY, MEI-CHAN.
MERRY CHRISTMAS!
EVERY TIME CHRISTMAS CAME AROUND...
...THE BUSTLE OF THE CITY...
...THE SPARKLING NEON LIGHTS...

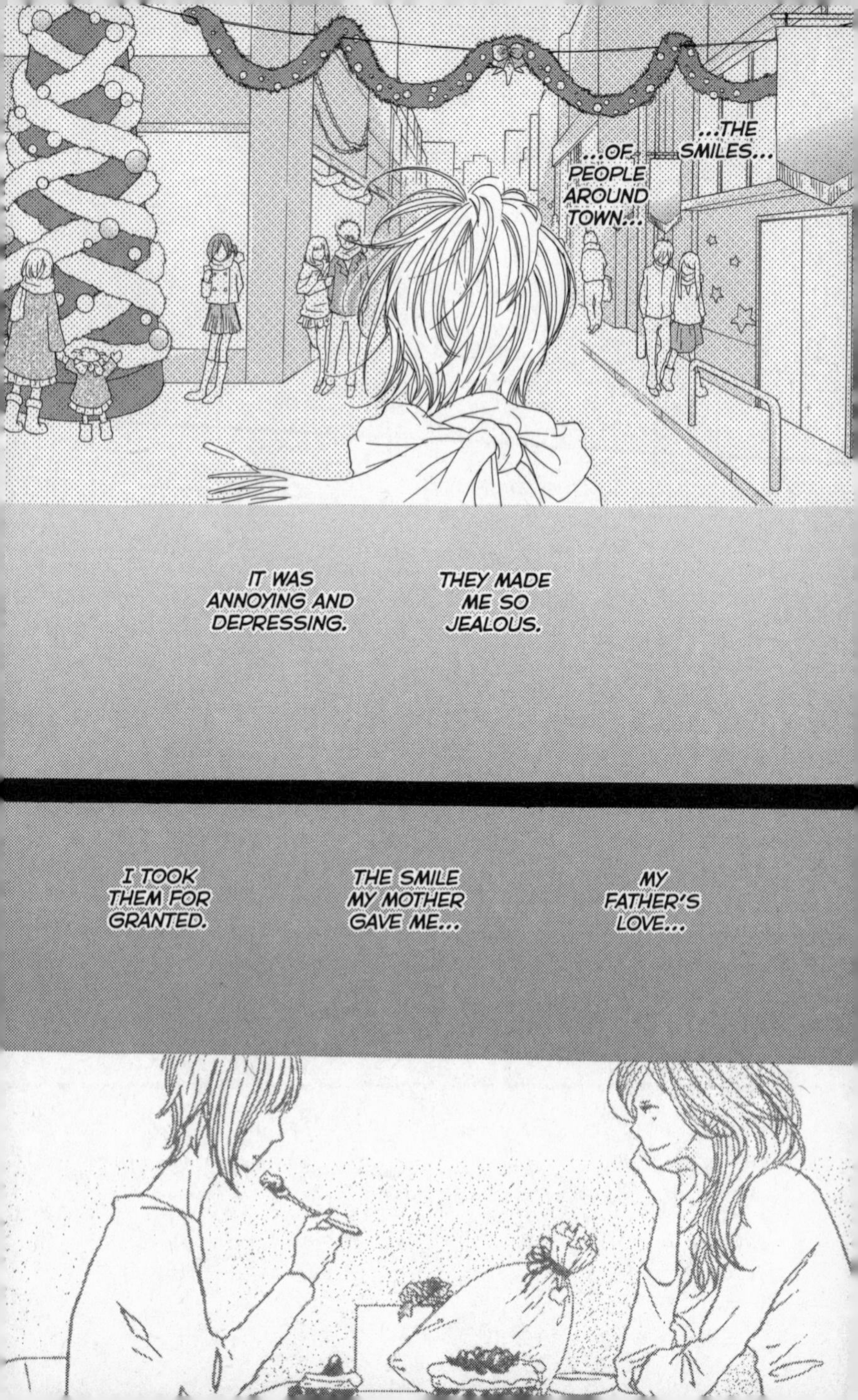
...THE SMILES...
...OF PEOPLE AROUND TOWN...
THEY MADE ME SO JEALOUS.
IT WAS ANNOYING AND DEPRESSING.
MY FATHER'S LOVE...
THE SMILE MY MOTHER GAVE ME...
I TOOK THEM FOR GRANTED.

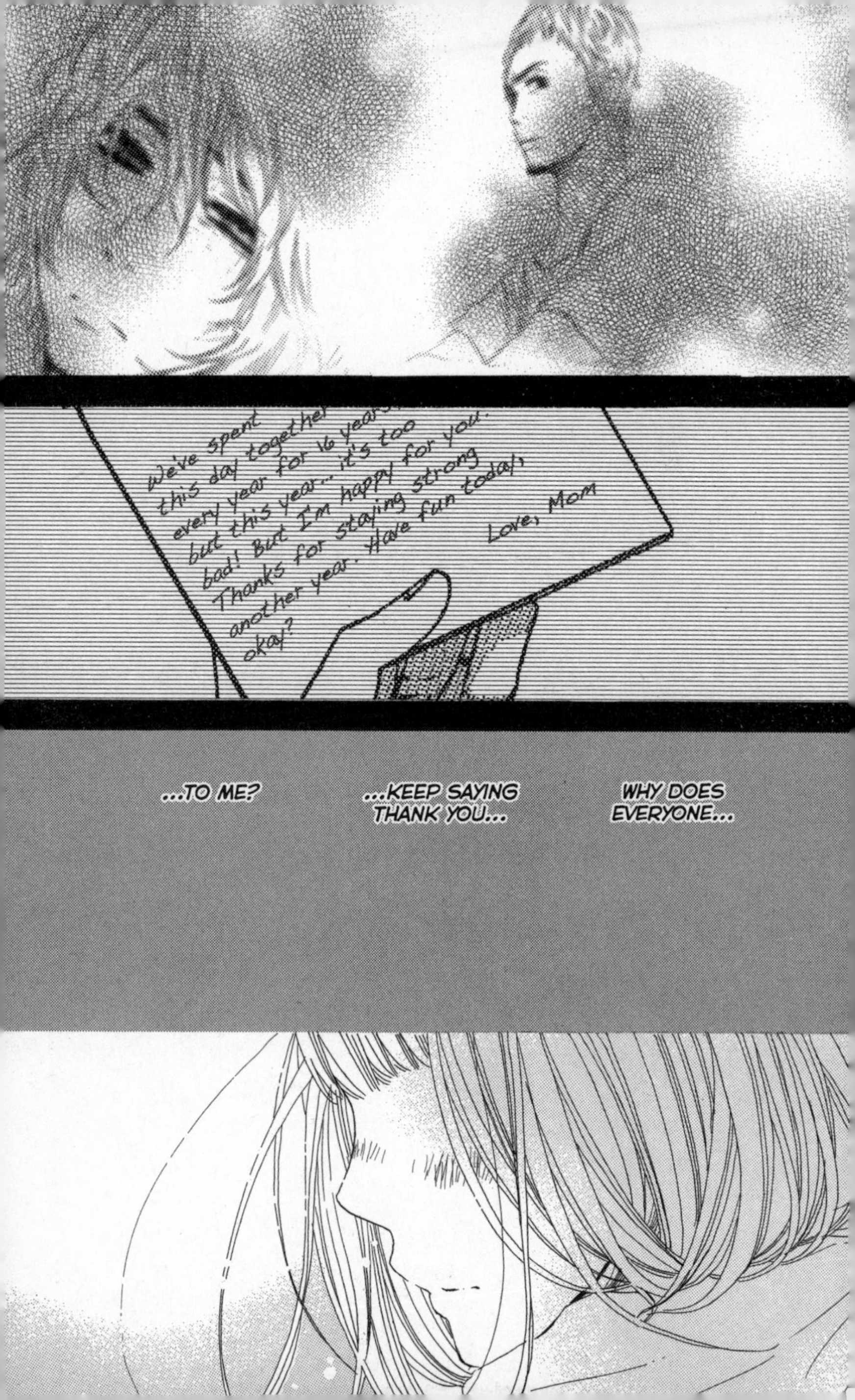
We've spent
this day together
every year for 16 years...
but this year... it's too
bad! But I'm happy for you.
Thanks for staying strong
another year. Have fun today,
okay?
Love, Mom
WHY DOES EVERYONE...
...KEEP SAYING THANK YOU...
...TO ME?

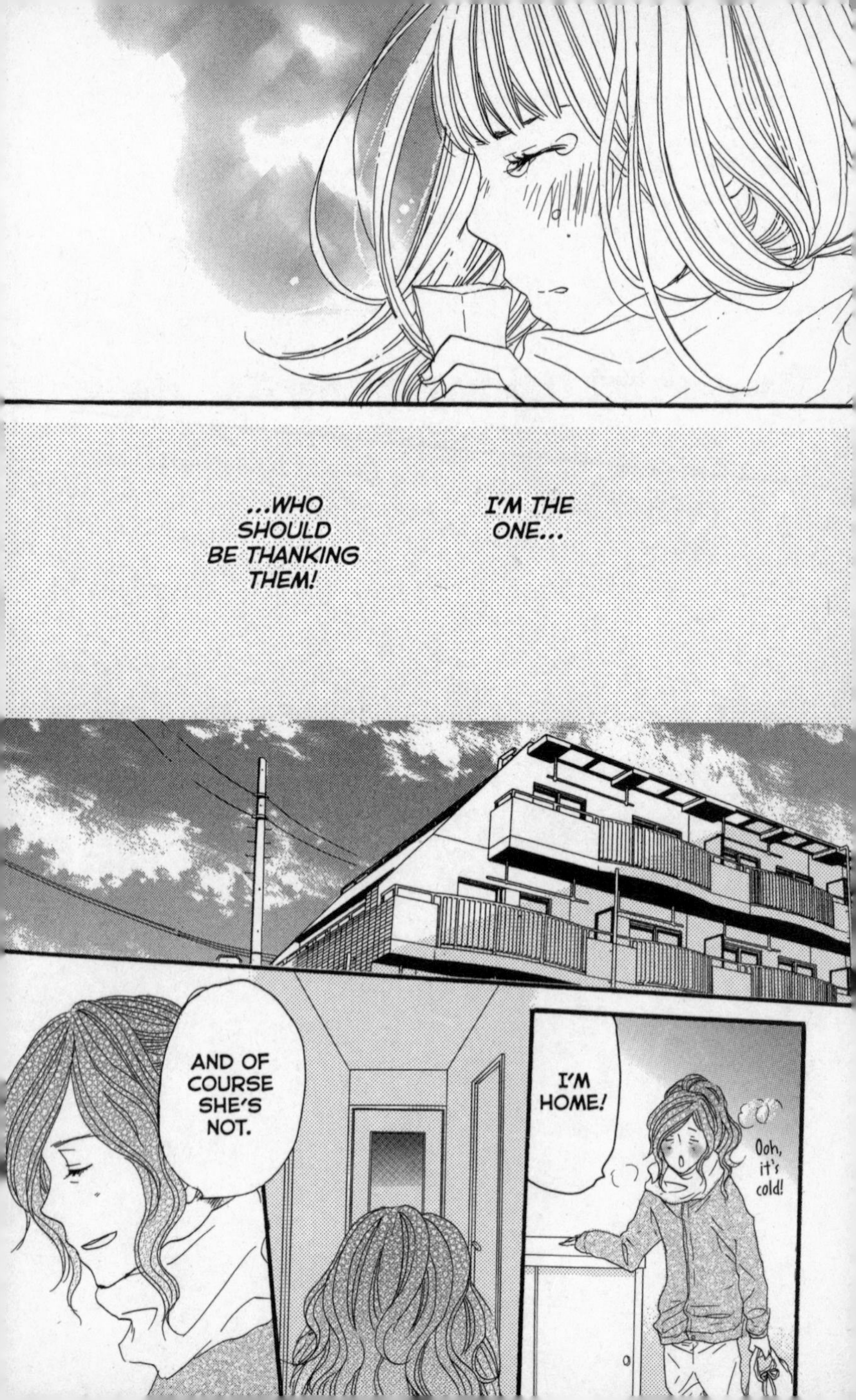
I'M THE ONE...
...WHO SHOULD BE THANKING THEM!
I'M HOME!
Ooh, it's cold!
AND OF COURSE SHE'S NOT.

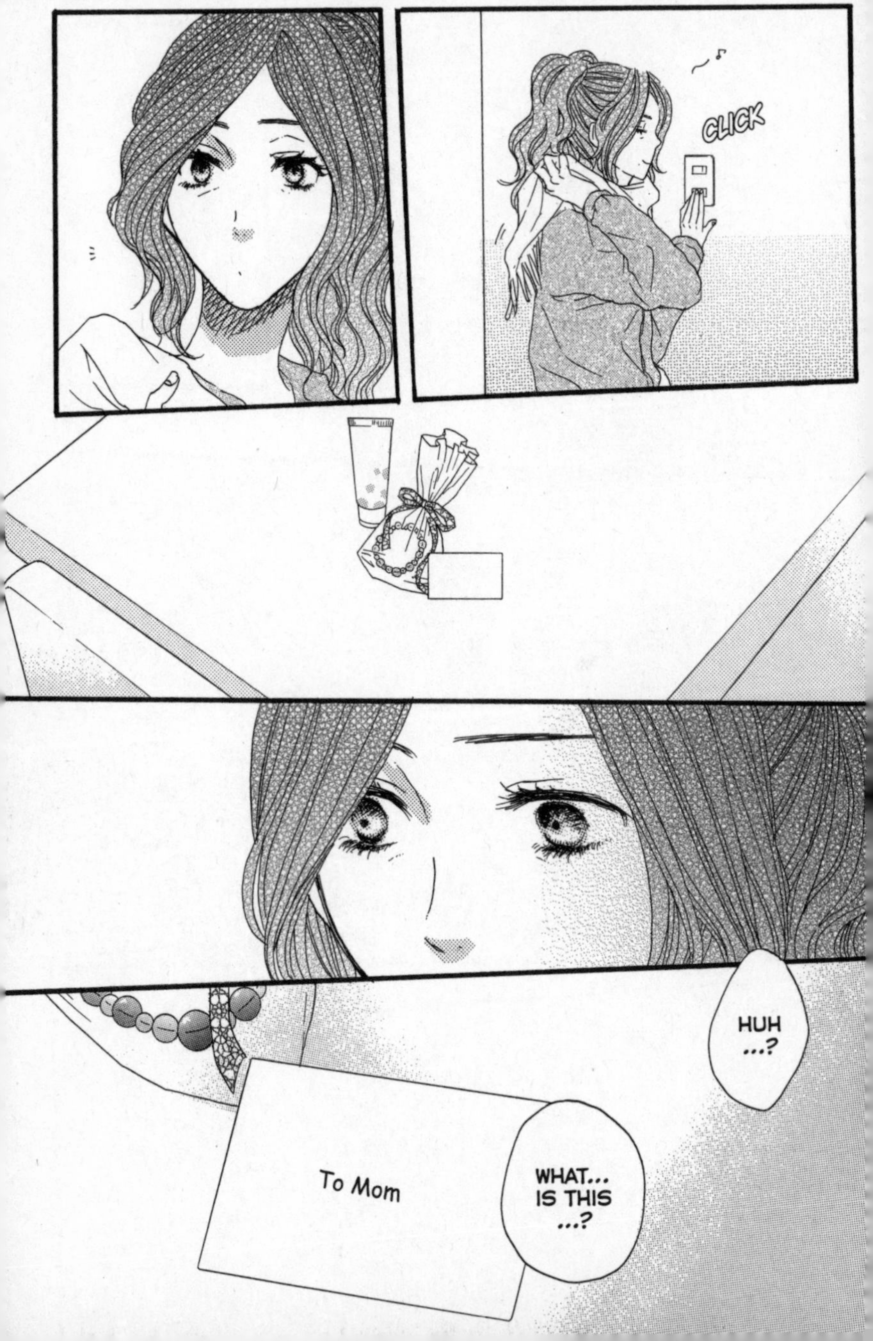
CLICK
HUH ...?
WHAT... IS THIS ...?
To Mom

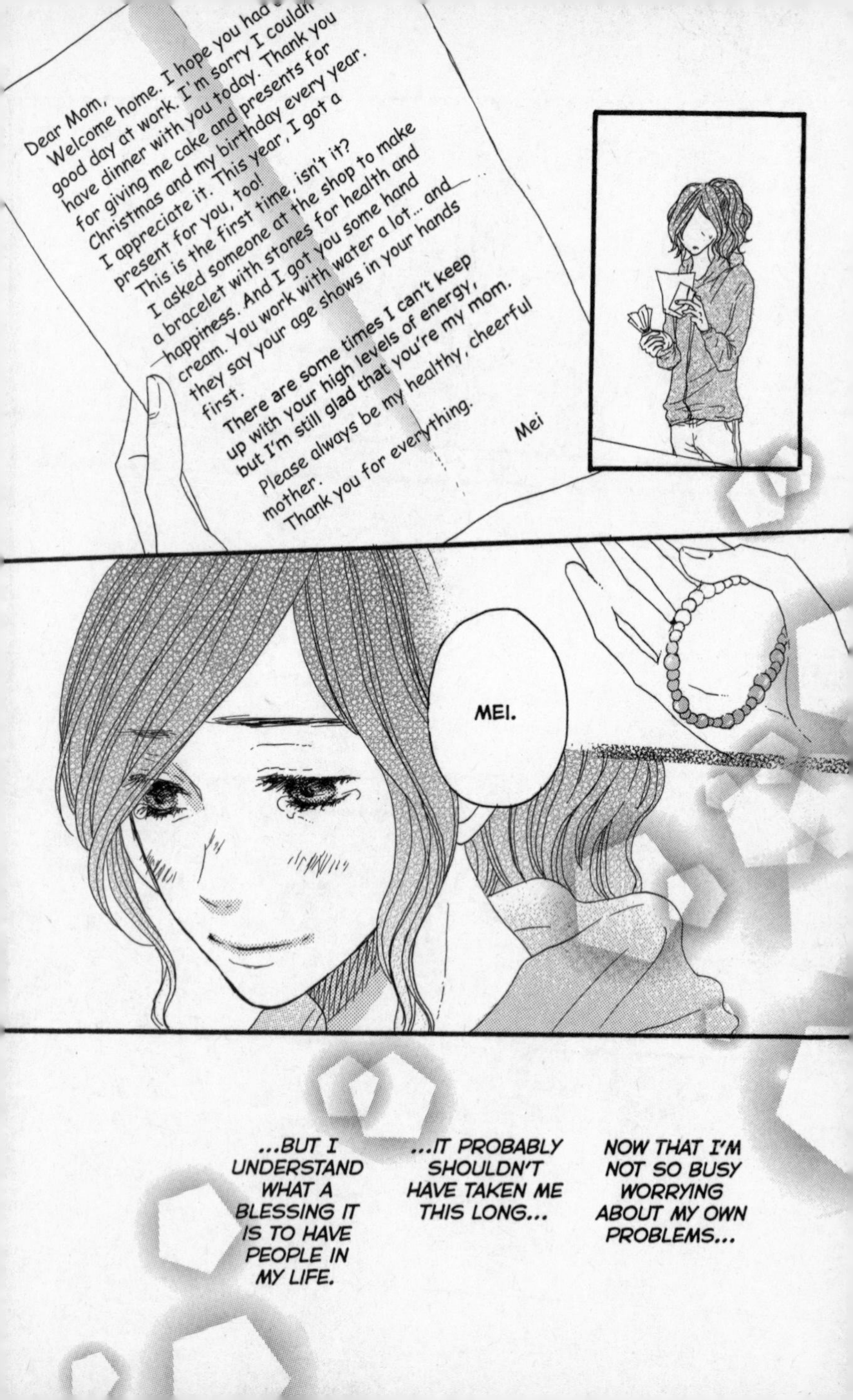
Dear Mom,
Welcome home. I hope you had
good day at work. I'm sorry I couldn
have dinner with you today. Thank you
for giving me cake and presents for
Christmas and my birthday every year.
I appreciate it. This year, I got a
present for you, too!
This is the first time, isn't it?
I asked someone at the shop to make
a bracelet with stones for health and
happiness. And I got you some hand
cream. You work with water a lot... and
they say your age shows in your hands
first.
There are some times I can't keep
up with your high levels of energy,
but I'm still glad that you're my mom.
Please always be my healthy, cheerful
mother.
Thank you for everything.
Mei
MEI.
NOW THAT I'M NOT SO BUSY WORRYING ABOUT MY OWN PROBLEMS...
...IT PROBABLY SHOULDN'T HAVE TAKEN ME THIS LONG...
...BUT I UNDERSTAND WHAT A BLESSING IT IS TO HAVE PEOPLE IN MY LIFE.

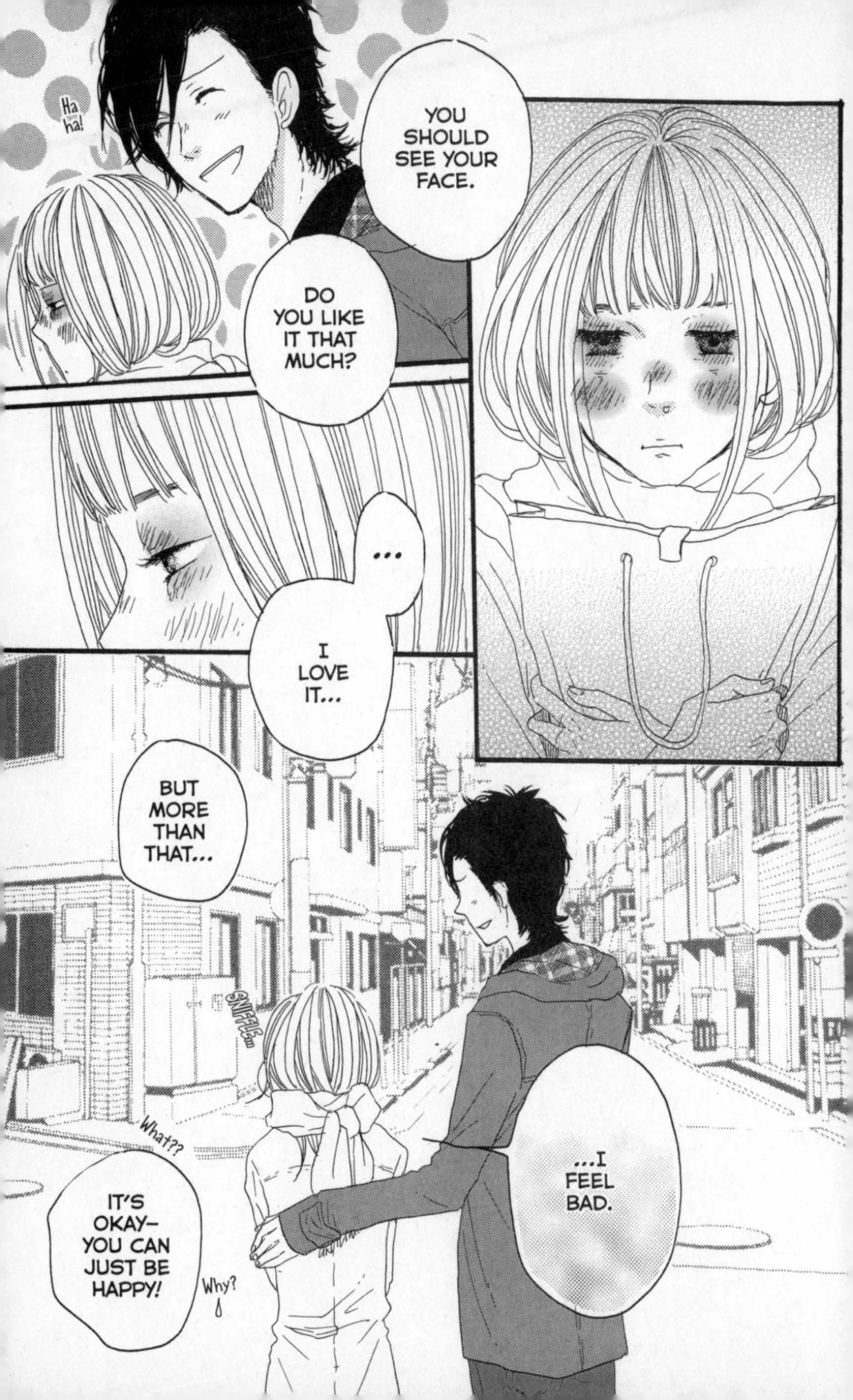
YOU SHOULD SEE YOUR FACE.
Ha ha!
DO YOU LIKE IT THAT MUCH?
...
I LOVE IT...
BUT MORE THAN THAT...
...I FEEL BAD.
SNIFFLE...
What??
IT'S OKAY— YOU CAN JUST BE HAPPY!
Why?

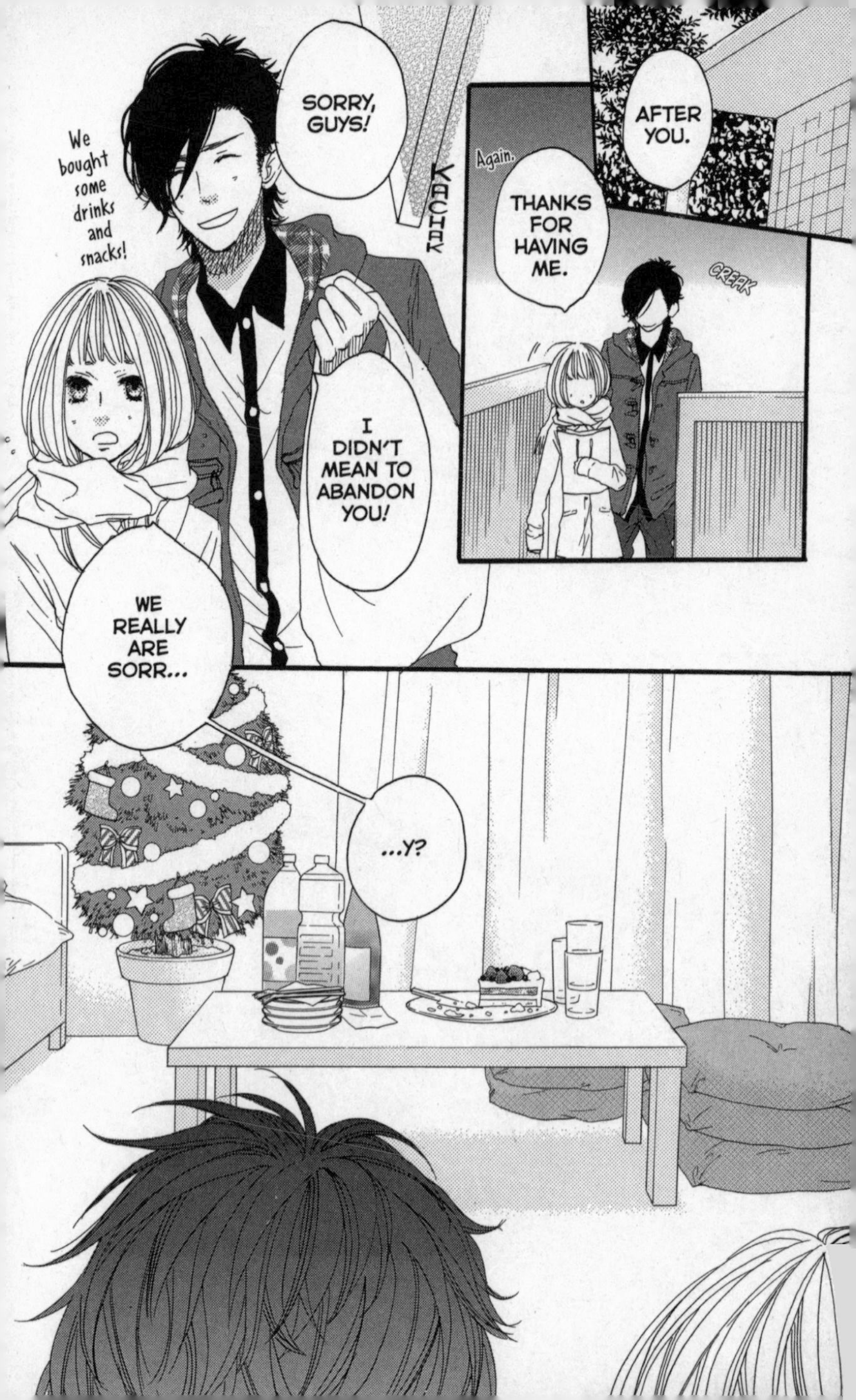
AFTER YOU.
Again.
THANKS FOR HAVING ME.
CREAK
SORRY, GUYS!
KACHAK
We bought some drinks and snacks!
I DIDN'T MEAN TO ABANDON YOU!
WE REALLY ARE SORR...
...Y?

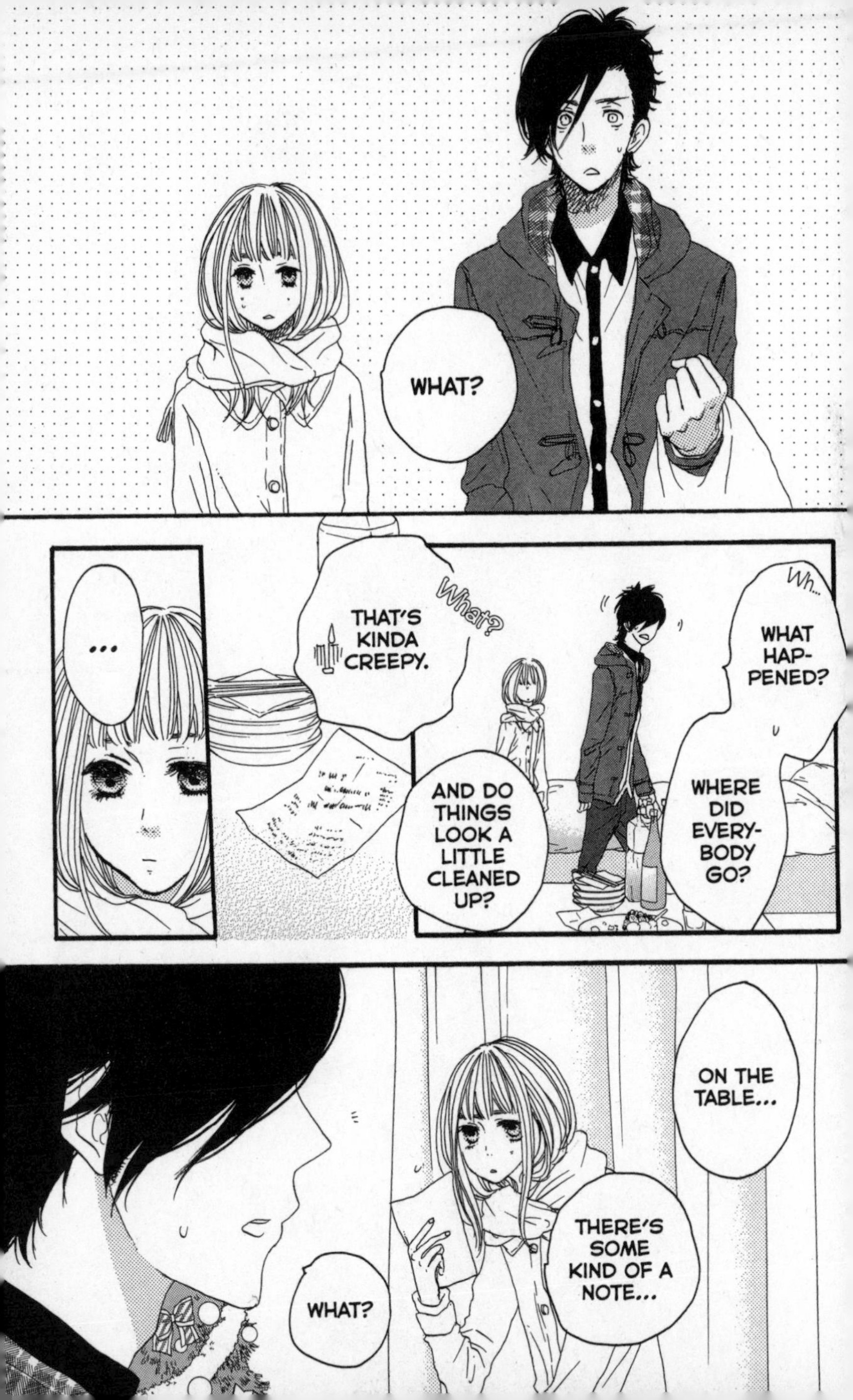
WHAT?
Wh...
WHAT HAPPENED?
WHERE DID EVERYBODY GO?
AND DO THINGS LOOK A LITTLE CLEANED UP?
What?
THAT'S KINDA CREEPY.
...
ON THE TABLE...
THERE'S SOME KIND OF A NOTE...
WHAT?

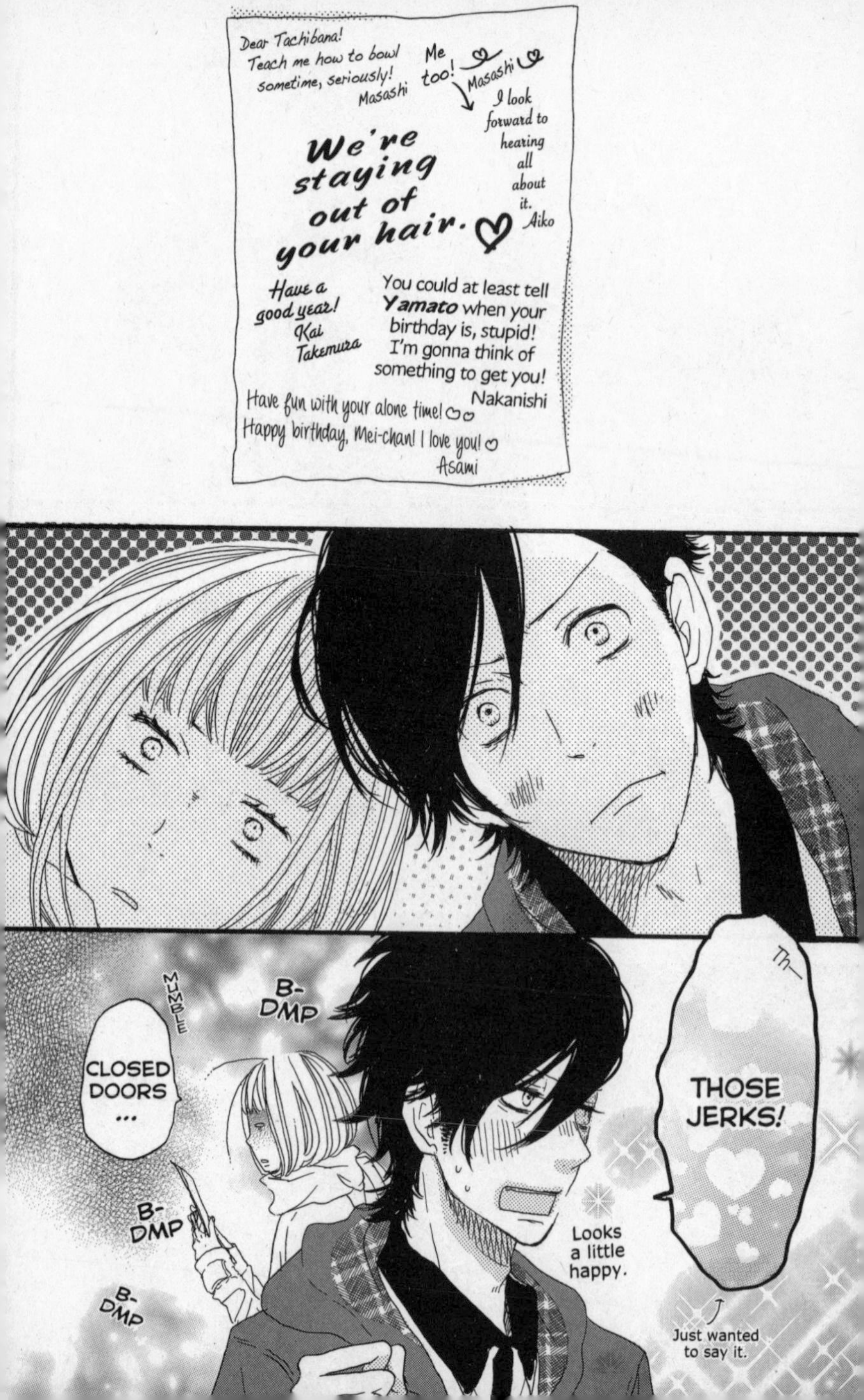
Dear Tachibana!
Teach me how to bowl sometime, seriously!
Masashi
Me too!
Masashi
I look forward to hearing all about it.
Aiko
We're staying out of your hair.
Have a good year!
Kai Takemura
You could at least tell Yamato when your birthday is, stupid! I'm gonna think of something to get you!
Nakanishi
Have fun with your alone time!
Happy birthday, Mei-chan! I love you!
Asami
Th—
THOSE JERKS!
Just wanted to say it.
Looks a little happy.
B-DMP
CLOSED DOORS...
MUMBLE
B-DMP
B-DMP

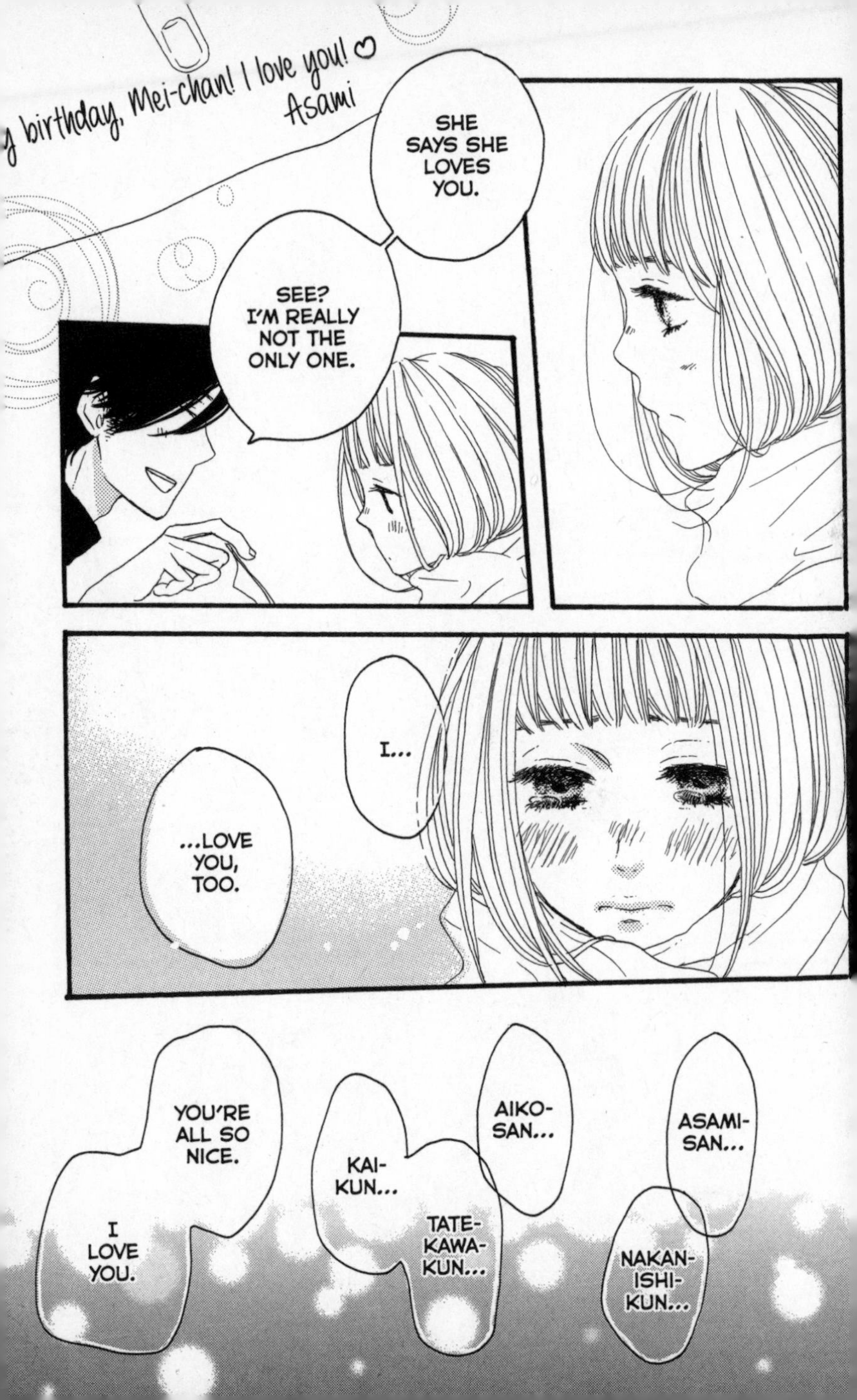
y birthday, Mei-chan! I love you!
Asami
SHE SAYS SHE LOVES YOU.
SEE? I'M REALLY NOT THE ONLY ONE.
I...
...LOVE YOU, TOO.
ASAMI-SAN...
NAKAN-ISHI-KUN...
AIKO-SAN...
KAI-KUN...
TATE-KAWA-KUN...
YOU'RE ALL SO NICE.
I LOVE YOU.

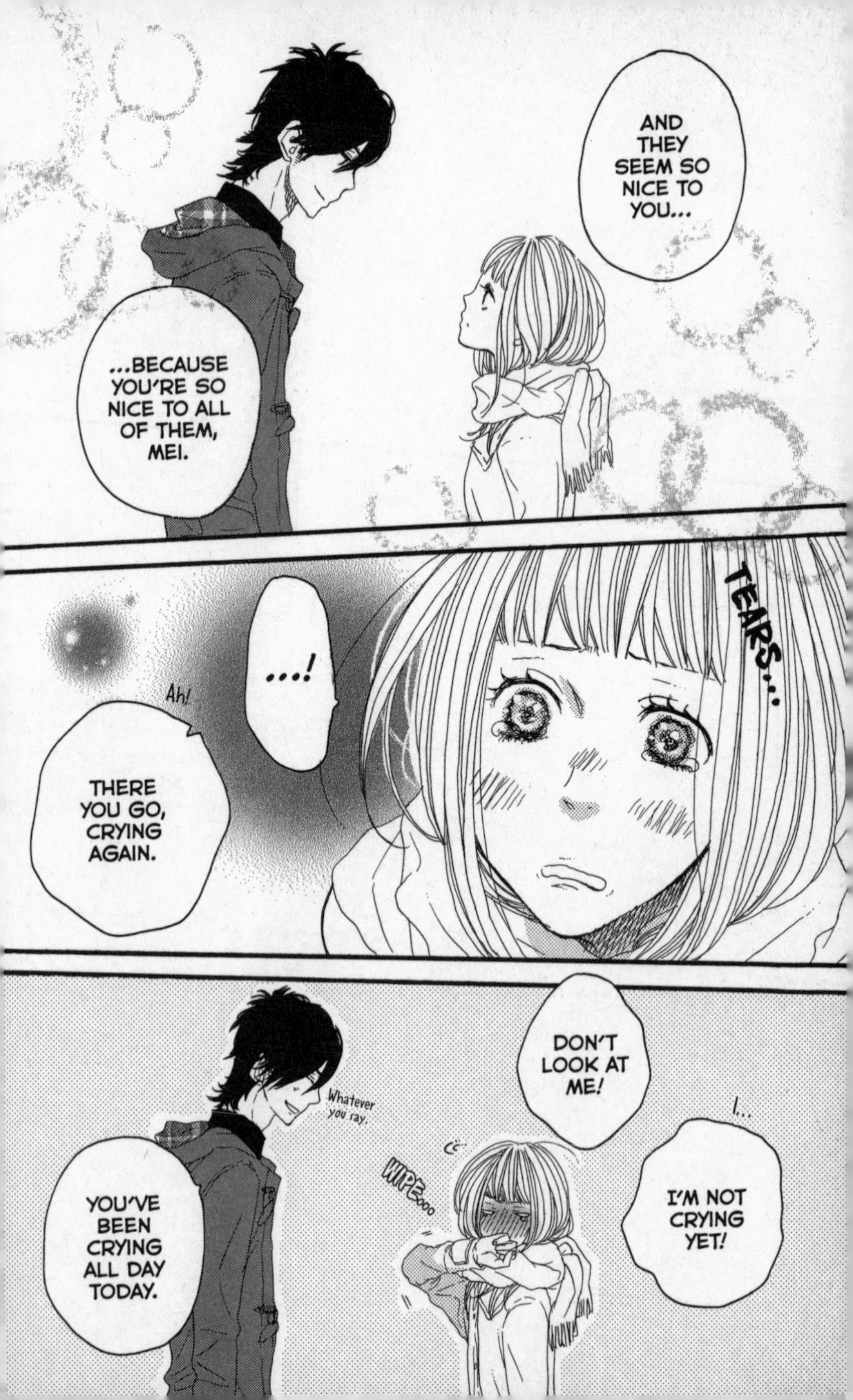
AND THEY SEEM SO NICE TO YOU...
...BECAUSE YOU'RE SO NICE TO ALL OF THEM, MEI.
TEARS...
...!
Ah!
THERE YOU GO, CRYING AGAIN.
DON'T LOOK AT ME!
I...
I'M NOT CRYING YET!
WIPE
Whatever you say.
YOU'VE BEEN CRYING ALL DAY TODAY.

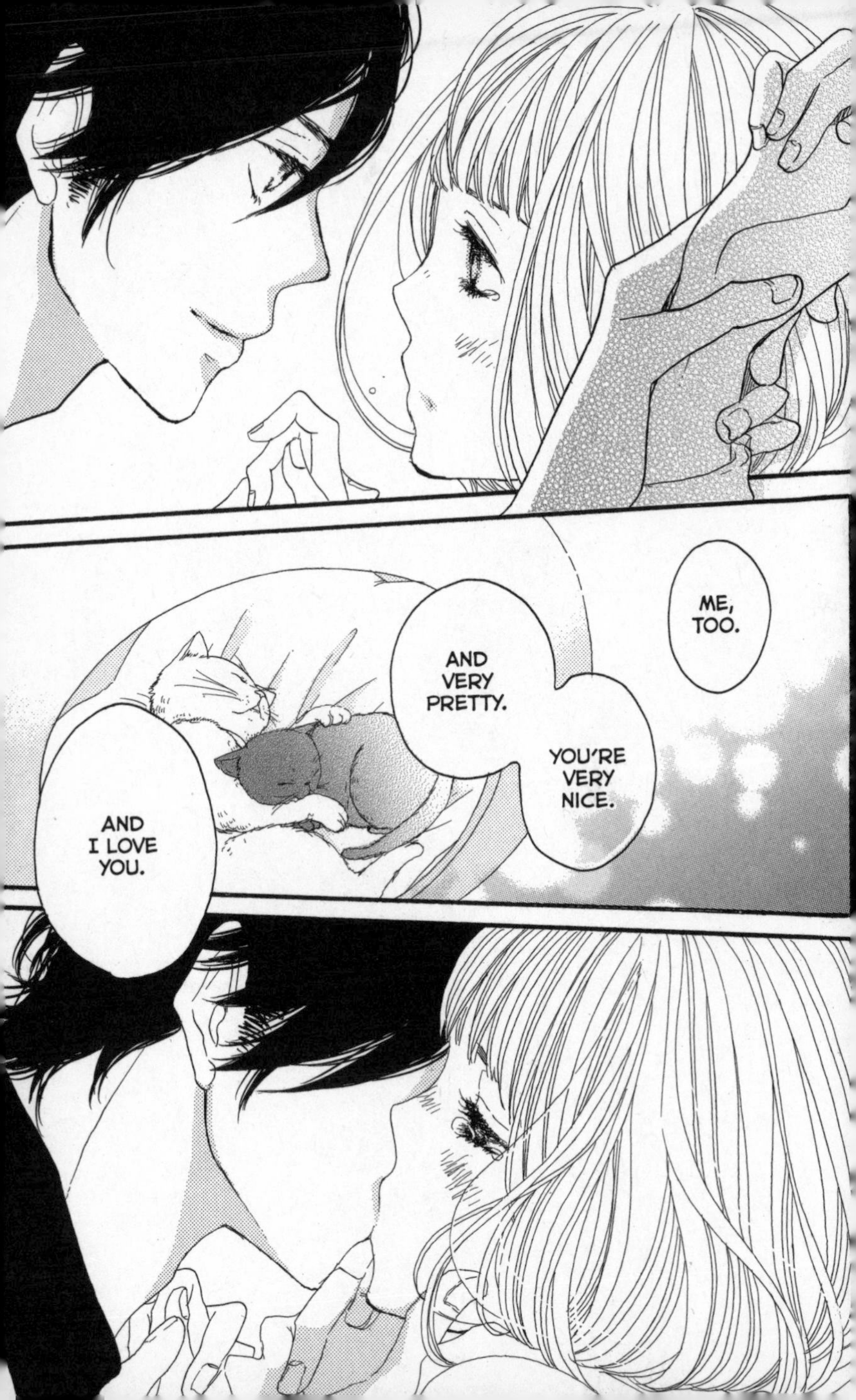

ME, TOO.
YOU'RE VERY NICE.
AND VERY PRETTY.
AND I LOVE YOU.

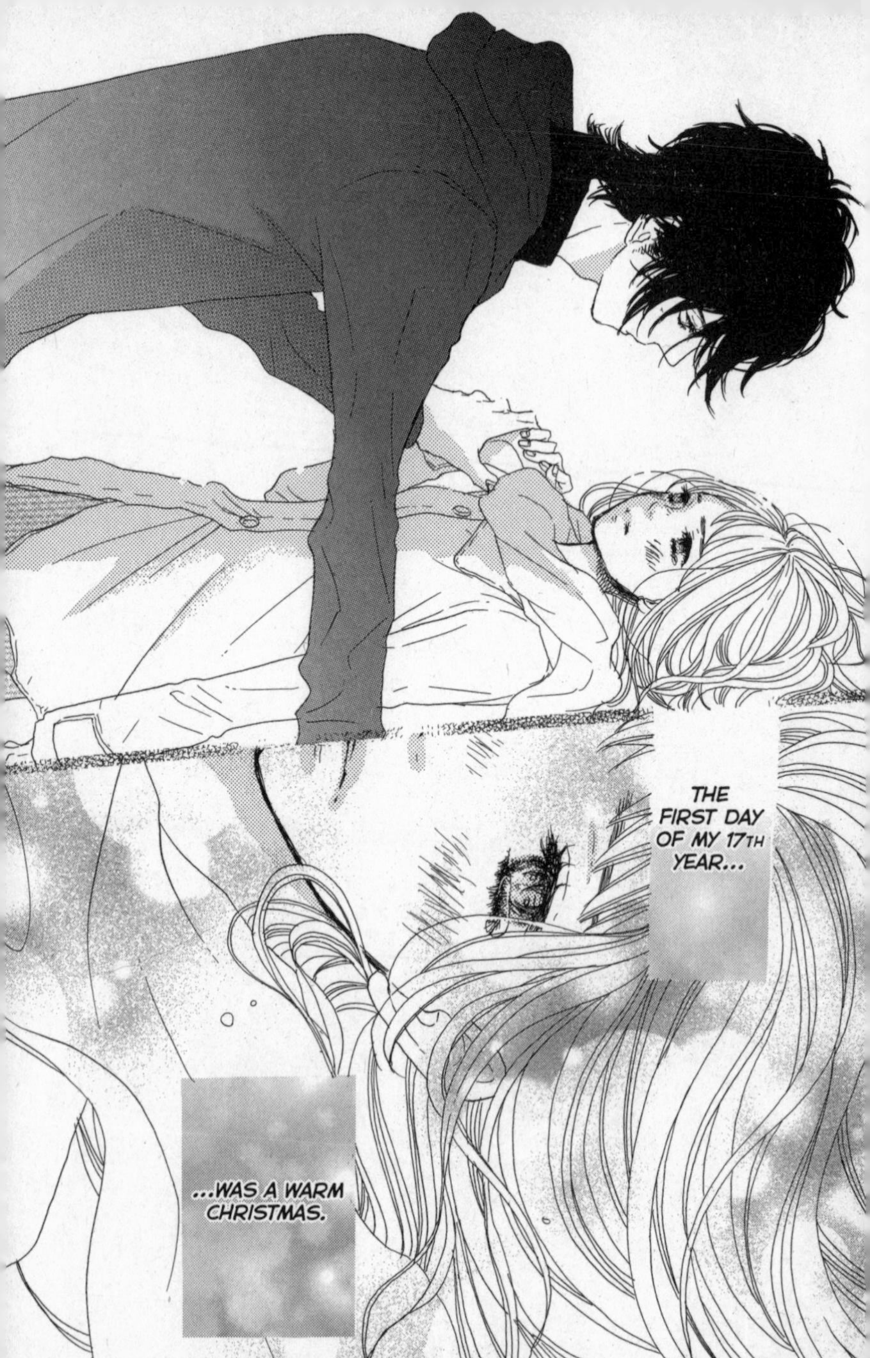
THE FIRST DAY OF MY 17TH YEAR...
...WAS A WARM CHRISTMAS.

Chapter 38 — End

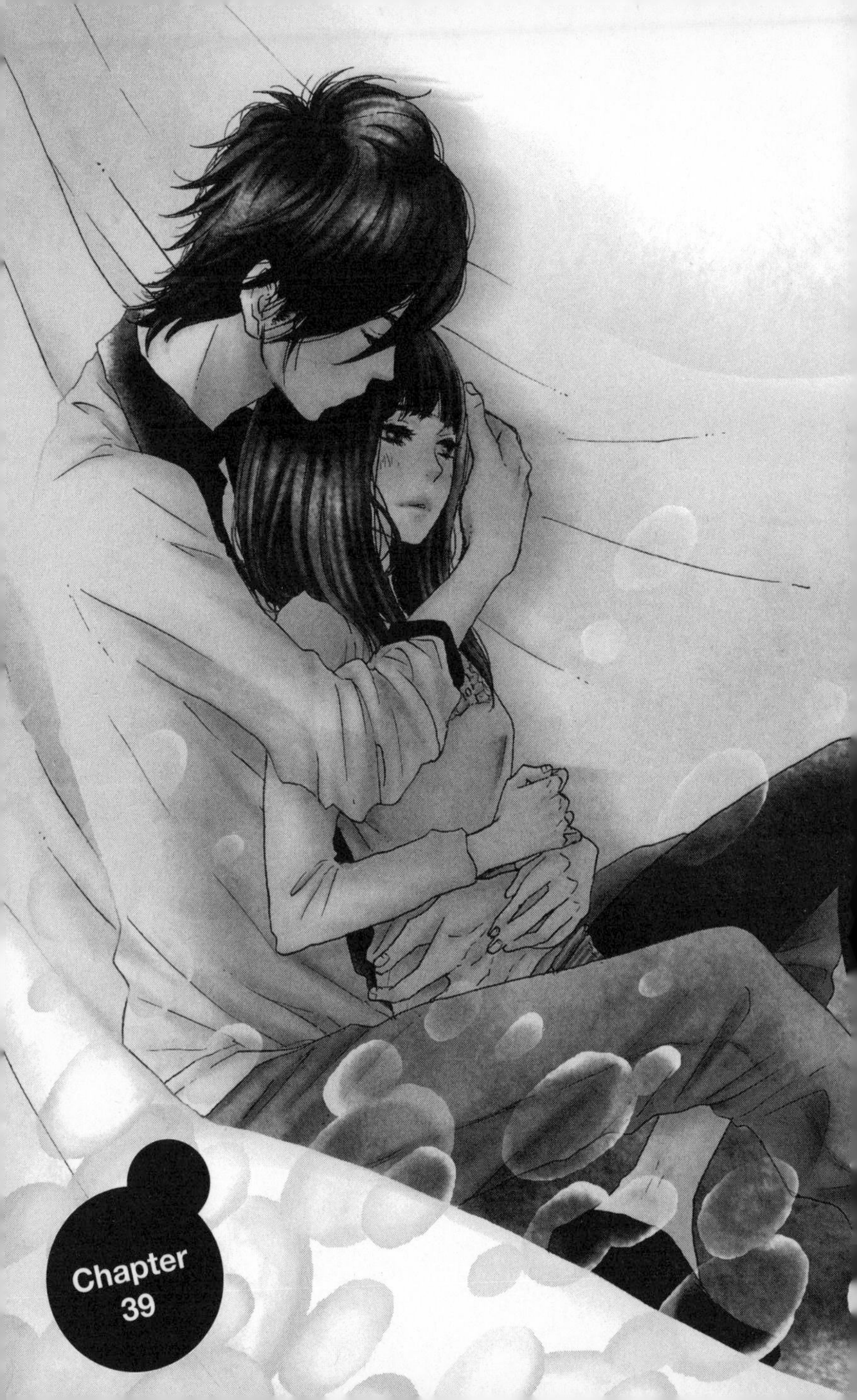
Chapter
39

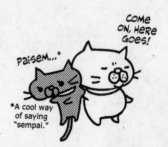

COME ON, HERE GOES!
PAISEM...*
*A cool way of saying "sempai."

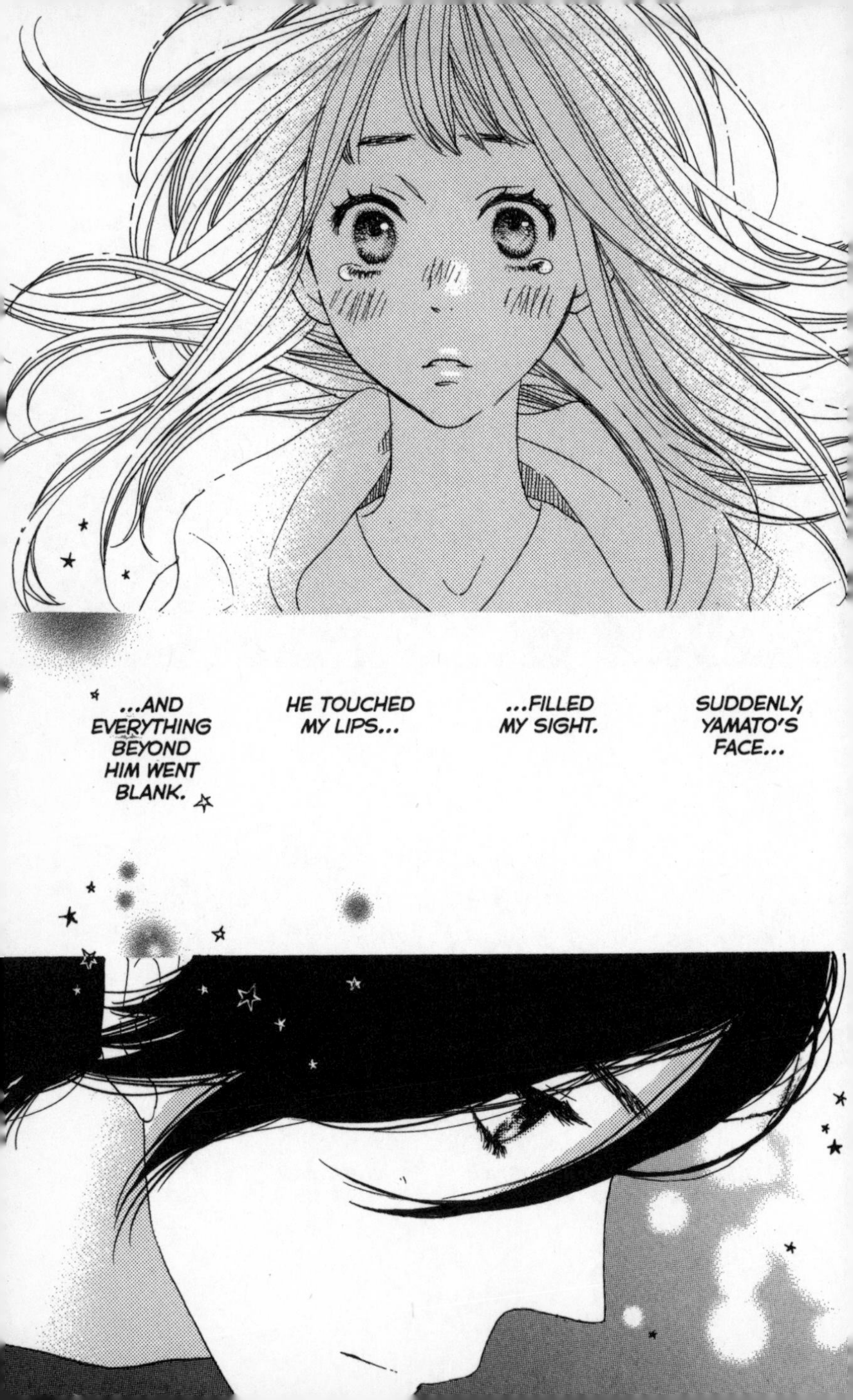
SUDDENLY, YAMATO'S FACE...
...FILLED MY SIGHT.
HE TOUCHED MY LIPS...
...AND EVERYTHING BEYOND HIM WENT BLANK.

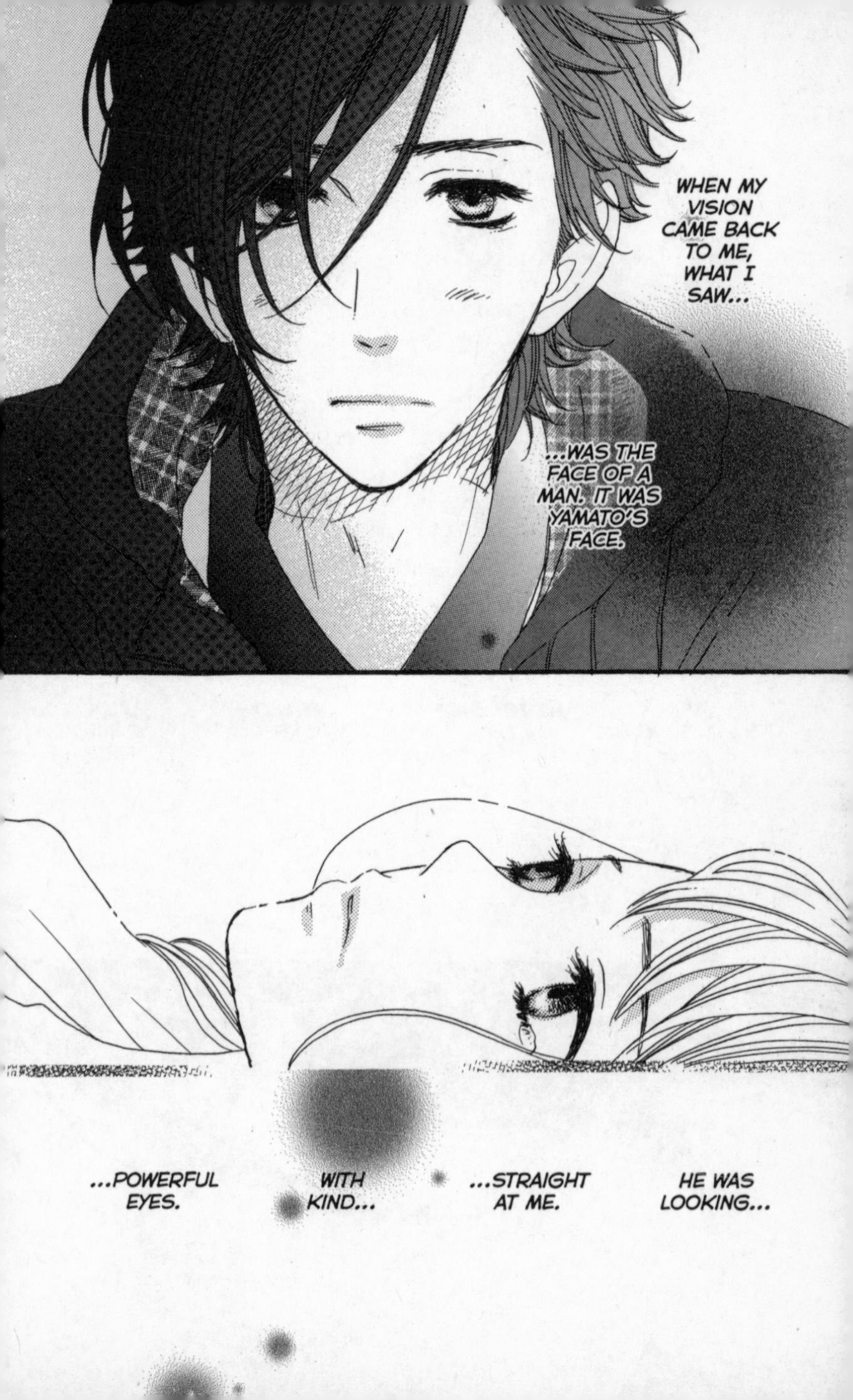
WHEN MY VISION CAME BACK TO ME, WHAT I SAW...
...WAS THE FACE OF A MAN. IT WAS YAMATO'S FACE.
HE WAS LOOKING...
...STRAIGHT AT ME.
WITH KIND...
...POWERFUL EYES.

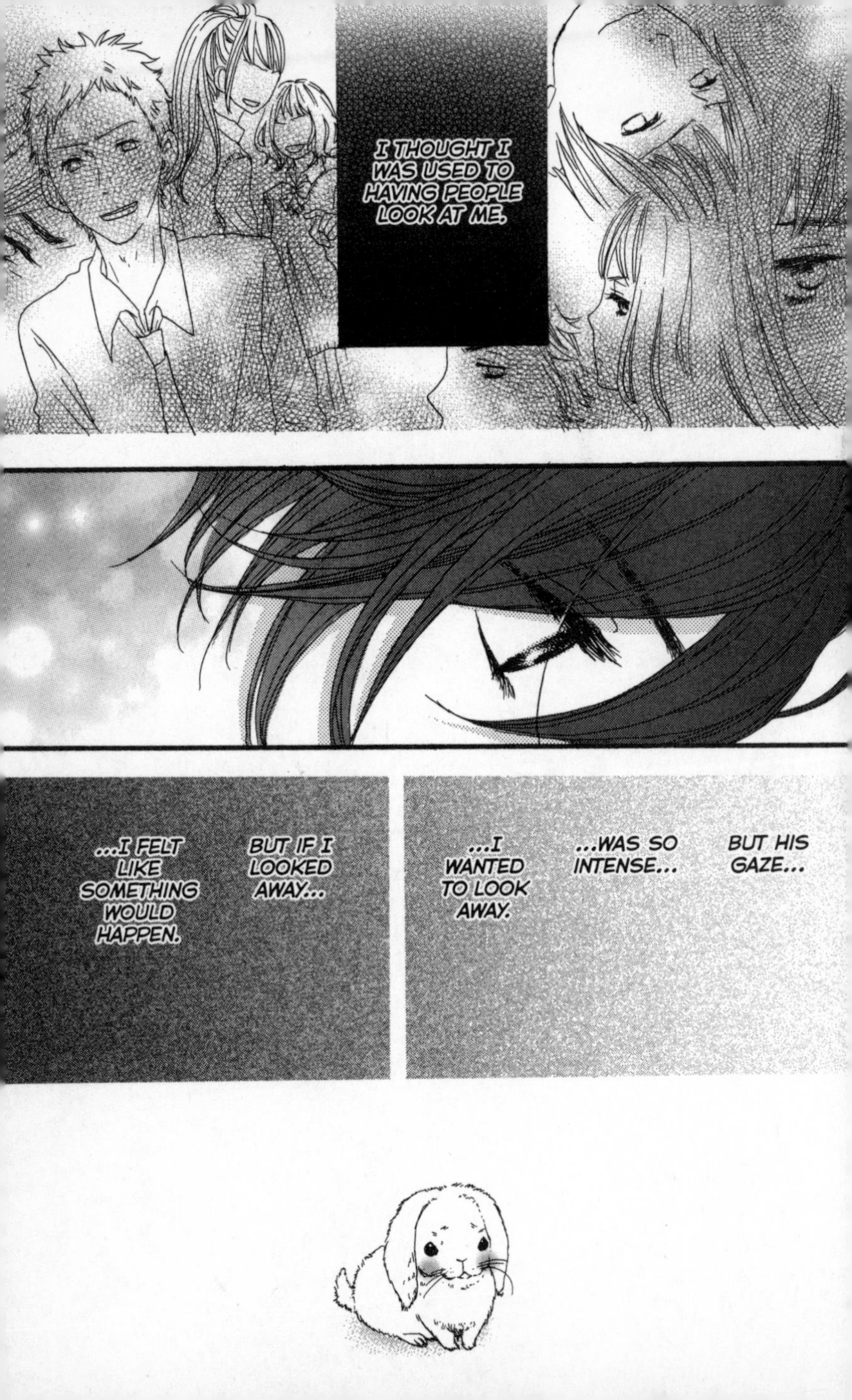
I THOUGHT I WAS USED TO HAVING PEOPLE LOOK AT ME.
BUT HIS GAZE...
...WAS SO INTENSE...
...I WANTED TO LOOK AWAY.
BUT IF I LOOKED AWAY...
...I FELT LIKE SOMETHING WOULD HAPPEN.

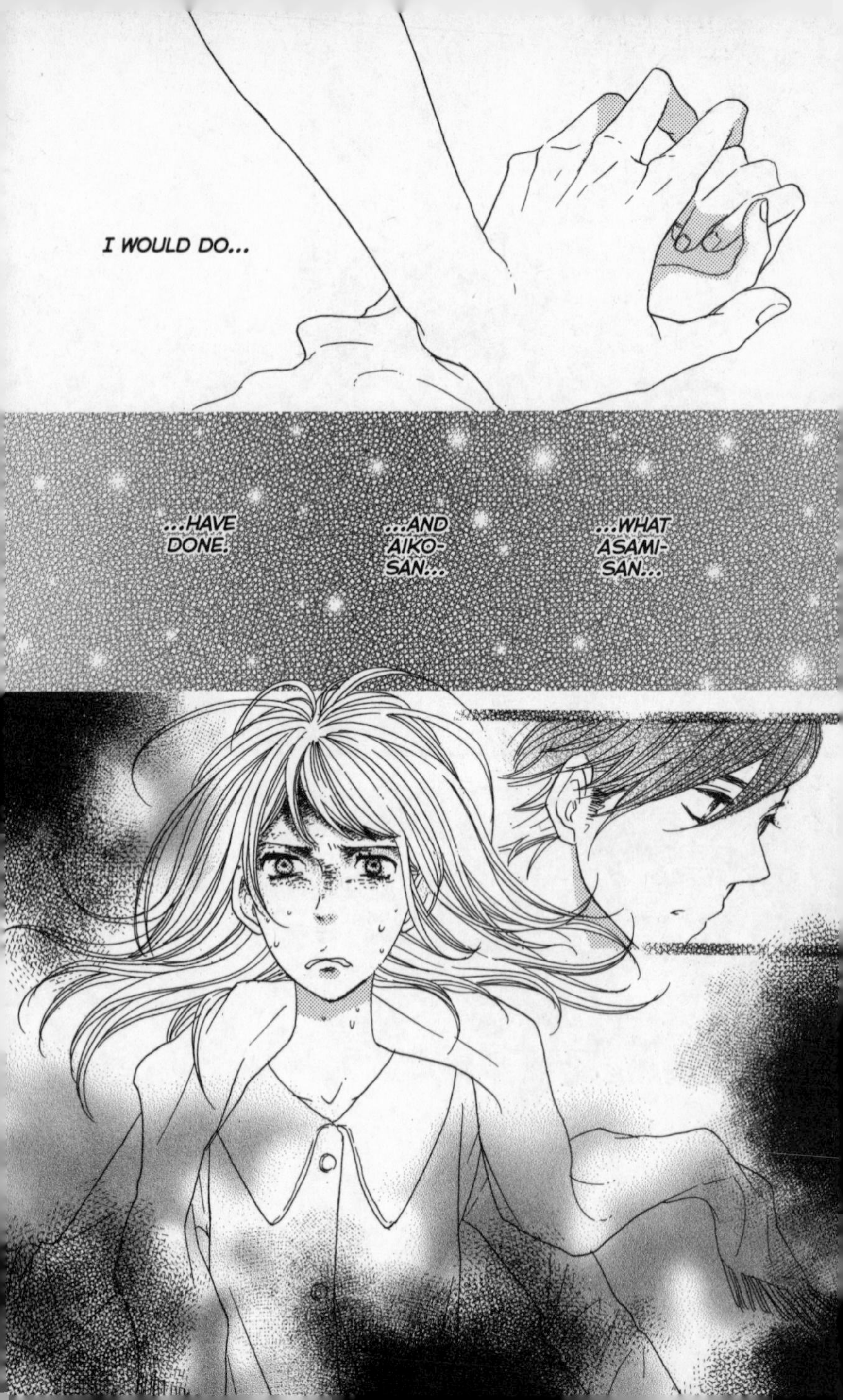
I WOULD DO...
...WHAT ASAMI-SAN...
...AND AIKO-SAN...
...HAVE DONE.

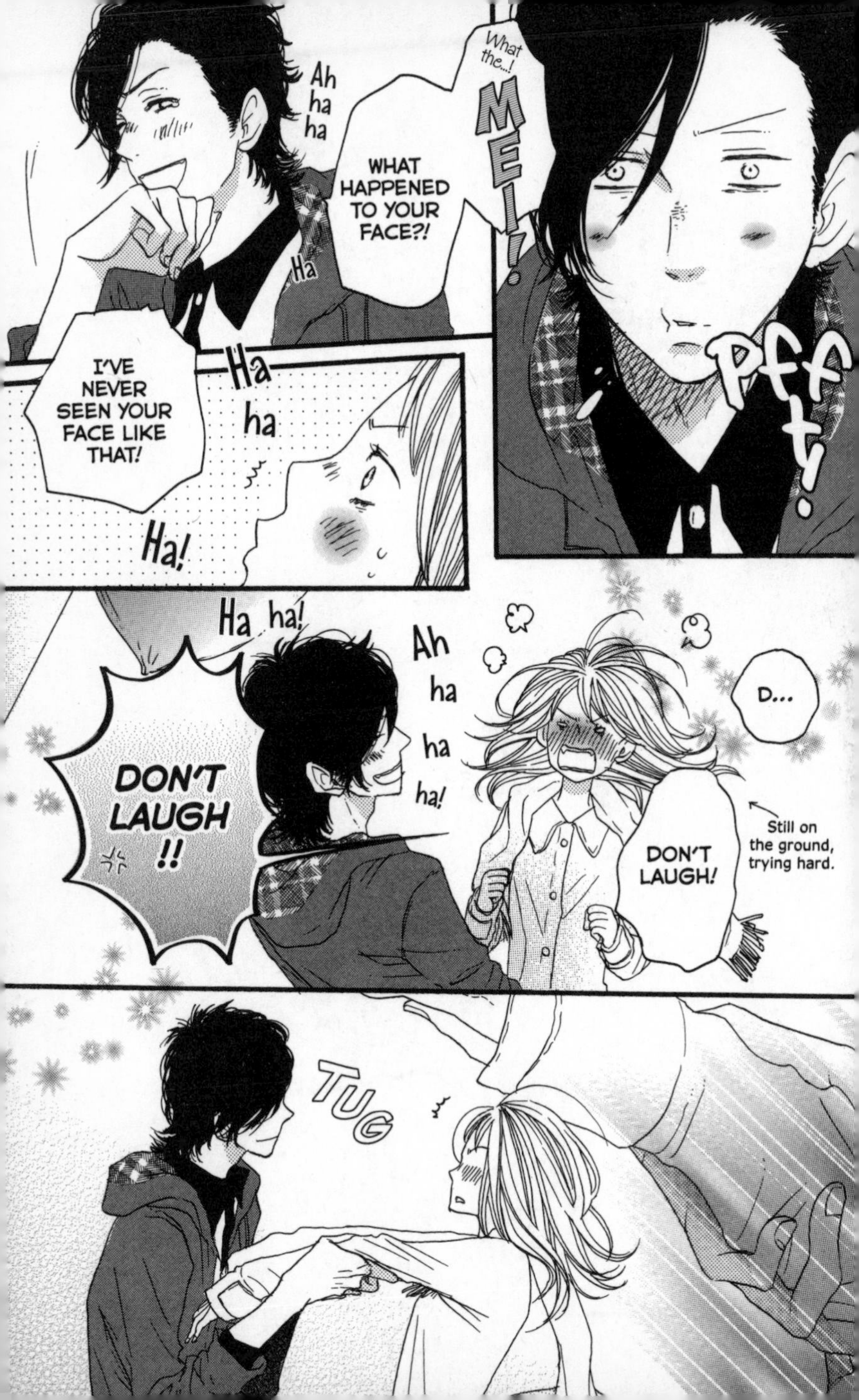

What the...!
MEI!!
Pfft!
Ah ha ha
WHAT HAPPENED TO YOUR FACE?!
Ha
I'VE NEVER SEEN YOUR FACE LIKE THAT!
Ha ha
Ha!
D...
DON'T LAUGH!
Still on the ground, trying hard.
Ah ha ha ha!
Ha ha!
DON'T LAUGH!!
TUG

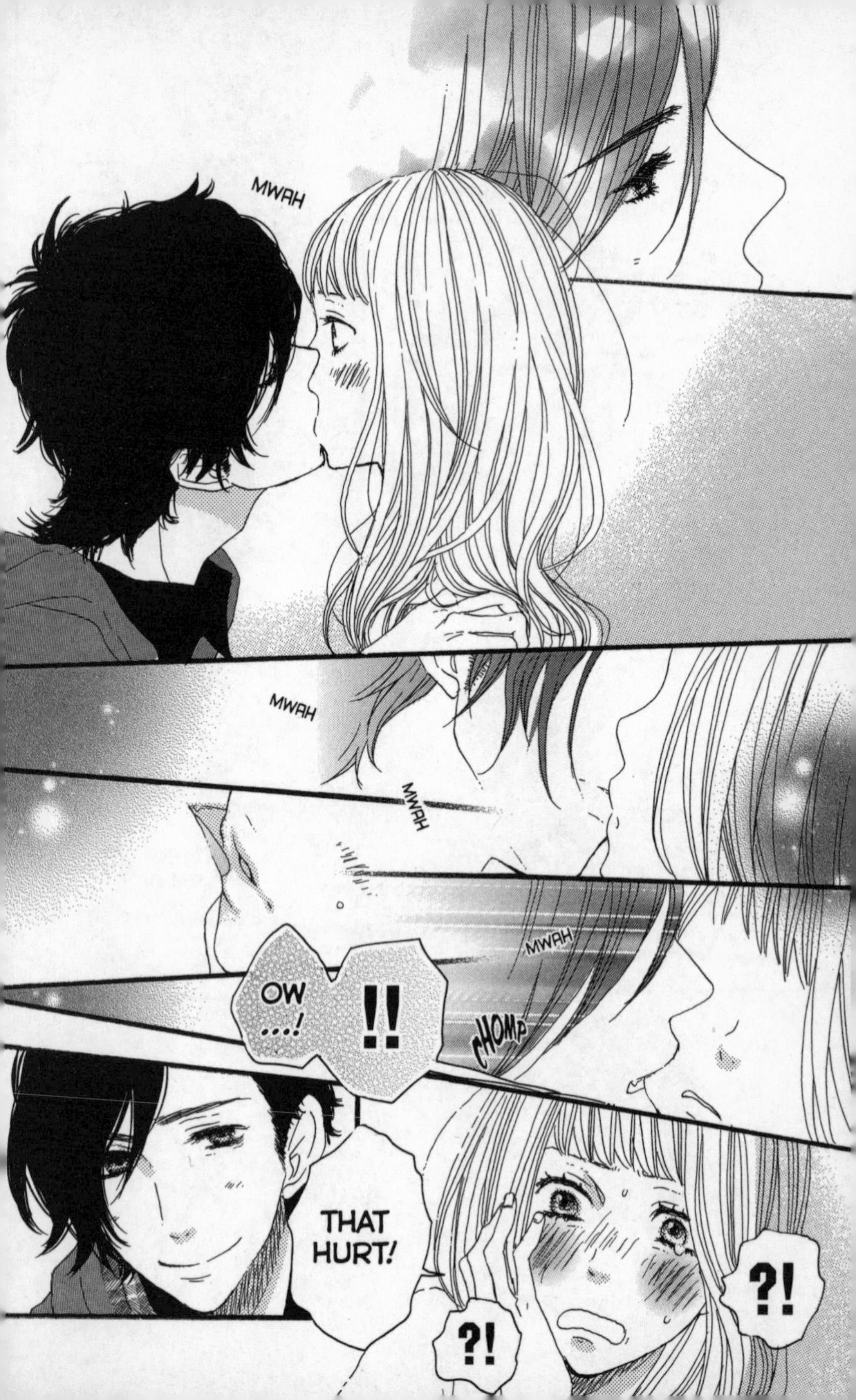
MWAH
MWAH
MWAH
MWAH
CHOMP
OW ...!
!!
?!
?!
THAT HURT!

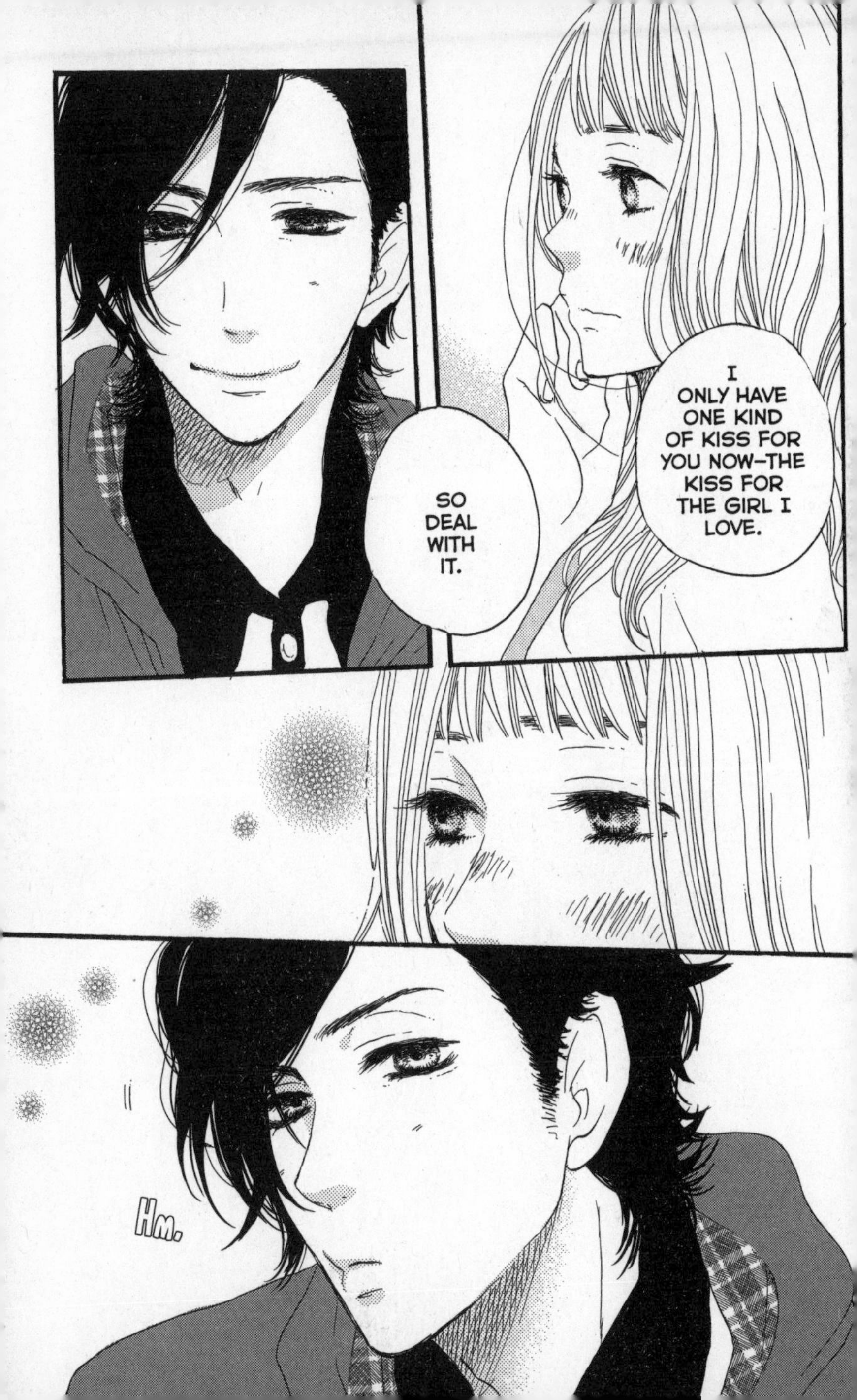
I ONLY HAVE ONE KIND OF KISS FOR YOU NOW–THE KISS FOR THE GIRL I LOVE.
SO DEAL WITH IT.
Hm.

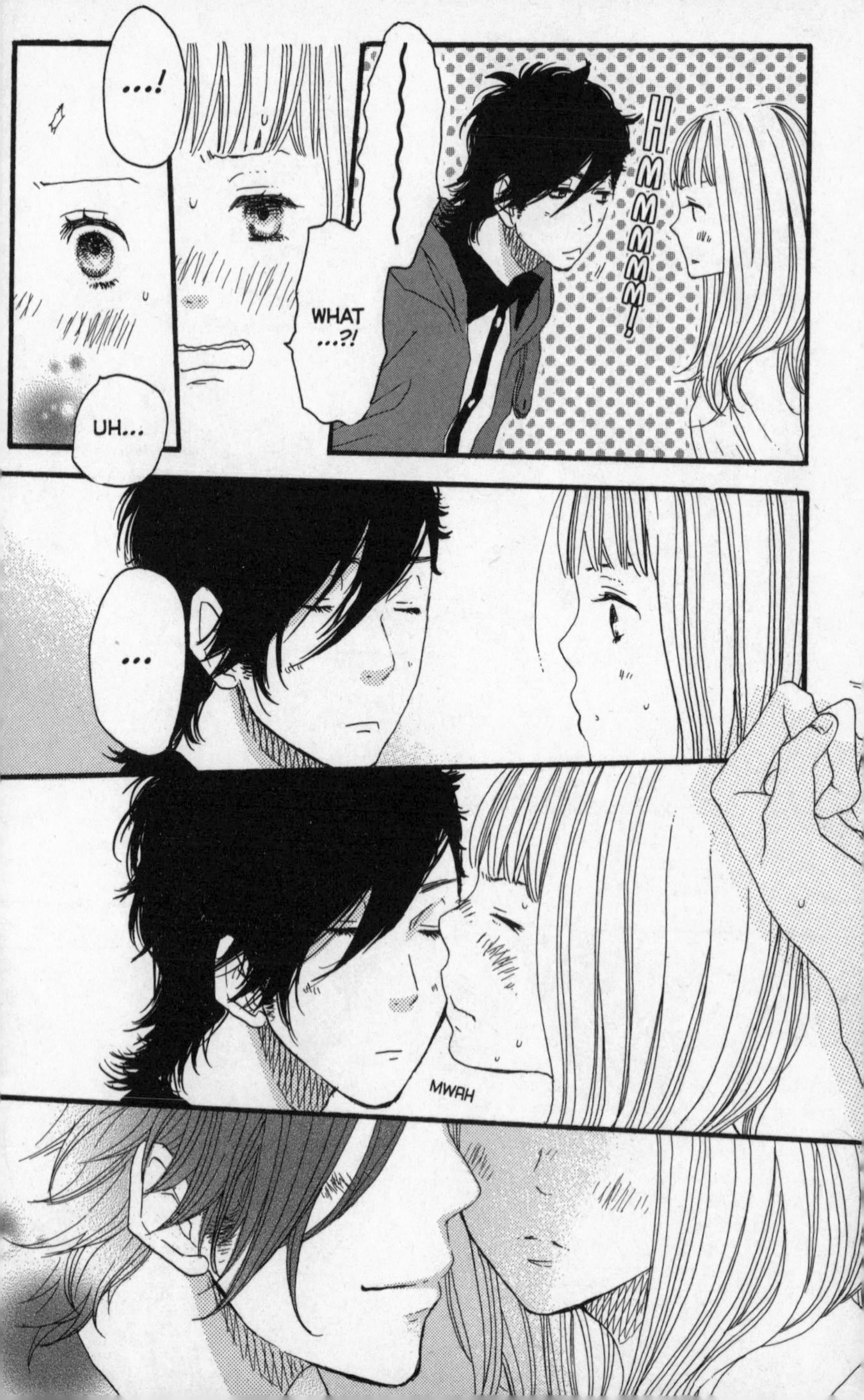
HMMMMMM!
WHAT ...?!
...!
UH...
...
MWAH

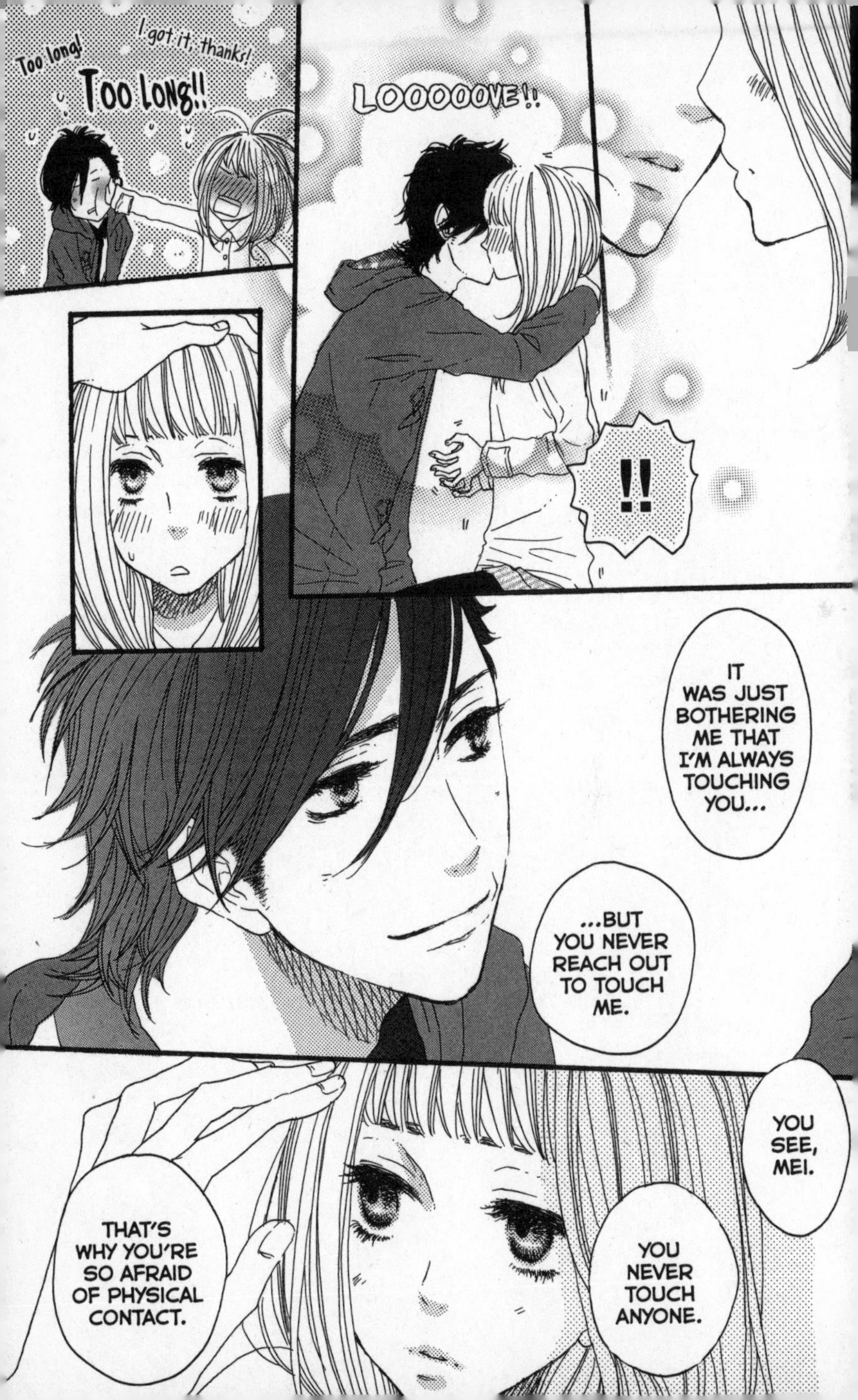
LOOOOOVE!!
!!
I got it, thanks!
Too long!
Too Long!!
IT WAS JUST BOTHERING ME THAT I'M ALWAYS TOUCHING YOU...
...BUT YOU NEVER REACH OUT TO TOUCH ME.
YOU SEE, MEI.
YOU NEVER TOUCH ANYONE.
THAT'S WHY YOU'RE SO AFRAID OF PHYSICAL CONTACT.

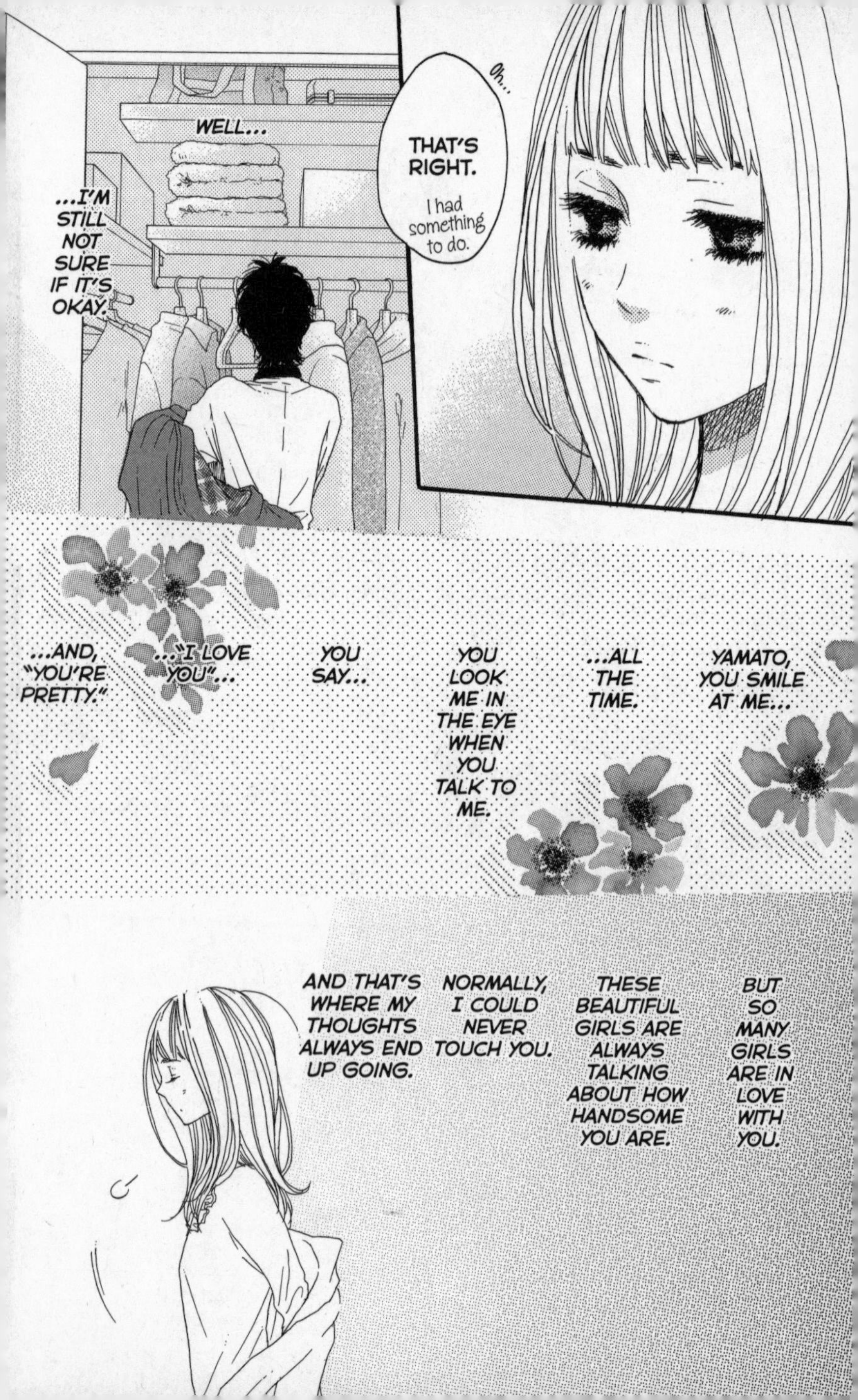
Oh...
THAT'S RIGHT.
I had something to do.
WELL...
...I'M STILL NOT SURE IF IT'S OKAY.
YAMATO, YOU SMILE AT ME...
...ALL THE TIME.
YOU LOOK ME IN THE EYE WHEN YOU TALK TO ME.
YOU SAY...
..."I LOVE YOU"...
...AND, "YOU'RE PRETTY."
BUT SO MANY GIRLS ARE IN LOVE WITH YOU.
THESE BEAUTIFUL GIRLS ARE ALWAYS TALKING ABOUT HOW HANDSOME YOU ARE.
NORMALLY, I COULD NEVER TOUCH YOU.
AND THAT'S WHERE MY THOUGHTS ALWAYS END UP GOING.

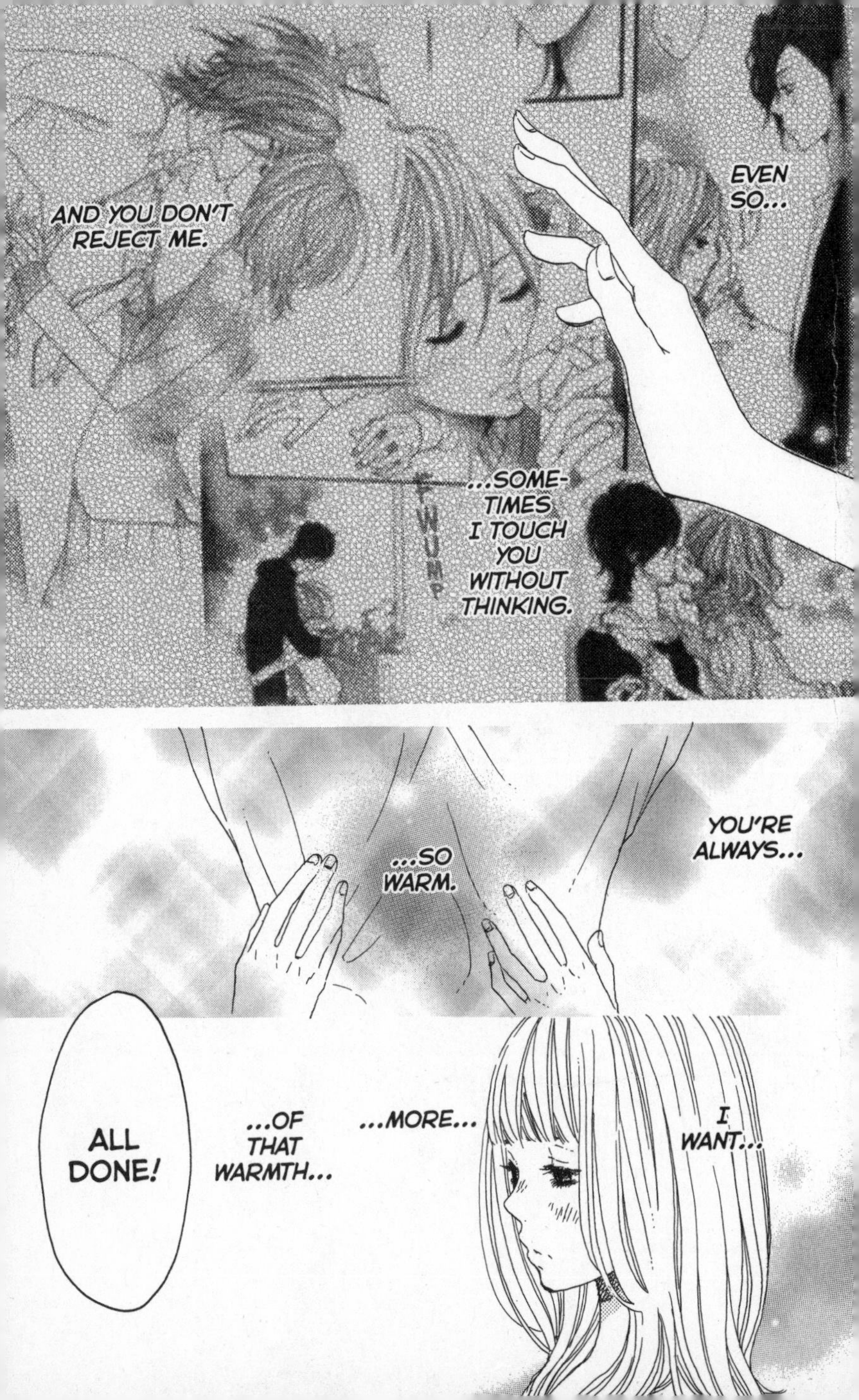
EVEN SO...
...SOME-TIMES I TOUCH YOU WITHOUT THINKING.
AND YOU DON'T REJECT ME.
FWUMP
YOU'RE ALWAYS...
...SO WARM.
I WANT...
...MORE...
...OF THAT WARMTH...
ALL DONE!

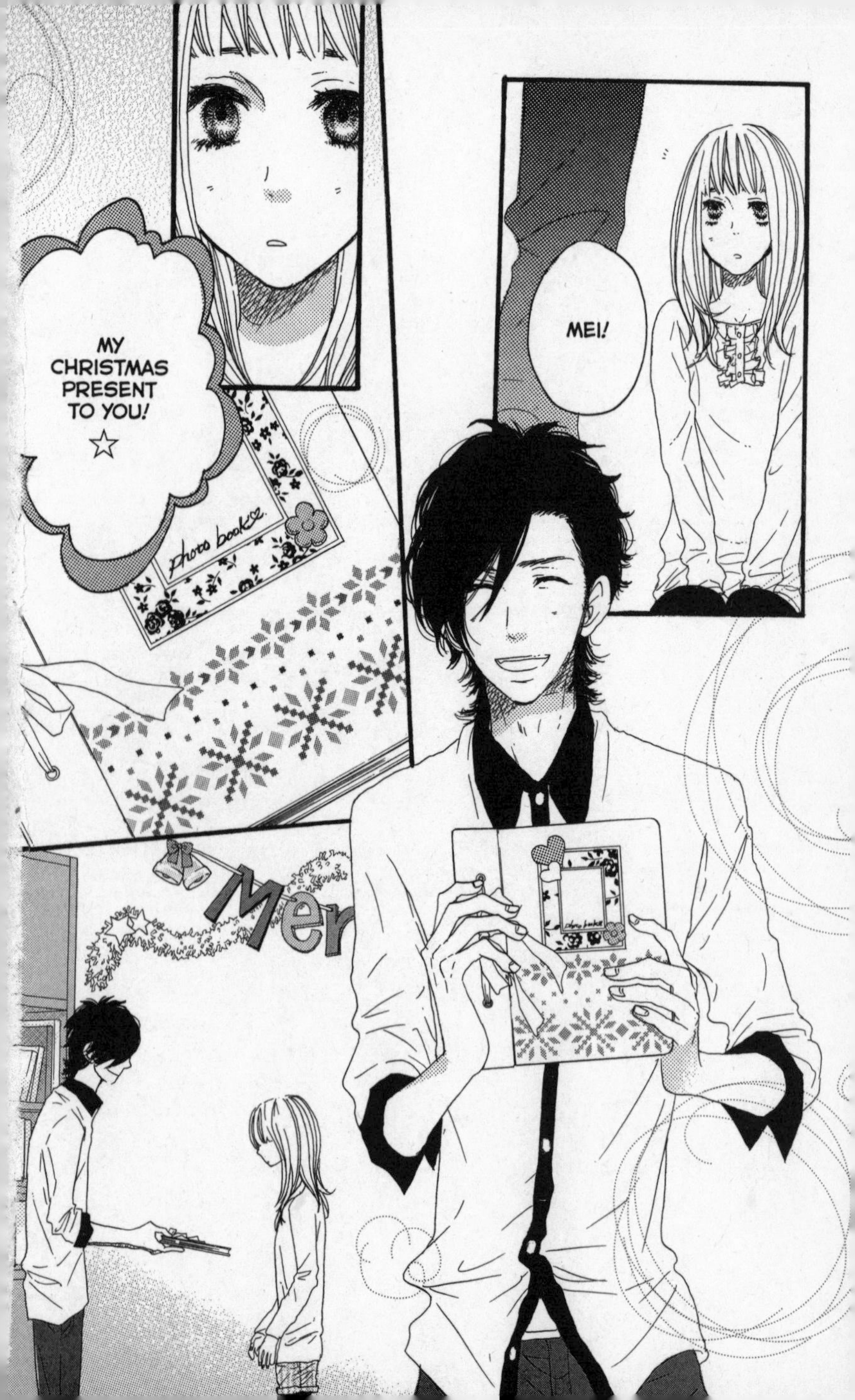
MEI!
MY CHRISTMAS PRESENT TO YOU! ☆
photo book
Mer

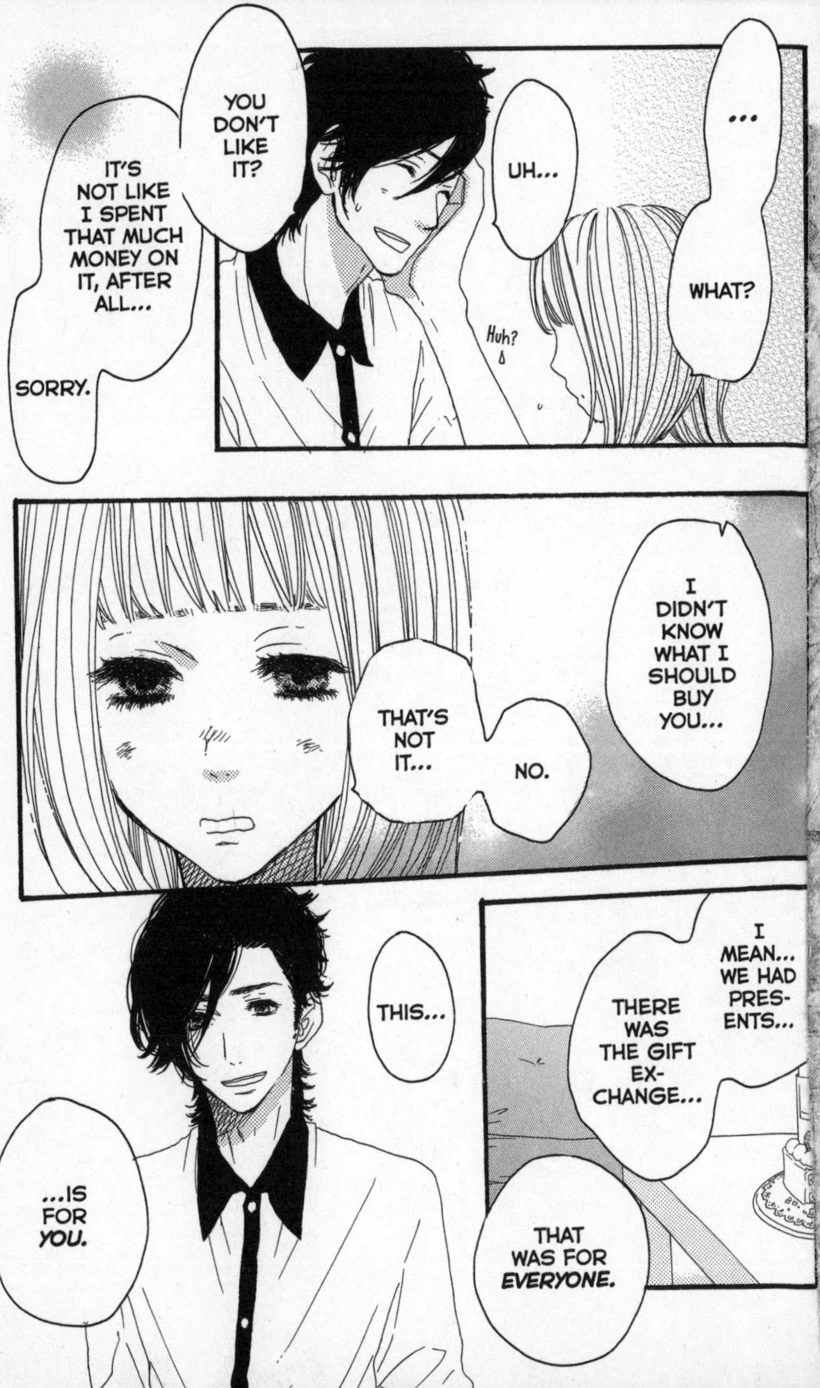
...
WHAT?
UH...
Huh?
YOU DON'T LIKE IT?
IT'S NOT LIKE I SPENT THAT MUCH MONEY ON IT, AFTER ALL...
SORRY.
I DIDN'T KNOW WHAT I SHOULD BUY YOU...
NO.
THAT'S NOT IT...
I MEAN... WE HAD PRES-ENTS...
THERE WAS THE GIFT EX-CHANGE...
THAT WAS FOR EVERYONE.
THIS...
...IS FOR YOU.

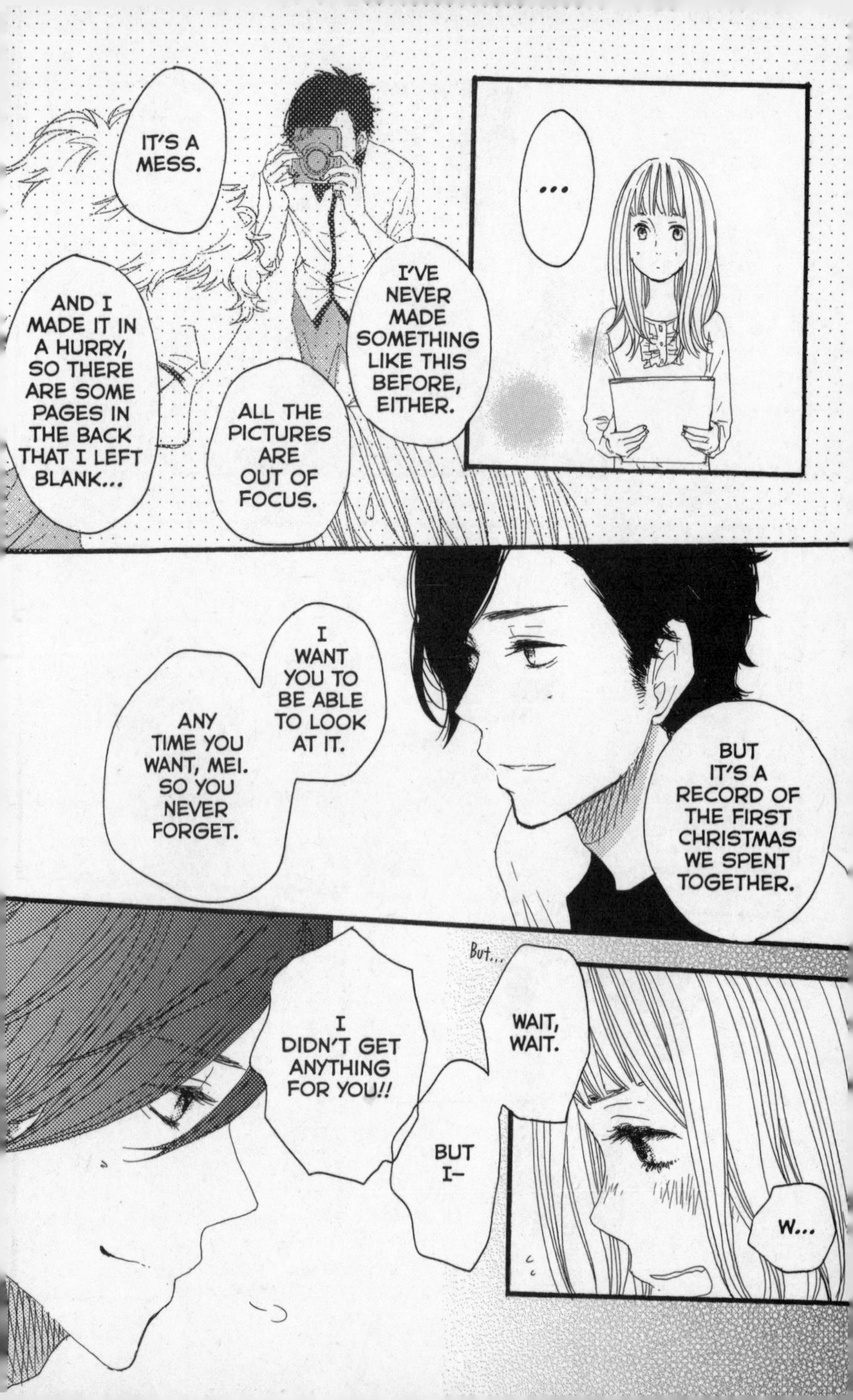
...
IT'S A MESS.
ALL THE PICTURES ARE OUT OF FOCUS.
AND I MADE IT IN A HURRY, SO THERE ARE SOME PAGES IN THE BACK THAT I LEFT BLANK...
I'VE NEVER MADE SOMETHING LIKE THIS BEFORE, EITHER.
BUT IT'S A RECORD OF THE FIRST CHRISTMAS WE SPENT TOGETHER.
I WANT YOU TO BE ABLE TO LOOK AT IT.
ANY TIME YOU WANT, MEI. SO YOU NEVER FORGET.
W...
WAIT, WAIT.
But...
I DIDN'T GET ANYTHING FOR YOU!!
BUT I–

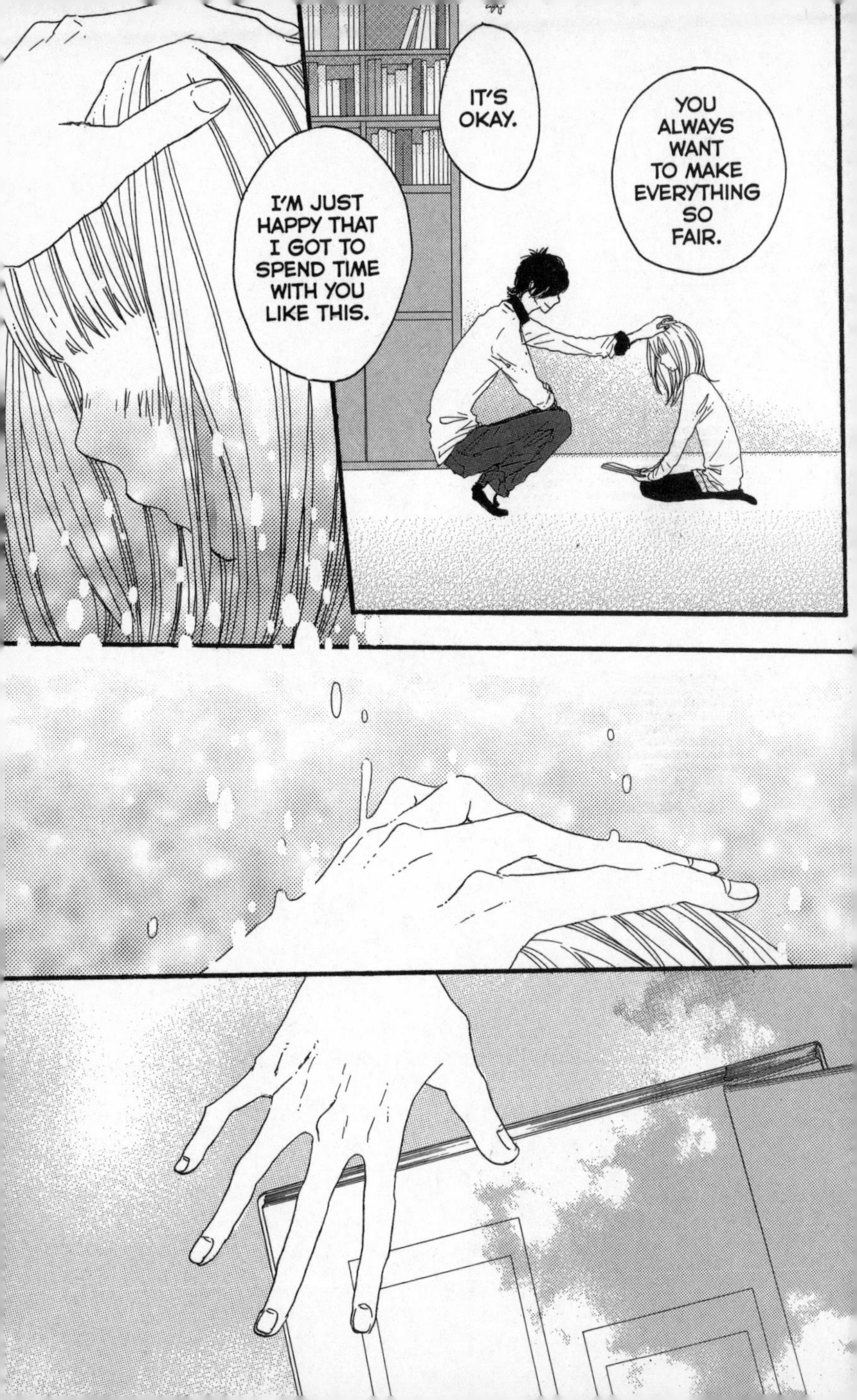
YOU ALWAYS WANT TO MAKE EVERYTHING SO FAIR.
IT'S OKAY.
I'M JUST HAPPY THAT I GOT TO SPEND TIME WITH YOU LIKE THIS.

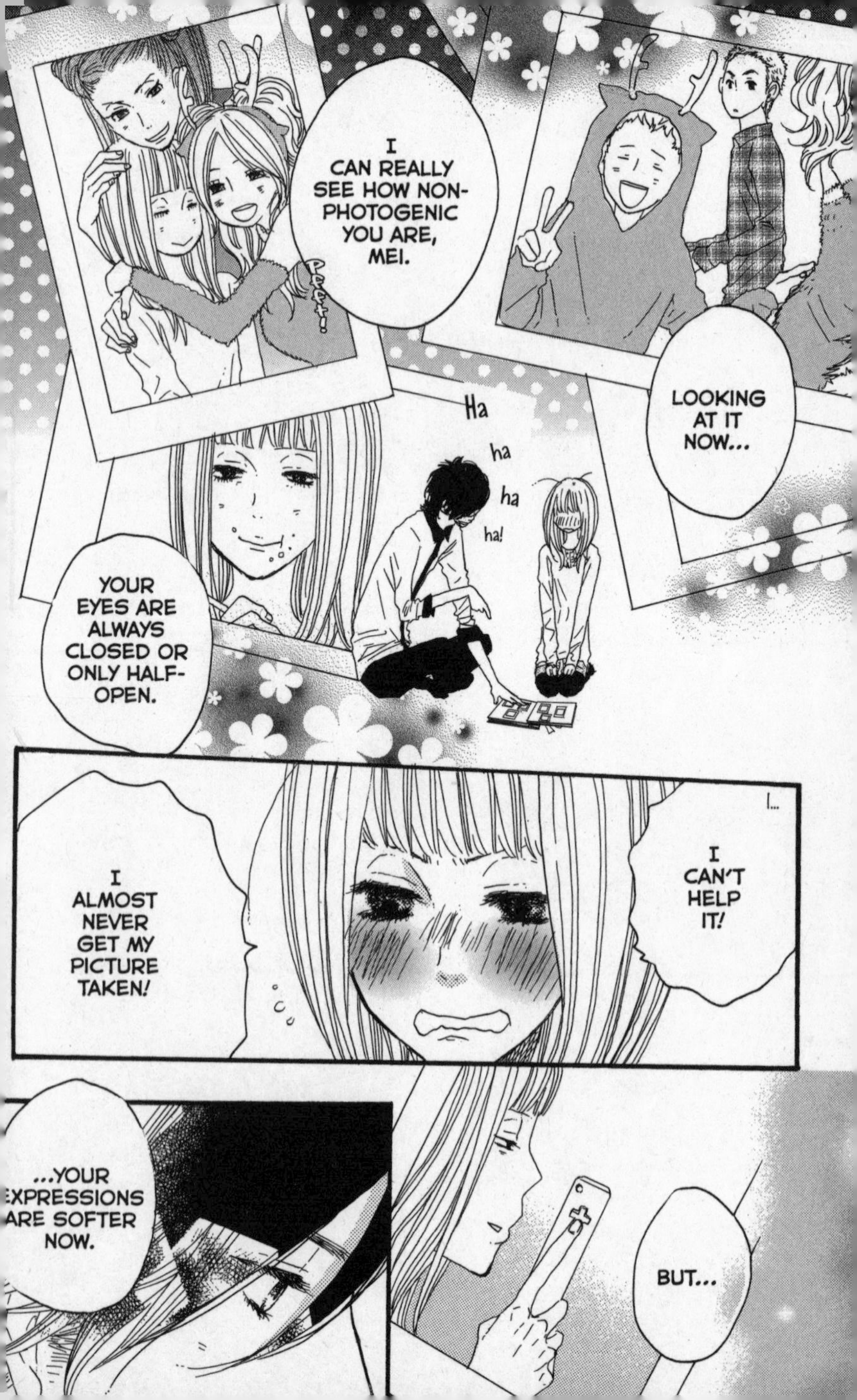
I CAN REALLY SEE HOW NON-PHOTOGENIC YOU ARE, MEI.
LOOKING AT IT NOW...
Ha ha ha ha!
YOUR EYES ARE ALWAYS CLOSED OR ONLY HALF-OPEN.
I...
I CAN'T HELP IT!
I ALMOST NEVER GET MY PICTURE TAKEN!
BUT...
...YOUR EXPRESSIONS ARE SOFTER NOW.

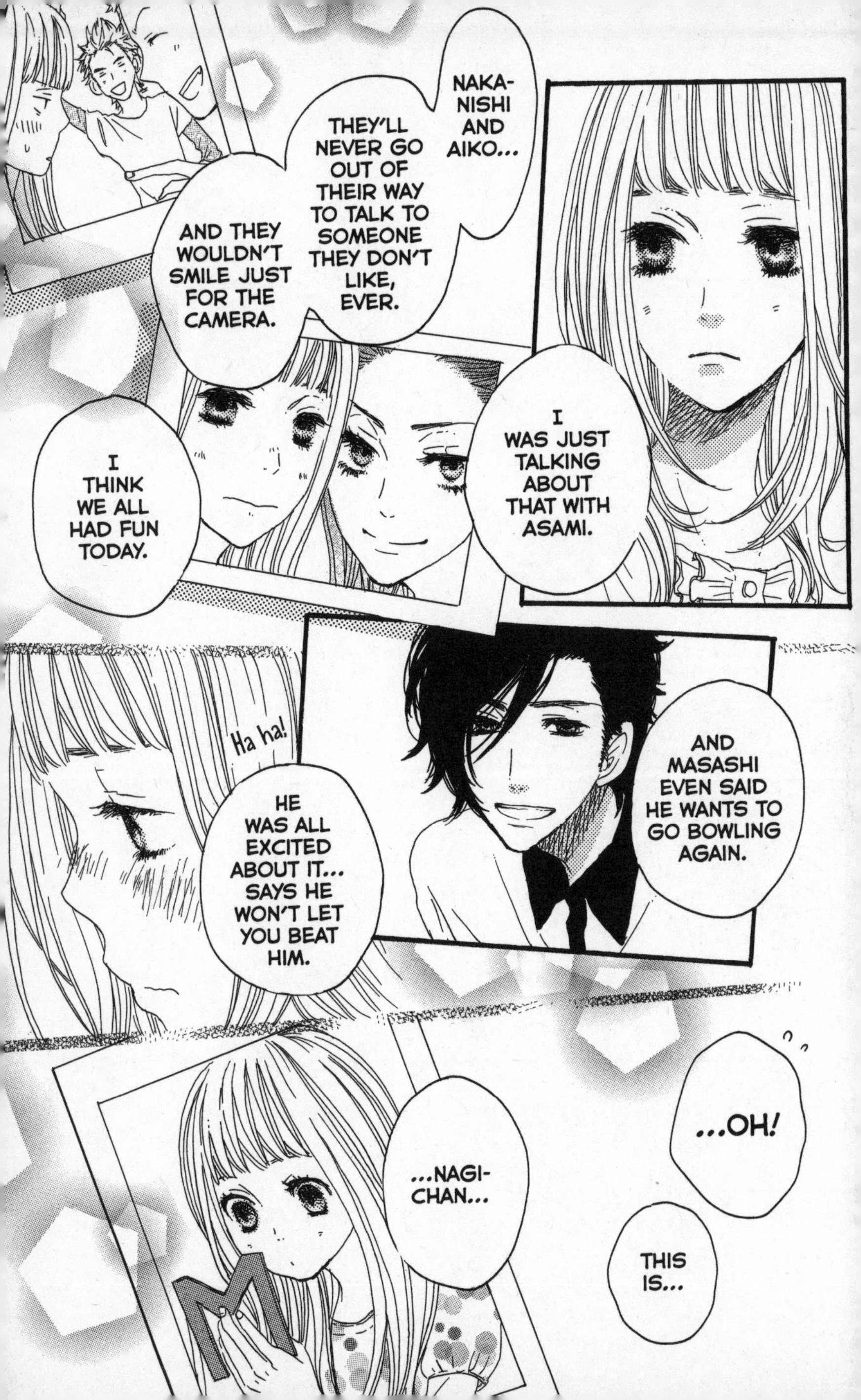
NAKA-NISHI AND AIKO...
THEY'LL NEVER GO OUT OF THEIR WAY TO TALK TO SOMEONE THEY DON'T LIKE, EVER.
AND THEY WOULDN'T SMILE JUST FOR THE CAMERA.
I WAS JUST TALKING ABOUT THAT WITH ASAMI.
I THINK WE ALL HAD FUN TODAY.
AND MASASHI EVEN SAID HE WANTS TO GO BOWLING AGAIN.
Ha ha!
HE WAS ALL EXCITED ABOUT IT... SAYS HE WON'T LET YOU BEAT HIM.
...OH!
THIS IS...
...NAGI-CHAN...

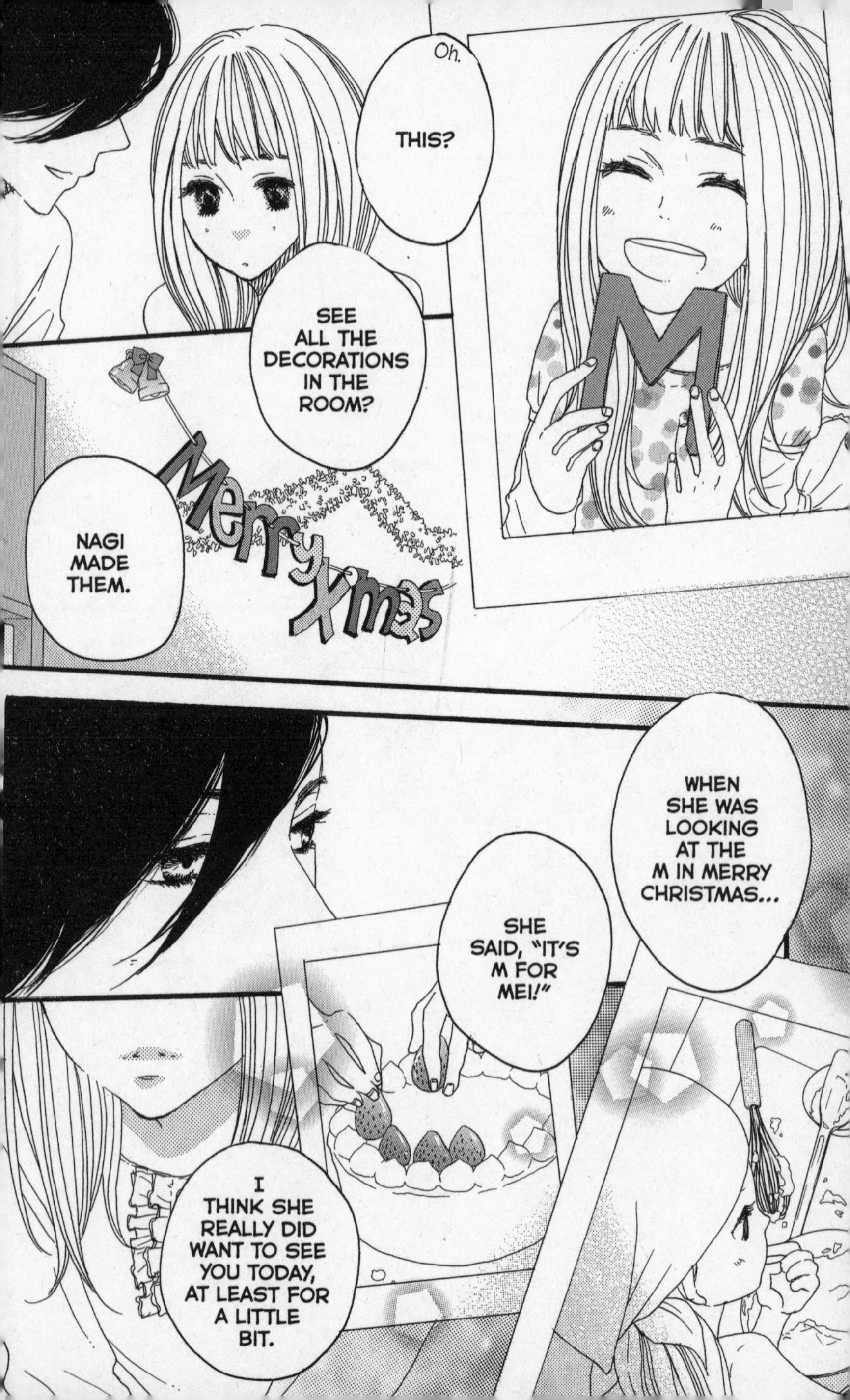
Oh. THIS?
SEE ALL THE DECORATIONS IN THE ROOM?
NAGI MADE THEM.
Merry X'mas
WHEN SHE WAS LOOKING AT THE M IN MERRY CHRISTMAS...
SHE SAID, "IT'S M FOR MEI!"
I THINK SHE REALLY DID WANT TO SEE YOU TODAY, AT LEAST FOR A LITTLE BIT.

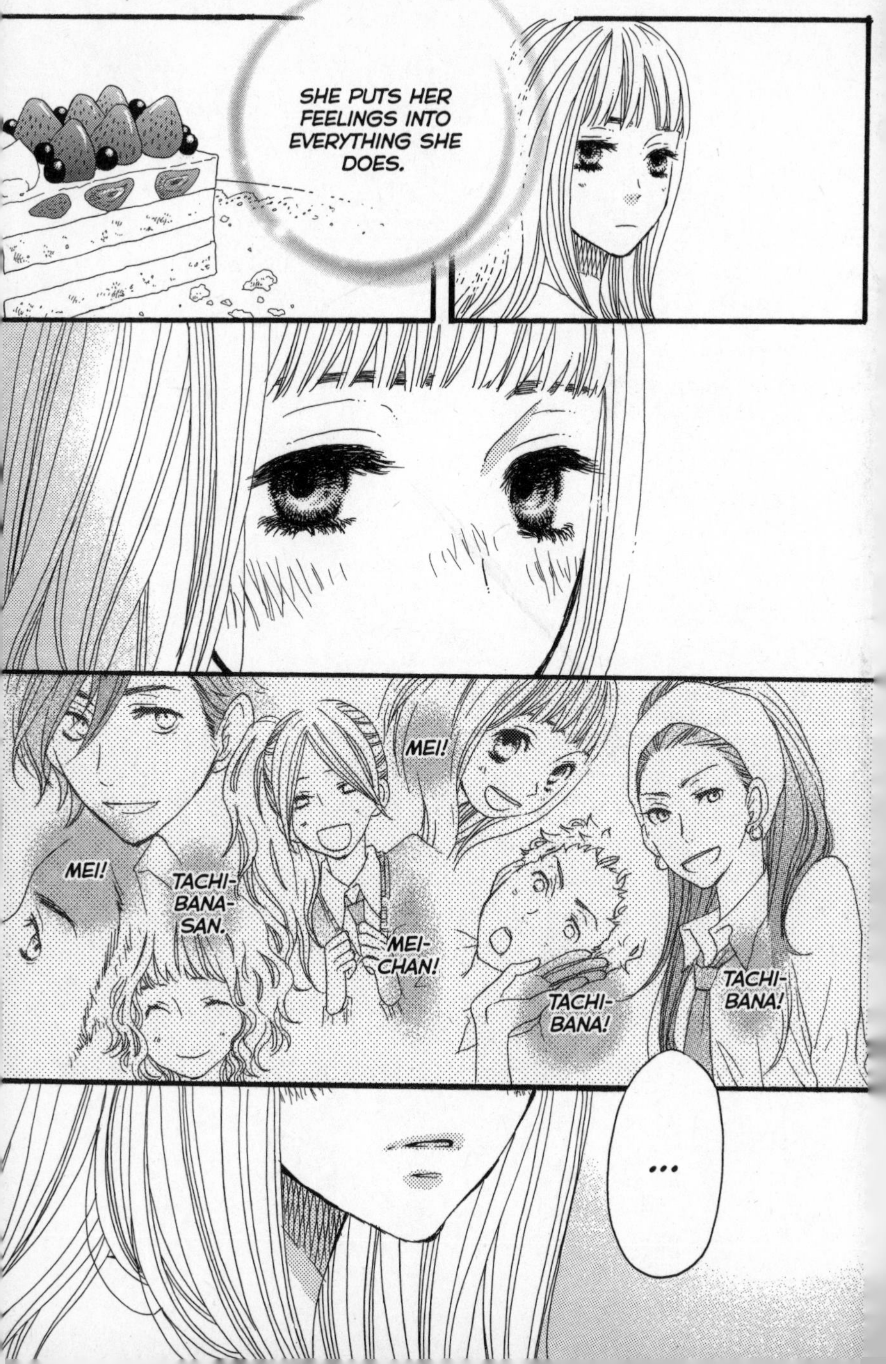
SHE PUTS HER FEELINGS INTO EVERYTHING SHE DOES.
TACHI-BANA!
MEI!
TACHI-BANA!
MEI-CHAN!
TACHI-BANA-SAN.
MEI!
...

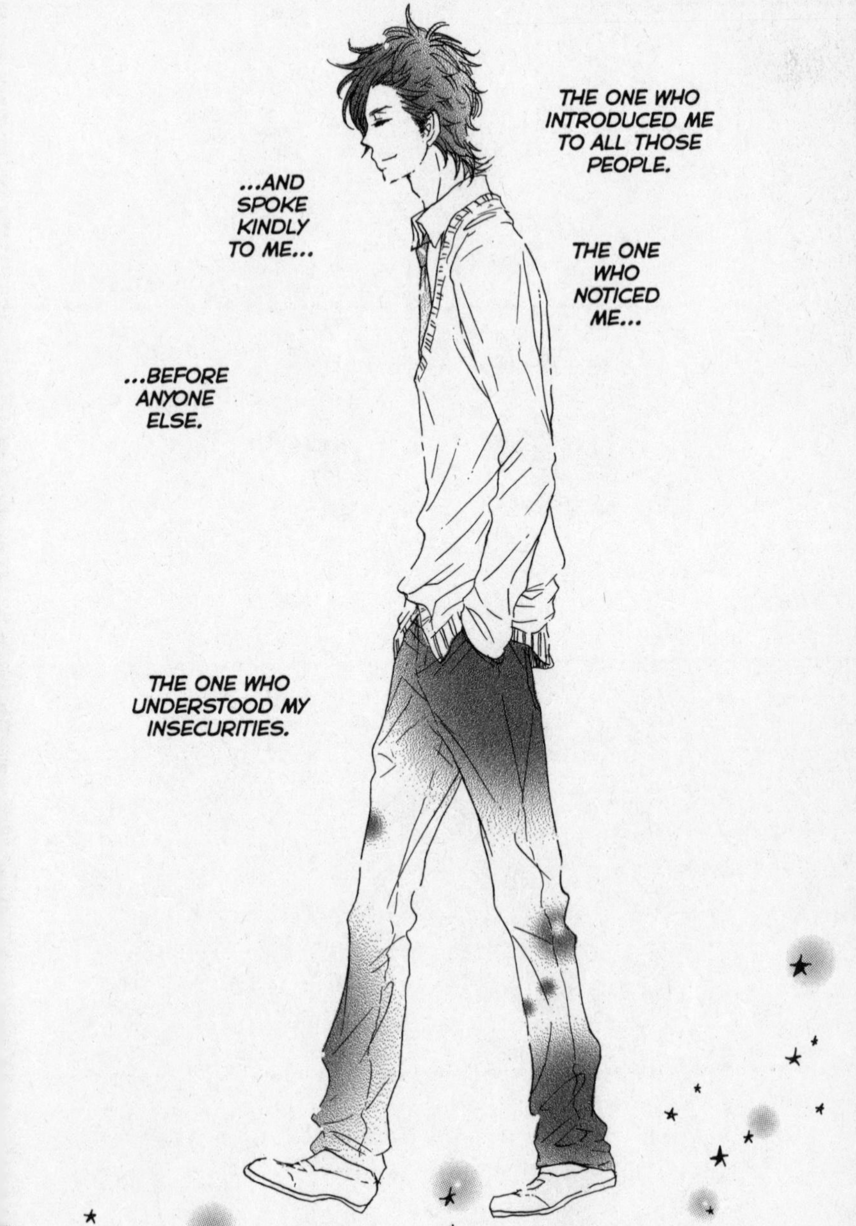
THE ONE WHO INTRODUCED ME TO ALL THOSE PEOPLE.
THE ONE WHO NOTICED ME...
...AND SPOKE KINDLY TO ME...
...BEFORE ANYONE ELSE.
THE ONE WHO UNDERSTOOD MY INSECURITIES.

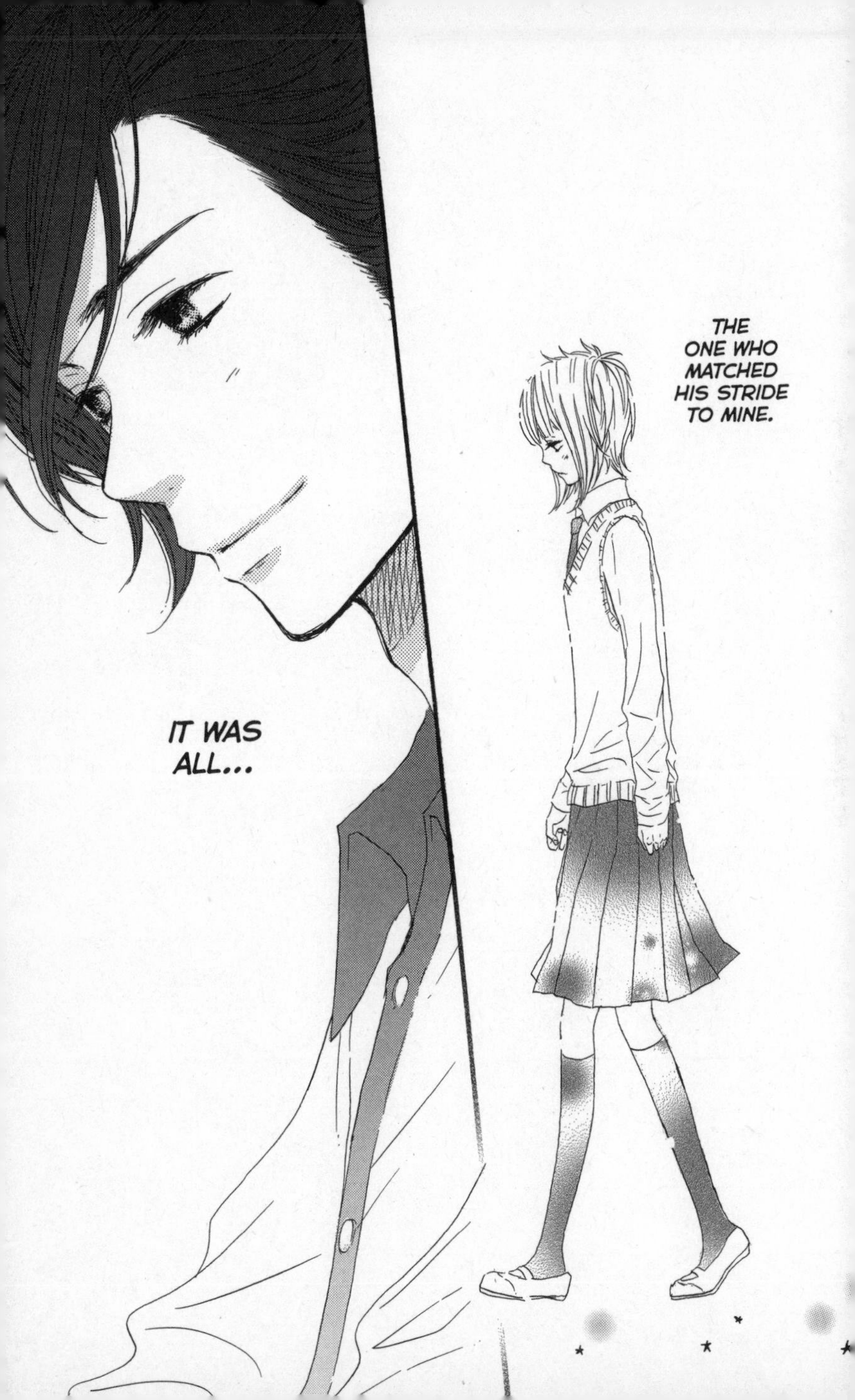
THE ONE WHO MATCHED HIS STRIDE TO MINE.
IT WAS ALL...

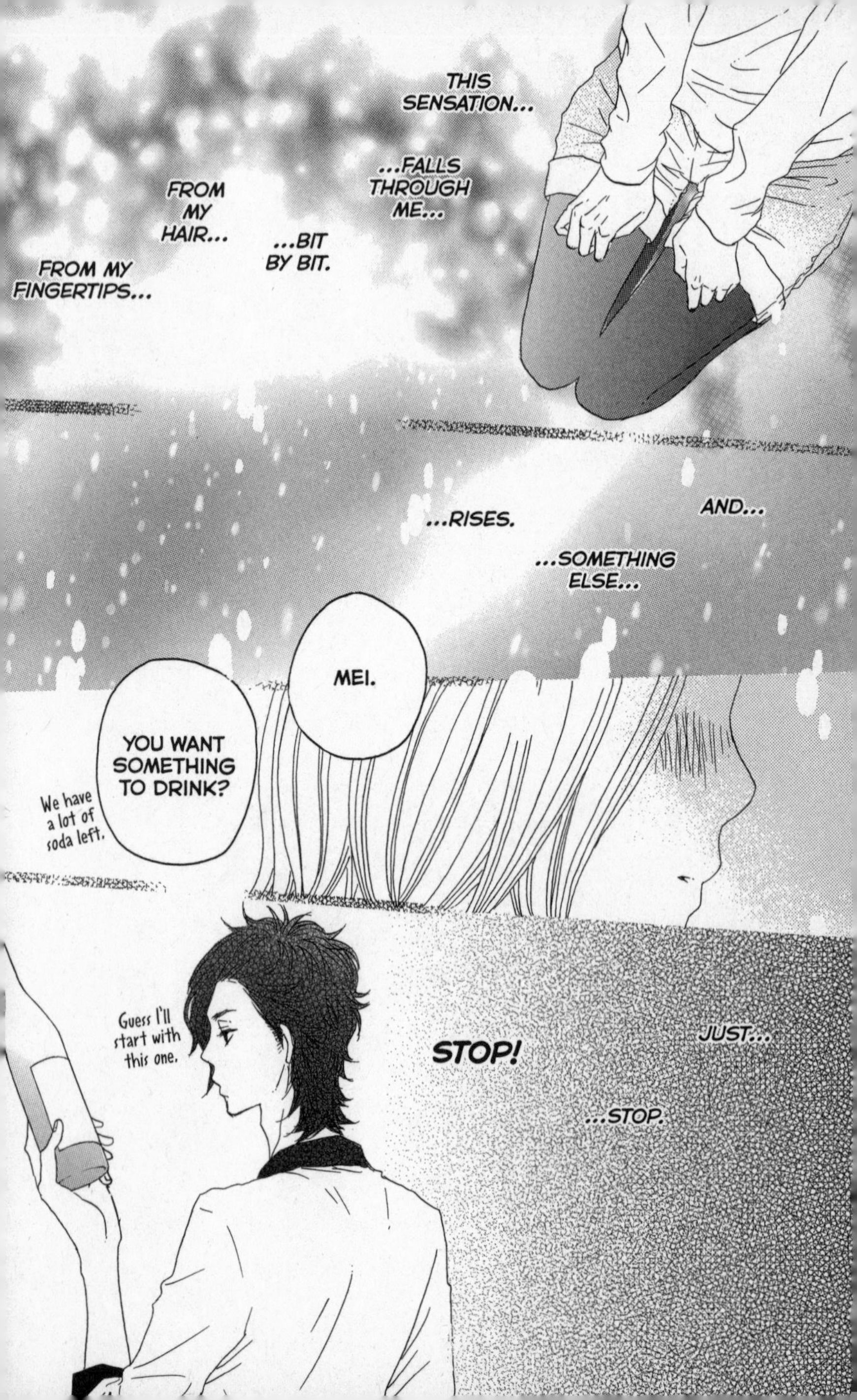
THIS SENSATION...
...FALLS THROUGH ME...
...BIT BY BIT.
FROM MY HAIR...
FROM MY FINGERTIPS...
AND...
...SOMETHING ELSE...
...RISES.
MEI.
YOU WANT SOMETHING TO DRINK?
We have a lot of soda left.
JUST...
...STOP.
STOP!
Guess I'll start with this one.

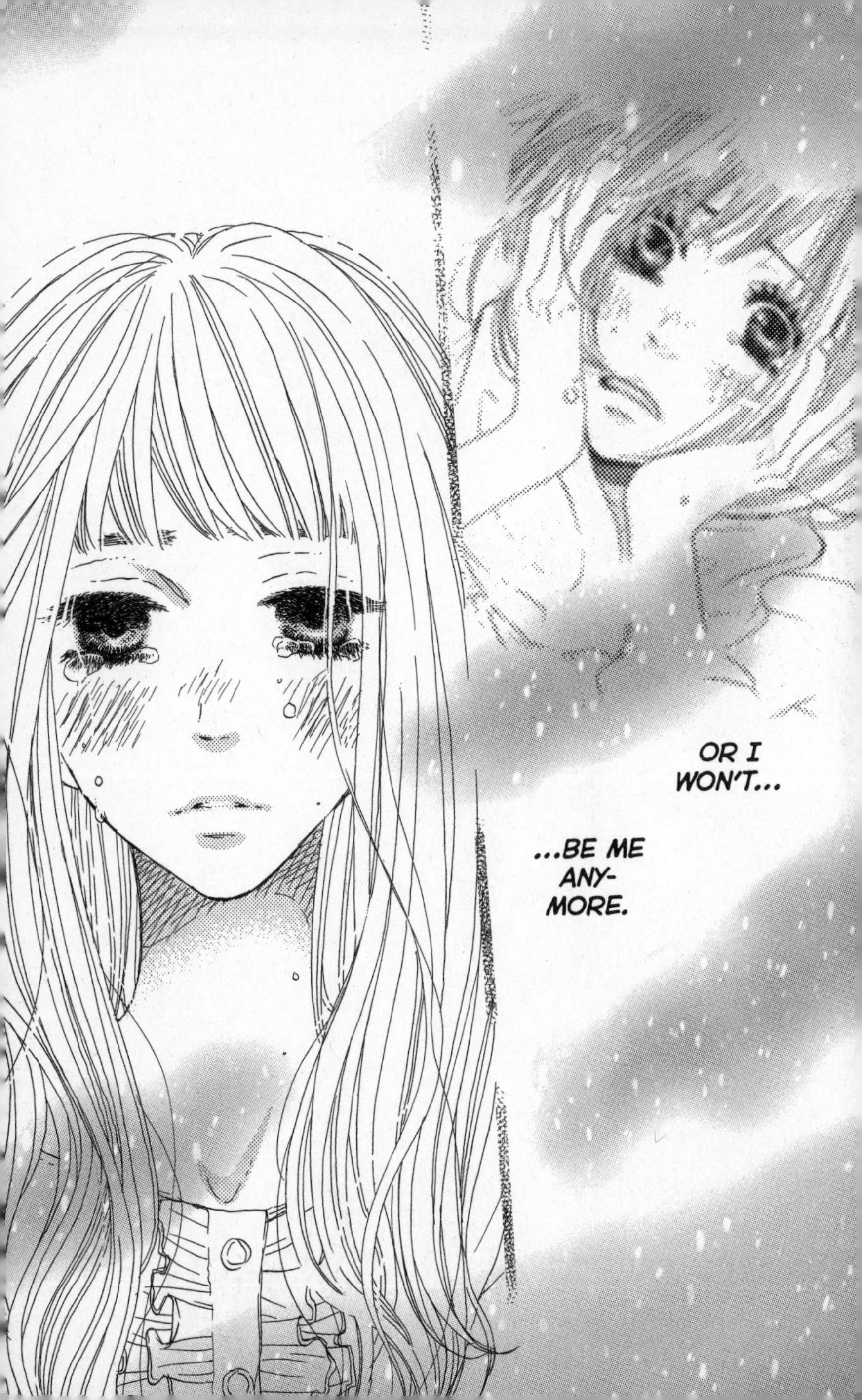
OR I WON'T...
...BE ME ANY-MORE.

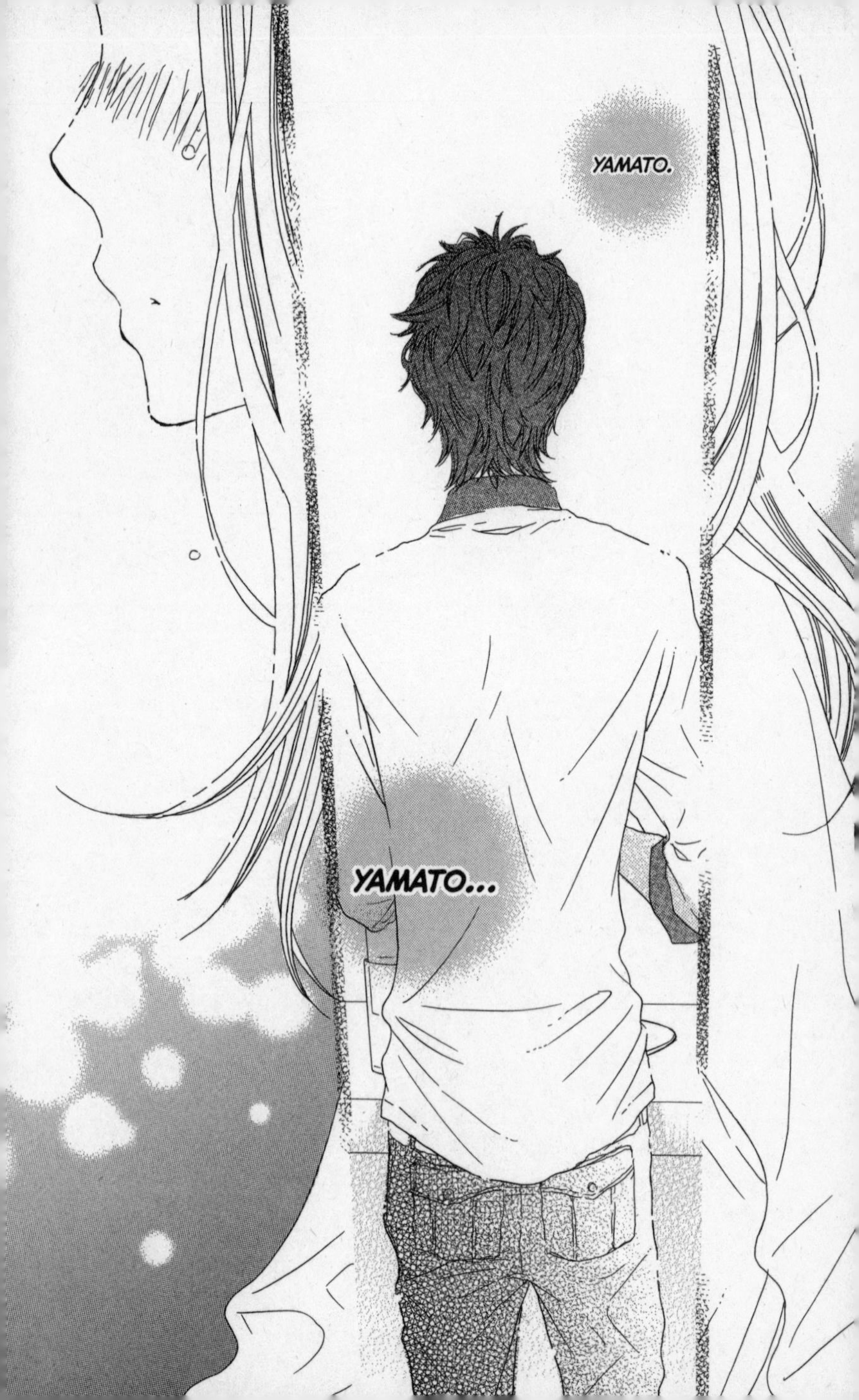
YAMATO.
YAMATO...

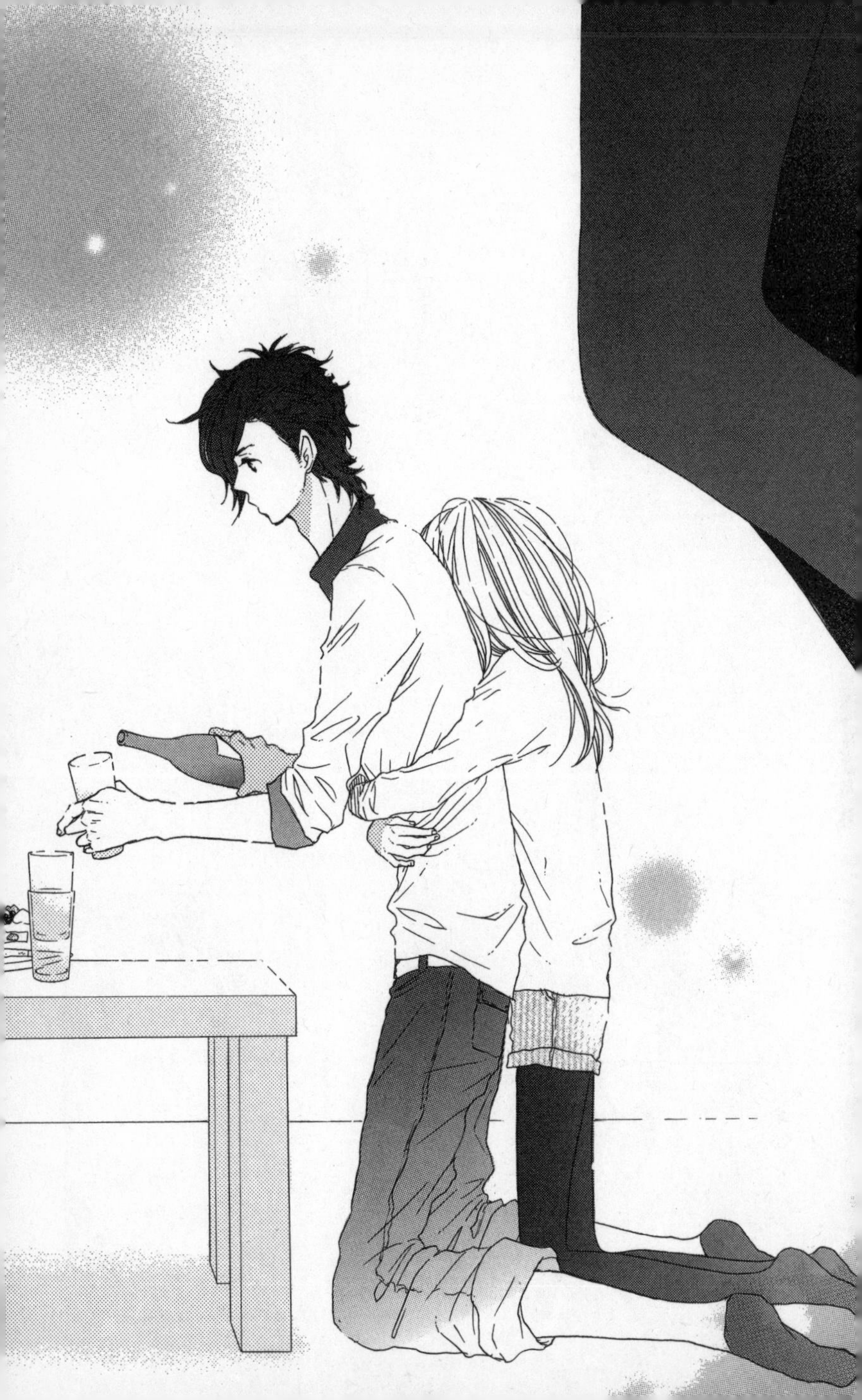

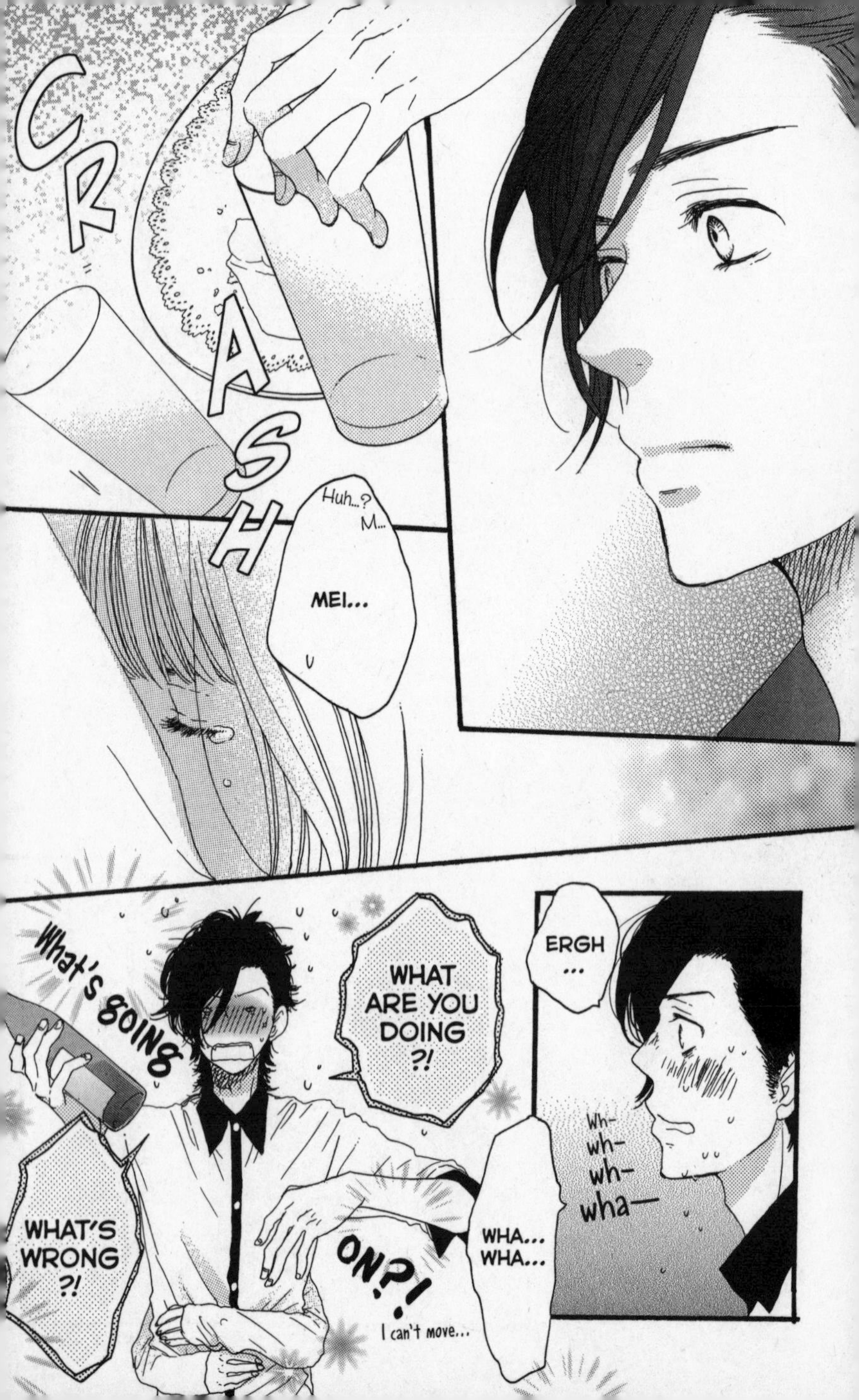
CRASH
Huh...? M...
MEI...
ERGH...
Wh- wh- wh- wha—
WHA... WHA...
WHAT ARE YOU DOING?!
What's going ON?!
WHAT'S WRONG?!
I can't move...

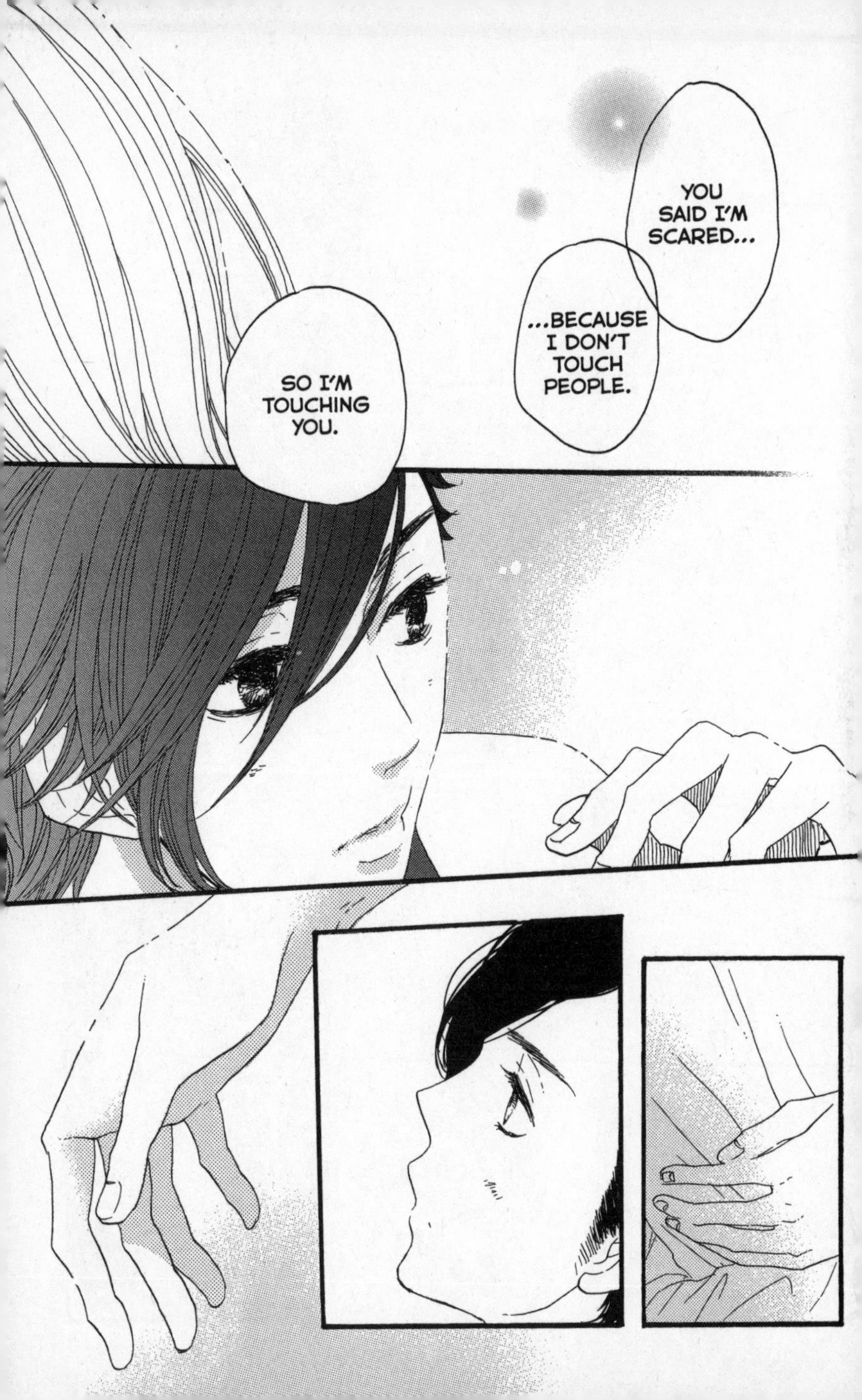
YOU SAID I'M SCARED...
...BECAUSE I DON'T TOUCH PEOPLE.
SO I'M TOUCHING YOU.

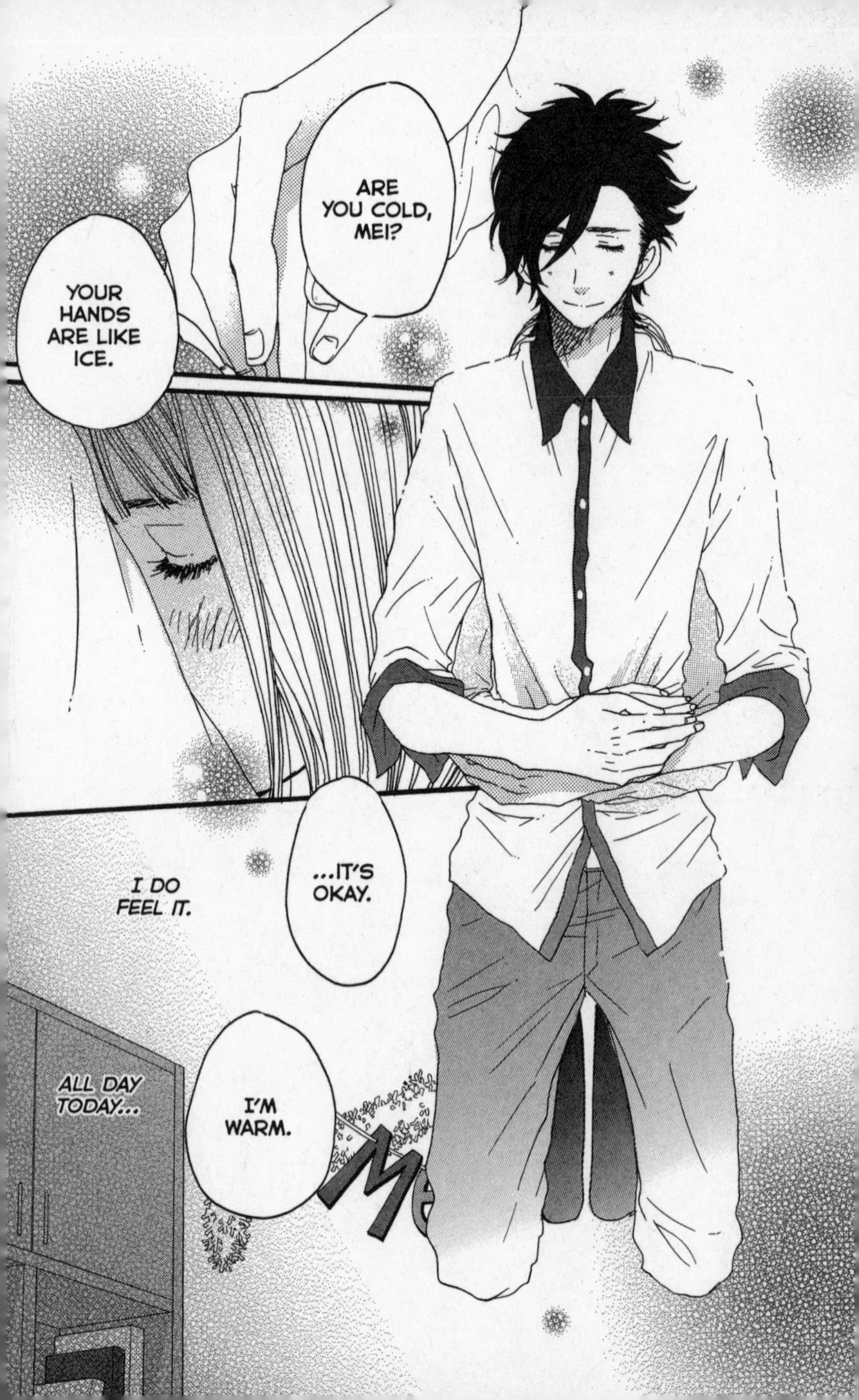
ARE YOU COLD, MEI?
YOUR HANDS ARE LIKE ICE.
...IT'S OKAY.
I DO FEEL IT.
I'M WARM.
ALL DAY TODAY...

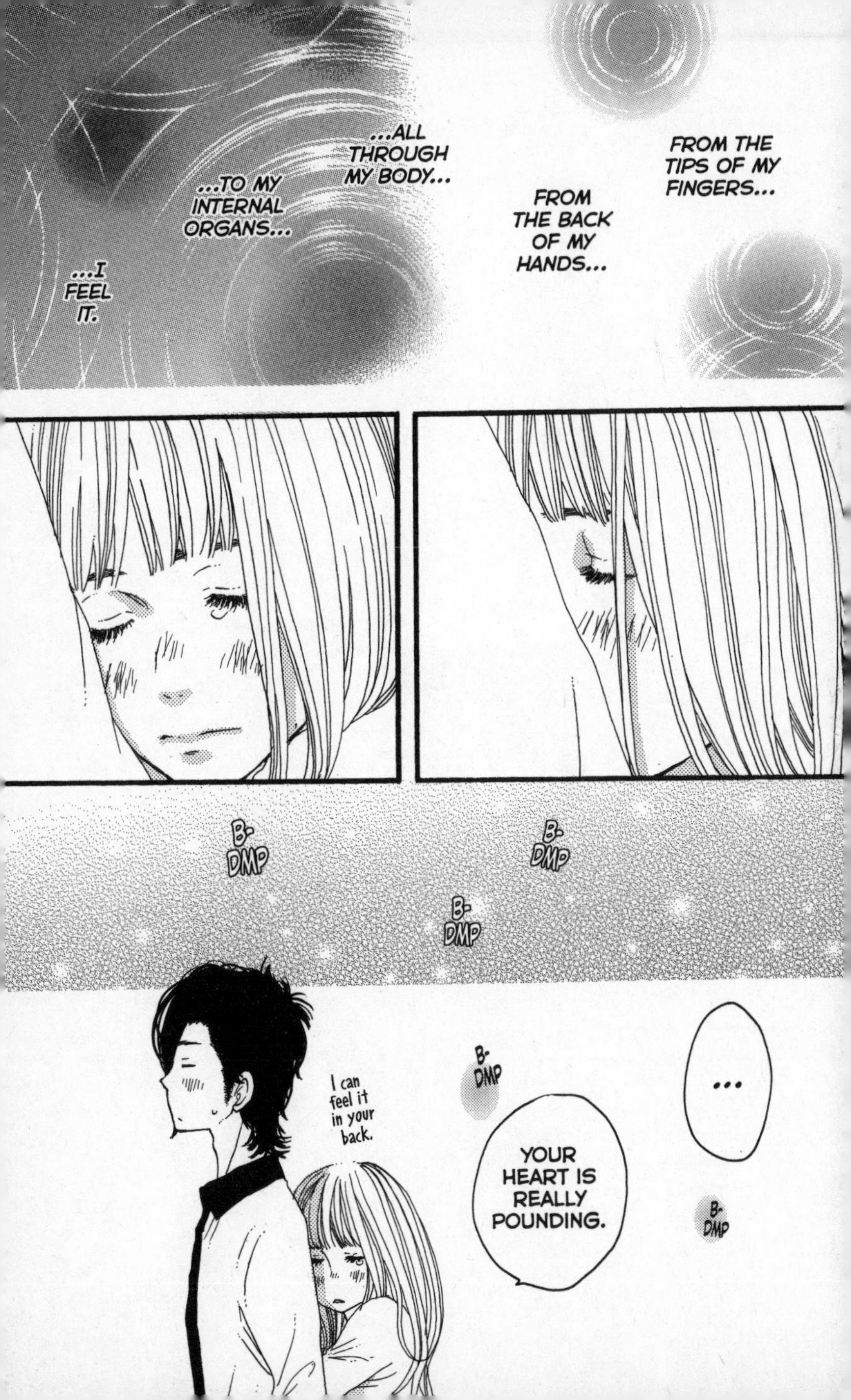
FROM THE TIPS OF MY FINGERS...
FROM THE BACK OF MY HANDS...
...ALL THROUGH MY BODY...
...TO MY INTERNAL ORGANS...
...I FEEL IT.
B-DMP
B-DMP
B-DMP
...
B-DMP
YOUR HEART IS REALLY POUNDING.
B-DMP
I can feel it in your back.

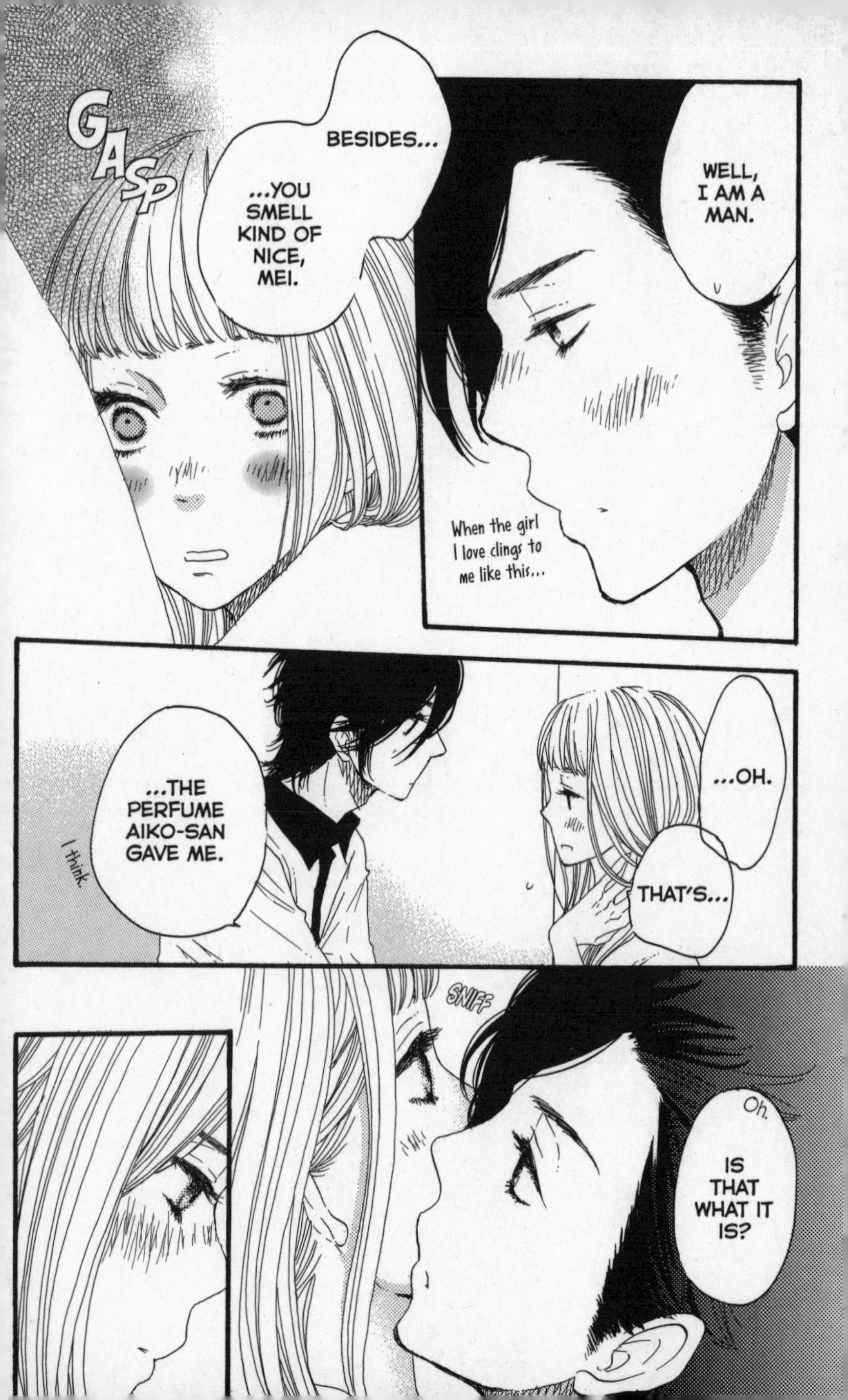
WELL, I AM A MAN.
When the girl I love clings to me like this...
BESIDES...
...YOU SMELL KIND OF NICE, MEI.
GASP
...OH.
THAT'S...
I think
...THE PERFUME AIKO-SAN GAVE ME.
SNIFF
Oh.
IS THAT WHAT IT IS?

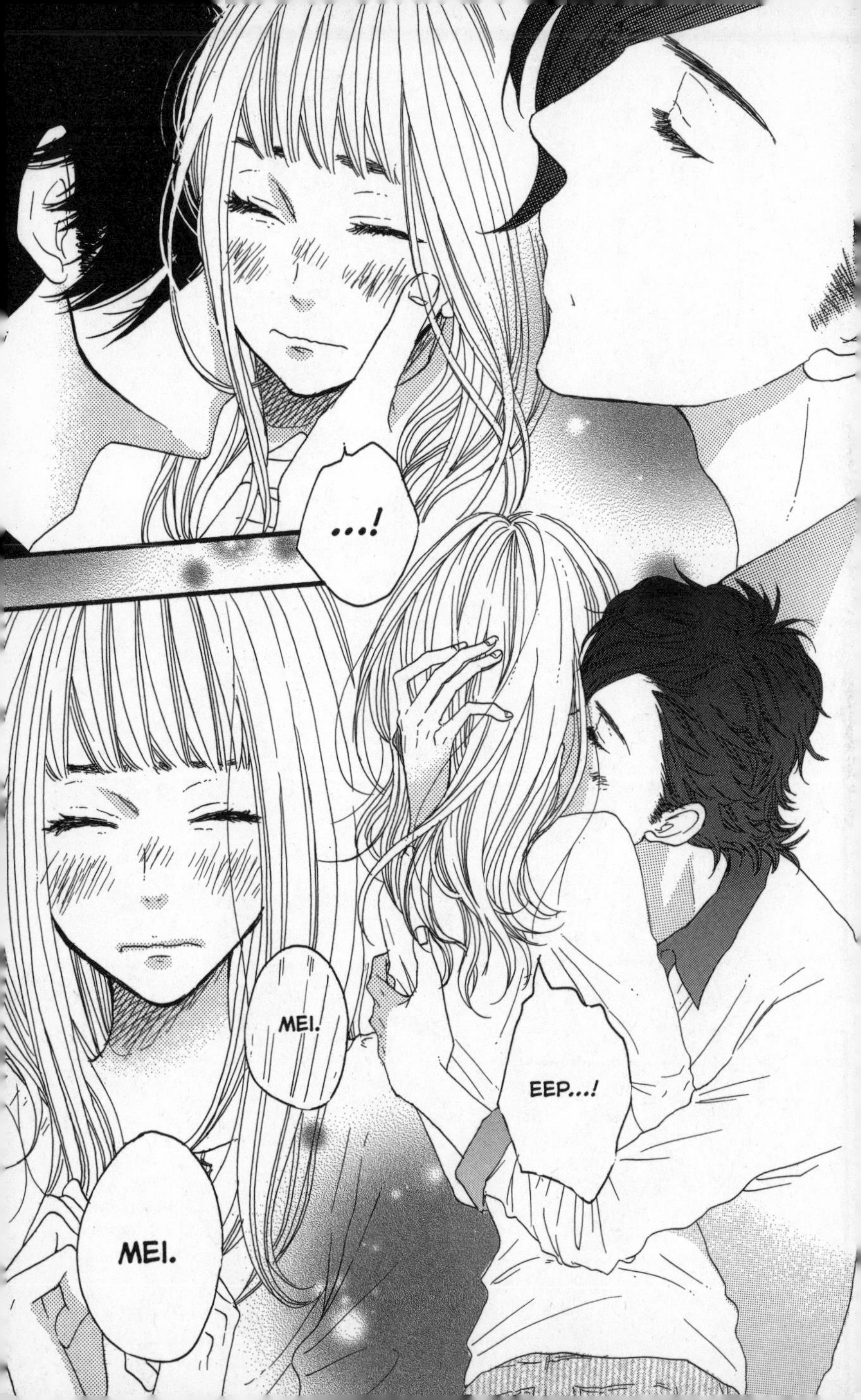
...!
EEP...!
MEI.
MEI.

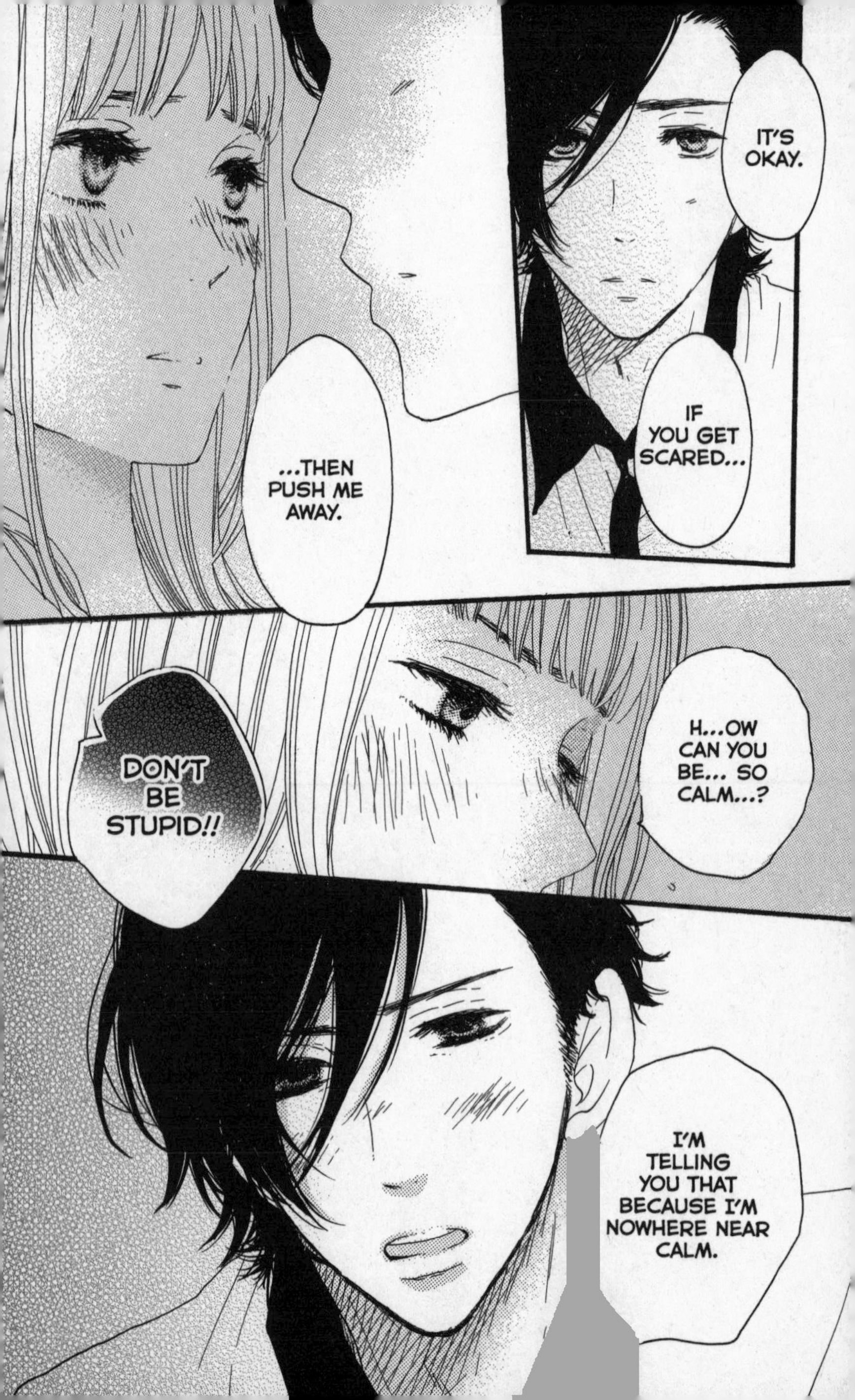
IT'S OKAY.
IF YOU GET SCARED...
...THEN PUSH ME AWAY.
H...OW CAN YOU BE... SO CALM...?
DON'T BE STUPID!!
I'M TELLING YOU THAT BECAUSE I'M NOWHERE NEAR CALM.

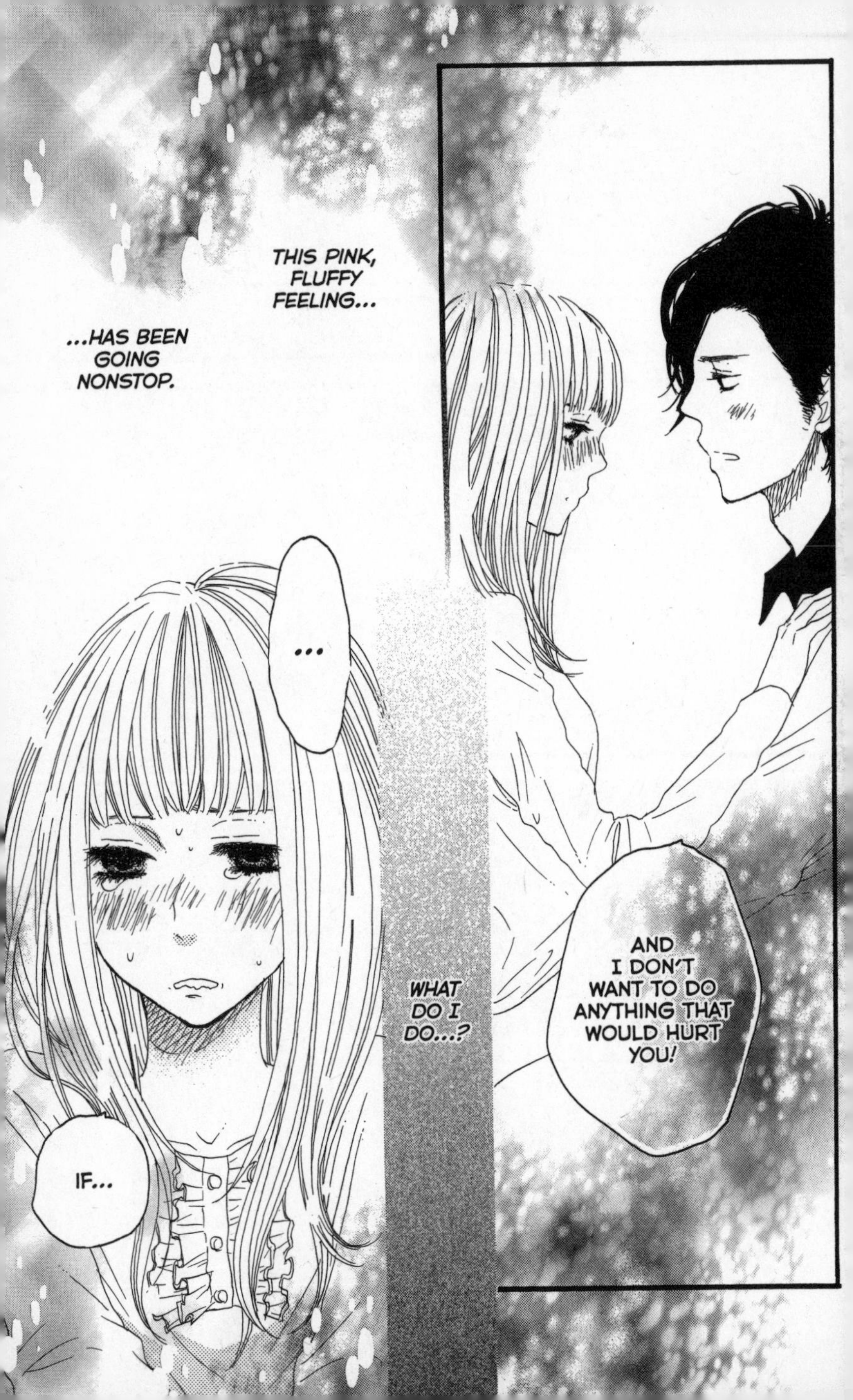
AND I DON'T WANT TO DO ANYTHING THAT WOULD HURT YOU!
THIS PINK, FLUFFY FEELING...
...HAS BEEN GOING NONSTOP.
...
WHAT DO I DO...?
IF...

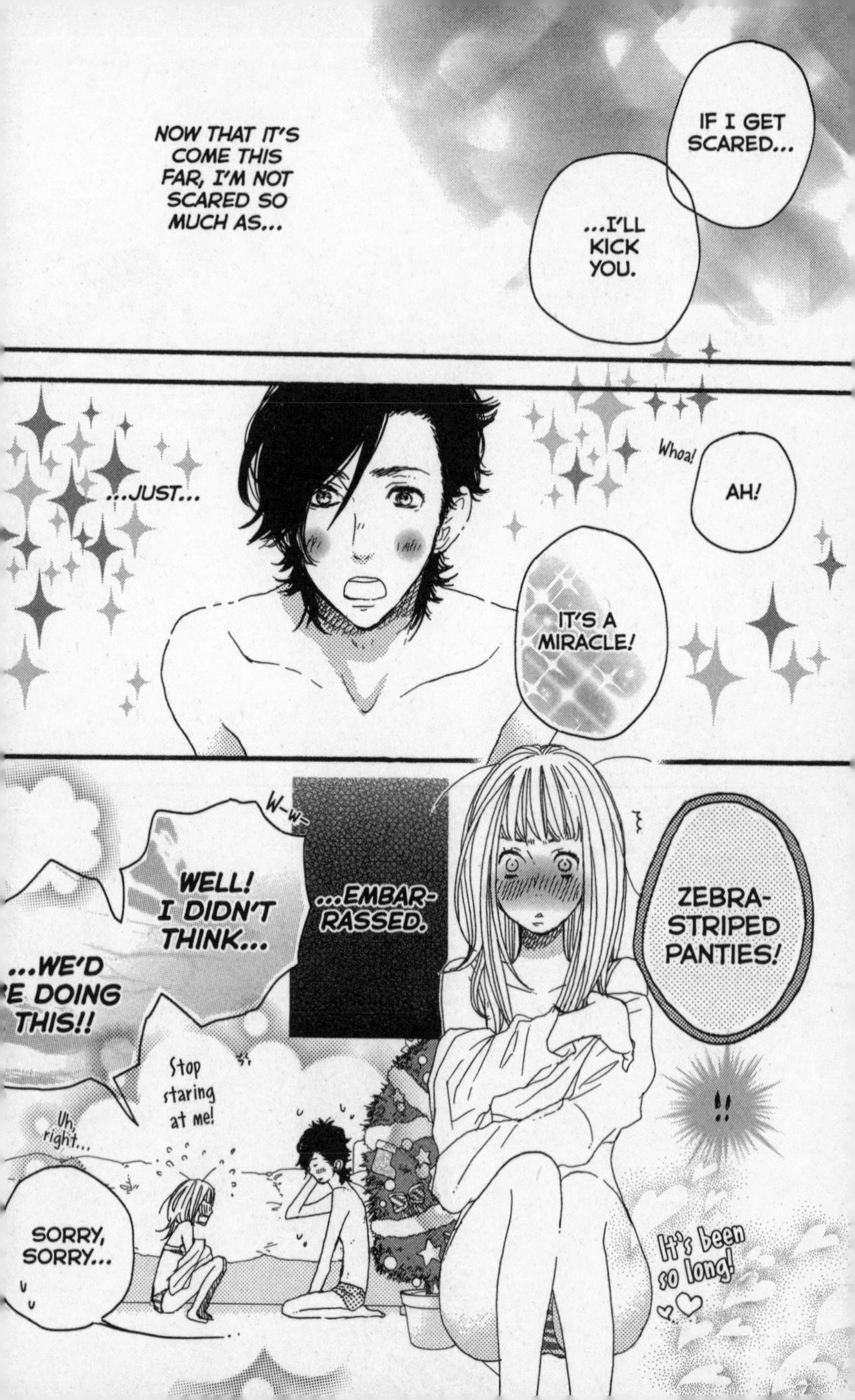
IF I GET SCARED...
...I'LL KICK YOU.
NOW THAT IT'S COME THIS FAR, I'M NOT SCARED SO MUCH AS...
Whoa!
AH!
IT'S A MIRACLE!
...JUST...
ZEBRA-STRIPED PANTIES!
...EMBARRASSED.
W-W-
WELL! I DIDN'T THINK...
...WE'D BE DOING THIS!!
It's been so long!
Stop staring at me!
Uh, right...
SORRY, SORRY...

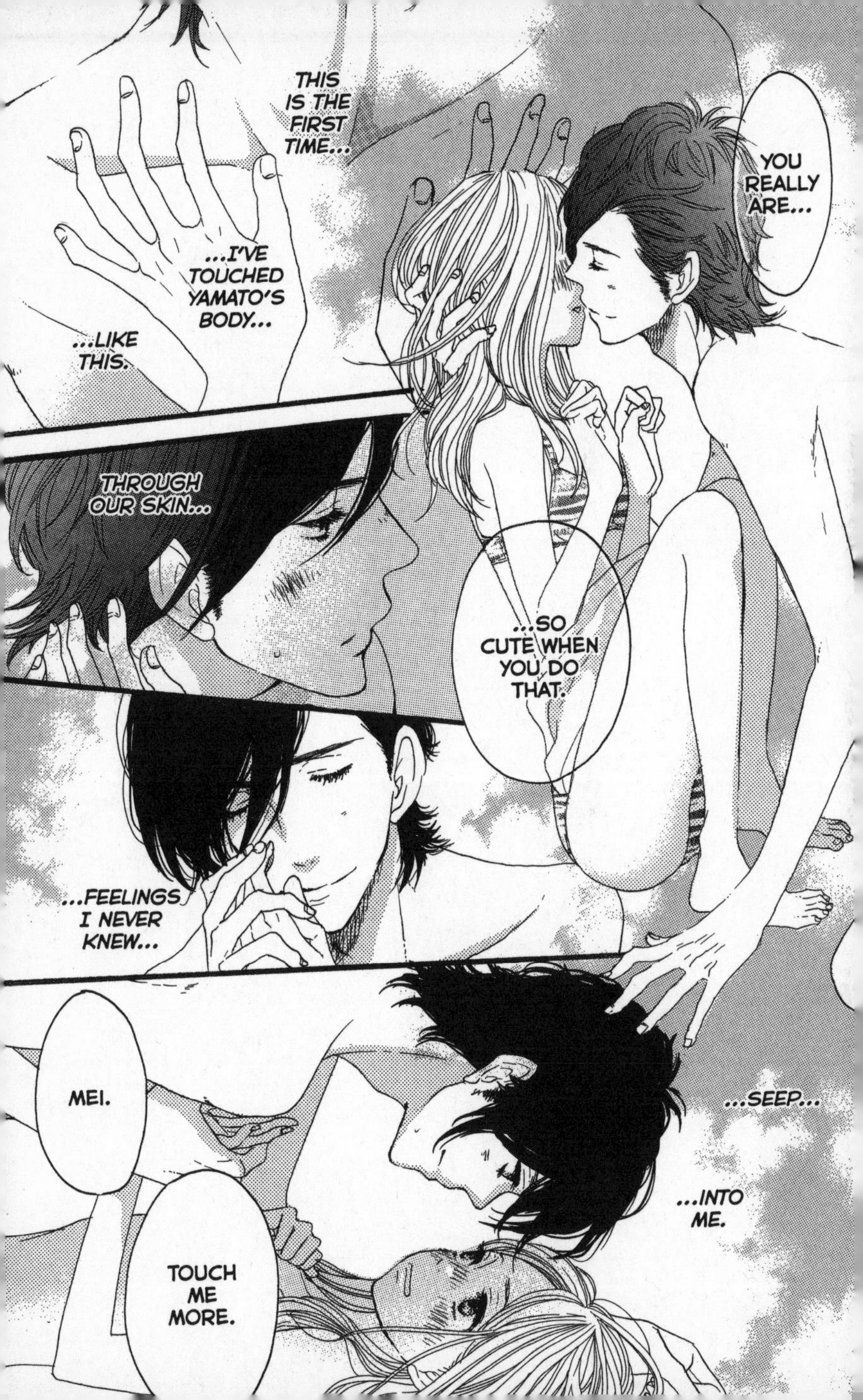
YOU REALLY ARE...
THIS IS THE FIRST TIME...
...I'VE TOUCHED YAMATO'S BODY...
...LIKE THIS.
...SO CUTE WHEN YOU DO THAT.
THROUGH OUR SKIN...
...FEELINGS I NEVER KNEW...
...SEEP...
...INTO ME.
MEI.
TOUCH ME MORE.

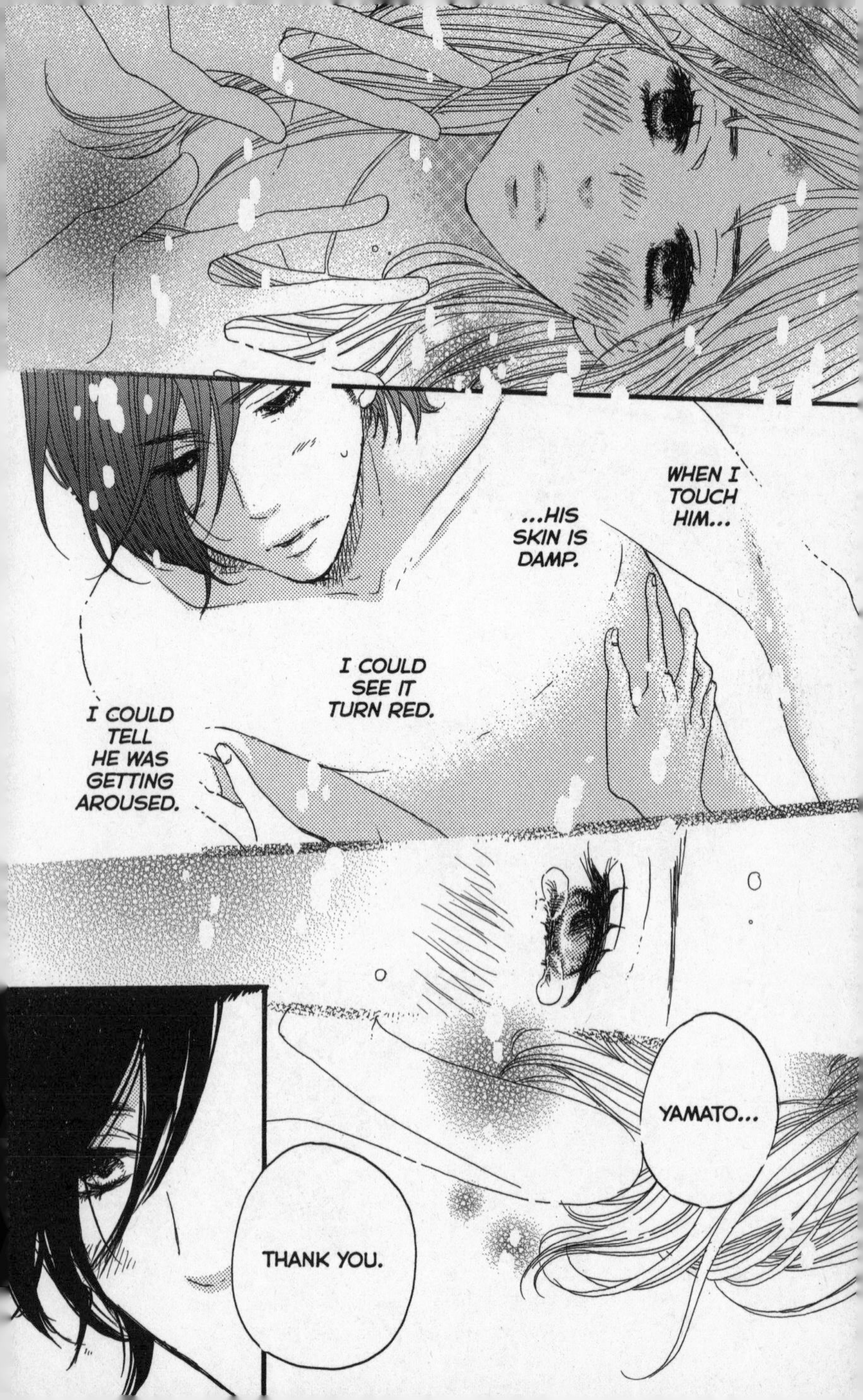
WHEN I TOUCH HIM...
...HIS SKIN IS DAMP.
I COULD SEE IT TURN RED.
I COULD TELL HE WAS GETTING AROUSED.
YAMATO...
THANK YOU.

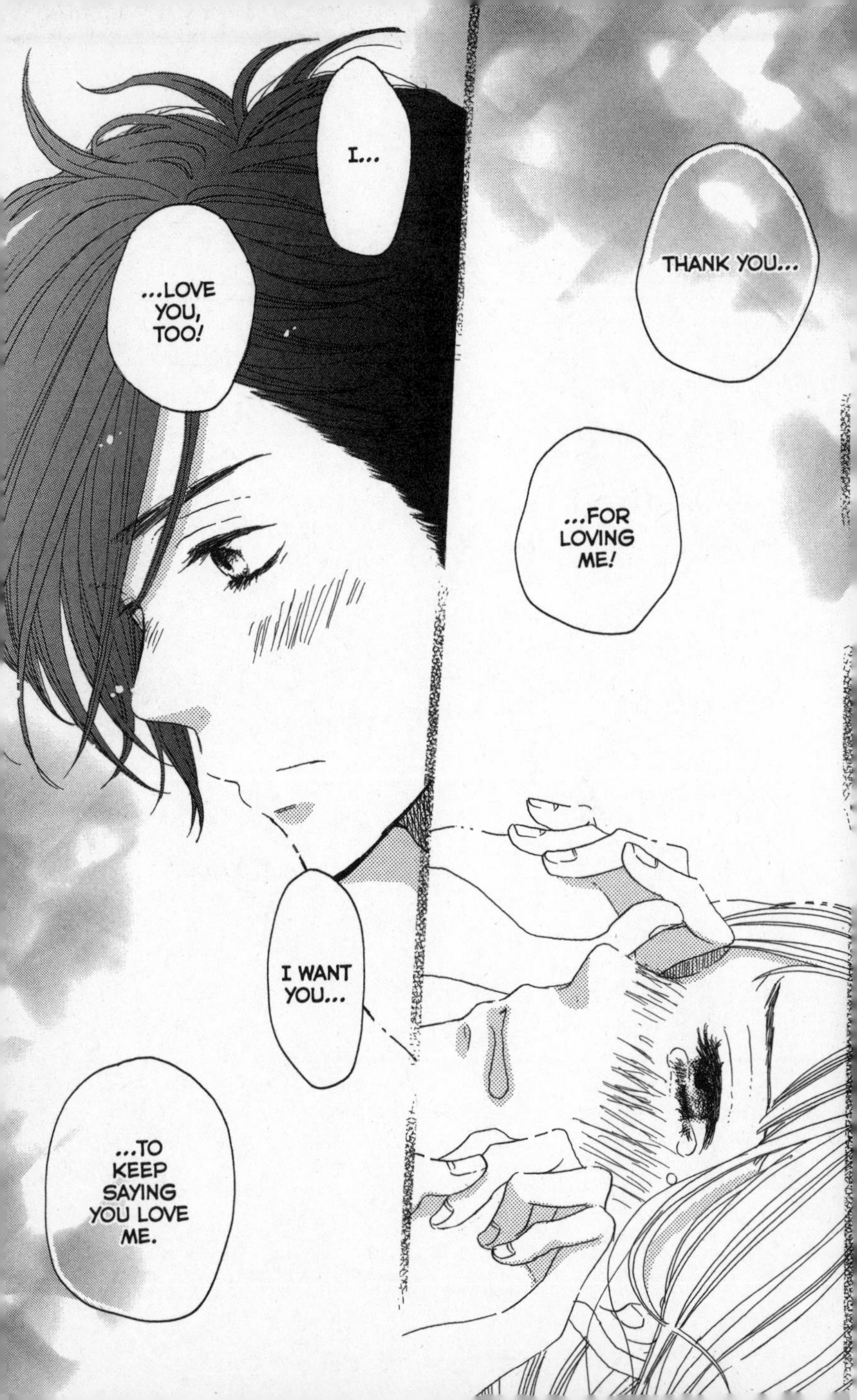
THANK YOU...
...FOR LOVING ME!
I...
...LOVE YOU, TOO!
I WANT YOU...
...TO KEEP SAYING YOU LOVE ME.

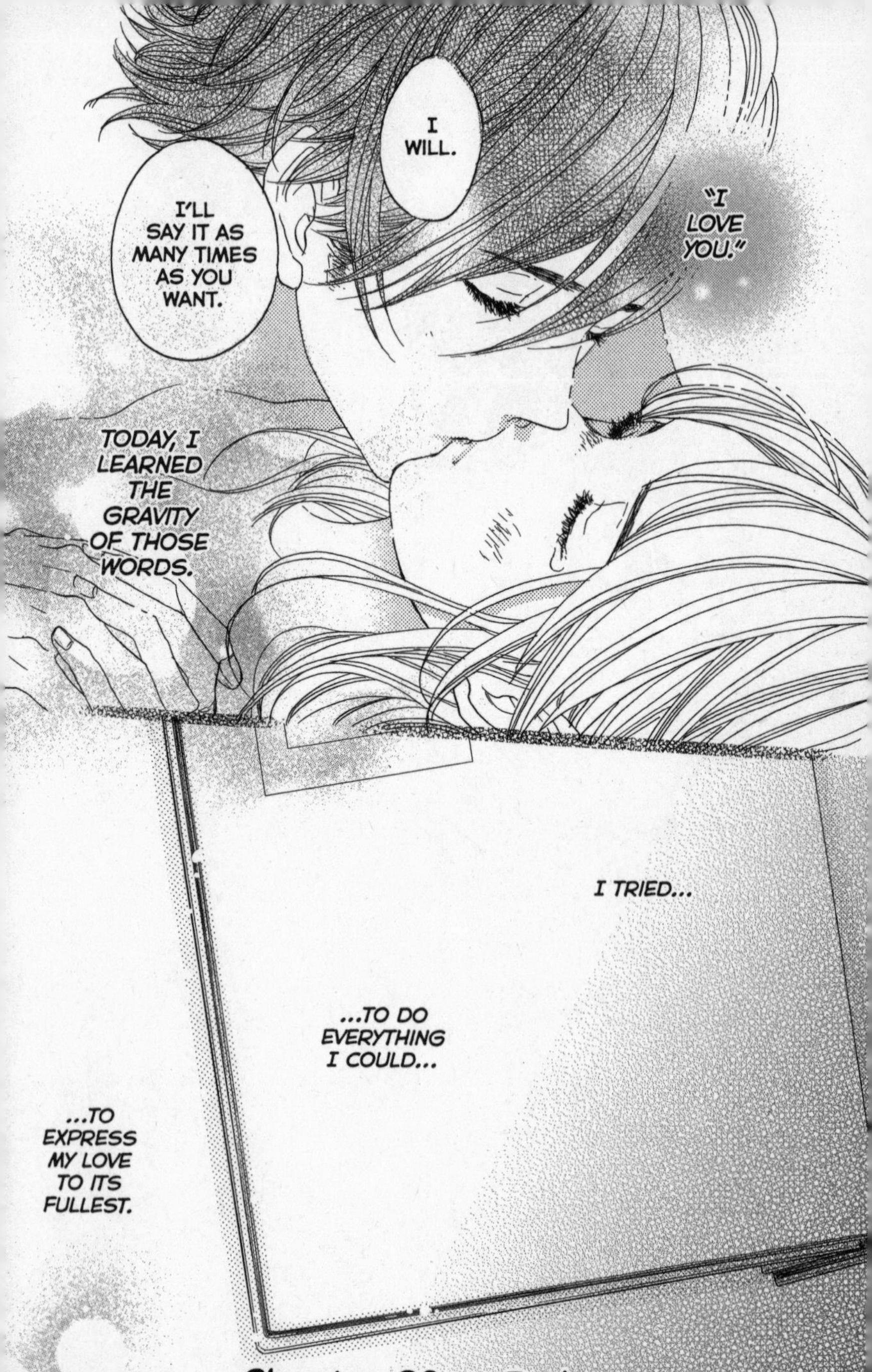
"I LOVE YOU."
I WILL.
I'LL SAY IT AS MANY TIMES AS YOU WANT.
TODAY, I LEARNED THE GRAVITY OF THOSE WORDS.
I TRIED...
...TO DO EVERYTHING I COULD...
...TO EXPRESS MY LOVE TO ITS FULLEST.

Chapter 39 — End

Chapter
40

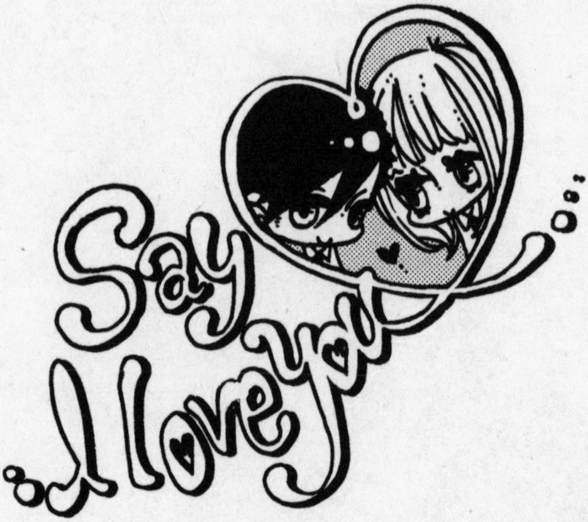
Say I love you

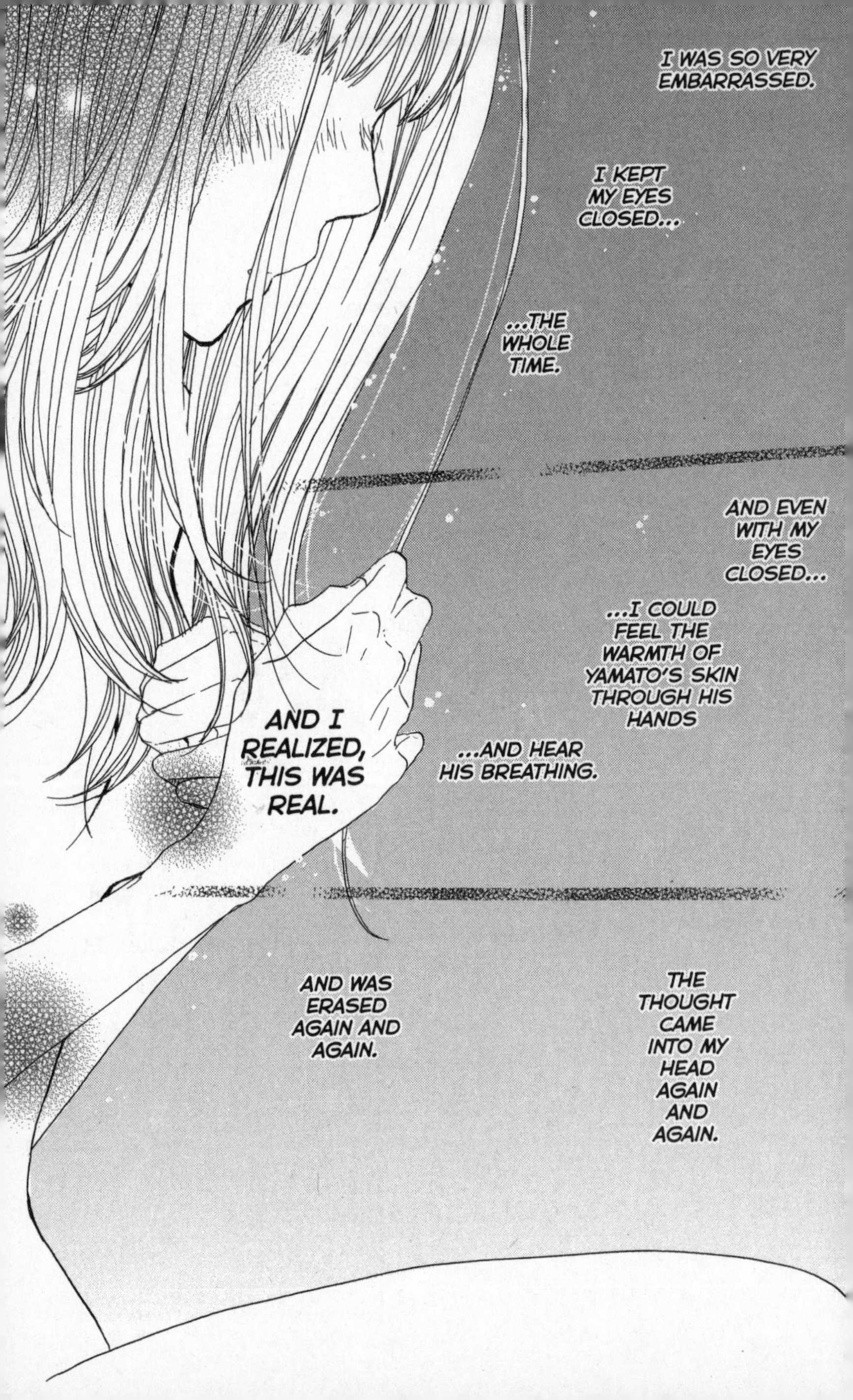
I WAS SO VERY EMBARRASSED.
I KEPT MY EYES CLOSED...
...THE WHOLE TIME.
AND EVEN WITH MY EYES CLOSED...
...I COULD FEEL THE WARMTH OF YAMATO'S SKIN THROUGH HIS HANDS
...AND HEAR HIS BREATHING.
AND I REALIZED, THIS WAS REAL.
THE THOUGHT CAME INTO MY HEAD AGAIN AND AGAIN.
AND WAS ERASED AGAIN AND AGAIN.

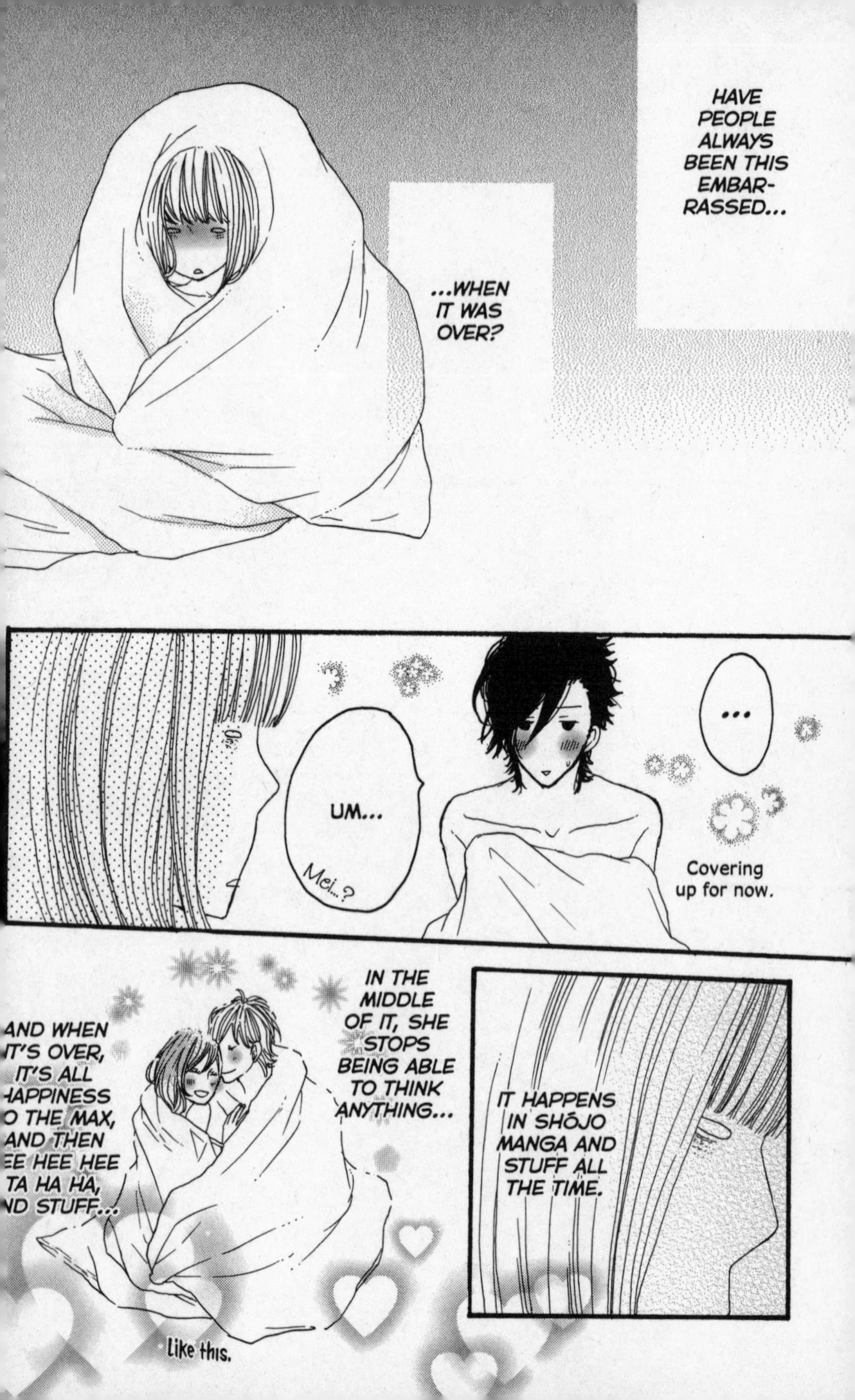
HAVE PEOPLE ALWAYS BEEN THIS EMBARRASSED...
...WHEN IT WAS OVER?
...
Covering up for now.
UM...
Mei...?
IT HAPPENS IN SHŌJO MANGA AND STUFF ALL THE TIME.
IN THE MIDDLE OF IT, SHE STOPS BEING ABLE TO THINK ANYTHING...
AND WHEN IT'S OVER, IT'S ALL HAPPINESS O THE MAX, AND THEN EE HEE HEE TA HA HA, ND STUFF...
Like this.

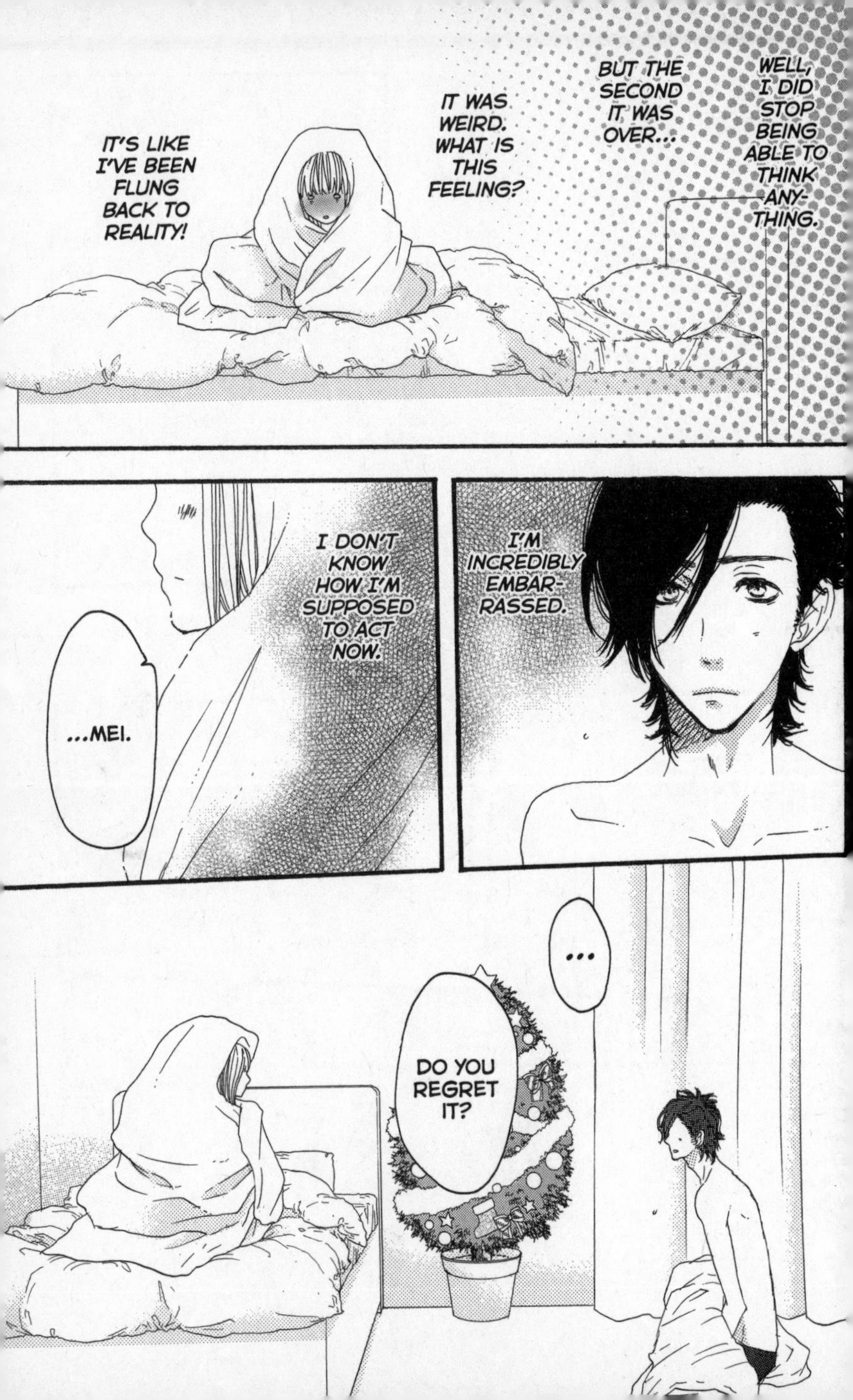
WELL, I DID STOP BEING ABLE TO THINK ANYTHING.
BUT THE SECOND IT WAS OVER...
IT WAS WEIRD. WHAT IS THIS FEELING?
IT'S LIKE I'VE BEEN FLUNG BACK TO REALITY!
I'M INCREDIBLY EMBARRASSED.
I DON'T KNOW HOW I'M SUPPOSED TO ACT NOW.
...MEI.
...
DO YOU REGRET IT?

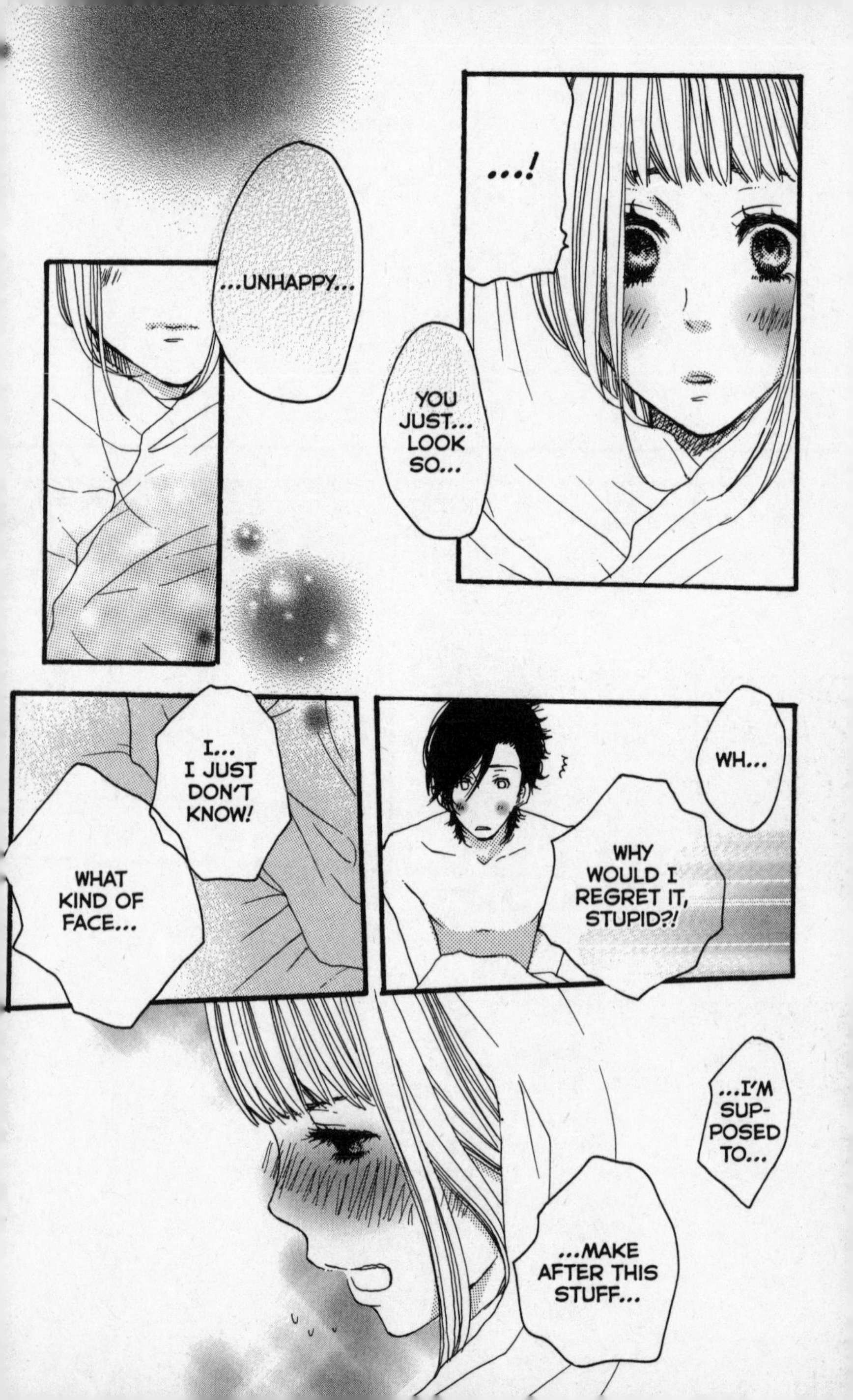
...!
YOU JUST... LOOK SO...
...UNHAPPY...
WH...
WHY WOULD I REGRET IT, STUPID?!
I... I JUST DON'T KNOW!
WHAT KIND OF FACE...
...I'M SUP-POSED TO...
...MAKE AFTER THIS STUFF...

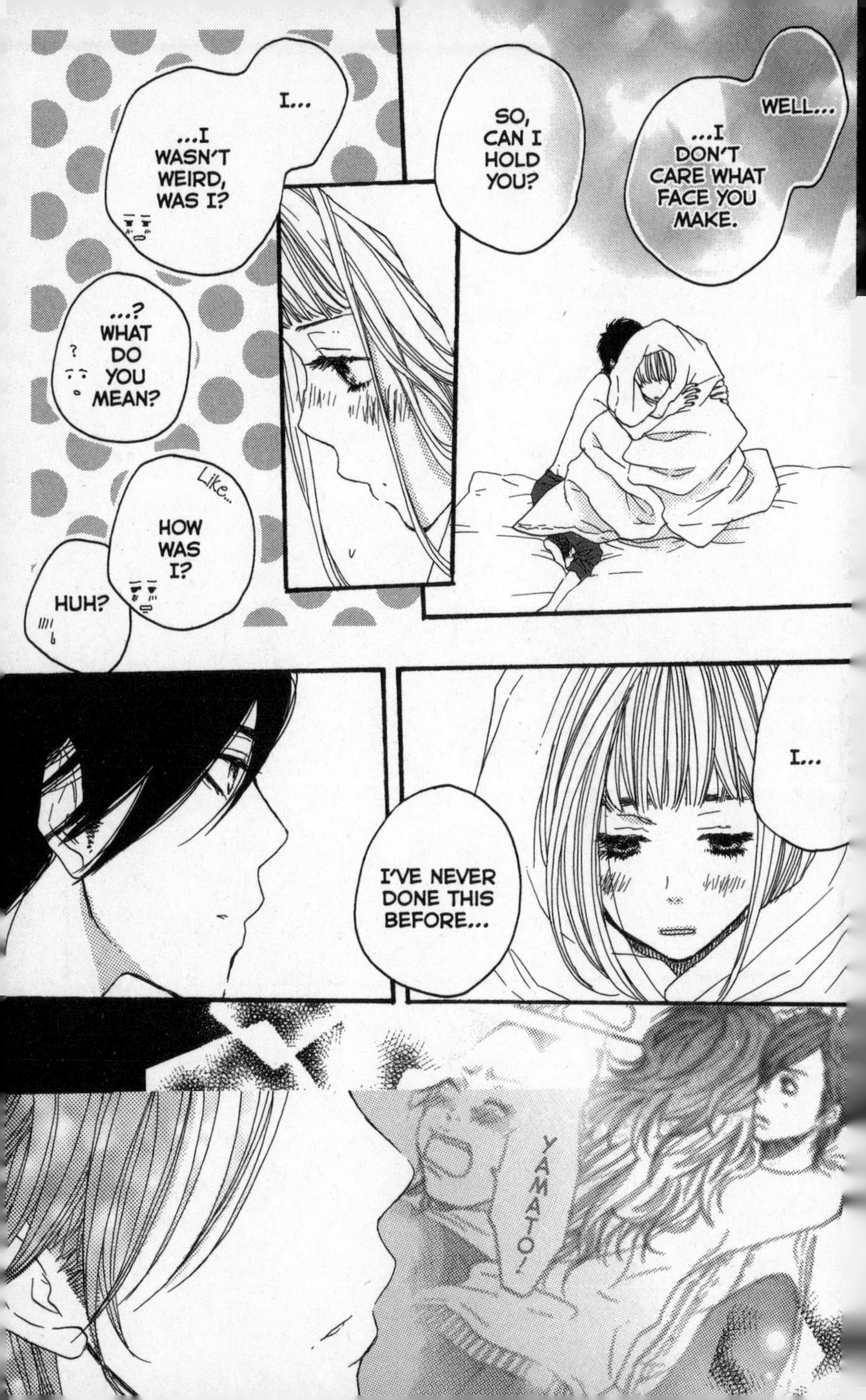
WELL...
...I DON'T CARE WHAT FACE YOU MAKE.
SO, CAN I HOLD YOU?
I...
...I WASN'T WEIRD, WAS I?
...? WHAT DO YOU MEAN?
Like...
HOW WAS I?
HUH?
I...
I'VE NEVER DONE THIS BEFORE...
YAMATO!

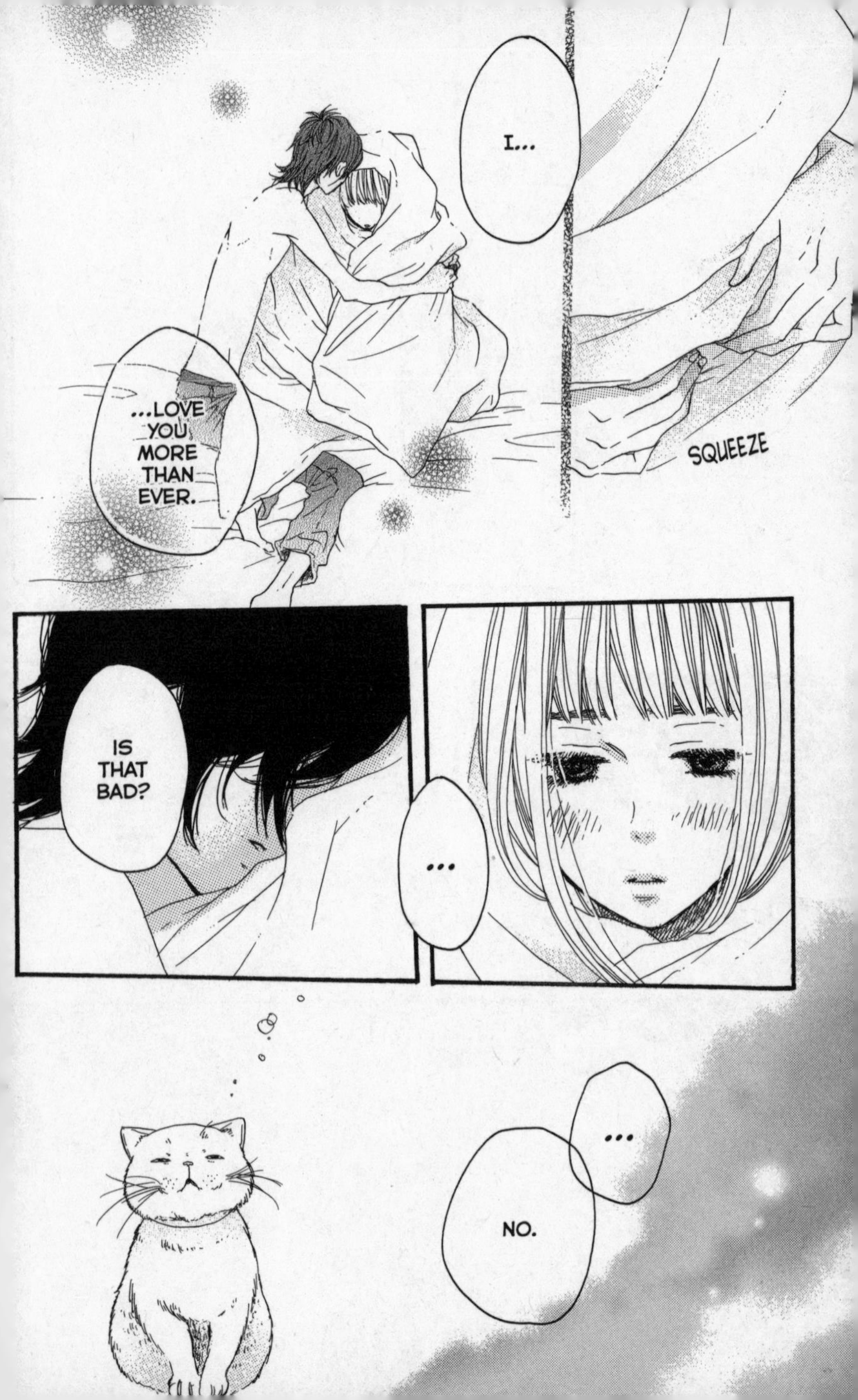
I...
SQUEEZE
...LOVE YOU MORE THAN EVER.
...
IS THAT BAD?
...
NO.

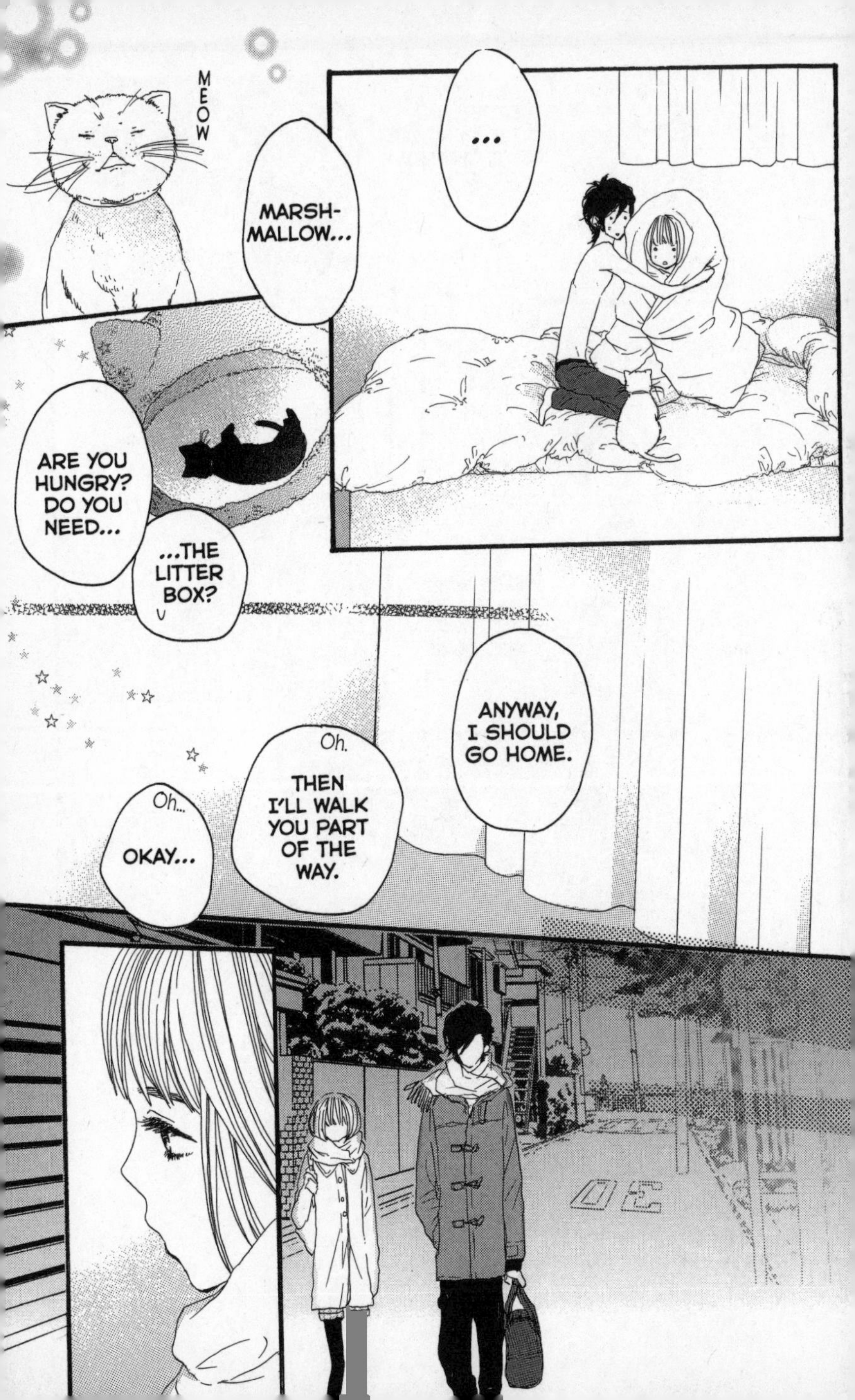
...
MARSH-MALLOW...
MEOW
ARE YOU HUNGRY? DO YOU NEED...
...THE LITTER BOX?
ANYWAY, I SHOULD GO HOME.
Oh.
THEN I'LL WALK YOU PART OF THE WAY.
Oh...
OKAY...

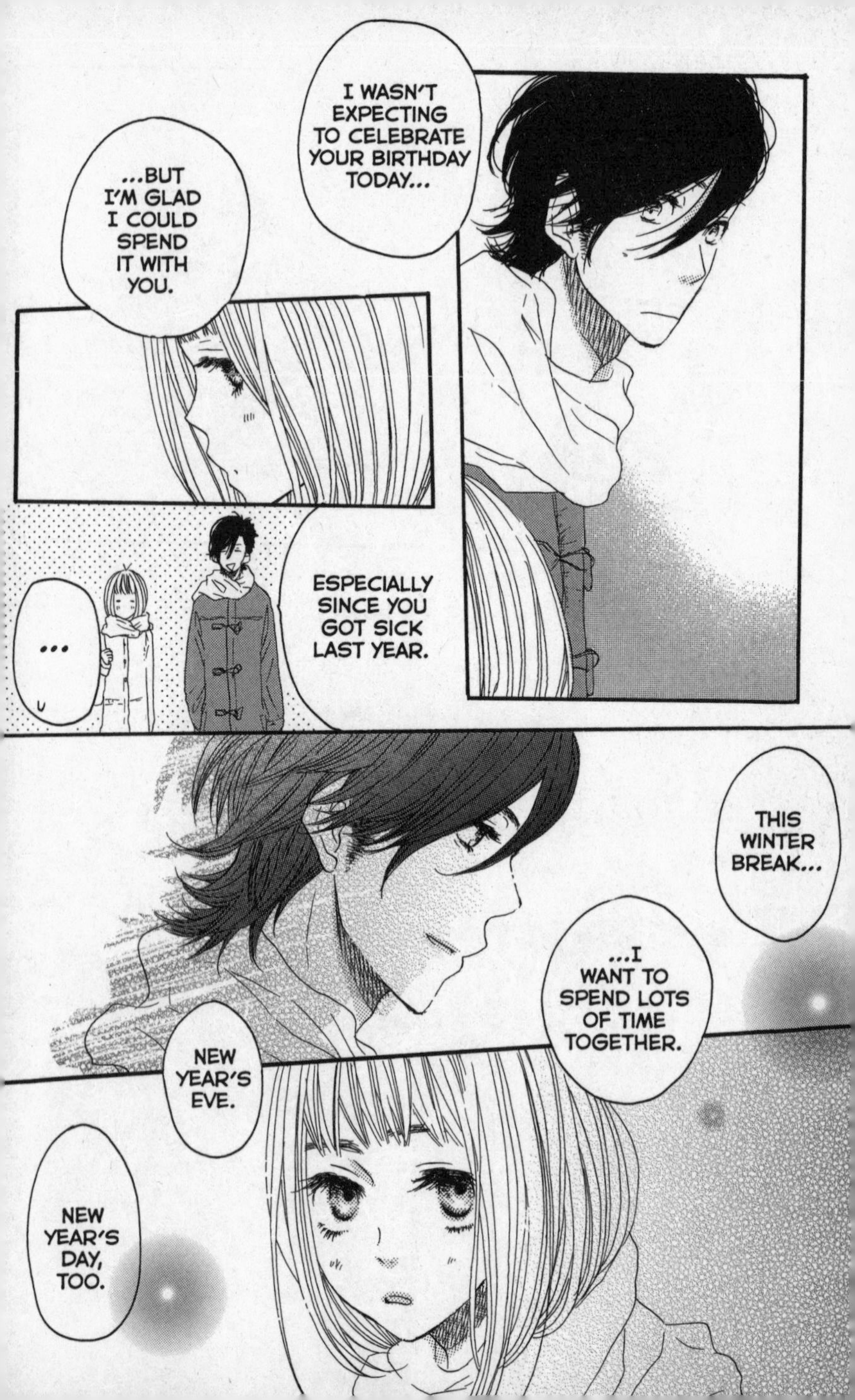
I WASN'T EXPECTING TO CELEBRATE YOUR BIRTHDAY TODAY...
...BUT I'M GLAD I COULD SPEND IT WITH YOU.
ESPECIALLY SINCE YOU GOT SICK LAST YEAR.
...
THIS WINTER BREAK...
...I WANT TO SPEND LOTS OF TIME TOGETHER.
NEW YEAR'S EVE.
NEW YEAR'S DAY, TOO.

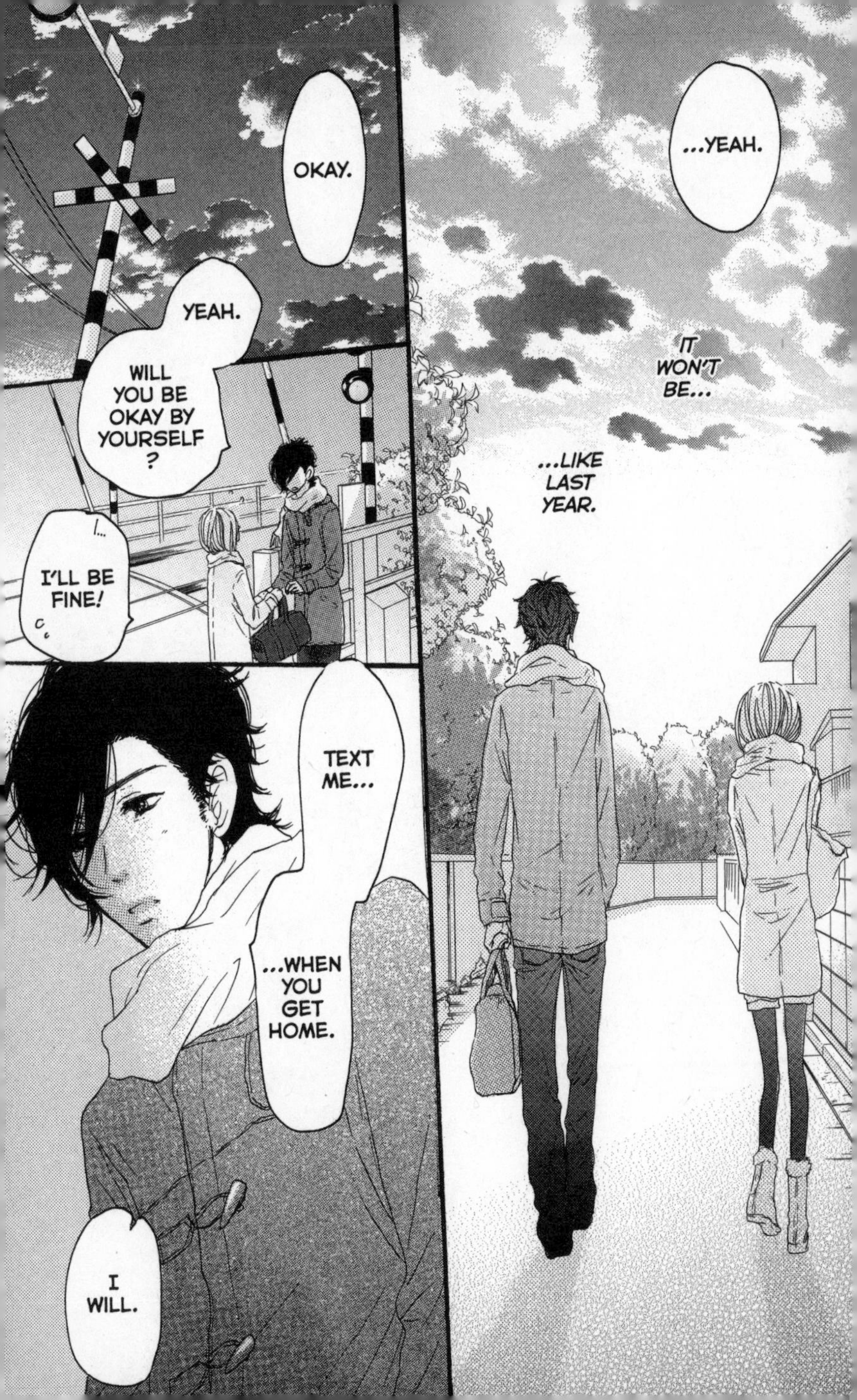
...YEAH.
IT WON'T BE...
...LIKE LAST YEAR.
OKAY.
YEAH.
WILL YOU BE OKAY BY YOURSELF?
I...
I'LL BE FINE!
TEXT ME...
...WHEN YOU GET HOME.
I WILL.

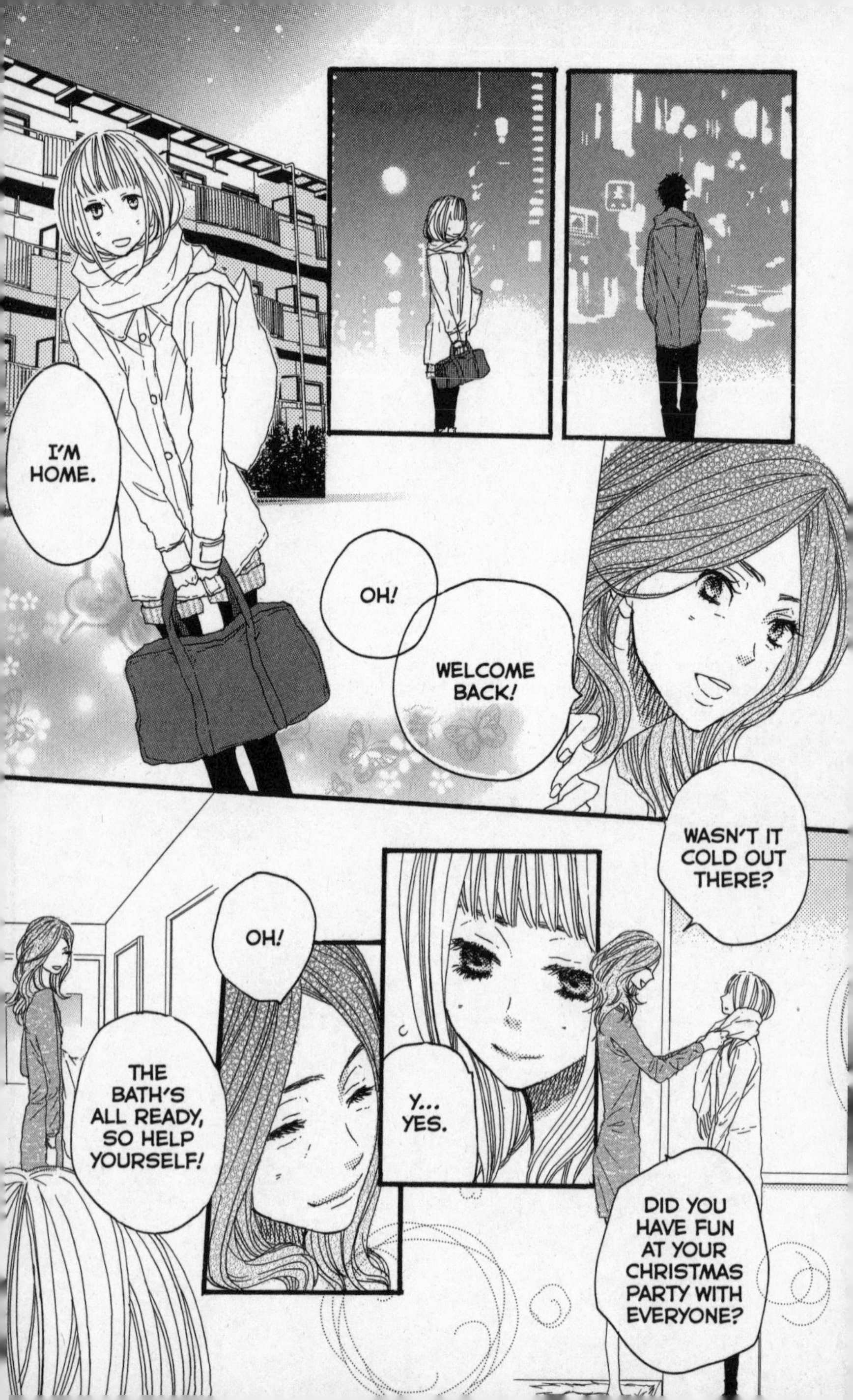
I'M HOME.
OH!
WELCOME BACK!
WASN'T IT COLD OUT THERE?
DID YOU HAVE FUN AT YOUR CHRISTMAS PARTY WITH EVERYONE?
Y... YES.
OH!
THE BATH'S ALL READY, SO HELP YOURSELF!

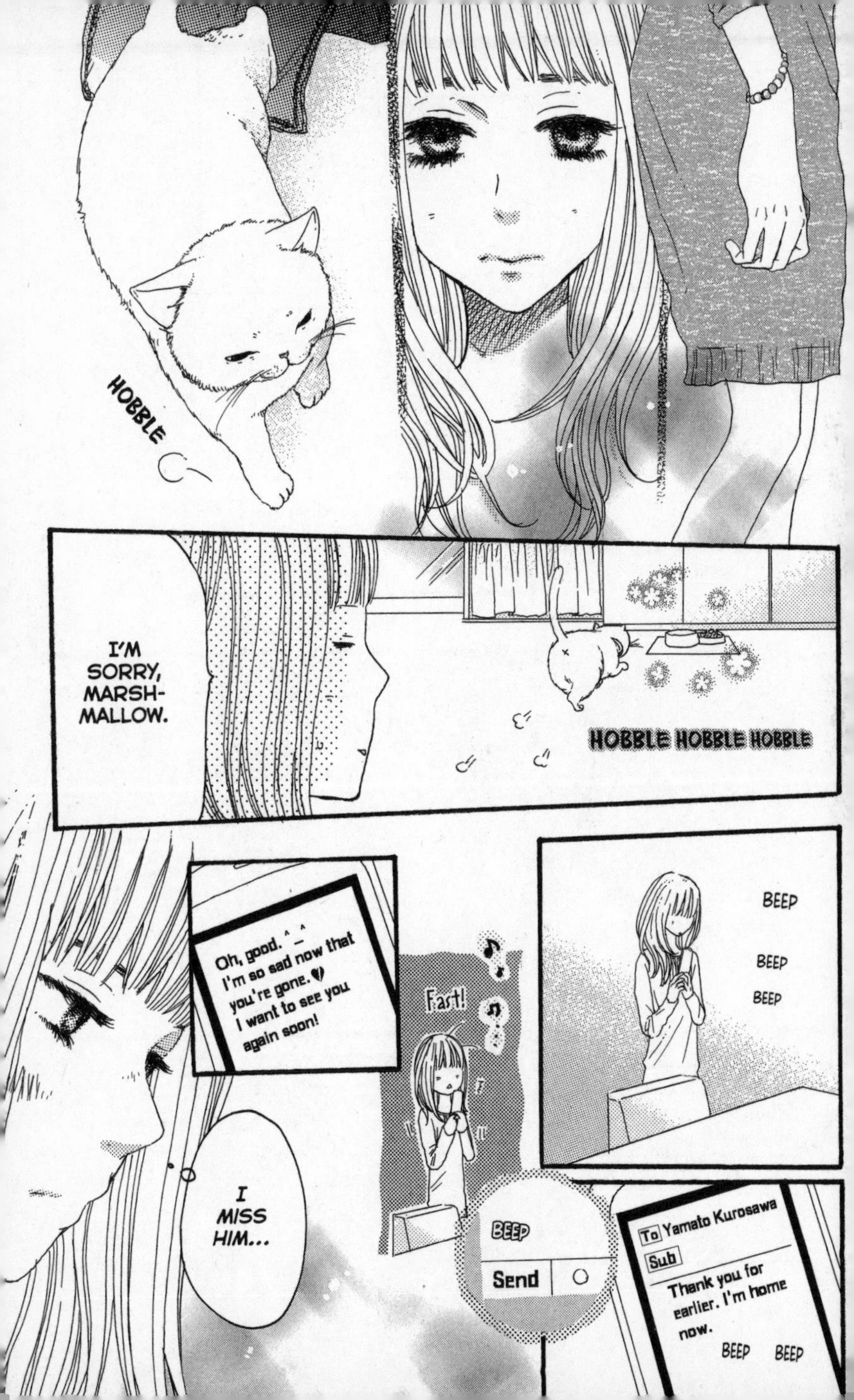
HOBBLE
HOBBLE HOBBLE HOBBLE
I'M SORRY, MARSH-MALLOW.
BEEP
BEEP
BEEP
To Yamato Kurosawa
Sub
Thank you for earlier. I'm home now.
BEEP BEEP
BEEP
Send
Fast!
Oh, good. ^_^ I'm so sad now that you're gone. I want to see you again soon!
I MISS HIM...

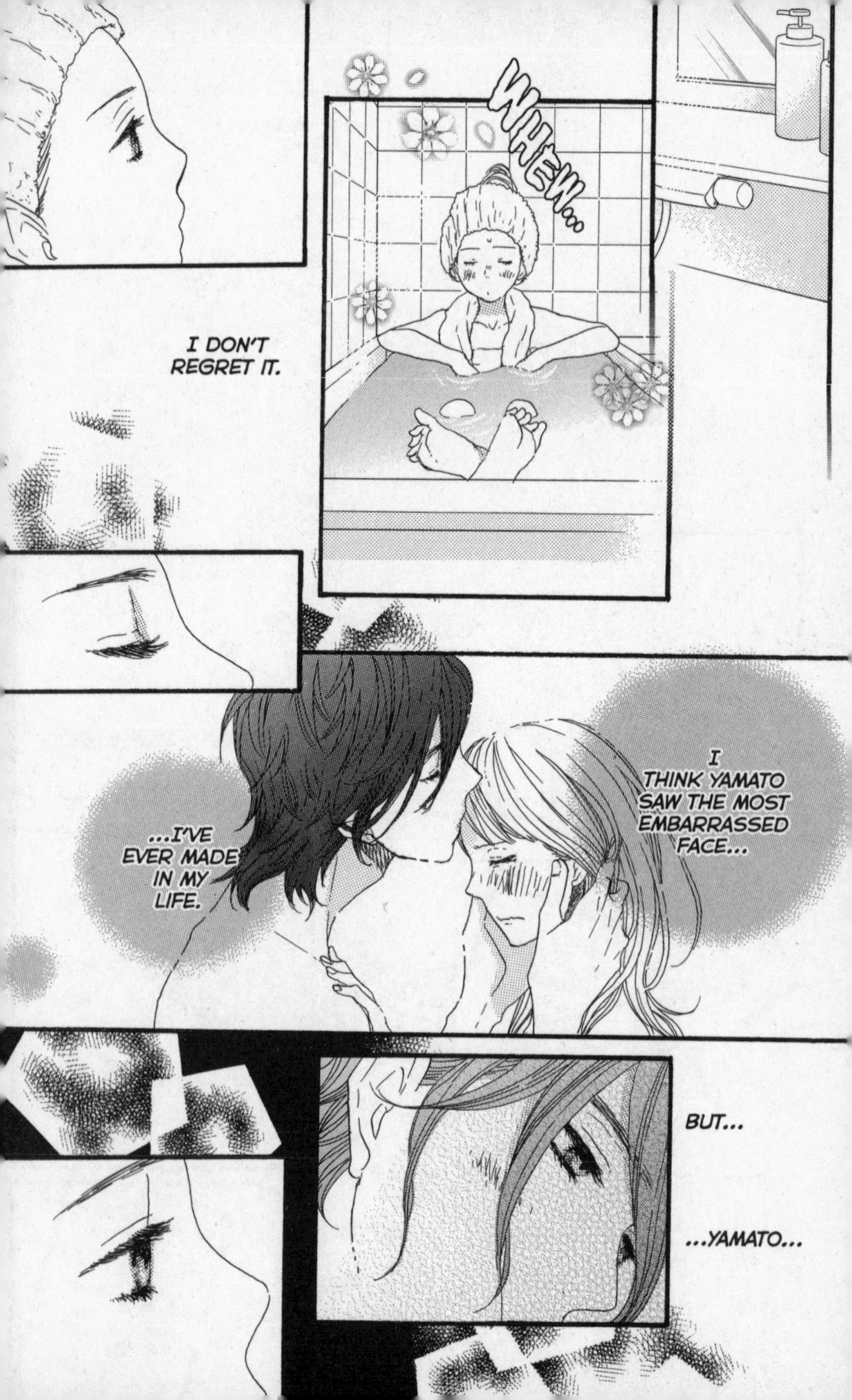
WHEW...
I DON'T REGRET IT.
I THINK YAMATO SAW THE MOST EMBARRASSED FACE...
...I'VE EVER MADE IN MY LIFE.
BUT...
...YAMATO...

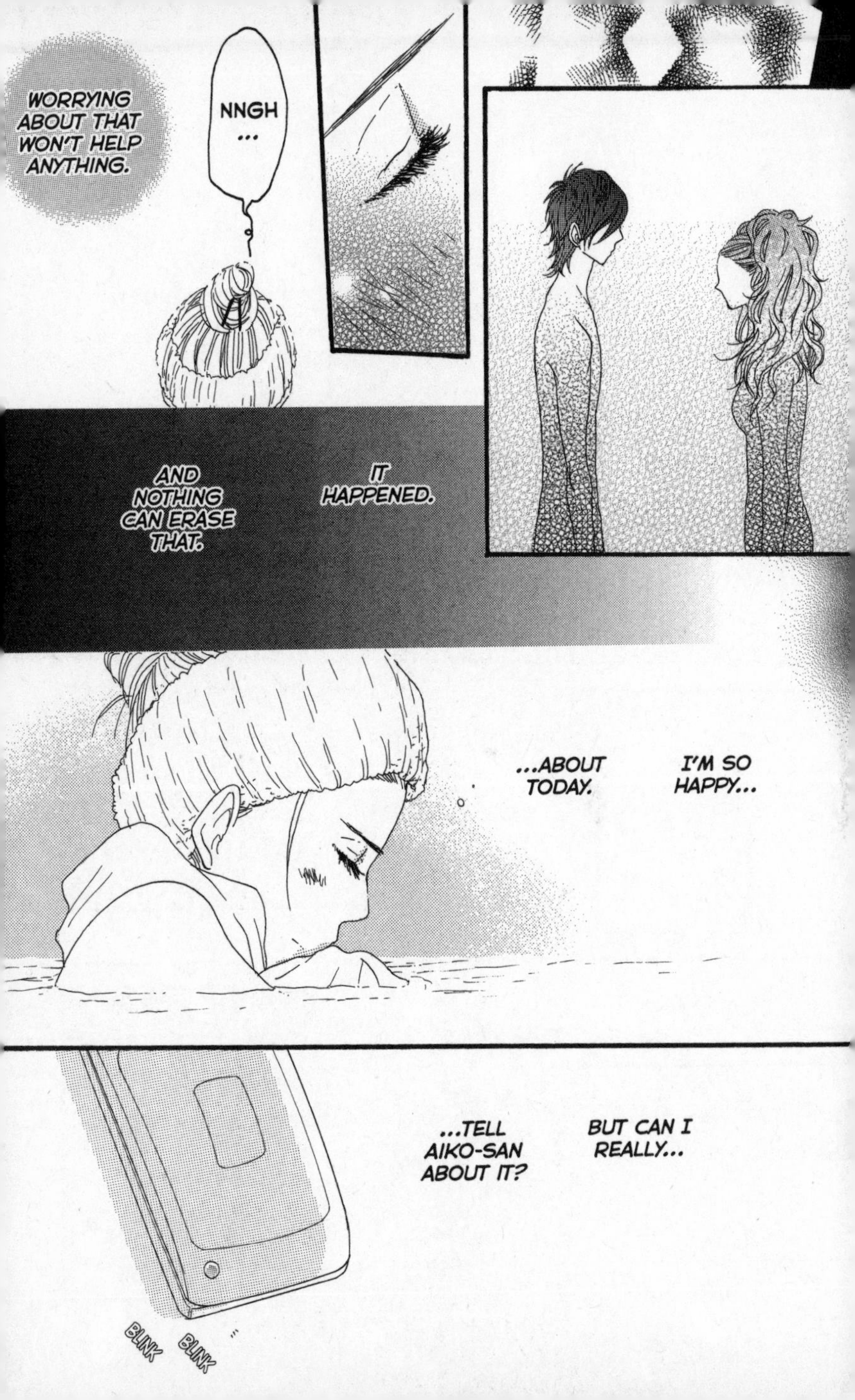
NNGH...
WORRYING ABOUT THAT WON'T HELP ANYTHING.
IT HAPPENED.
AND NOTHING CAN ERASE THAT.
I'M SO HAPPY...
...ABOUT TODAY.
BUT CAN I REALLY...
...TELL AIKO-SAN ABOUT IT?
BLINK
BLINK

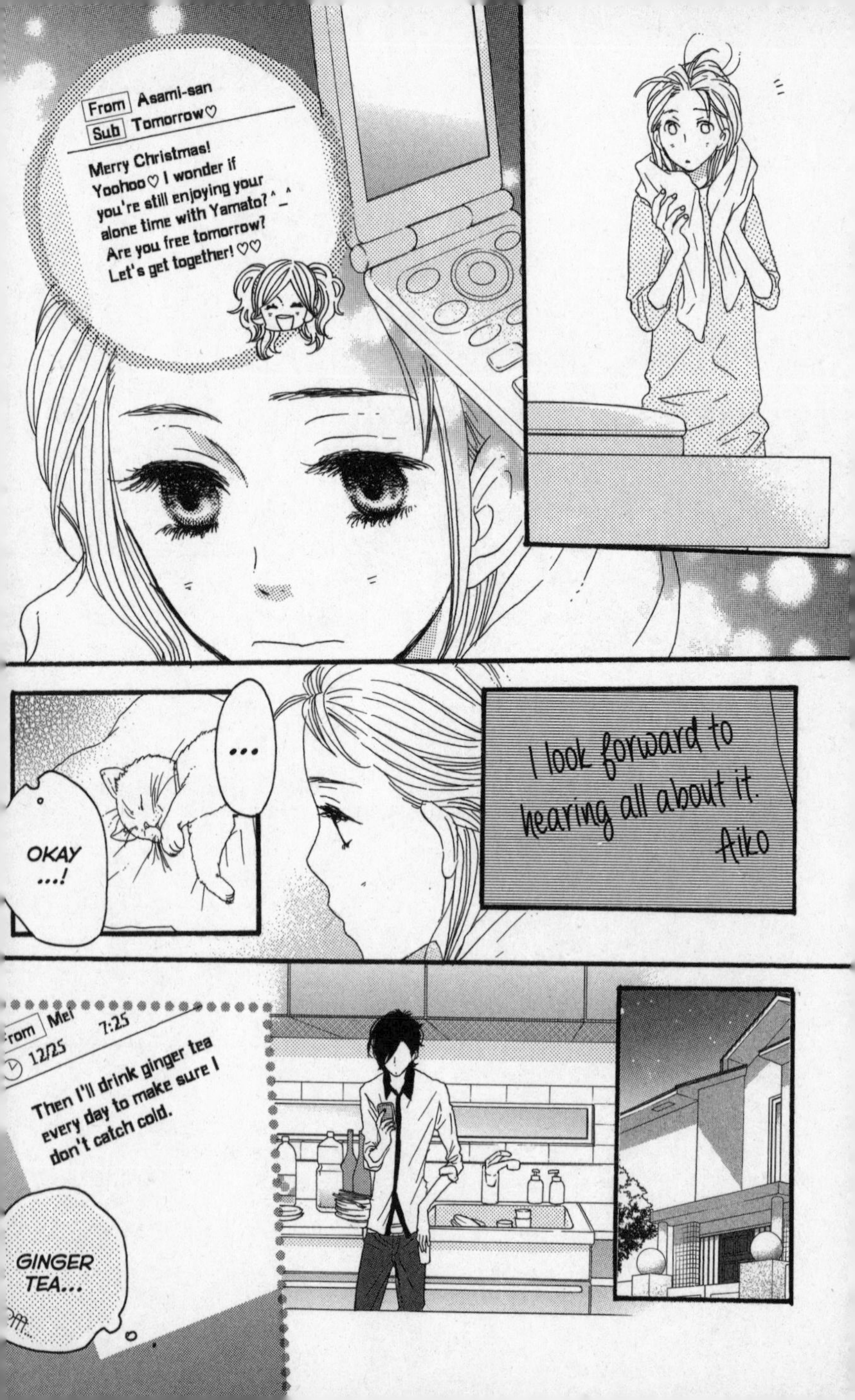
From Asami-san
Sub Tomorrow♡
Merry Christmas! Yoohoo♡ I wonder if you're still enjoying your alone time with Yamato? ^_^ Are you free tomorrow? Let's get together! ♡♡
I look forward to hearing all about it. Aiko
...
OKAY ...!
From Mei 12/25 7:25
Then I'll drink ginger tea every day to make sure I don't catch cold.
GINGER TEA...

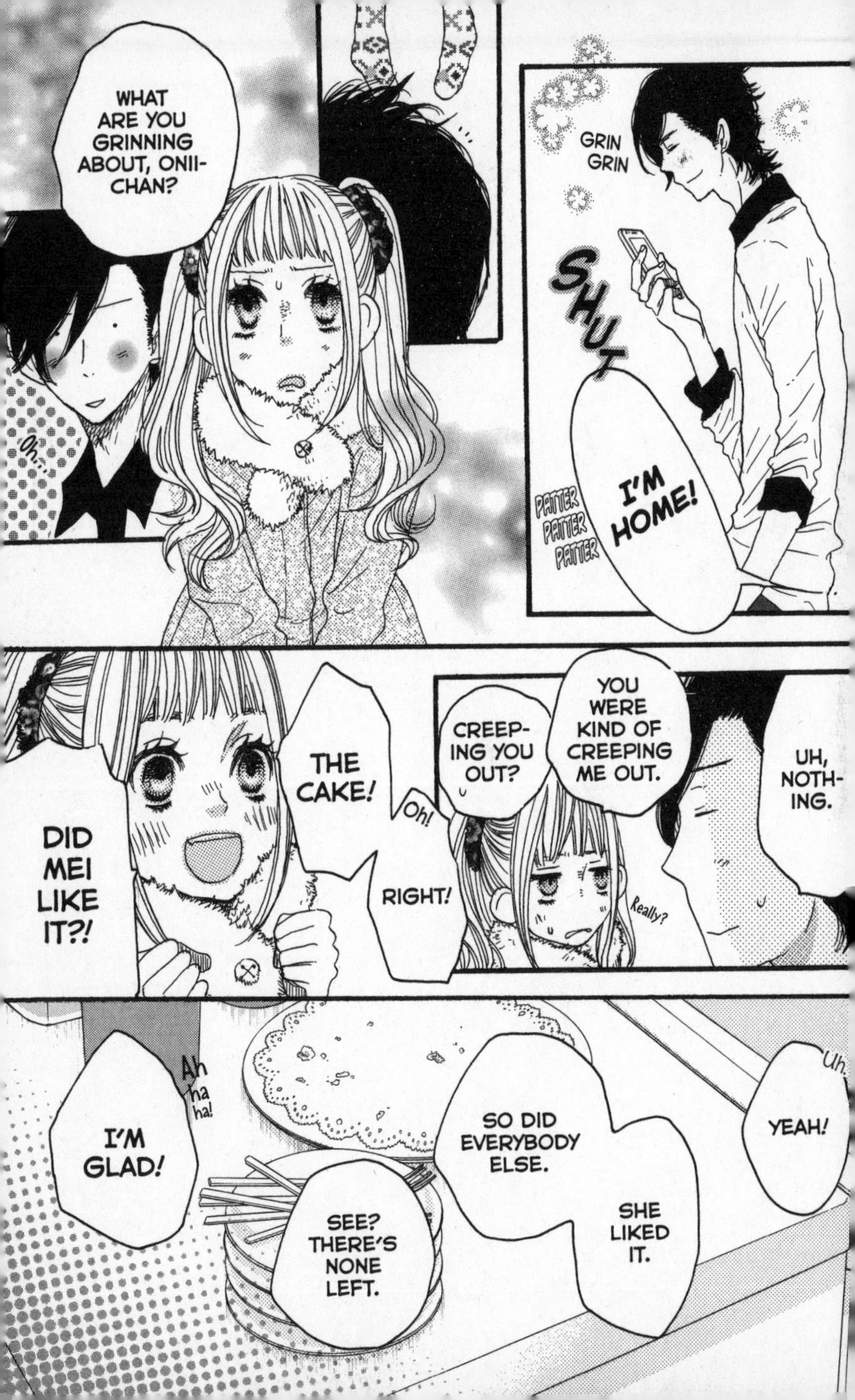
GRIN GRIN
SHUT
I'M HOME!
PATTER PATTER PATTER
WHAT ARE YOU GRINNING ABOUT, ONII-CHAN?
Oh...
UH, NOTHING.
YOU WERE KIND OF CREEPING ME OUT.
CREEPING YOU OUT?
Really?
Oh!
THE CAKE!
RIGHT!
DID MEI LIKE IT?!
Uh
YEAH!
SHE LIKED IT.
SO DID EVERYBODY ELSE.
SEE? THERE'S NONE LEFT.
I'M GLAD!
Ah ha ha!

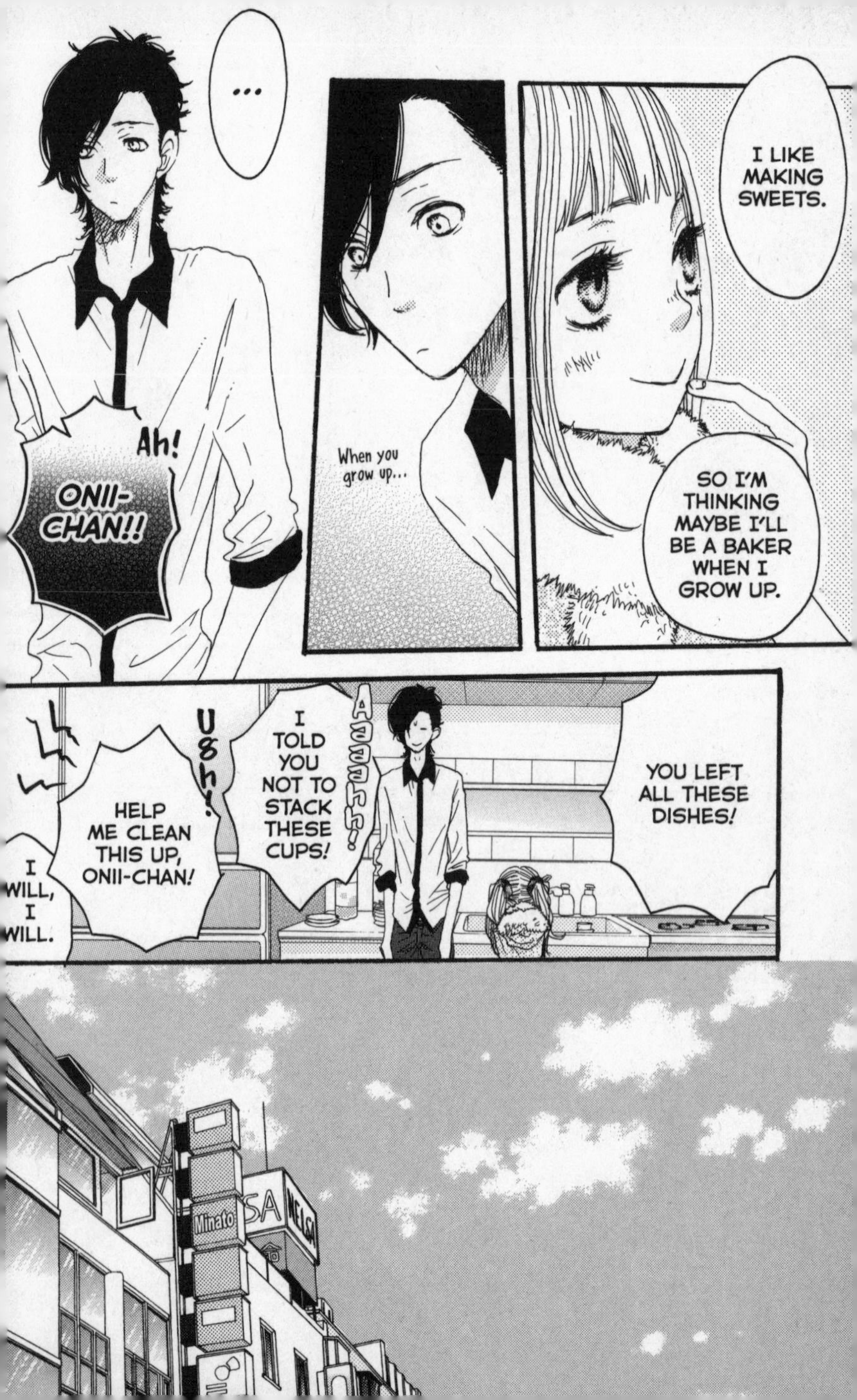

I LIKE MAKING SWEETS.
SO I'M THINKING MAYBE I'LL BE A BAKER WHEN I GROW UP.
When you grow up...
...
Ah!
ONII-CHAN!!
YOU LEFT ALL THESE DISHES!
Aaaahh!
I TOLD YOU NOT TO STACK THESE CUPS!
Ugh!
HELP ME CLEAN THIS UP, ONII-CHAN!
I WILL, I WILL.
Minato

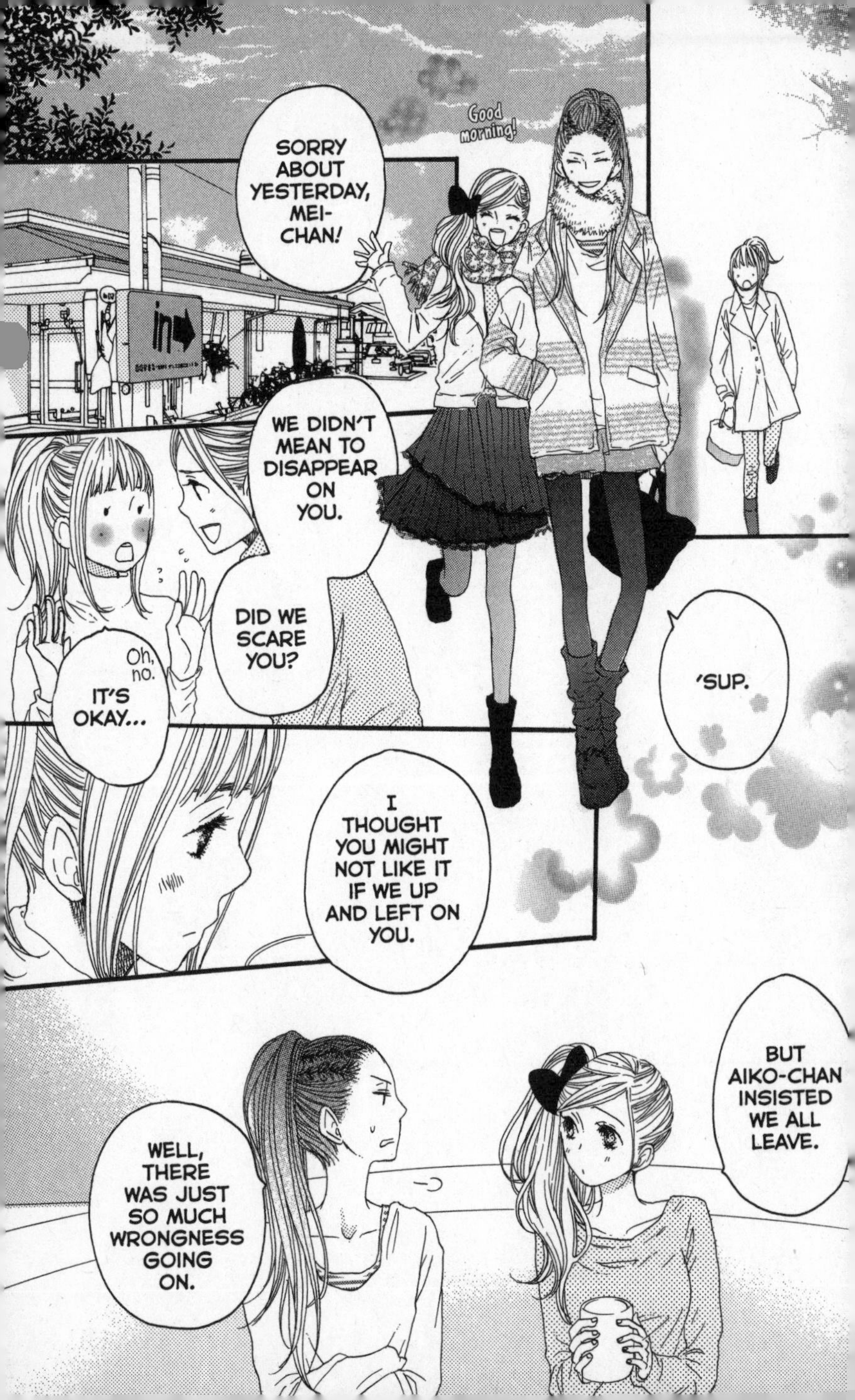

Good morning!
SORRY ABOUT YESTERDAY, MEI-CHAN!
in
'SUP.
WE DIDN'T MEAN TO DISAPPEAR ON YOU.
DID WE SCARE YOU?
Oh, no.
IT'S OKAY...
I THOUGHT YOU MIGHT NOT LIKE IT IF WE UP AND LEFT ON YOU.
BUT AIKO-CHAN INSISTED WE ALL LEAVE.
WELL, THERE WAS JUST SO MUCH WRONGNESS GOING ON.

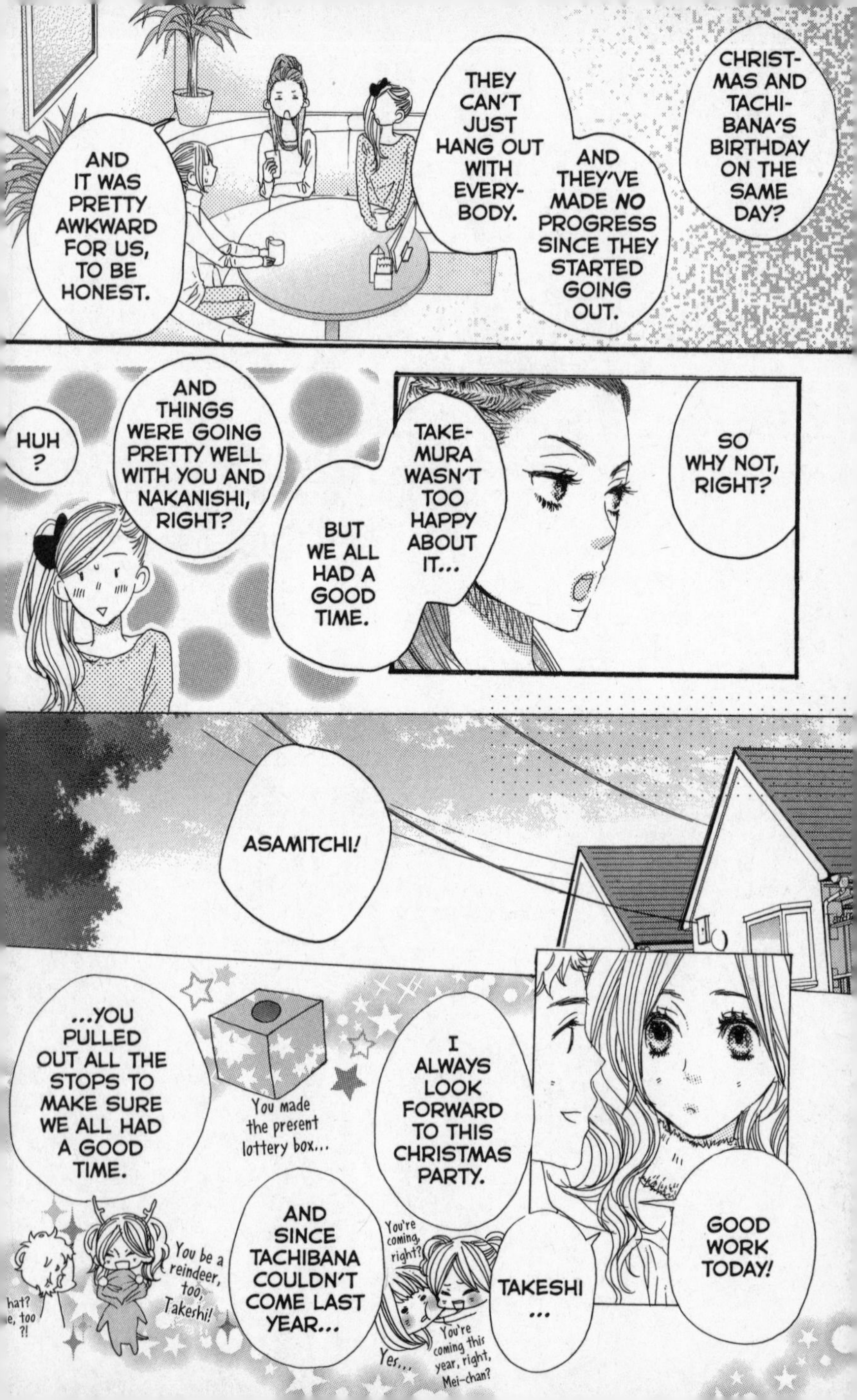
CHRISTMAS AND TACHIBANA'S BIRTHDAY ON THE SAME DAY?
THEY CAN'T JUST HANG OUT WITH EVERYBODY.
AND THEY'VE MADE *NO* PROGRESS SINCE THEY STARTED GOING OUT.
AND IT WAS PRETTY AWKWARD FOR US, TO BE HONEST.
SO WHY NOT, RIGHT?
TAKEMURA WASN'T TOO HAPPY ABOUT IT...
BUT WE ALL HAD A GOOD TIME.
AND THINGS WERE GOING PRETTY WELL WITH YOU AND NAKANISHI, RIGHT?
HUH?
ASAMITCHI!
GOOD WORK TODAY!
TAKESHI...
I ALWAYS LOOK FORWARD TO THIS CHRISTMAS PARTY.
...YOU PULLED OUT ALL THE STOPS TO MAKE SURE WE ALL HAD A GOOD TIME.
You made the present lottery box...
AND SINCE TACHIBANA COULDN'T COME LAST YEAR...
You're coming, right?
You're coming this year, right, Mei-chan?
Yes...
You be a reindeer, too, Takeshi!

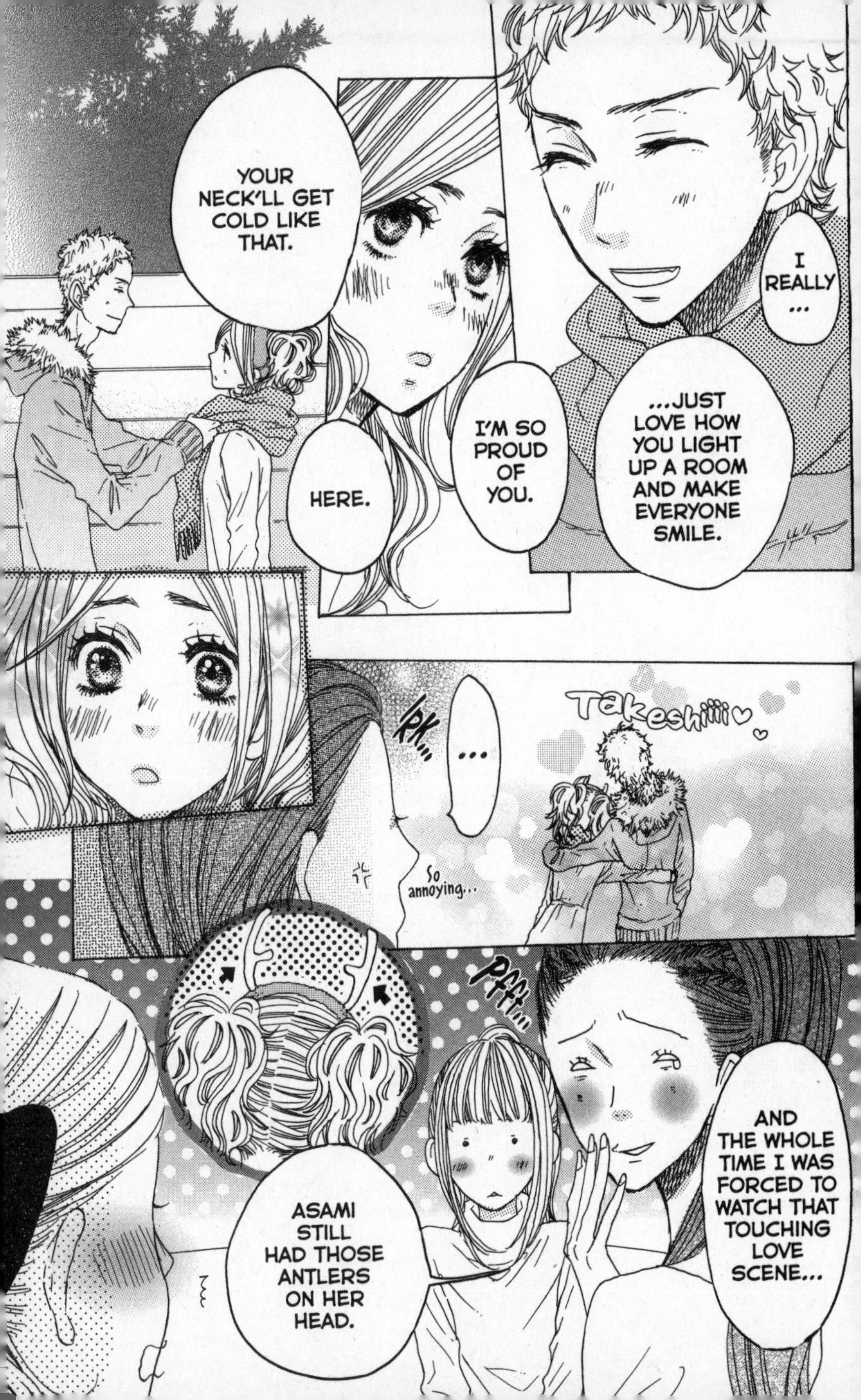
I REALLY...
...JUST LOVE HOW YOU LIGHT UP A ROOM AND MAKE EVERYONE SMILE.
I'M SO PROUD OF YOU.
YOUR NECK'LL GET COLD LIKE THAT.
HERE.
Takeshiiii♥
...
IRK...
So annoying...
AND THE WHOLE TIME I WAS FORCED TO WATCH THAT TOUCHING LOVE SCENE...
Pfft...
ASAMI STILL HAD THOSE ANTLERS ON HER HEAD.

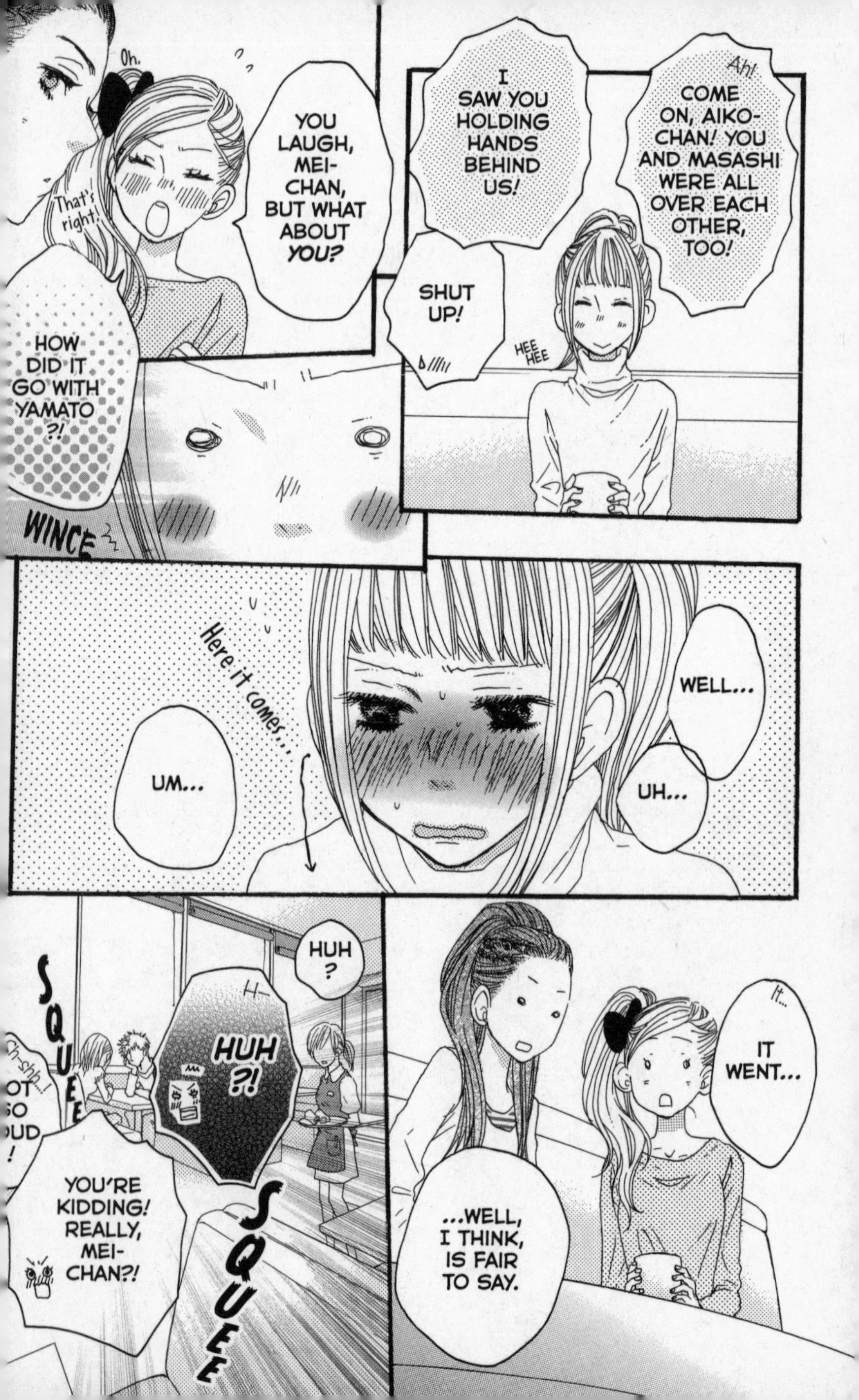
Ah!
COME ON, AIKO-CHAN! YOU AND MASASHI WERE ALL OVER EACH OTHER, TOO!
I SAW YOU HOLDING HANDS BEHIND US!
SHUT UP!
HEE HEE
Oh.
YOU LAUGH, MEI-CHAN, BUT WHAT ABOUT YOU?
That's right!
HOW DID IT GO WITH YAMATO?!
WINCE
WELL...
UH...
Here it comes...
UM...
It...
IT WENT...
...WELL, I THINK, IS FAIR TO SAY.
HUH?
HUH?!
SQUEE
ch-shh..!
OT SO OUD!
YOU'RE KIDDING! REALLY, MEI-CHAN?!
SQUEE

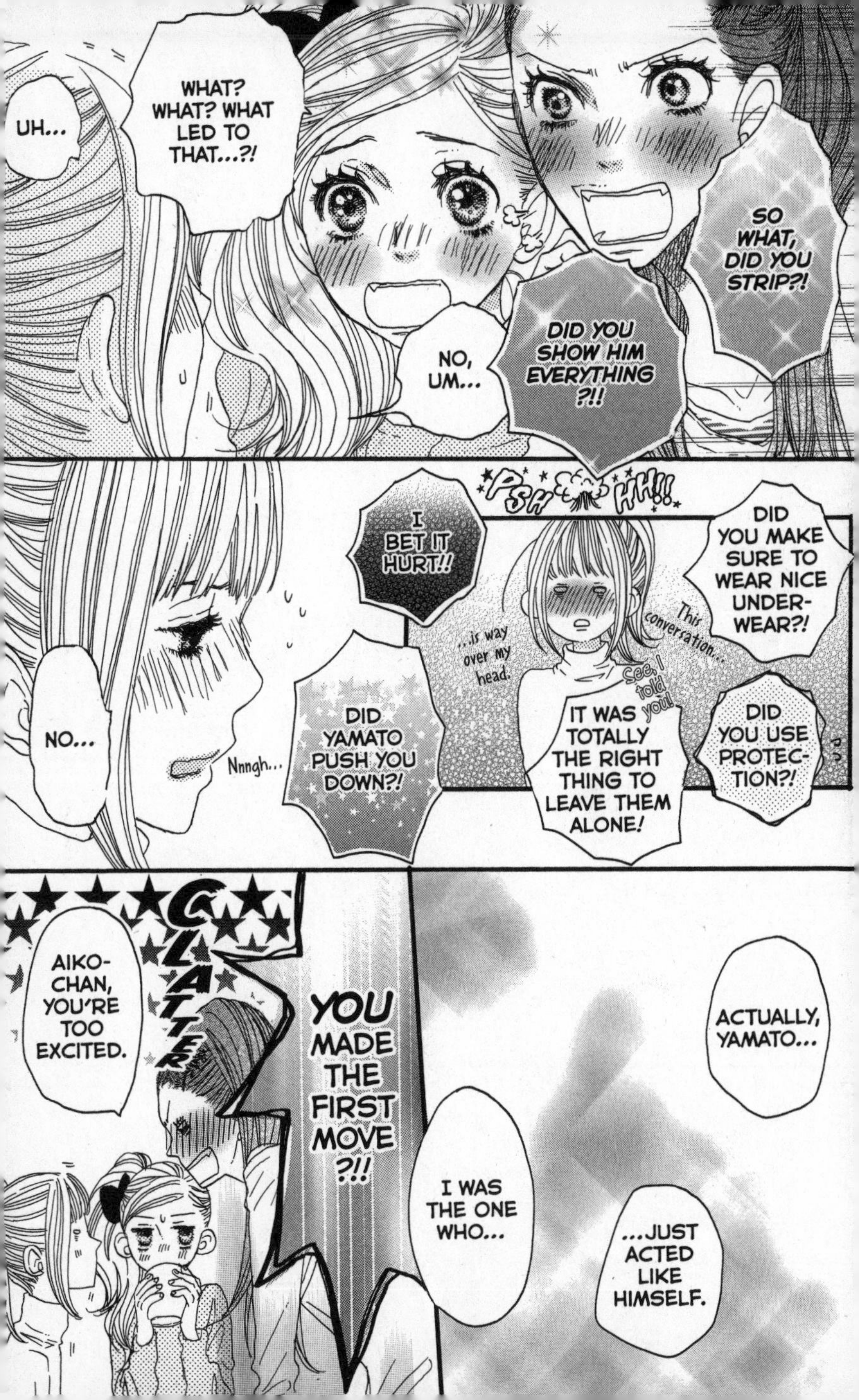
SO WHAT, DID YOU STRIP?!
DID YOU SHOW HIM EVERYTHING?!!
WHAT? WHAT? WHAT LED TO THAT...?!
NO, UM...
UH...
PSH HH!!
DID YOU MAKE SURE TO WEAR NICE UNDER-WEAR?!
This conversation...
...is way over my head.
DID YOU USE PROTEC-TION?!
See, I told you!
IT WAS TOTALLY THE RIGHT THING TO LEAVE THEM ALONE!
I BET IT HURT!!
DID YAMATO PUSH YOU DOWN?!
Nnngh...
NO...
ACTUALLY, YAMATO...
...JUST ACTED LIKE HIMSELF.
I WAS THE ONE WHO...
YOU MADE THE FIRST MOVE?!!
CLATTER
AIKO-CHAN, YOU'RE TOO EXCITED.

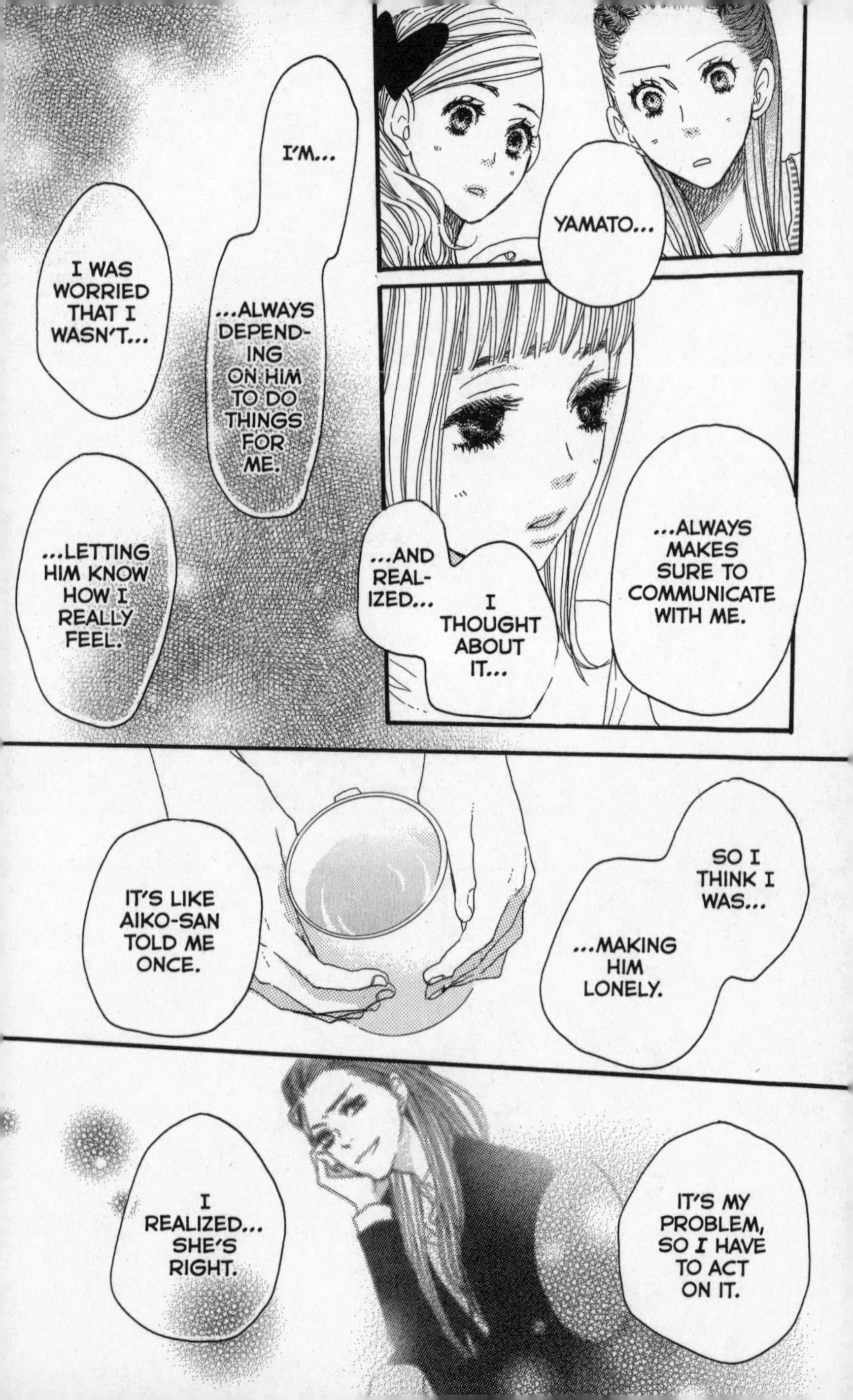
YAMATO...
...ALWAYS MAKES SURE TO COMMUNICATE WITH ME.
I THOUGHT ABOUT IT...
...AND REALIZED...
I'M...
...ALWAYS DEPENDING ON HIM TO DO THINGS FOR ME.
I WAS WORRIED THAT I WASN'T...
...LETTING HIM KNOW HOW I REALLY FEEL.
SO I THINK I WAS...
...MAKING HIM LONELY.
IT'S LIKE AIKO-SAN TOLD ME ONCE.
IT'S MY PROBLEM, SO *I* HAVE TO ACT ON IT.
I REALIZED... SHE'S RIGHT.

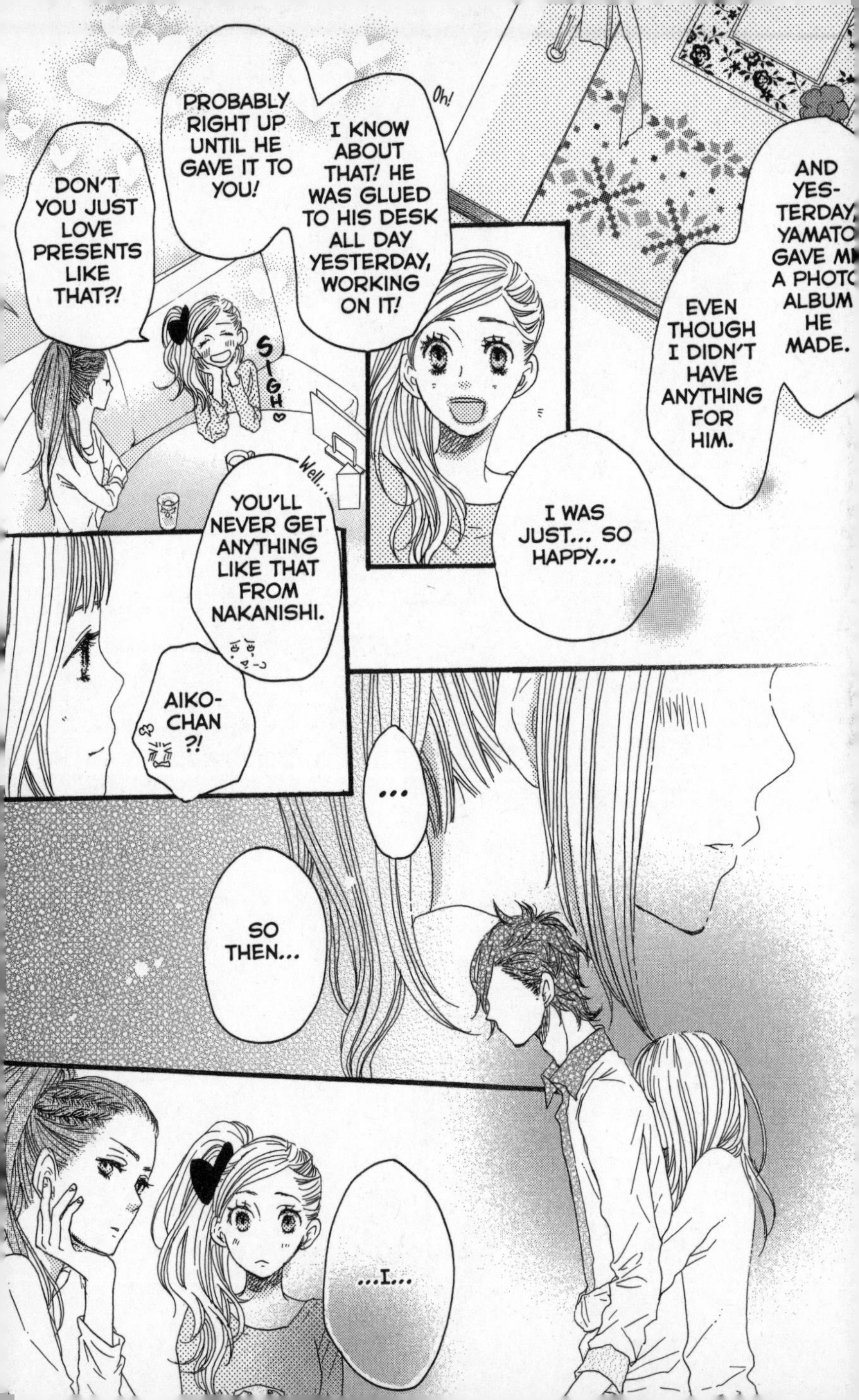
AND YES-TERDAY, YAMATO GAVE M A PHOTO ALBUM HE MADE.
EVEN THOUGH I DIDN'T HAVE ANYTHING FOR HIM.
I WAS JUST... SO HAPPY...
Oh!
I KNOW ABOUT THAT! HE WAS GLUED TO HIS DESK ALL DAY YESTERDAY, WORKING ON IT!
PROBABLY RIGHT UP UNTIL HE GAVE IT TO YOU!
SIGH
DON'T YOU JUST LOVE PRESENTS LIKE THAT?!
Well...
YOU'LL NEVER GET ANYTHING LIKE THAT FROM NAKANISHI.
AIKO-CHAN?!
...
SO THEN...
...I...

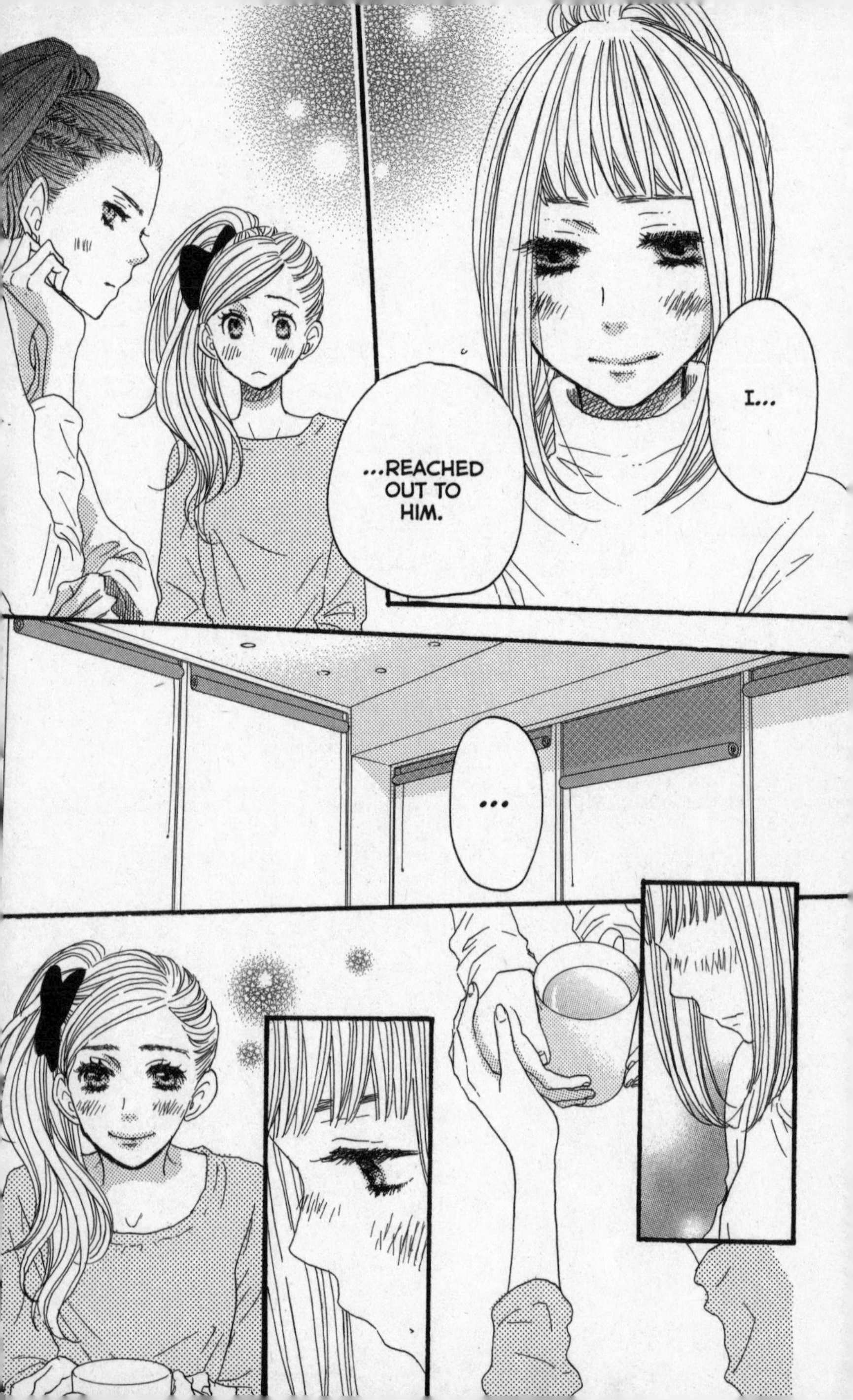
I...
...REACHED OUT TO HIM.
...

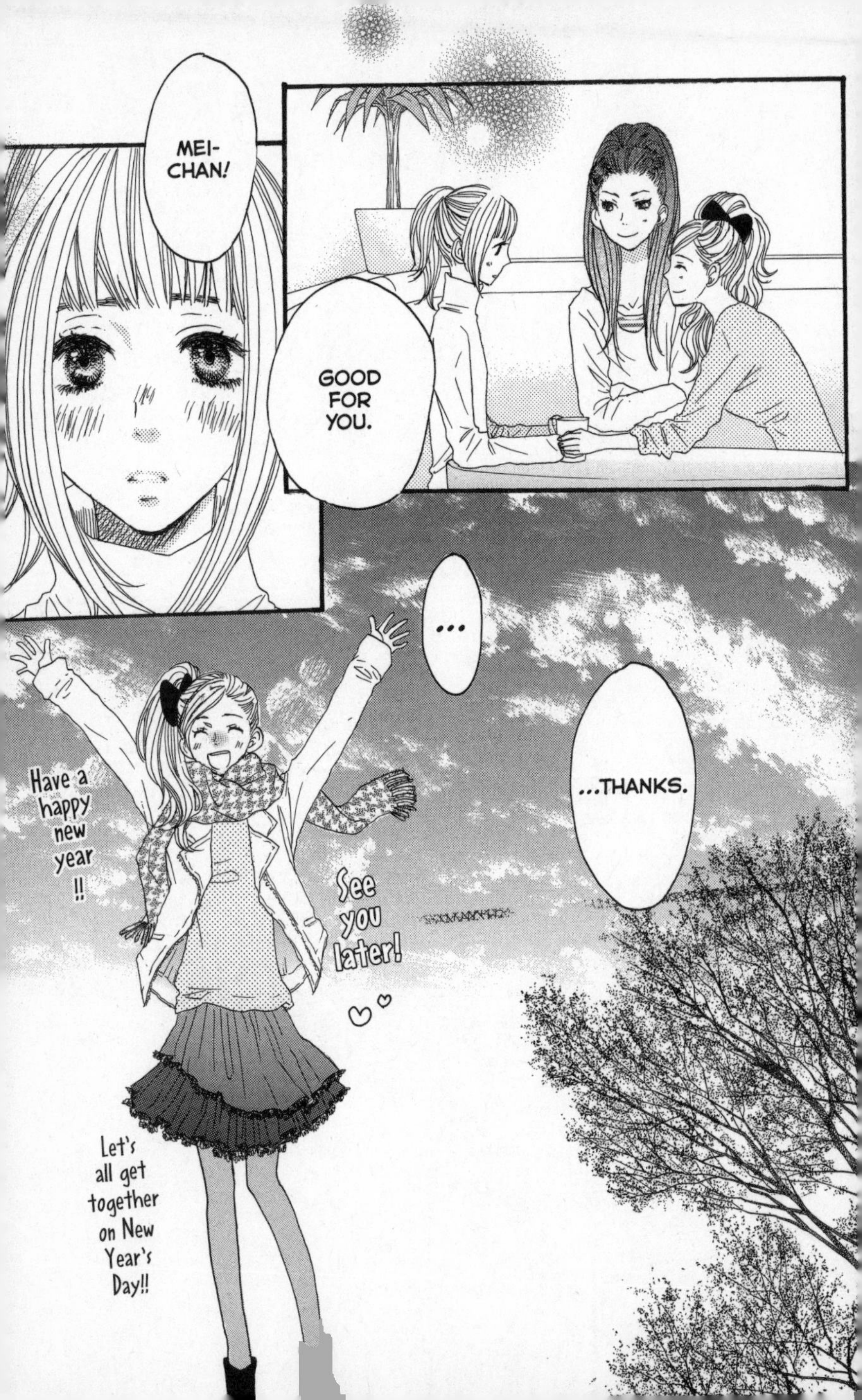
MEI-CHAN!
GOOD FOR YOU.
...
...THANKS.
See you later!
Have a happy new year !!
Let's all get together on New Year's Day!!

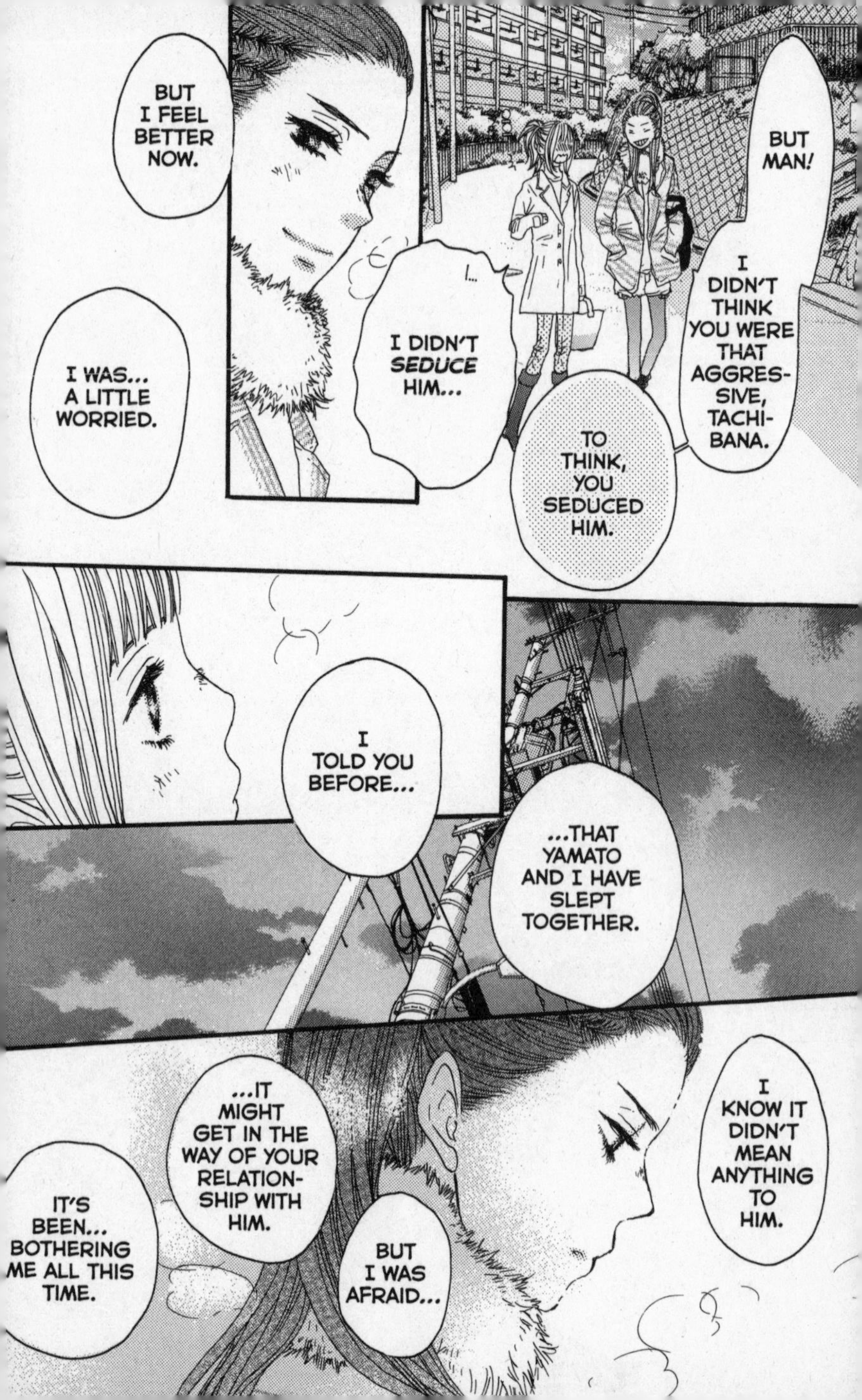
BUT MAN!
I DIDN'T THINK YOU WERE THAT AGGRES-SIVE, TACHI-BANA.
TO THINK, YOU SEDUCED HIM.
I...
I DIDN'T *SEDUCE* HIM...
BUT I FEEL BETTER NOW.
I WAS... A LITTLE WORRIED.
I TOLD YOU BEFORE...
...THAT YAMATO AND I HAVE SLEPT TOGETHER.
I KNOW IT DIDN'T MEAN ANYTHING TO HIM.
BUT I WAS AFRAID...
...IT MIGHT GET IN THE WAY OF YOUR RELATION-SHIP WITH HIM.
IT'S BEEN... BOTHERING ME ALL THIS TIME.

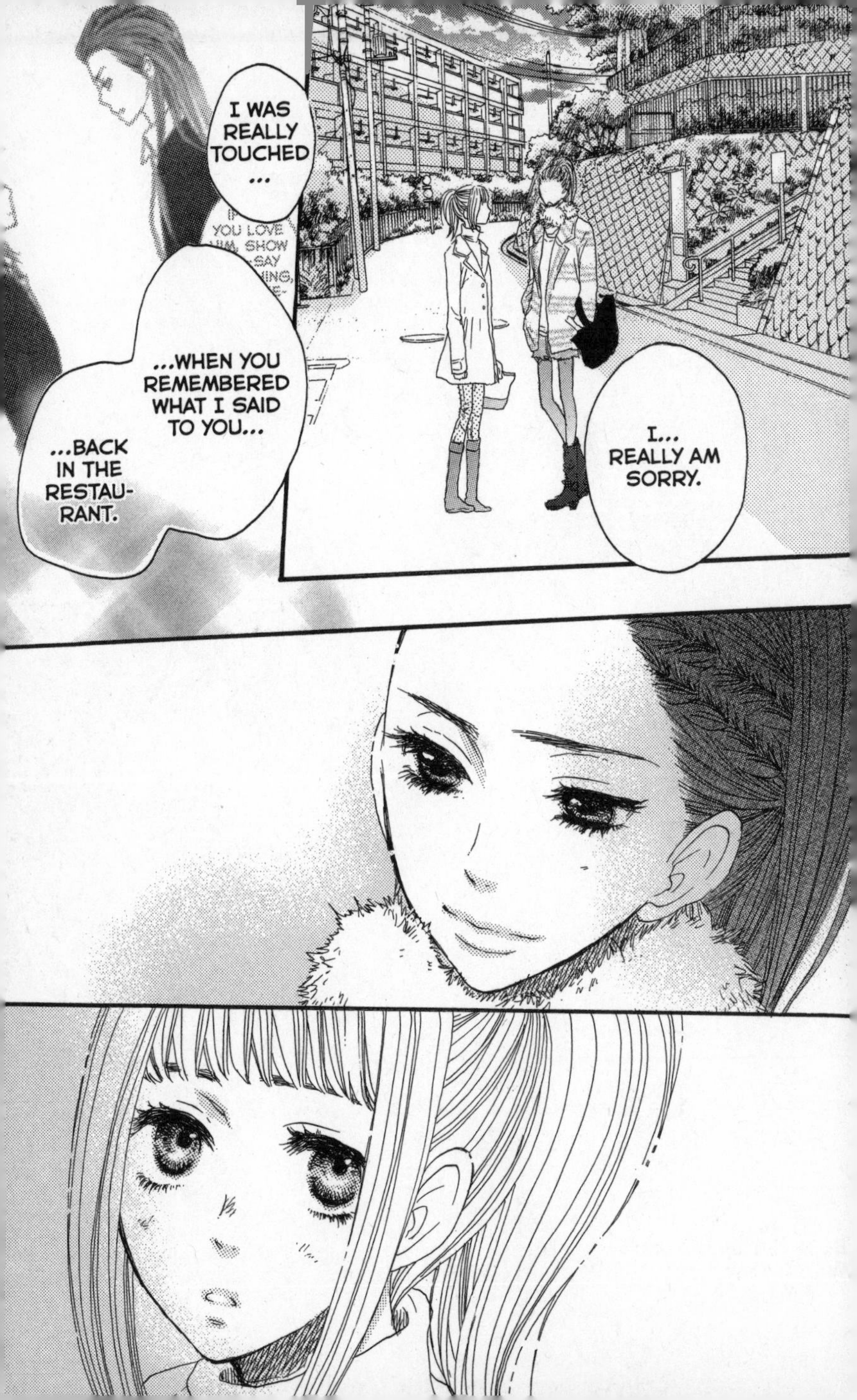
I... REALLY AM SORRY.
I WAS REALLY TOUCHED...
...WHEN YOU REMEMBERED WHAT I SAID TO YOU...
...BACK IN THE RESTAURANT.

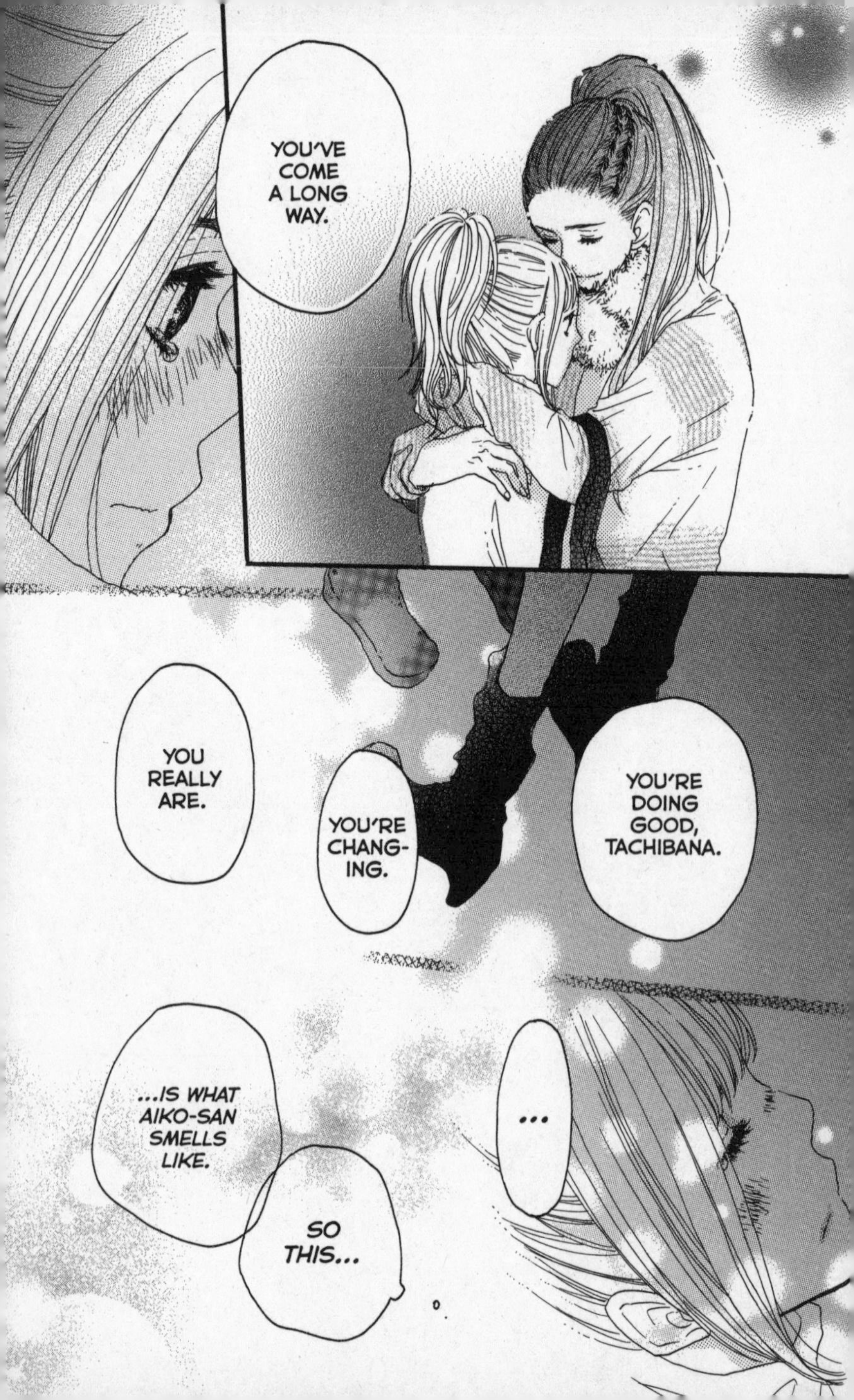
YOU'VE COME A LONG WAY.
YOU'RE DOING GOOD, TACHIBANA.
YOU'RE CHANGING.
YOU REALLY ARE.
...
SO THIS...
...IS WHAT AIKO-SAN SMELLS LIKE.

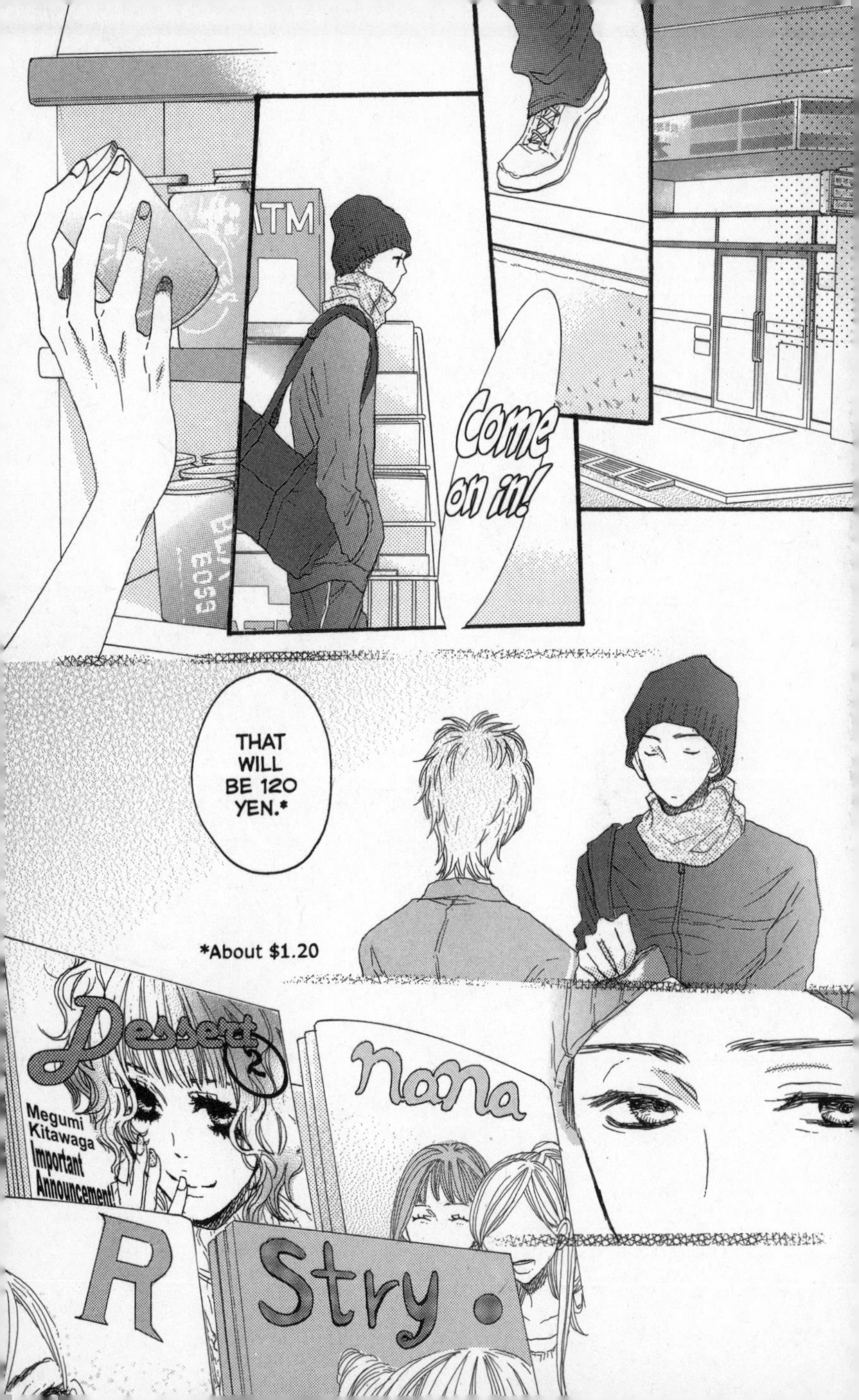
Come on in!
THAT WILL BE 120 YEN.*
*About $1.20
Dessert 2
Megumi Kitawaga
Important Announcement!
nana
R
Stry

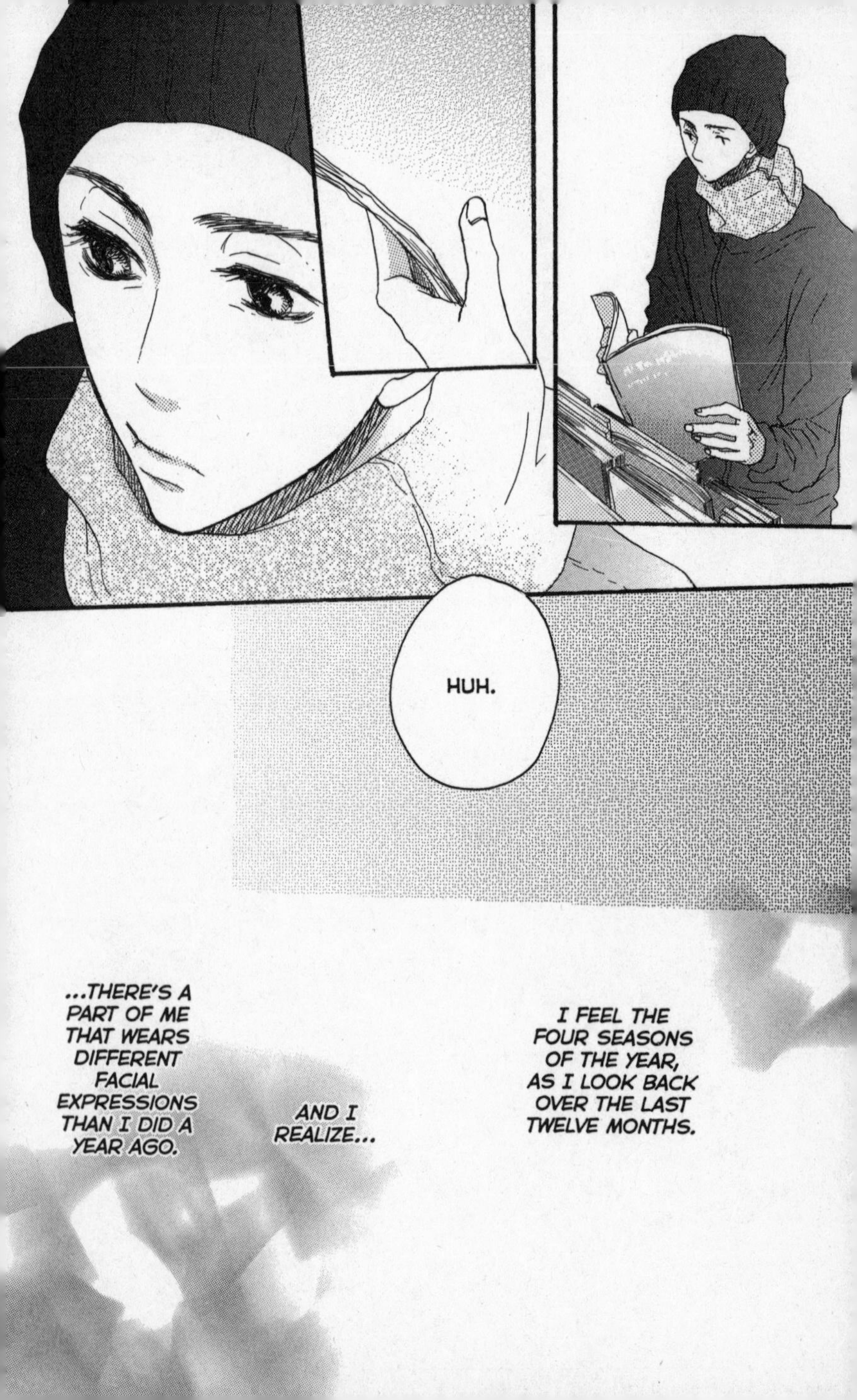
HUH.
I FEEL THE FOUR SEASONS OF THE YEAR, AS I LOOK BACK OVER THE LAST TWELVE MONTHS.
AND I REALIZE...
...THERE'S A PART OF ME THAT WEARS DIFFERENT FACIAL EXPRESSIONS THAN I DID A YEAR AGO.

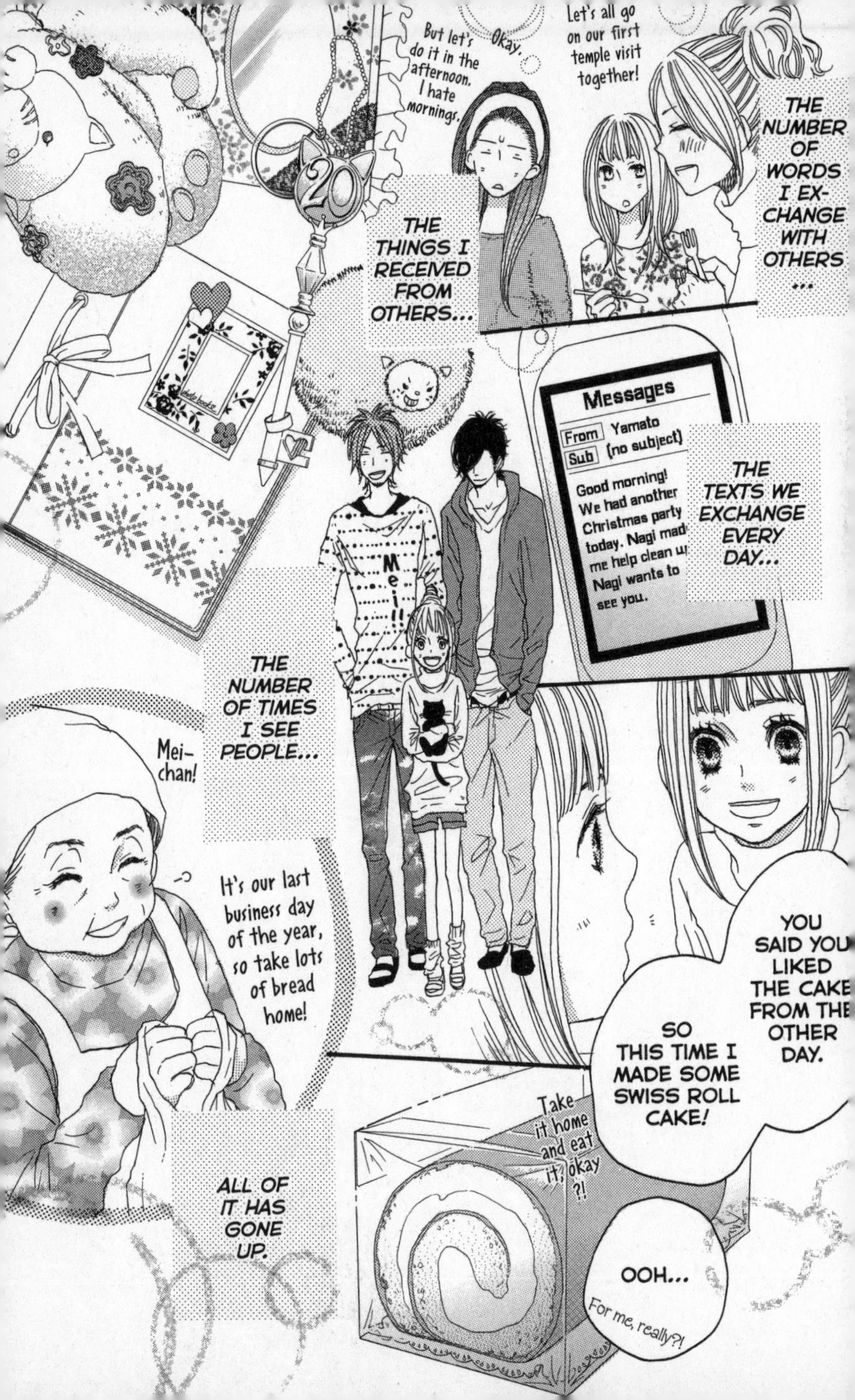
THE NUMBER OF WORDS I EXCHANGE WITH OTHERS...
Let's all go on our first temple visit together!
Okay.
But let's do it in the afternoon. I hate mornings.
THE THINGS I RECEIVED FROM OTHERS...
Messages
From Yamato
Sub (no subject)
Good morning! We had another Christmas party today. Nagi mad me help clean u Nagi wants to see you.
THE TEXTS WE EXCHANGE EVERY DAY...
Mei!!
THE NUMBER OF TIMES I SEE PEOPLE...
Mei-chan!
It's our last business day of the year, so take lots of bread home!
YOU SAID YOU LIKED THE CAKE FROM THE OTHER DAY.
SO THIS TIME I MADE SOME SWISS ROLL CAKE!
Take it home and eat it, okay?!
OOH...
For me, really?!
ALL OF IT HAS GONE UP.

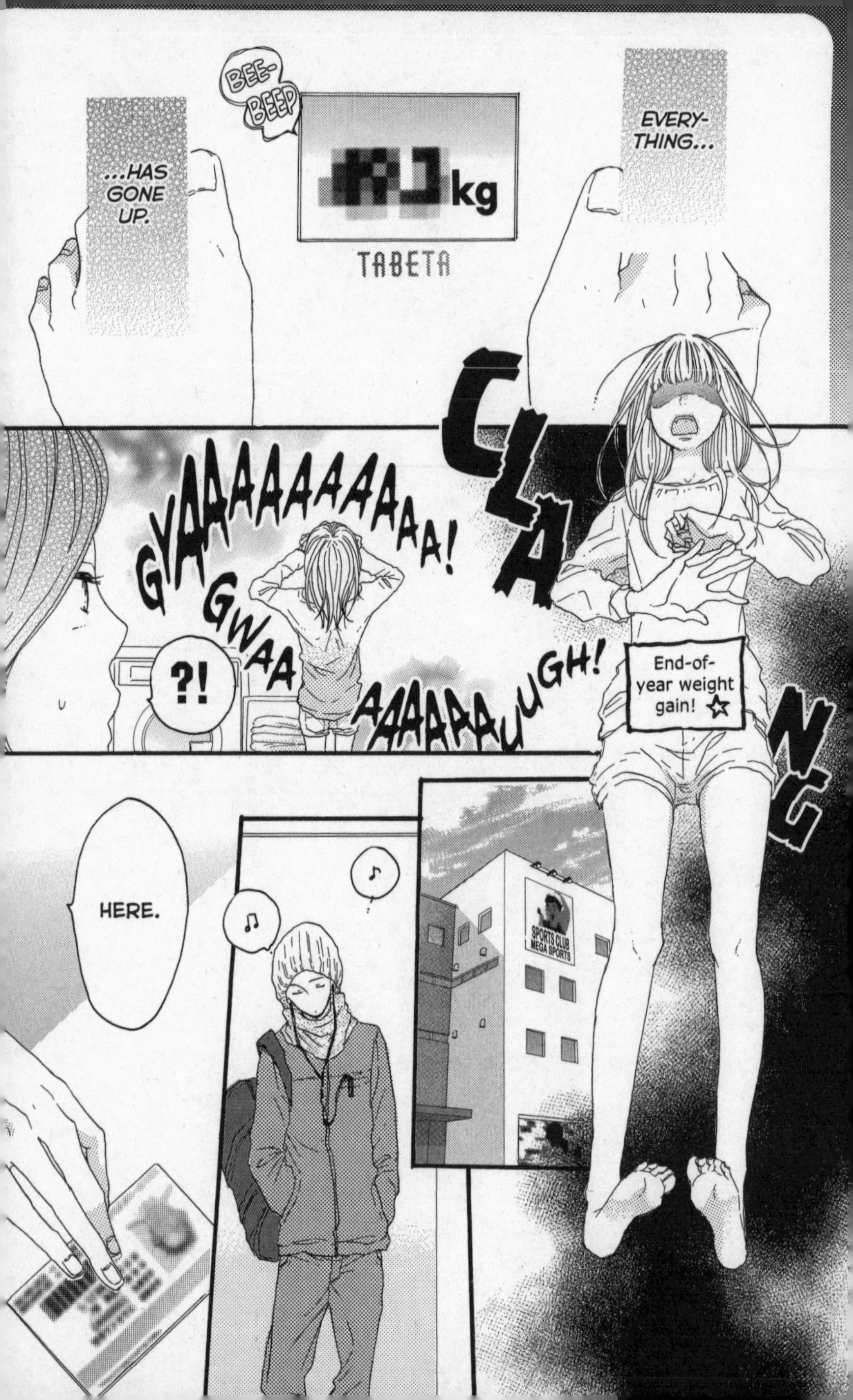
EVERY-THING...
BEE-BEEP
kg
TABETA
...HAS GONE UP.
CLANG
End-of-year weight gain! ☆
GYAAAAAAAAAAAA!
?!
GWAAAAAAAAAUUGH!
SPORTS CLUB MEGA SPORTS
♪
♫
HERE.

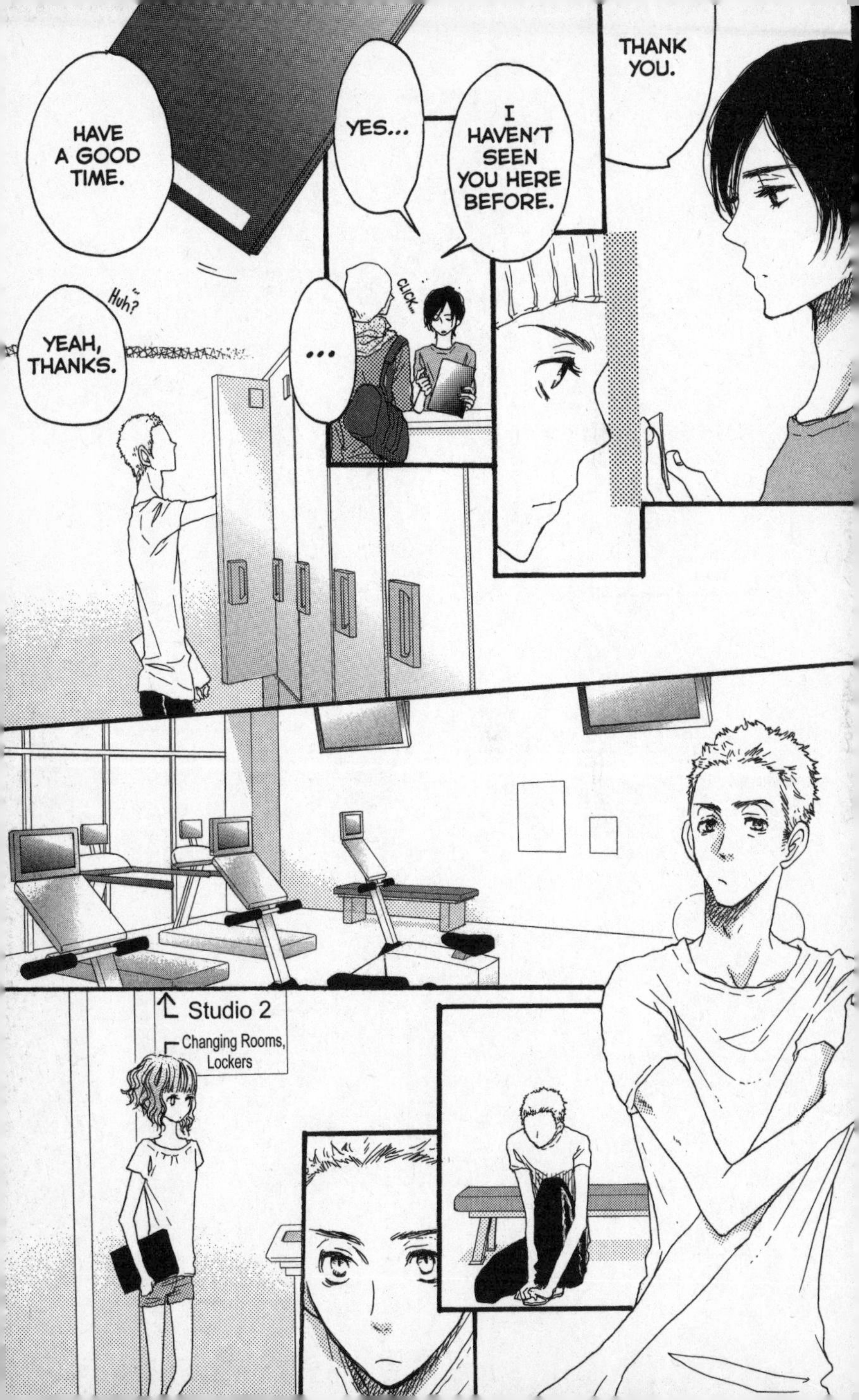
THANK YOU.
I HAVEN'T SEEN YOU HERE BEFORE.
YES...
...
CLICK...
HAVE A GOOD TIME.
Huh?
YEAH, THANKS.
Studio 2
Changing Rooms, Lockers

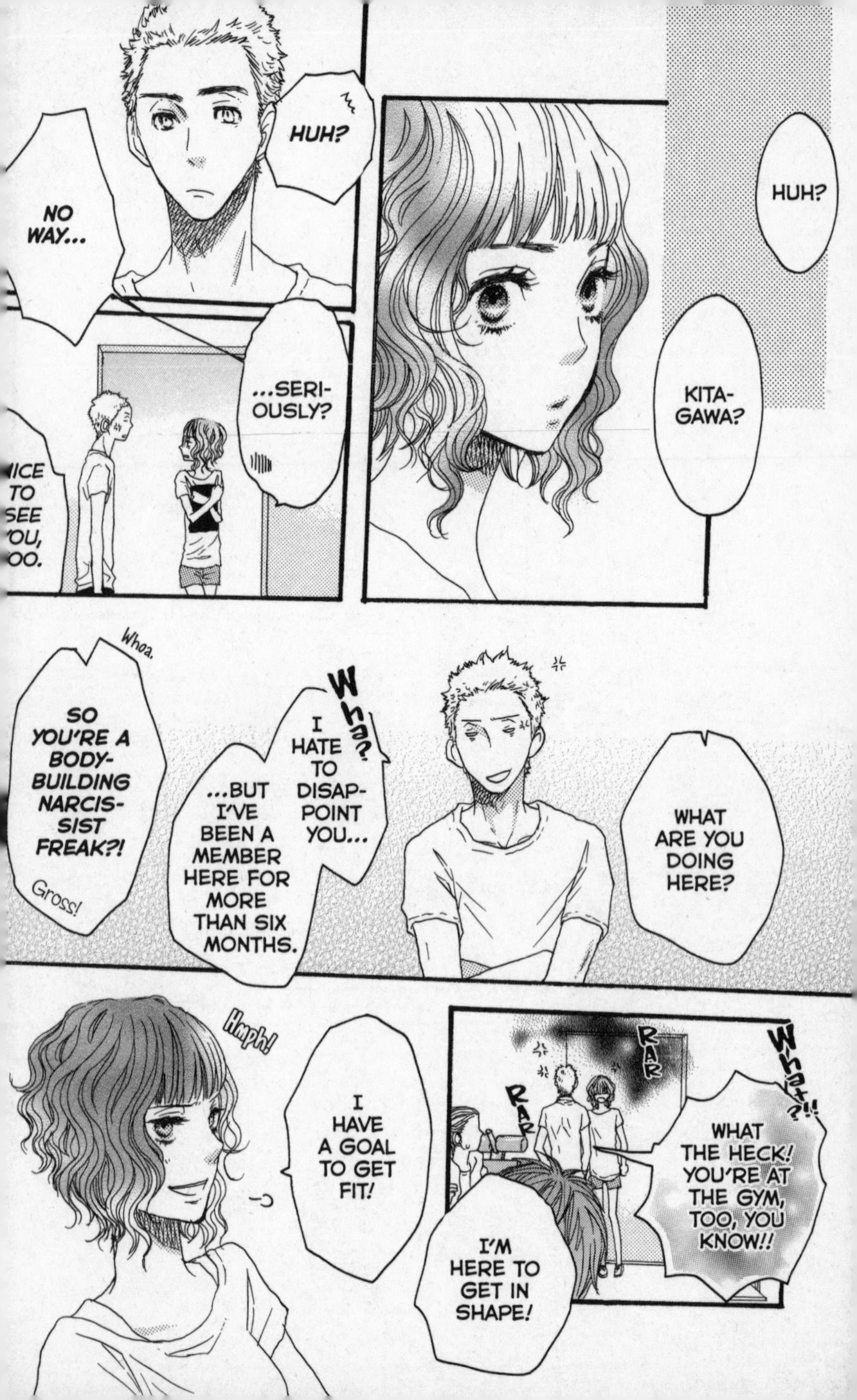
HUH?
KITA-GAWA?
HUH?
NO WAY...
...SERI-OUSLY?
NICE TO SEE YOU, TOO.
WHAT ARE YOU DOING HERE?
I HATE TO DISAP-POINT YOU...
Wha?
...BUT I'VE BEEN A MEMBER HERE FOR MORE THAN SIX MONTHS.
Whoa.
SO YOU'RE A BODY-BUILDING NARCIS-SIST FREAK?!
Gross!
What?!!
WHAT THE HECK! YOU'RE AT THE GYM, TOO, YOU KNOW!!
RAR
RAR
I'M HERE TO GET IN SHAPE!
Hmph!
I HAVE A GOAL TO GET FIT!

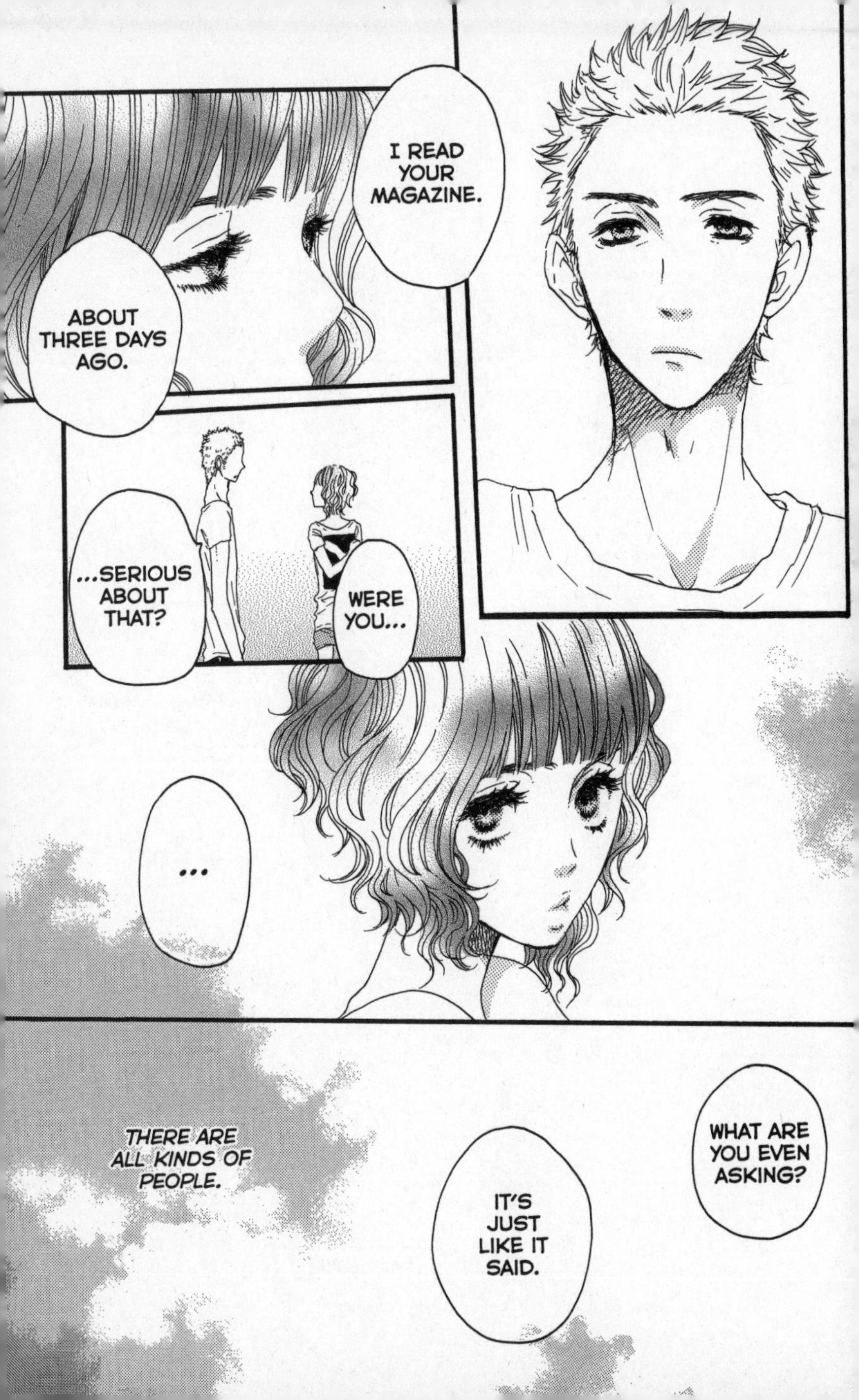

I READ YOUR MAGAZINE.
ABOUT THREE DAYS AGO.
WERE YOU...
...SERIOUS ABOUT THAT?
...
WHAT ARE YOU EVEN ASKING?
IT'S JUST LIKE IT SAID.
THERE ARE ALL KINDS OF PEOPLE.

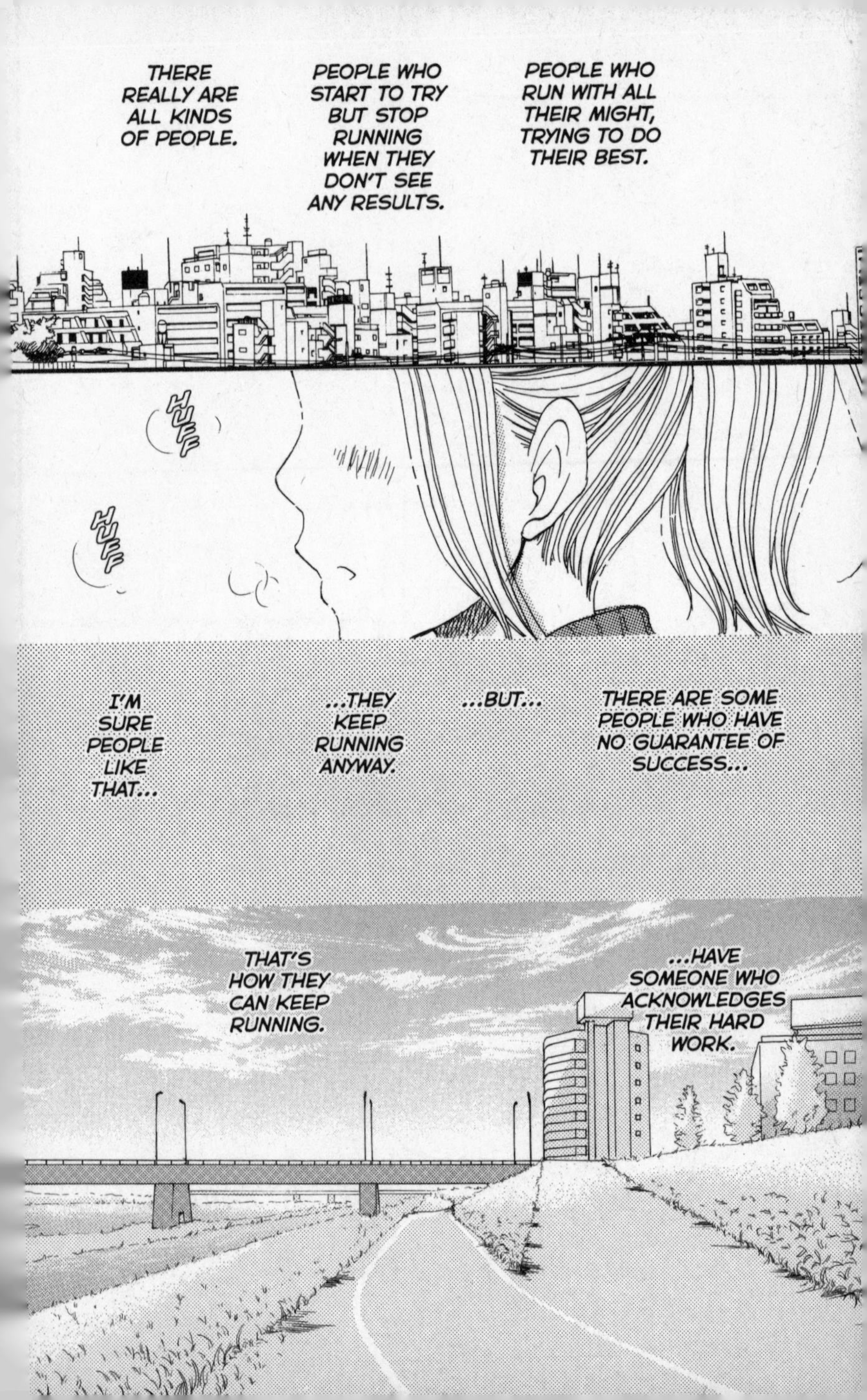
PEOPLE WHO RUN WITH ALL THEIR MIGHT, TRYING TO DO THEIR BEST.
PEOPLE WHO START TO TRY BUT STOP RUNNING WHEN THEY DON'T SEE ANY RESULTS.
THERE REALLY ARE ALL KINDS OF PEOPLE.
HUFF
HUFF
THERE ARE SOME PEOPLE WHO HAVE NO GUARANTEE OF SUCCESS...
...BUT...
...THEY KEEP RUNNING ANYWAY.
I'M SURE PEOPLE LIKE THAT...
...HAVE SOMEONE WHO ACKNOWLEDGES THEIR HARD WORK.
THAT'S HOW THEY CAN KEEP RUNNING.

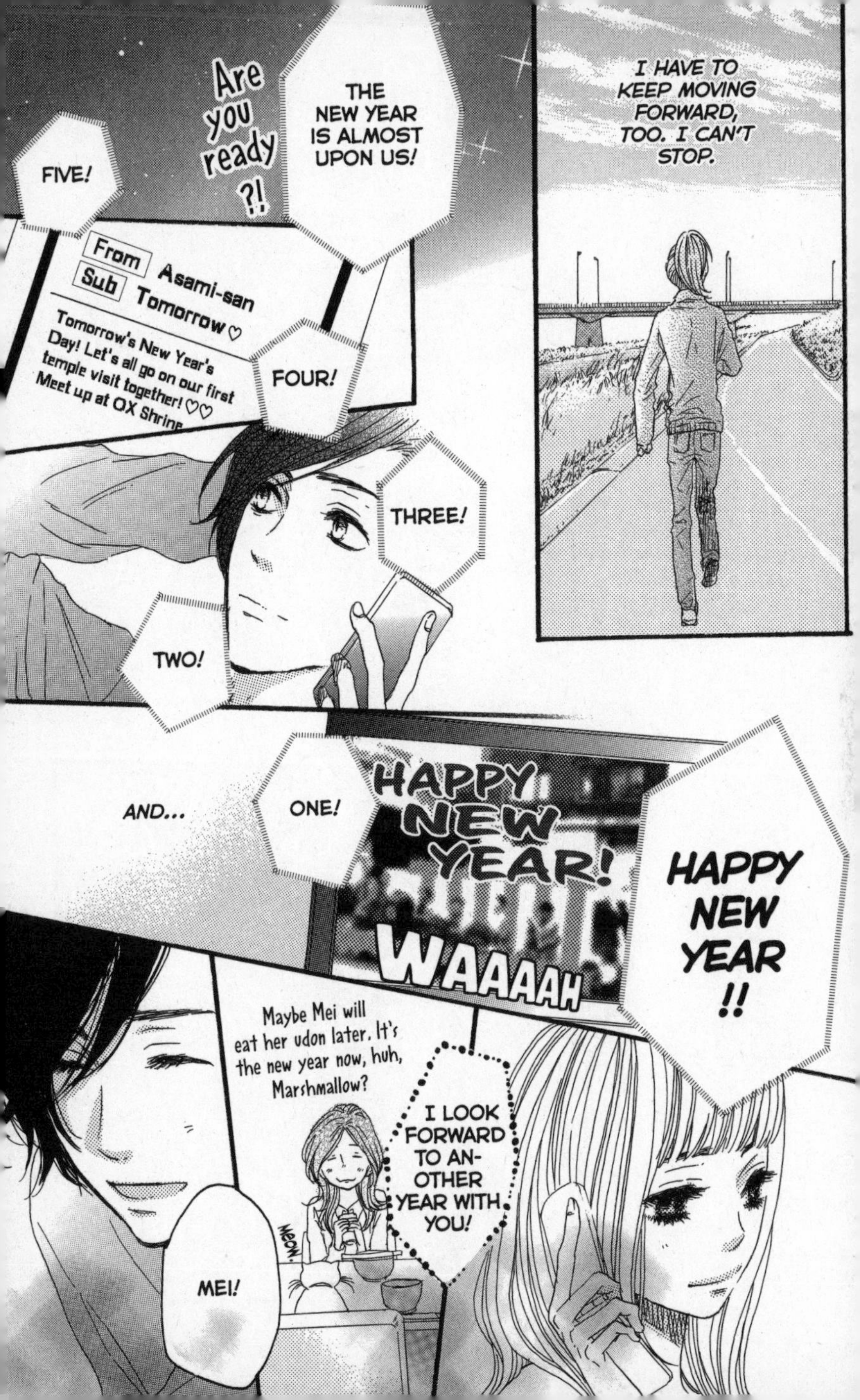
I HAVE TO KEEP MOVING FORWARD, TOO. I CAN'T STOP.
THE NEW YEAR IS ALMOST UPON US!
Are you ready ?!
FIVE!
From Asami-san
Sub Tomorrow ♡
Tomorrow's New Year's Day! Let's all go on our first temple visit together! ♡♡ Meet up at OX Shrine
FOUR!
THREE!
TWO!
HAPPY NEW YEAR !!
HAPPY NEW YEAR!
WAAAAH
ONE!
AND...
I LOOK FORWARD TO AN-OTHER YEAR WITH YOU!
Maybe Mei will eat her udon later. It's the new year now, huh, Marshmallow?
MEOW
MEI!

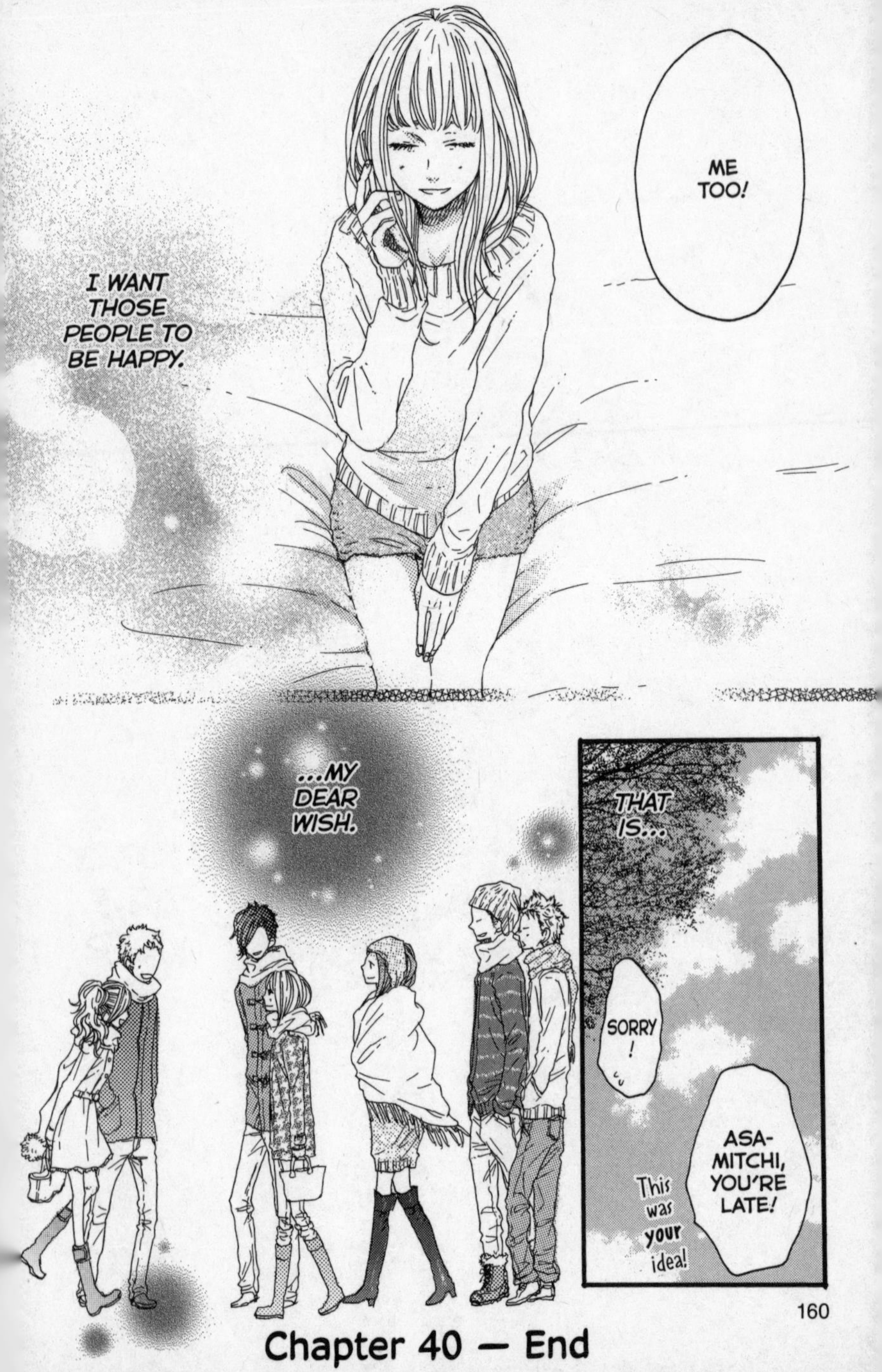
ME TOO!
I WANT THOSE PEOPLE TO BE HAPPY.
THAT IS...
ASA-MITCHI, YOU'RE LATE!
This was **your** idea!
SORRY!
...MY DEAR WISH.

Chapter 40 — End

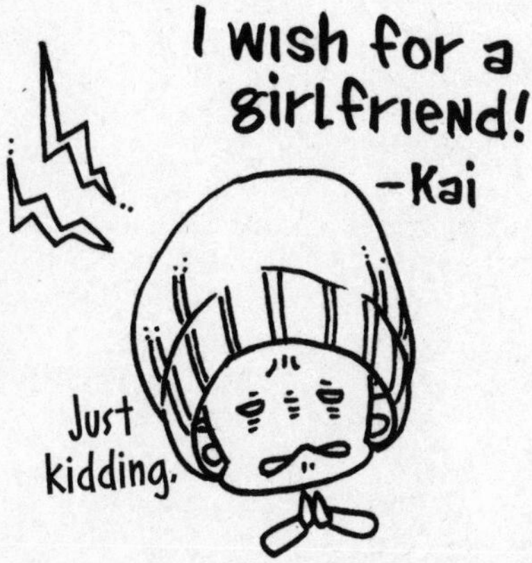
I wish for a girlfriend!
-Kai
Just kidding.

Hello, I'm Kanae Hazuki. We made it to volume ten. We're in the double digits now!

Last October, the anime started, and I was in so much awe of what was going on that the next thing I knew, it was the middle of winter! The anime...

They came to me with the idea a year before the anime was broadcast. I remember my first meeting with the director and the production staff like it was yesterday. For my part, I requested that they take care with the ambiance and timing, and with words. The director understood me right away, and I saw him again at the voice recordings after production started, and we talked. He understood *Say I Love You* more than I thought, so I was assured that I could trust Director Sato.

The sound director, Aketagawa-san, put such detailed sound into the animated pictures. Every time I watched him direct the voice actors, I thought, "He is a sound pro!"

And all of the voice actors took time out of their busy schedules to come to the studio and give such passionate performances, breathing life into the characters in the form of their voices. Just listening to them made me tear up every time. I was so excited to go to the recordings every week that I could hardly stand it.

And the opening and ending themes. Unfortunately, it's no longer possible for me to meet Okazaki-san, but it was her song that was provided for the opening song, and I was reminded that good music never fades over time. I think it really did work as the opening song, and it really enhanced the feeling of the opening sequence. And Suneohair-san, who wrote the ending theme, "Slow Dance," read the manga before he wrote the lyrics. I've always loved Suneohair-san's songs, so I was really very happy to hear that.

The *Love You* anime was created through the hard work of all these various professionals. And because the anime staff was so careful to maintain the nuance of the manga, I cried so often when I watched it. I've gotten many, many kind words from all the readers who watched it, too. I have only words of gratitude for everyone who helped make the anime, and everyone who watched it.

The anime is over now, but Mei and Yamato's story has a long way to go, so I hope you'll keep watching over them.

Now, this volume. Last time, I said Mei and Yamato would make progress, *and they did!!!!* Kanae Hazuki is a woman of her word, haha. I wasn't really confident about it, but it worked out... right? ^_^

The Christmas story turned out to be pretty long, but it was a really big event for Mei, so I couldn't leave anything out. If I couldn't draw it just the way I wanted, I didn't want to draw it at all. That sounds really cool, but I can only say it now that it's all over.

Before I started this series, I pretty much only did one-shots, so I guess I still have some of those habits. I would always try to cram a whole story—beginning, middle, conclusion—into 32 pages. So for this Christmas episode, at first, I thought about putting it all into one chapter. Before I started actually drawing, I was really worried. I kept thinking, "There's too much! What do I do? How do I fit it in?" But Shiigeru-san, my editor from Dessert, said, "It's an important event for Mei—for both of them—so I think it's okay to take it slow." Oh, how that one sentence made an impact and lifted the load off my chest. Thanks to Shiigeru-san's advice, I really was able to take it slow and draw all the characters and all the things that I wanted to draw, and it was a lot of fun.

This time, my theme was "thank you." The thank yous you say out loud, the thank yous you feel in your heart. All kinds of thank yous. The big thank you I feel more and more is for everyone involved with the animated series. These words don't come out of your mouth unless you're thinking of others. And I just—I wanted Mei to feel that in this volume. But I didn't want it to just be Mei's thank yous—I thought it would be nice if they all felt grateful to each other. I wanted to draw that kind, gentle atmosphere. And while I was drawing it, I kept thinking "thank you," too. I felt gratitude for my editor, who is always patient with my selfishness; my assistants, who help me with the manga; and the characters in the manga.

Lately, I really have felt gratitude for so many people whom I've met. I am extremely grateful that I can be placed in such an environment. Thinking back, I realize that my old self would only ever look at the bad things in people. Because it's easier for people to be impressed by the bad than the good. Especially because of my body, I always felt like people were talking about me behind my back. I think that's why I would always look for the faults in others. I didn't think about thank you as much as I do now. But now, it's the other way around, and I try to look at the good in people. I think it's a really good thing if you can see the good in someone, then spend some time with them and have fun and feel good about it. But, well, unfortunately, maybe some people just don't get along. But I'm trying to stop letting those people leave only a bad impression on me. Because I think I just wouldn't like to have too many bad impressions of people in my heart. I find the good in people, respect them, and appreciate them. I think that's all it takes for me to have a much easier life. I think some of you may be thinking, "Would you shut up about all this thank you and gratitude junk?!" ^_^

But nevertheless, thank you for reading.

TRANSLATION NOTES

Page 36: The kashiwa mochi duck

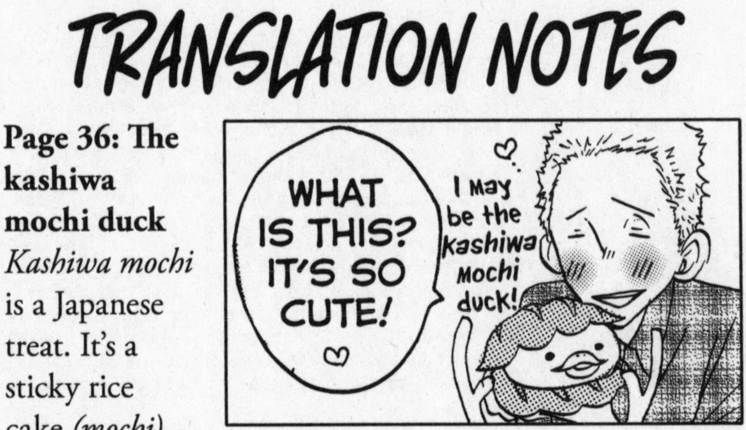
I may be the kashiwa mochi duck!
WHAT IS THIS? IT'S SO CUTE!

Kashiwa mochi is a Japanese treat. It's a sticky rice cake *(mochi)* wrapped in an oak *(kashiwa)* leaf. The duck seems uncertain of its identity because the Japanese word for duck *(kamo)* also means "maybe."

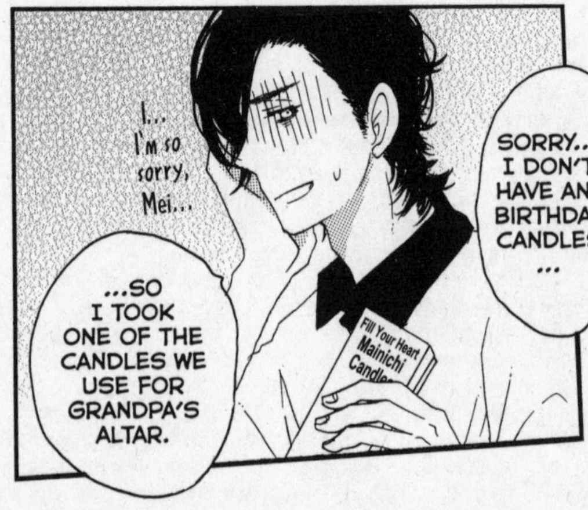
SORRY... I DON'T HAVE ANY BIRTHDAY CANDLES ...
I... I'm so sorry, Mei...
...SO I TOOK ONE OF THE CANDLES WE USE FOR GRANDPA'S ALTAR.
Fill Your Heart Mainichi Candle

Page 47: Grandpa's altar

Specifically, Yamato is referring to a *butsudan*, or Buddhist altar. This is basically a home shrine, with various items used for Buddhist worship and for remembering deceased relatives. Among these items are candles.

EVERY-
THING...
BEE-
BEEP
kg
TABETA
...HAS
GONE
UP.

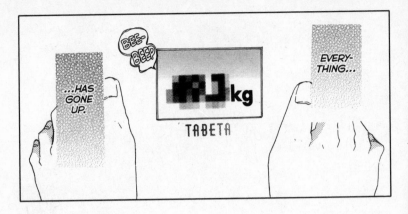

Page 156: Tabeta

The scale's brand may be a parody version of the Tanita brand of bathroom scales. The name Tabeta is fitting, as it is Japanese for "you ate."

Say I Love You.

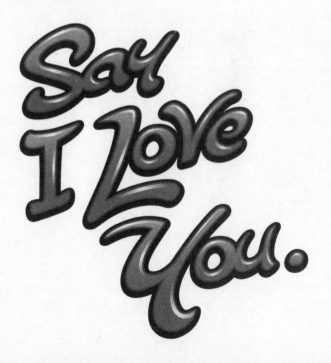

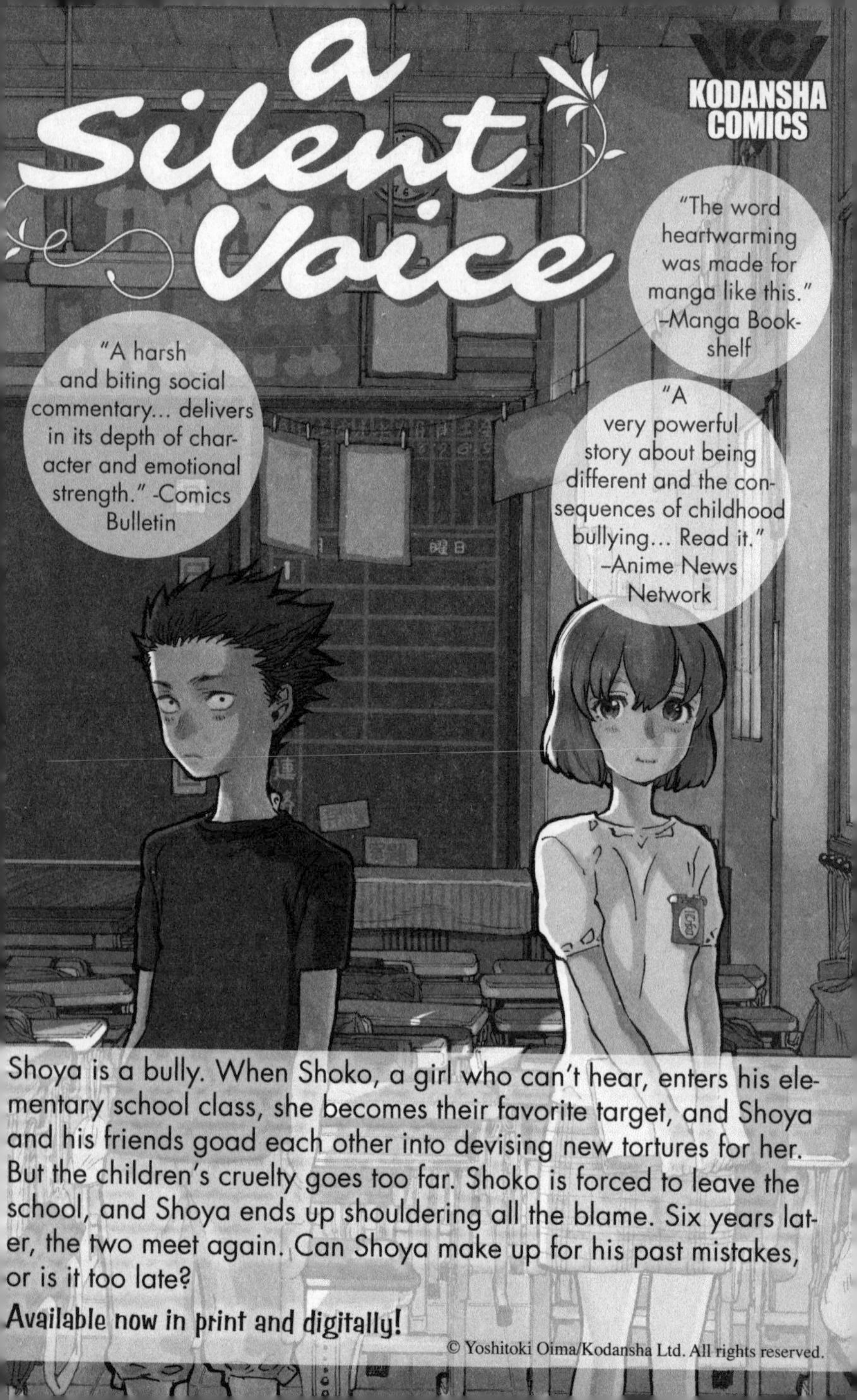
a Silent Voice
KC
KODANSHA COMICS
"The word heartwarming was made for manga like this." –Manga Bookshelf
"A harsh and biting social commentary... delivers in its depth of character and emotional strength." -Comics Bulletin
"A very powerful story about being different and the consequences of childhood bullying... Read it." –Anime News Network
Shoya is a bully. When Shoko, a girl who can't hear, enters his elementary school class, she becomes their favorite target, and Shoya and his friends goad each other into devising new tortures for her. But the children's cruelty goes too far. Shoko is forced to leave the school, and Shoya ends up shouldering all the blame. Six years later, the two meet again. Can Shoya make up for his past mistakes, or is it too late?
Available now in print and digitally!
© Yoshitoki Oima/Kodansha Ltd. All rights reserved.

OPPOSITES ATTRACT...MAYBE?

Haru Yoshida is feared as an unstable and violent "monster." Mizutani Shizuku is a grade-obsessed student with no friends. Fate brings these two together to form the most unlikely pair. Haru firmly believes he's in love with Mizutani and she firmly believes he's insane.

A Kodansha Comics Trade Paperback Original
Say I Love You. volume 10 copyright © 2013 Kanae Hazuki
English translation copyright © 2015 Kanae Hazuki

Published in the United States by Kodansha Comics, an imprint of Kodansha USA Publishing, LLC, New York.

Publication rights for this English edition arranged through Kodansha Ltd, Tokyo.

First published in Japan in 2013 by Kodansha Ltd., Tokyo as *Sukitte iinayo.* volume 10.

ISBN 978-1-61262-675-8

Printed in the United States of America.

www.kodanshacomics.com

9 8 7 6 5 4 3 2 1
Translation: Alethea and Athena Nibley
Lettering: John Clark
Editing: Ajani Oloye
Kodansha Comics edition cover design by Phil Balsman